Dedicated
(BY PERMISSION)
TO
COLONEL H.R.H. THE PRINCE OF WALES AND DUKE OF
CORNWALL, K.G., K.T., G.C.S.I., G.C.M.G., G.C.I.E.,
G.C.V.O., G.B.E., M.C.
COLONEL-IN-CHIEF OF THE REGIMENT.

THE HISTORY *of the* PRINCE OF WALES'S LEINSTER REGIMENT ..
(*Royal Canadians*)

Late THE 100TH PRINCE OF WALES'S ROYAL CANADIAN REGIMENT *descended from* THE 100TH PRINCE REGENT'S COUNTY OF DUBLIN REGIMENT OF FOOT *disbanded in Canada in* 1818: *And* THE 109TH FOOT *formerly* THE HONOURABLE EAST INDIA COMPANY'S 3RD BOMBAY EUROPEAN REGIMENT: *To which were added in* 1881 *as* 3RD, 4TH *and* 5TH BATTALIONS *respectively* THE KING'S COUNTY MILITIA: THE QUEEN'S COUNTY MILITIA *and* THE ROYAL MEATH MILITIA: *And the* 6TH *and* 7TH SERVICE BATTALIONS *raised in* 1914 *on the Outbreak of the Great War:*

Compiled and Edited by
LIEUTENANT-COLONEL
FREDERICK ERNEST WHITTON, C.M.G.
Late of the Regiment

PART I
The Old Army

ALDERSHOT :
GALE & POLDEN LTD., WELLINGTON WORKS
ALSO AT LONDON AND PORTSMOUTH

**PRINTED AND BOUND BY
ANTONY ROWE LTD,
EASTBOURNE.**

PREFACE

THE Editor desires to express his profound gratitude to those members of all ranks of the Regiment who supplied him with anecdotes, narratives and sketches, or placed letters and diaries at his disposal. They are too numerous to mention individually, but, in thanking them all collectively, the Editor wishes to place on record the acknowledgment that, without their generous assistance, this History could not have been written.

The Editor is also indebted to Captain F. D. Grierson, who compiled a useful digest of the War Diaries of the various battalions, which served as an admirable framework for the story of the Regiment in the Great War. The existence of this digest did not, however, absolve the Editor from the necessity of consulting the War Diaries himself, and those records have been thoroughly explored by him in the case of every battalion.

To Mr. Gorman, of Sarnia, Ontario—one of the few surviving Royal Canadians—a special meed of thanks is due for his invaluable narrative dealing with 1858 and the years immediately following.

Much of the portion dealing with the formation of the earlier 100th Regiments is based upon an article which appeared in the *Journal of the Society of Army Research*, from the pen of Mr. Baldry, of the War Office Library. The Editor wishes to acknowledge his sense of indebtedness to that magazine and also to thank Mr. Baldry for his researches in connexion with the earlier 109th Regiments, and for much useful advice as to research and inquiry generally.

PREFACE

In the account of the German Legion considerable use was made of an excellent article by Lieut.-Colonel Arthur Egerton, D.S.O., on the subject, which appeared in the *Journal of the Royal United Service Institution*, of August, 1921. Some valuable information regarding the very early days of the Irish Militia was obtained from " The Midland Septs and the Pale," by the Rev. F. R. Montgomery Hitchcock, D.D.

Although every effort has been made to ensure accuracy in personal and place names, some minor variations will still be found to exist. In the case of the latter, the variations are given on the maps; and, as regards personal names, where a minor error was discovered too late for correction in the text, the correct rendering has been given in the index when possible.

Finally, a tribute is due to Mr. C. S. Seager, managing director of Messrs. Gale & Polden, Ltd., for the close personal interest he has taken in the production of the History ever since its inception, and for the valuable advice on technical points of publication which he has always been ready to afford.

July, 1924.

CONTENTS

CHAPTER	PAGE
I. THE EARLIER 100TH REGIMENTS	1
II. THE 100TH PRINCE REGENT'S COUNTY OF DUBLIN REGIMENT—THE WAR WITH AMERICA, 1812–1814	14
III. THE 100TH PRINCE REGENT'S COUNTY OF DUBLIN REGIMENT—THE WAR WITH AMERICA, 1812–1814 (*continued*)	26
IV. THE 100TH THE PRINCE OF WALES'S ROYAL CANADIAN REGIMENT — 1858–1859 — MONTREAL — QUEBEC — SHORNCLIFFE—ALDERSHOT	44
V. THE 100TH ROYAL CANADIANS — GIBRALTAR, 1859–1863	65
VI. THE 100TH ROYAL CANADIANS—MALTA, 1863–1866 ...	75
VII. THE 100TH ROYAL CANADIANS—CANADA, 1866–1868	82
VIII. THE 100TH ROYAL CANADIANS—THE UNITED KINGDOM, 1869–1877	88
IX. THE 100TH ROYAL CANADIANS—INDIA, 1877–1894 ...	97
X. THE 1ST BATTALION, 1894-1900—IRELAND—THE REPATRIATION QUESTION—HALIFAX	120
XI. THE 1ST BATTALION, 1900–1902—SOUTH AFRICA ...	133
XII. THE 1ST BATTALION, 1902–1914—THE UNITED KINGDOM—INDIA	150
XIII. THE EARLIER 109TH REGIMENTS	170
XIV. THE EAST INDIA COMPANY	176
XV. THE OUTBREAK OF THE INDIAN MUTINY	186
XVI. THE 3RD BOMBAY EUROPEANS—CENTRAL INDIA ...	196
XVII. THE 3RD BOMBAY EUROPEANS—CENTRAL INDIA (*continued*)	210
XVIII. THE 3RD BOMBAY EUROPEANS—CENTRAL INDIA (*continued*)—THE STORMING OF JHANSI	222
XIX. THE 3RD BOMBAY EUROPEANS—CENTRAL INDIA (*continued*)	231
XX. THE 109TH BOMBAY INFANTRY	243
XXI. THE 109TH REGIMENT—ADEN, 1864–1866	257
XXII. THE 109TH REGIMENT—INDIA, 1867–1874	266
XXIII. THE 109TH REGIMENT—INDIA (*continued*), 1874–1877	277

CONTENTS

CHAPTER		PAGE
XXIV. THE 109TH REGIMENT—ENGLAND, 1878–1882	...	289
XXV. THE 2ND BATTALION—IRELAND, 1882–1887	...	317
XXVI. THE 2ND BATTALION—ENGLAND, 1888–1894	...	330
XXVII. THE 2ND BATTALION—THE MEDITERRANEAN, 1894–1895	...	348
XXVIII. THE 2ND BATTALION—BERMUDA, 1895–1897 ...	...	361
XXIX. THE 2ND BATTALION—HALIFAX, 1897–1898	...	372
XXX. THE 2ND BATTALION—JAMAICA, 1898	...	382
XXXI. THE 2ND BATTALION—BARBADOS, 1898–1901	...	389
XXXII. THE 2ND BATTALION—SOUTH AFRICA, 1901–1905 ...		411
XXXIII. THE 2ND BATTALION—MAURITIUS, 1905–1907	...	441
XXXIV. THE 2ND BATTALION—INDIA, 1907–1911	...	447
XXXV. THE 2ND BATTALION—CORK, 1911–1914	...	452
XXXVI. THE 3RD, 4TH, AND 5TH BATTALIONS	...	456

ILLUSTRATIONS

	FACING PAGE
H.R.H. THE PRINCE OF WALES, K.G. ...	*Frontispiece*
GENERAL SIR JAMES WILLCOCKS, G.C.B., G.C.M.G., K.C.S.I., D.S.O. ...	166
MESS PLATE OF THE 2ND BATTALION	452
COLONEL CHARLES PEPPER, M.B.E.	466

MAPS

	FACING PAGE
SKETCH MAPS, FORT NIAGARA AND CHIPPAWA	40
GENERAL MAP, CANADIAN FRONTIER	42
GENERAL MAP, CENTRAL INDIA CAMPAIGN	242
1ST, 2ND, AND 3RD BATTALIONS, SOUTH AFRICAN WAR	460

THE PRINCE OF WALES'S LEINSTER REGIMENT (ROYAL CANADIANS).
[100]
No. 12 District.

The Plume of the Prince of Wales. In each of the four corners a Maple Leaf.

" Niagara," " Central India," " South Africa, 1900–02."

THE GREAT WAR—7 BATTALIONS.

"**Armentières, 1914,**" "**Ypres, 1915,** '**17,** '**18,**" " Gravenstafel," " St. Julien," " Frezenberg," "**Somme, 1916,** '**18,**" "Delville Wood," "**Guillemont,**" " Ginchy," " Arras, 1917," " **Vimy, 1917,**" "**Messines, 1917,**" " Pilckem," " Langemarck, 1917," "**St. Quentin,**" " Rosières," " Courtrai," " France and Flanders, 1914–18," " Kosturino," " Struma," "**Macedonia, 1915–17,**" " Suvla," " Sari Bair," "**Gallipoli, 1915,**" " Gaza," "**Jerusalem,**" " Tell 'Asur." " Megiddo," " Nablus," " Palestine, 1917–18."

Agents—Messrs. Cox & Co.

Regular, Militia and Service Battalions.
Uniform—Scarlet. *Facings*—Blue.

1st Bn. (100th Foot).	5th Bn. (Royal Meath Militia).
2nd ,, (109th ,,).	6th ,, (Service Battalion).
3rd ,, (King's County Militia).	7th ,, (Service Battalion).
4th ,, (Queen's County Militia).	
Depot ... ... *Birr*.	Record Office ... ... *Cork*.

Allied Regiments of Canadian Militia.

The Royal Grenadiers ... ... *Toronto, Ontario.*
The Winnipeg Grenadiers ... ... *Winnipeg, Manitoba.*

Colonel-in-Chief :—Col. H.R.H. *the Prince of* Wales and *Duke of* Cornwall, *K.G., G.C.S.I., G.C.M.G., G.C.I.E., G.C.V.O., G.B.E., M.C.*, Col. W. Gds., Colonel-in-Chief : 12th L., R. S. Fus., D.C.L.I., Midd'x. R., Seaforth, and R. Wilts. Yeo. (*Personal A.D.C. to the King*).

Colonel ... Boyd, Maj.-Gen. Sir G. F., *K.C.B., C.M.G., D.S.O., D.C.M., p.s.c., s.*

I would have History familiar rather than heroic.

Esmond.

[Photo] [Bassano]

H.R.H. THE PRINCE OF WALES, K.G.
Colonel-in-Chief of the Regiment

THE
LEINSTER REGIMENT

CHAPTER I

The Earlier 100th Regiments.

IN almost every war in which England has been engaged history may be said to repeat itself. Invariably she has found herself without sufficient troops when the contest begins. The requisite numbers are eventually obtained, though not until much blood has been uselessly shed. Victory is ultimately secured; and then almost before the last peal of the joy-bells of thanksgiving has died away she sets herself once again to whittle down her armed forces below danger point.

The evils of this system, from a military point of view, are beyond the purview of these volumes. But from the point of view of the regimental historian it may be said that this concertina process adds greatly to his difficulties when his task is concerned with a unit bearing—or, rather, which has borne—a number near the end of the roll of regiments of the line. Assuming that the number of infantry regiments of the Army—in the days when figures and not territorial titles distinguished infantry regiments—was roughly one hundred, it follows that regiments in the danger zone near those digits were in a perpetual state of being born, being put to death, and being, sooner or later, recalled from the tomb. Britannia stamped upon the ground in a moment of peril—and panic, and armed men sprang from the ground. Britannia labelled them with the first vacant number, invariably somewhere near 100 and sent them to fight for her, usually in pestilential climates. So soon as the matter had been successfully accomplished the regiment was disbanded, the survivors were dismissed, and the surplus number plates were put away ready for the next unit to be raised.

In British regiments whose numbers approximated to the fatal three figures continuity of history is, therefore, not to be expected. In all, six regiments have at different times borne the digits 100, the last, in course of time, becoming the 1st Battalion of the Leinster Regiment. With four of these older Hundredths, whose history will now be summarized, the Leinster Regiment has no direct connexion nor has it ever claimed any, though it is proper that their story should be related here. With one, however, there has always existed a link. From it the battle honour " Niagara " has been inherited, and the history of that forbear of the 1st Leinster Regiment will therefore, be dealt with at some length in these opening chapters.

To go back to the very beginning, the first 100th Regiment was the 100th Highlanders. In August and September, 1760, four Independent Companies of Highlanders for foreign service, each of 100 men, were raised for rank in Argyllshire by Lieutenants Alexander Ross, Neil Campbell, Alexander Macdonald and John MacHarg, and were placed on the establishment on 25th August, 5th, 23rd and 24th September, respectively. The men were armed with side-pistols, as well as firelocks. Early in 1761 these four companies marched from Scotland to Newcastle, where, in May, they were ordered to be formed into a corps under the command of Major Colin Campbell, late of the 4th Foot, which was placed on the establishment on the 25th of that month. Shortly afterwards it was sent by sea to Portsmouth, destined for Guadeloupe. On arrival at Portsmouth, however, its destination was changed to Jersey, where it disembarked on 20th July, being then only 14 men under strength. Five days later the establishment of the

Regiment was augmented by the addition of Captain Nightingale's Independent Company. This company was one of several, of 100 men each, authorized for the augmentation of the regiments in Germany. The orders for raising it were issued to Lieutenant Gerard Moore (11th Foot) on 31st July, 1760, but Moore, having failed to complete it by April, 1761, was superseded by Thomas Nightingale, and the company was placed on the establishment from the 6th of that month. Whilst stationed at Enfield in July, 1761, it received orders to march to Portsmouth and embark for Jersey to join Campbell's Corps, into which it was incorporated on 25th July. It again became an independent company from 25th December, 1761, the privates (described as being chiefly old men and boys) being drafted at Guadeloupe into the 4th, 63rd, and 64th Regiments, the officers and non-commissioned officers returning to England to recruit. On 25th July, 1762, it was incorporated into Fitzroy's Regiment (119th), which was disbanded in January, 1763. The clothing for independent companies at this period was scarlet, lined with scarlet, with white buttons and without lace.

At the end of September, 1761, Campbell's Corps received orders to embark for Guadeloupe, being then 521 strong, but, on arrival there, it was detached to reinforce Monckton's expedition against Martinique, being included in Brigadier-General Haviland's brigade. Early in January, 1762, the expedition sailed from Barbados, and on the 16th January the whole force (eighteen regiments of infantry, etc.) landed in the neighbourhood of Cas de Navire. On the 24th a general attack was made on the Morne Tortensen and Morne Grenier, two eminences which completely commanded the town and citadel of Fort Royal. Morne Tortensen was first attacked and carried, the attack on the centre of it being made by the united grenadier companies of the force and the Highlanders (42nd, Montgomery's and Campbell's). On the 25th the troops began to throw up batteries on Morne Tortensen to bombard the citadel, and on the 27th the French took the offensive from Morne Grenier, debouching in three columns, which came on with great spirit and dash. The weight of their attack fell on General Haviland's brigade, which included the 100th Highlanders and the light infantry companies, but the column exposed its flank to the Highlanders, who " drawing their swords, rushed forward like furies, and, being supported by the Grenadiers, under Colonel Grant, and a party of Lord Rollo's brigade, the hills were mounted and the batteries seized, and numbers of the enemy, unable to escape from the rapidity of the attack, were taken." The other two French columns were also forced to retire, and Morne Grenier remained in the hands of the British. The batteries on both Mornes were then completed, and on the 3rd February Fort Royal surrendered.

A detachment of the Regiment took part in Lord Albemarle's expedition to Havannah, destined to inflict a blow on the power of Spain, against whom Great Britain had in 1762 also declared war. The troops landed in Cuba on the 7th June, and proceeded to attack Fort Moro, which defends on the north side the entrance to Havannah Harbour. The ground and the climate were all against the British, and it was only on the 30th July that the fort was stormed, and on the 10th August that Havannah surrendered. The losses of the expedition were appalling. At the date of the surrender, out of 12,000 men composing the Earl of Albemarle's force originally, 1,000 had been killed and wounded, and 5,000 had died of disease, and most of the remainder were in a feeble state of health. Little is on record of the doings of the detachment of the 100th, which was in Lord Rollo's brigade and is believed to have been attached to the 42nd Highlanders, but it lost heavily, and, after the expedition, rejoined regimental headquarters at Martinique.

In 1763 the Regiment returned home, and was disbanded on the 23rd September, 1763, at Stirling, although part of the process took place evidently at

Plympton, its major-commandant being then John Broughton.

Thus ended the short but eventful life of the 100th Highlanders. The Regiment does not appear to have been of a very high standard. Whilst stationed in Jersey Captain MacHarg embezzled his company's pay, the men starving and publicly begging in the streets of St. Heliers, and the paymaster's office was set on fire and robbed of £1,100. When in Martinique it was several times reported as being unfit for service, being composed of very young boys or old men. Whilst there Captain MacHarg was killed by Major Campbell, who was tried by court-martial for murder, but managed to escape from the island. Owing to some irregularities in the court-martial, the proceedings were not confirmed by the King, but Campbell was dismissed from the Service. He was succeeded by John Broughton on 20th August, 1762, who remained major-commandant until the Regiment was disbanded.

The second regiment bearing the number 100 was raised by Lieutenant-Colonel Francis Mackenzie Humberstone in England, for service in India. It had ten companies, and its first majors were Henry Rooke (9/1/81) and John Campbell (7/2/81), the adjutant being James Fraser, and the quartermaster Richard Brown. The regimental agents were "Messrs. Cox, Mair, and Cox," of Craig's Court, London. No mention of its uniform is made in any of the contemporary Army Lists. The Regiment was placed on the establishment from 5th August, 1780, and was numbered the 100th Regiment of Foot. On 23rd August a warrant was issued to augment the Regiment with five more companies upon the same terms, a second major being added and two fifers allowed for the Grenadier Company. These were brought upon the establishment on 9th January, 1781. On 25th December, 1781 (the Regiment then being in India), a company was added for the purpose of recruiting at home, consisting of 100 men with twice the usual non-commissioned officers, of which the officers and

96 privates (with arms, clothing, etc.) were ordered to be transferred from the 2nd recruiting company (reduced at this date) of the 102nd Regiment (Rowley's). The Regiment was largely raised in Scotland and was stationed at Inverness in August, 1780 (the five companies being already practically complete), and was at Dundee in October. In November and December it was sent, in detachments, by sea to Gravesend, from whence it marched to Hilsea, near Portsmouth.

There it joined an expedition fitting out under the command of Major-General William Meadows for an attack on the Cape of Good Hope, and consisting of the 2nd Battalion 42nd Highlanders, 98th, and 100th Regiments, together with one company each of the 8th, 9th, 20th, and 47th Regiments. The expedition sailed on the 12th of March, 1781, convoyed by a squadron under Commodore Johnstone. About the same time the French had despatched a squadron, under Admiral Suffren, with reinforcements for their troops in India, but also with the Cape of Good Hope as an intermediary objective. The British expedition had the start, and was lying in the neutral port of Porto Praya in the Cape Verde Islands, when it was attacked by Suffren on the 16th April. The attack was beaten off with some loss—the 100th suffering 28 casualties, and Suffren proceeded on his voyage to the Cape. Commodore Johnstone then returned to England with his frigates, but sent the remainder of his ships to escort the transports on their further voyage. On arriving off the Cape it was ascertained that Suffren had landed reinforcements there, and so the nut proved too hard to crack, and General Meadows's expedition continued on its voyage to India. However, a valuable convoy of Dutch East Indiamen, which had taken shelter in Saldanha Bay, was captured there, and the troops shared the prize money. Scurvy attacked the troops on the voyage, and to obtain fresh provisions they were landed on the island of Joanna, but here, unfortunately, they contracted a local fever, and, on returning on board to continue the voyage many men fell victims to it. Early in 1782—the dates given by different authorities ranging from 22nd January to 5th March—after a year's voyage, the expedition arrived at Bombay.

It came in the nick of time to be of service in the operations against Hyder Ali, against whom and his French allies General Coote had been operating from the Coromandel Coast with varying success. The 100th were sent at once to Calicut, and, moving from that as a base, Colonel Humberstone, whose force, consisting of his own regiment and a few native troops who had defended Tellicherry, did not exceed 1,000 men, during April, 1782, twice defeated a force of 7,000 Mysoreans, capturing 2 guns and inflicting a loss in killed, wounded and prisoners of 2,000 men. Hitherto Coote had naturally disapproved of the employment of troops which he so sorely needed himself, in desultory operations, but he now placed Humberstone's force definitely under the orders of the Governor of Bombay, and begged that the diversion on the western coast might be pushed home with all possible vigour. Humberstone therefore again took the field in September, this time using Panianee, forty miles south of Calicut, for his base, but he effected little, and in November was forced to retreat rapidly before an army under Tippoo Sahib and Lally, which had been sent by Hyder from Tanjore. So hardly was he pressed that he made his escape only by passing his troops across a ford which was for an ordinary man chin-deep. Marvellous to say, he accomplished this feat without the loss of a man, and marched safely into Panianee.

On arrival at Panianee, on the 20th November, the 100th found the 2nd Battalion of the 42nd, whose commander, Lieutenant-Colonel Macleod, being senior to Lieutenant-Colonel Humberstone, assumed command of all the troops. As it was evident that Tippoo Sahib and Lally, whose forces amounted to 10,000 cavalry and 14,000 infantry, including two battalions of French infantry, would press their advantage, the position round Panianee was hastily fortified, but the works were unfinished when, on the 29th November, an attack was made by the entire hostile army in four columns. Lally led the attack with great spirit at the head of the French battalions, but the British dispositions were excellent, the Mysoreans were no match for the 42nd and 100th, and the attack was repulsed with a loss of 8 officers and 88 men killed and wounded. The share of the 42nd was 22 men killed and 3 officers and 33 men wounded, so it may be assumed that the remainder of the loss fell on the 100th. The Mysoreans left 200 dead on the field, and retired from the scene of action to a distance to await reinforcements. On the 12th December news came of the death of Hyder Ali, the ruler of Mysore, and the army at once withdrew into the interior. The battle of Panianee appears to have been most creditable to the British troops, who were fighting against heavy odds, and Fortescue writes that "a single company of British did not hesitate to charge with the bayonet a column of whatever weight, without calculating numbers." It is by gallantry like this, by the unflinching assumption of the offensive, regardless of odds, that our troops have always triumphed over Oriental enemies, and it is instructive to note that most of our failures have been due to the force concerned adopting a purely defensive attitude.

It was about this time that Colonel Humberstone gave up command of the Regiment, as his cousin, Lord Seaforth, who had raised and who commanded the 78th or Seaforth Highlanders (later the 72nd Regiment, and now the 1st Battalion Seaforth Highlanders) now died during the voyage of that regiment to India, and Colonel Humberstone succeeded to the family estates and to the command of the 78th. He himself was killed in an action at sea in 1783. His successor in the command of the 100th was Colonel the Honourable Thomas Bruce, whose commission as lieutenant-colonel was dated 13th February, 1781. Among other changes in the

Regiment may be noted that Major Rooke was succeeded by Major Adam Colt on 28th January, 1783, and Major Campbell (who was promoted brevet lieutenant-colonel on 19th February, 1783) by Major Hugh Lamont on 9th April, 1783. Thomas Dale became quartermaster on 4th October, 1783.

The share of the 100th in the operations which followed the battle of Panianee on the Malabar Coast is difficult to ascertain. On learning of Colonel Humberstone's force having been forced back on Panianee, the Bombay Government despatched their commander-in-chief, General Matthews, with what forces could be collected, to its relief, but on receiving the report of the retreat of Tippoo Sultan's army, General Matthews landed his forces at Rajaman Droog, and was about to undertake further operations in that vicinity when he received orders from Government to abandon all operations on the coast, and make an immediate push for the possession of Bednore. He sent transports to bring up the troops from Panianee, and then landed his force at Coondapore, whence he moved on Bednore. Strong opposition was met with on the way, line after line of defences on the successive terraces of the Ghauts had to be carried, and finally the fort of Hyder Ghar, in which were found 8,000 stand of new arms, was taken by storm, upon which Bednore surrendered on the 27th January, 1783. A detachment of the 100th took part in these operations. Anantpoor, a fort thirty miles north-east of Bednore, was captured on the 15th February, and on the 9th March Mangalore, a strong fort on the coast, was taken by a force detached for the purpose. Meanwhile Tippoo's main army had been steadily advancing on Bednore, and on the 7th April appeared before that place, and, by the capture of Hyder Ghar, cut General Matthews's communications with the sea. Bednore was now closely invested, and, the outer defences being too extensive to be held, the British were forced, after the first assault had penetrated those works, to retire into the citadel. In this a desperate defence was made, till the whole of the fortifications were in ruins and further resistance hopeless, when a capitulation was arranged, under which the garrison was to receive safe conduct to the coast. In consequence, however, of an alleged breach of the conditions as to public property being surrendered, the entire garrison was put in irons and marched off as prisoners.

Mangalore was next attacked by the victorious Mysoreans, and on the 20th May it was invested. The garrison consisted of the 2nd Battalion 42nd Highlanders, a detachment of the 100th, a detachment of artillery and the 1st and 8th Battalions of Bombay sepoys, the whole under Major John Campbell, of the 42nd. The defence lasted till the 30th January, 1784, and is to this day commemorated by the inscription "Mangalore" on the colours of the Black Watch, and 101st (late 1st Bombay) Grenadiers. The outposts, about a mile distant from the place, were first driven in, and then Tippoo's troops proceeded to a siege in form, and in a short time the fortress was breached on all sides, and the defences reduced to ruins. Assault after assault was repulsed, and daily fighting went on until on 2nd August an armistice was agreed to, as, in consequence of the peace signed between Great Britain and France, the French troops, under M. de Cossigny, were withdrawn from the besieging force. The garrison was to be supplied with provisions, ten days' stock at a time, but Tippoo contrived to evade this condition in the hope of starving out the garrison, and on the 9th October he threw off the mask and resumed the siege. Three attempts at relief by a fleet were made, but on each occasion General Macleod, who commanded the relief forces, declined to land supplies, out of a scrupulous respect for the terms of the armistice, and of negotiations for peace which were going on, scruples which were not shared by Tippoo, who pushed his siege works and pursued his starving policy. At last the garrison was starved into submission, and on the 30th January, 1784, after standing an eight-months' siege, it capitulated on conditions of safe conduct to Tellicherry, where it was landed on 4th February.

Peace with Mysore was signed on the 11th March, 1784, and shortly afterwards the 100th were ordered home and disbanded in 1785, the only relics of it in the 1786 Army List being two captains, five lieutenants, and an ensign shown as "on English half pay." The life of the second 100th had thus lasted over five years, and had been not without much hard fighting and much honour. During its three years' service in India the Regiment had lost in action or from disease 39 officers and 1,200 men.

The history of the third 100th need not detain us long, for the corps still exists as the 2nd Battalion of the Gordon Highlanders, which has carved its name deep on the roll of fame of the British Army. Embodied on the 24th June, 1794, at Aberdeen, the Gordons were shortly moved by sea to Southampton, and on 5th September were embarked there for Gibraltar, where they arrived on the 27th, and remained till the 11th June, 1795. On that date they left for Corsica, and garrisoned Bastia till 6th September, 1796, when they sailed for Gibraltar. On their voyage the transports and the fleet convoying them were fired on by a Spanish fleet in greatly superior force, and one transport, with 2 officers and 51 other ranks on board, was captured. This was the only time during their period of service as the 100th that the Gordon Highlanders came under fire. On the 4th October the Regiment landed at Gibraltar, and remained there till 16th March, 1798, when it embarked for Portsmouth, where it arrived on 15th May only, so slow and so affected by winds and seasons were sea voyages in those days. The Regiment was, in consequence of the threatened French invasion of Ireland, hurriedly ordered over to Dublin, where it arrived on the 15th June, but it was not engaged against General Humbert's forces, and gained the goodwill of the people everywhere by its conduct in quarters and the good behaviour of its men. On the 16th October, 1798, in consequence of the disbandment of the then existing

91st to 97th and 99th Regiments, the 98th Highlanders became the 91st, and the 100th the 92nd Highlanders, under which number it continued to win fame until 1881, when it became the 2nd Battalion Gordon Highlanders.

The story now turns to the short but honourable life of another 100th, the immediate forbear of the 1st Leinster Regiment. In April, 1804, Frederick John Falkiner, Esq., was authorized to recruit an Irish Levy of which he was to be the commandant, and on 14th May, 1804, a Letter of Service was granted to him for raising a corps of 1,000 rank and file in Ireland. By the end of the year over 700 recruits had been obtained, and on 28th February, 1805, with a view to doing away with the idea of it being drafted, which might prevent its early completion, the King was pleased to approve of it being numbered the 100th Regiment of Foot, with Falkiner as colonel. It was transferred to the British establishment from 25th March, 1805, its establishment then being 10 companies of 100 rank and file. The lieutenant-colonel commanding was John Murray, who had served in the 37th Regiment in Holland in 1793-4, and been wounded and taken prisoner there. He subsequently served in the 4th and 39th Regiments and was gazetted lieutenant-colonel of the 100th on 21st March, 1805. The first majors were Archibald Bertram and Christopher Hamilton, but the former was succeeded by the Honourable Alexander Abercromby on 12th July, 1806. The first adjutant was Lieutenant Wynne Fawcett and the quartermaster John A. Hearne. The regimental agents were " Messrs. Greenwood, Cox, and Hamersley," Craig's Court, London, and the uniform was red, with deep yellow facings. The title was simply the " 100th Regiment of Foot," and it was not till 1812 that the title of " 100th or H.R.H. the Prince Regent's County of Dublin Regiment of Foot," was conferred upon it.

On the 19th March, 1805, the Regiment embarked at Warrenpoint for the Isle of Wight. It proceeded to Gosport in June and embarked thence for Canada on

10th August with an effective strength of 560 rank and file. The voyage was most unfortunate, for on the 21st October, 1805, the day of the Battle of Trafalgar, one of the transports conveying three companies of the Regiment was wrecked in a violent gale off the coast of Newfoundland, and 8 officers and 184 men lost their lives. Two other companies were wrecked off the Island of Cape Breton where they remained until they joined the Regiment in Quebec in June, 1806. Headquarters of the Regiment moved to Montreal in October, 1807, to Fort George in August, 1809, Three Rivers, August, 1811, and returned to Quebec in May, 1812. During this time W. S. Plenderleath became major (1/1/07), *vice* Abercromby, and George Taylor major (9/6/08), *vice* Plenderleath, while on 4/1/10 Ensign Samuel Kingston succeeded Lieutenant Fawcett as adjutant. Lastly, on 18th July, 1811, Malcolm MacPherson became lieutenant-colonel of the Regiment in place of Lieutenant-Colonel Murray, who was appointed inspecting field officer of the Canadian Militia.

CHAPTER II

THE 100TH PRINCE REGENT'S COUNTY OF DUBLIN REGIMENT—THE WAR WITH AMERICA, 1812–1814.

THE year 1812 found England in a position of some anxiety. For twenty years almost without a break she had been engaged in war with France whose armies were commanded by possibly the greatest soldier the world has ever seen. Her strength was now taxed to the utmost; the campaign on land was a severe drain both in men and money; the blockade of the French ports imposed a serious strain on the Navy; trade was depressed; and to a shrewd observer like Metternich it seemed that the empire of England was on the verge of collapse. Napoleon was on the eve of his great invasion of Russia and it looked as if the balance of power on the Continent, for which England had vigorously striven, was beyond her reach. It was at this critical period that she was confronted with a new danger and involved in a fresh and distant struggle.

Although divided by thousands of miles of ocean from the prolonged contest in the Old World the war in America was a direct sequel to it. The United States were, it is true, neutral, and in that capacity were probably the chief carriers of the time. So fierce, however, was the contest between England and Napoleon that the rights of neutrals were apt to be treated with but scant respect. To a maritime nation like England, to whom sea communications were vital, command of the sea was of the first importance and this necessary command had by no means been secured at Trafalgar, for since that battle the losses inflicted on England's sea-borne trade by French privateers had been staggering.

Napoleon, although he was at his weakest in maritime questions, could scarcely fail to see the crippling effect he might achieve by strangling England's sea-borne trade, and, as a result, England and France took active measures, the one to maintain her sea communications and the other to cripple them. In a *guerre à outrance* between Great Powers smaller nations and their rights are apt to be disregarded; and it soon followed that American commerce was severely hampered not only by Napoleon's decrees but by the retaliatory British Orders in Council. The United States had, therefore, a grievance against both France and England.

Just as was to prove to be the case a century later America was forced to abandon her attitude of neutrality and to be involved in a world struggle, and for the same reason in both cases, interference with her neutral rights at sea. In 1812 she threw down the gage of defiance to England. American sympathy with Napoleon was strong, particularly in the south, which then and for years afterwards dominated the union. There was thus a bias in favour of France which was increased by irritation over high-handed action by England. British naval officers undoubtedly showed severity in searching American ships for deserters and British seamen, and something more than severity in impressing American sailors. Two encounters between English and American ships of war had already taken place. The steadily increasing friction between the two Powers had become intensified by the summer of 1812; and, although the British Government revoked the Orders in Council on 23rd June, the news arrived too late to avert the conflict which came about by the declaration of war by America on 18th June, 1812.

The struggle thus brought about lasted more than two years and had within it the germs of a great war, a status it would have reached had it not been fought in a little way. It was, however, inevitable that it should have been so fought in view of the paucity of the forces engaged—certainly at first; the immense size of the potential theatre of war; and the mediocrity which characterized the leading on both sides, particularly the American.

As regards numbers the army of the United States at the declaration of war amounted to less than 7,000 regular troops. Congress had previously sanctioned the further enlistment of 25,000 men but only 4,000 raw recruits had been enrolled by June, 1812. The President was further empowered to call up 50,000 volunteers and 100,000 militia from the various states but these numbers were never reached and the quality of the militia was poor. There was not even unanimity on the American side, for the New England States were bitterly opposed to the war; and there was a serious deficiency in arms, ammunition, transport and equipment. Small as were the numbers available to the United States the force at England's disposal was more exiguous still. The British regular forces in the Canadas consisted of the 8th, 41st, 49th and 100th Regiments, a small detachment of artillery, the 10th Royal Veteran Battalion and the Canadian, Newfoundland and Glengarry Fencibles, the total being assessed by different authorities at a figure varying from 4,500 to 7,000 men. This force had not even the advantage of concentration. It was strung out from a point about 250 miles below Quebec to the head of Lake Huron. And so unequally was it divided that in the upper province of Ontario, along a front of 1,300 miles, there were but 1,450 men. Further, the closing of the St. Lawrence by ice in the winter months left little hope of the arrival of reinforcements before the following summer; and with so many troops locked up in the Peninsula the chance of receiving such assistance was still further diminished.

As for the potential theatre of war, reference to a map of North America will convey, better than any mere words, the vastness of the territory. At the same time it would be entirely fallacious to assume that the common frontier, for military purposes, extended from the Gulf of St. Lawrence to the Pacific. If the map of North

America be consulted the frontier existing to-day may be divided into three sharply defined sectors. Working from east to west there is first the line of the St. Lawrence as far as Kingston, protected by an immense bridgehead formed by portion of the province of Quebec and by New Brunswick. Secondly, there come the Great Lakes. The compiler of these volumes would rejoice could he know that his readers are immune from a mental affliction which obsesses him—an inability to visualize a " lake " as any sheet of water larger than that which can be crossed in a couple of hours in a sculling boat. As a matter of fact, the five Great Lakes, taken together, form an immense inland sea of some 100,000 square miles. Lake Superior is the largest sheet of fresh water on the globe. Among its several islands is one nearly two-thirds the size of Jamaica. The width of Lake Huron is 180 miles. Lake Ontario, the baby of the group, has a circumference of 470 miles. The existence of these great areas of water made the contest here an amphibious war. Then, still working westwards comes the arbitrarily delimitated frontier to the Pacific. For the purpose of this history the territory divided by it may be entirely ignored for in 1812 it was uninhabited, save by Indians, roadless, trackless, entirely undeveloped and practically unexplored. The head of Lake Huron may be taken as marking the extreme western boundary of the frontier fighting in the war of 1812.

With these topographical conditions it might be thought that, since America was the aggressor, her best chance was to move down by Lake Champlain, force the passage of the St. Lawrence, and thus cut off all the scattered British detachments west of it. The project was rejected, partly through fear of the menace exerted by the alliance of Red Indians, under Tecumseh, with the British which rendered the United States anxious for their left or western flank; and partly from the lack of outstanding military talent on the American side. In 1812 America brought forth no leader of the calibre of Lee or Grant or Jackson or Sherman. On land, therefore, the war centred mainly about the two extremities of Lake Erie, command of which by naval force was the deciding factor of success. The American plan was to invade Ontario—or Upper Canada—from each end of Lake Erie. And there followed a queer, confused, unco-ordinated and rather futile war with surprising alternations and unexpected happenings; a war fought with unusual bitterness; a war which broke out after the cause of it had ceased to exist, and in which the biggest action was fought weeks after peace was declared; a war in which battle was delivered on frozen rivers in winter, and in summer gunboats were captured by infantry; a war in which several of the States were pro-English and hundreds of Canadians fought on the American side; a war in which each side burned the capital of the other; a war in which the Americans failed completely in what they imagined was an easy task, the conquest of Canada, and in which they secured considerable success, to their complete surprise, at sea; a war which, though almost entirely confined to the neighbourhood of the Great Lakes, yet spread to New Orleans; an odd jumble of unexpected victories and mortifying defeats; a war of prods and pin-pricks rather than one of grand operations; not, indeed, so much a war as samples of fighting.

When the war broke out the 100th Regiment was stationed at Quebec—or, rather, the headquarters were at that city, with outlying detachments. The Regiment was not called upon to play an active part in the 1812 campaign which may, therefore, be recapitulated merely in such detail as will make clear the operations of the two following years. The American plan was to invade Upper Canada from each end of Lake Erie. The first move was made by the American general Hull who after a tedious and difficult march through the wild forests of Ohio crossed the Detroit in July, 1812, with 1,850 men. News of the capture of a small post at the head of Lake Huron by the British and Indians disconcerted him and left him a prey to anxiety for his communications.

He hurriedly retired to Detroit. Attacked by the British with their allies, Hull surrendered and for his conduct was subsequently sentenced to death by court-martial, the extreme sentence being, however, commuted. At the other end of Lake Erie two further pin-pricks, grandiloquently called " invasions of Canada " were dealt with. The British troops re-crossed the St. Lawrence, the militia returned to their homes, the few regulars went into winter quarters and thus ended the campaign of 1812.

The year 1813 opened with further American reverses but the tide now began to turn. As a result of an American victory on the waters of Lake Erie that lake henceforth became American and later in the year the gallant Indian chief Tecumseh fell gallantly while striving to retrieve the day in an action where the British met defeat. Meanwhile on Lake Ontario the Americans had also secured command of its waters and in the spring they utilized the advantage for an attack upon York, now known as Toronto. On 27th April the place with 300 prisoners fell into the hands of the Americans who burnt the Houses of Parliament. Exactly a month later the American victor, General Chauncey, moved down to the western end of Lake Ontario and compelled the British to abandon the line of the River Niagara, which in its course formed a portion of the frontier between Canada and the United States.

The naval base which the Americans had been using for the operations just described was Sackett's Harbour on the southern shores of Lake Ontario. This base was now weakened by the absence of Chauncey with his flotilla and the time seemed favourable to make an attack upon the place. Thanks chiefly to the strenuous exertions of Admiral Sir James Yeo the British vessels in Kingston were put into a state which enabled them once more to appear upon the lake. A combined expedition was resolved upon, the military element being composed of the grenadier company of the 100th Regiment (the headquarters of which regiment were now at Isle-aux-Noix a small island on the Richelieu River which flows from Lake Champlain to the St. Lawrence); a section of the Royal Scots; 2 companies of the 8th King's; 4 companies of the 104th; 1 company of the Glengarry Fencibles; 2 companies of the Canadian Voltigeurs and a small detachment of the Newfoundland Regiment. Two 6-pounders formed the artillery and the strength of the military portion of the expedition was something less than 750 rank and file.

Early on the morning of the 27th May the flotilla set sail arriving off Sackett's Harbour the same afternoon, but thanks to some unaccountable hesitation the vessels were kept uselessly manœuvring and it was not until the morning of the 29th that the troops were set ashore. Being without proper guides the troops were disembarked in error upon Horse Island north-west of the actual harbour. The grenadier company of the 100th had the post of honour and right well did they merit the distinction by their conduct in this the first action of their career. "The advance was led by the grenadiers of the 100th Regiment with undaunted gallantry which no obstacle could arrest"—so runs the official narrative of the engagement. The island was connected with the mainland by a narrow causeway, in many places under water, about 400 paces in length and under four feet in width. This formidable defile was commanded by an American 6-pounder and by the rifles of 300 to 400 American militia. But in spite of the odds the company of the 100th pressed on capturing the gun and driving the militia headlong into the woods. The remainder of the British force now landed though exposed to fire from a heavy gun from an American fort.

The British now moved due east in two columns towards the buildings and stores which were their objective, one column advancing along the shore road while the other cleared the woods to the right. Junction was successfully established and the whole American force—regular, volunteers and militia—was driven back within the log-barrack and stockaded fort. So hopeless did the situation appear to the Americans that the naval barracks and several ships were set on fire; but at this time a report that a party of the enemy had placed itself between the British and their boats so unnerved the British commander Sir George Prevost that he gave the order for immediate retreat and by the morning of the 30th the expedition was back at Kingston. The losses in this regrettable incident were severe. Out of a total of about 750 the British had 50 killed and 211 wounded, the casualties in the grenadier company of the 100th being 1 sergeant and 5 other ranks killed while the wounded totalled 24.

Meanwhile another portion of the Regiment was about to achieve success about 150 miles from the scene of the unfortunate expedition against Sackett's Harbour. It will be remembered that the headquarters of the Regiment was now at Isle-aux-Noix. This island was on the Richelieu about ten miles from the frontier which intersected that river at a distance of several miles from Lake Champlain the whole of which belonged to the United States. Upon that lake the Americans had equipped some vessels, and, probably with the intention of nipping in the bud any attempt on the part of the British to pass ships on to its waters, two American sloops entered the Richelieu and appeared off Isle-aux-Noix on the morning of 1st June. The troops at Isle-aux-Noix were, in the absence of Lieutenant-Colonel Hamilton, under the command of Major Taylor of the 100th who acted with remarkable promptitude. So soon as the American vessels came in sight Major Taylor ordered three British gun-boats to get under way, and these opened fire upon the intruders. Then, realizing that musketry might be employed with advantage, Major Taylor left the island with a force distributed in two *batteaux* and two rowing boats, and ordered their crews which consisted of a small detachment from the troops to land on each side of the river and fire upon the enemy ships. After a spirited action which lasted for three hours and a half the American sloops struck their colours. They proved to be the United States armed vessels *Growler* and *Eagle*, of from 90 to 100 tons burthen each, carrying 11 guns apiece, and with a crew of 50 men on board each vessel. The Americans had one man killed and eight wounded while the casualties on the side of the attackers were but three wounded, one of them severely from grape shot directed against the garrison on shore.

Thus ended an incident remarkable in the history of an infantry regiment and one which loses nothing of its remarkable character by the vagueness which characterizes the official record and despatch which mention it, for the doubtful point is whether the 100th Regiment formed the crews of the three gun-boats as well as of the " *batteaux* and row boats." One official document expressly states that " detachments of the Royal Artillery and 100th under Major Taylor from garrison of Isle-aux-Noix manned 3 gun-boats 2 *batteaux* and 2 row boats," and one historian goes so far as to say that the 100th " acted as marines " upon this occasion. But James in his " Military Occurrences between Great Britain and America " distinctly states that the gun-boats had Canadian crews assisted by three artillerymen on each. Major Taylor's own despatch does not elucidate the point but as it is clear that the gun-boats were under military control, and as there is no mention of sailors, it is not unreasonable to suppose that Major Taylor embarked some of his men on board them. It may be noted that on the American side the sloops were manned by naval personnel and commanded by Lieutenant Sidney Smith formerly of the *Chesapeake*.

The fortunate possession of these captured sloops, which were promptly renamed the *Broke* and the *Shannon*, suggested the idea of sending a combined naval and military expedition against the American ports on the shores of Lake Champlain. No seamen being at this time at Isle-aux-Noix, and none to be spared from Lake Ontario, the commander of H.M. brig *Wasp*, then lying at Quebec, volunteered with himself and crew to man the sloops and gun-boats. For the military operations along the shores there were available about 1,000 officers and men of the 13th and 100th Regiments and these embarked on the 29th July in the *Broke* and *Shannon*, the three gun-boats, and about 40 *batteaux* provided for the purpose. Next day the flotilla arrived at the American town of Plattsburg. The American militia, some 400 strong, quickly decamped and the arsenal, barracks and stores were destroyed by the British. Four days later a detachment of the 100th Regiment under the command of Captain Elliot landed at Champlain town and destroyed two blockhouses and a quantity of stores. The naval contingent pushed farther down the lake, burning an enemy sloop and doing further damage. The Americans made no attempt to assert their command of the waters of the lake and shortly afterwards, having fulfilled its mission, the British expeditionary force was withdrawn.

The next incident to be described, in which the 100th Regiment took part, occurred on the St. Lawrence. On the 15th or 16th July two ships from the American fleet at Sackett's Harbour each armed with a 16-pounder, and manned by 50 sailors, besides 20 soldiers, were sent to cruise in the St. Lawrence. On the following day these vessels captured a small British gun-boat and her convoy of 15 *batteaux* laden with stores. So soon as intelligence of this event reached Kingston three gun-boats under a naval lieutenant, with a detachment of the 100th Regiment under Captain Martin, proceeded to intercept the American vessels with their booty. The enemy took refuge in a creek, and, although the British were reinforced by another gun-boat and a detachment of the 41st, they were unable to get at the lair where the Americans had esconced themselves. The creek was obstructed by large felled trees across the stream. An attempt was made to land the British troops and these, led by Lieutenant Fawcett, leaped into the water, and carrying their arms and ammunition over their heads, gained the land. The Americans were driven back, but the impossibility of obtaining co-operation from his gun-boats induced Major

Frend of the 41st to order the re-embarkation of the troops. In this skirmish the British had 4 killed and 18 wounded. The casualties in the 100th are not known but none of the killed came from the Regiment.

The British military forces in Canada at this time were disposed in what were rather grandiloquently called three " divisions," right, centre and left. By the middle of September, 1813, the 100th was sent to reinforce the centre on the Niagara frontier. On the 9th October intelligence was received of a disaster to the right division on the Thames (on the northern shore of Lake Erie), where the British were completely defeated losing 8 guns and 600 prisoners. The centre division now fell back from the Niagara towards Burlington Heights where it was joined by fragments of the right division and by two detached companies of the 100th which had been stationed at Charlotteville. So soon as the news of the disaster to the right division had reached General Headquarters orders were sent to the centre division to retire at once along the northern shores of Lake Ontario and to evacuate all ports west of Kingston. Fortunately, these orders were disregarded by a council of war held at Burlington Heights and it was decided not to take a single step to the rear in the existing circumstances.

About the 1st November General Harrison, the victor of the action on the Thames, arrived at Newark with about 1,700 of his troops from whence he shortly embarked for Sackett's Harbour leaving General McClure with a few regulars and some 2,700 militia in command at St. George. The Americans seemed to have behaved with frightfulness to the population. These atrocities came to the ears of the British troops at Burlington Heights some 35 miles away and their commander was strongly urged to allow a small regular and Indian force to be marched against McClure. Consent was given and a force of 379 rank and file of the 100th, about 20 volunteers and 70 Indians, led by Colonel Elliot marched on Fort George. The Americans at first took up a position to bar the British advance but retired without firing a shot. McClure's next move was to burn Newark to the ground callously leaving the inhabitants to the horrors of an exceptionally severe Canadian winter. Elliot's reply was to push on with all speed and McClure now thought only of fleeing from vengeance. "The cowardly wretch with the whole of his minions abandoned Fort George and fled across the river. Not the slightest opposition did he make. He was in too much haste to destroy the whole of his magazines or even to remove his tents." And thus, thanks to the resolution of the council of war on Burlington Heights, the Niagara frontier was cleared of the enemy.

CHAPTER III

THE 100TH PRINCE REGENT'S COUNTY OF DUBLIN REGIMENT—THE WAR WITH AMERICA, 1812–1814 (*continued*).

A FEATURE of a war without strategy is that it tends to be played in a series of "hands" the scores in which cancel each other out as in bridge. This is what was happening at the end of 1813 in North America. The success gained by the Americans on the River Thames, on the north of Lake Erie, was discounted by the failure of another "Invasion of Canada" directed against Montreal, over 400 miles away. Up till now the war, so far as leadership and direction went, had been singularly futile. One American general had been court-martialed and sentenced to death. The British commander-in-chief, Sir George Prevost, had broken off an engagement at Sackett's Harbour and had issued orders for the evacuation of all territory west of Kingston; General Proctor, who had been defeated on the Thames, " escaped by the fleetness of his horses "—as an American despatch tersely puts it; in other words he drove off the field in his carriage, while the Indian chief Tecumseh sacrificed his life in an attempt to retrieve the day. What was wanted was an infusion of fresh blood and on the British side a more vigorous outlook was the result of the arrival of two generals. Early in November Lieutenant-General Drummond and Major-General Riall had arrived from England; the former to relieve Major-General de Rottenburg in the command of the upper province. They joined the centre division of the army soon after the capture of Fort George and at a time when

Colonel Murray's prompt and decisive measures had given a new aspect to affairs.

Murray was all for retaliation on the American bank of the River Niagara and Drummond agreed. Not only so, but, knowing full well that the delay in communicating with Prevost at Quebec, 530 miles away, would give time to the enemy to recover from their panic, he gave the project his immediate sanction. The plan was to attack and seize Fort Niagara on the American shore, just opposite Fort George. In a war when the word *fort* was vaguely applied to any building surrounded merely by a palisade as a protection against Indians, Fort Niagara stood out in a class by itself. It had been built by the French in 1751, and, unlike all the other frontier forts, it was a regular fortification built of stone, mounting 27 heavy guns with a furnace for heating shot and garrisoned by 450 men. For the attack of this formidable post the British force consisted of a small detachment of artillery. the grenadier company of the Royal Scots, the flank companies of the 41st (*i.e.*, of the 2nd Battalion which had recently arrived from Europe), and all the effectives of the 100th Regiment, the whole under the command of Colonel Murray, a former commanding officer of the Regiment and one of the most brilliant leaders the war produced.

Preparations for crossing the river had already been begun by Murray on his own responsibility immediately after recovering Fort George, but billeting difficulties and the extremely cold weather had caused some delay. The enemy had taken the precaution of destroying almost all the river craft, and but two boats fit for use could be found on the spot. The local Canadian militia, however, burning for an opportunity to avenge the horror of Newark, eagerly volunteered to bring a sufficient number of *batteaux* from Burlington, some 50 miles away. This duty was assigned to Captain Elliot, the D.A.Q.M.G., who with the help of Captain Kirby succeeded in smuggling down by night the necessary number of boats to Four Mile Creek and Twelve Mile Creek, whence they were hauled across the snow on sleighs to Longhurst Ravine, where they were placed in a suitable position for launching on the Niagara, while being hidden from view of the American bank. The night of the 17th December was originally fixed for the passage of the river and the troops were kept under arms for several hours, but a heavy gale caused the attempt to be postponed. Meanwhile, some non-combatants had been released by the Americans and allowed to cross to the Canadian side of the river. From these Drummond gained much useful intelligence as to the numbers and disposition of the enemy on which to base his plans. On the other hand, in spite of all the precautions as to secrecy, rumours of the British project came to the ears of the American general, and during the nights of the 17th and 18th Fort Niagara was on the alert. McClure, indeed, issued a proclamation to the militia on the 18th emphasizing the danger which threatened the frontier and calling upon the militia to come forward *en masse* to his support.

The same day Colonel Murray received final instructions for the assault. The troops were assembled at St. Davids where the configuration of the ground concealed them from watchers on the American shore. In addition to a party of volunteers from the Canadian militia, bearing axes and escalading ladders, the force consisted of 562 men made up as follows: Royal Artillery detachment, 12; grenadier company Royal Scots, 100; flank companies 2/41st, 100; 100th Regiment, 350. These troops constituted the storming party who were to be conveyed across in two trips, and were to be followed by the remaining regulars and the contingent of Indians. "The men must be silent, not load without orders, and rely chiefly on the bayonet" was the order, and strict instructions were issued to the Indians to abstain from plunder and from acts of violence to women or children.

At 10 p.m. on the night of the 18th-19th December, in bitterly cold weather, the troops silently fell in at St. Davids and marched off. The night was dark, but the troops moving over the snow showed up faintly. After a march of about an hour and a half they disappeared into the shadows of Longhurst Ravine, where a halt was made to give time for the boats to be quietly slipped down the slope and launched into the stream. By midnight all the troops were embarked, with muskets unloaded but bayonets fixed, and an hour later the whole force was successfully landed, and the move on the fort began. First went the forlorn hope, who slipped away like shadows into the dark, still forest. This party consisted of Lieutenant Dawson and Sergeant Spearman of the 100th, the latter a man of stupendous physical strength, and twenty picked men from Canadian troops, among whom were numbered some of the most celebrated names in Canadian history :—Sir John B. Robinson, Judge McLean, Colonel Kirby, Sir Allen McNabb, Captain Bullock, Lieutenant Knowland, Captain Ball and Lieutenant Daniel K. Servois, who carried a stick of cordwood on his shoulder to throw into the gateway to prevent it being closed. Then came the grenadiers of the 100th, under Captain Fawcett; with them went a few artillerymen and men equipped with axes and ladders. Behind came the main body, consisting of five companies of the 100th, under Lieutenant-Colonel Hamilton, and with these marched the commander of the force, Colonel Murray.

All these troops were destined to storm the main gate. Behind moved three companies of the 100th, under Captain Martin, who were told off to storm the demibastion, and the grenadier company of the 1st Royal Scots, who were to attack the salient angle. The two companies of the 41st moved as a support to the main attack.

The troops moved silently and quickly, without causing any alarm, until the forlorn hope reached Youngstown, where stood a large tavern at the door of which was posted an American sentry. The snow made it possible for a man of the forlorn hope to get close up to the back of the tavern, where, peering through a window, he discovered a party of American soldiers playing cards. Lieutenant

Dawson at once decided to deal with the sentry before he had time to give the alarm. Sergeant Spearman and a grenadier were sent forward to silence the sentry, which they did most successfully; before the wretched man suspected danger he was seized by the throat, the countersign demanded and given, and he lay dead in the snow. Simultaneously with the capture of the sentry the forlorn hope dashed into the tavern and bayoneted the inmates. Although 20 men were killed, the noise did not reach the fort. A second picquet of similar strength occupying a house midway between Youngstown and the fort was dealt with in the same way.

The assault of the fort now began in accordance with the carefully devised arrangements made beforehand. The principal attack directed against the main gate and adjacent works was headed by Lieutenant Dawson's forlorn hope. These were followed by the grenadier company of the 100th under Captain Fawcett, a dozen artillerymen carrying grenades and under the command of Lieutenant Charlton. Behind these came five companies of the 100th, led by Lieutenant-Colonel Hamilton. This column, which moved along the road close to the river bank, was guided by Captain Elliot of the quartermaster-general's department—for in those days that branch performed what are known to-day as " G " duties. Following in support by the same road were the two companies of the 41st Regiment under Lieutenant Bullock. To the right of this column were the grenadiers of the Royal Scots, directed against the salient angle, and farther to the right again were three companies of the 100th Regiment with the eastern demi-bastion as their objective. Both these detachments were guided by officers of Canadian militia. It will be seen that at least nine companies of the 100th were engaged in this important enterprise and the Regiment found the greater part of the troops engaged upon it.

In the various accounts available, from which this narrative of the capture of Fort Niagara is compiled, there are numerous discrepancies, but no more numerous and no less inevitable than such discrepancies usually are. The main facts, however, seem to have been as follows. The whole business was nearly wrecked by an untoward incident. Having lost a leg in Holland many years before, Lieutenant-Colonel Hamilton was unable to accompany the Regiment on foot. As he obstinately insisted on leading it into action on every possible occasion his charger had been ferried over with considerable difficulty. The various columns moved forward in complete silence, arms being carried at the shoulder to minimize any risk of clashing bayonets. Now, when the main column had nearly approached the ditch and while every man held his breath the colonel's charger did what every horse invariably does at these moments of tension—emitted a long, shrill, nerve-shattering neigh. It was immediately answered by a similar shrillness from within the fort. In an agony of suspense the stormers stood stock still muttering unutterable blasphemies upon the horse, but to their unspeakable relief no alarm was given. Fortune now relented and one incident occurred of immense advantage to the attack. The drawbridge was found to be down, and almost immediately the gate opened and the guard marched out to relieve the sentries at the waterside. The gate remained open and at once the gigantic Sergeant Spearman of the 100th advanced across the bridge alone. When he reached the entrance a sentry came out of his box and challenged. Spearman promptly gave the countersign and added that he came with a message from Youngstown. As the sentry turned Spearman flung himself upon him and strangled him in his iron grasp. With a loud yell the storming party now rushed across the drawbridge and raced headlong inside the fort, driving the American guard before them like chaff.

Here, at the cost of interrupting a dramatic narrative, it is necessary to give another version, of which, although the ultimate result is similar, the details are entirely different. According to this second version the grenadiers of the 100th, before they got to the fort, suddenly came upon a picquet of the enemy. They were immediately challenged and the countersign demanded, and Captain Kirby, or Kerby, an officer of Canadian militia, gave the countersign and stated that they were an American relief sent from the Falls. The answer was not believed, an alarm was raised, and the grenadiers of the 100th flung themselves on the picquet. About 20 men escaped and ran for their lives to the main gate of the fort which was opened for them to come in, but the attackers were too swift and friend and foe reached the gate together. Lieutenant Servois, who had been carrying a bundle of cordwood for just this contingency, now threw it into the partially opened entrance to prevent it being shut. There was a moment of fierce fighting, but the door was forced full open and the storming party, followed by the entire main body, found itself within the fort.

About the same time the grenadiers of the Royal Scots had carried the salient angle and Captain Martin with his three companies of the 100th Regiment had succeeded in escalading the eastern demi-bastion. Practically the whole of the attacking force was now within the fort. The darkness and confusion that ensued render it practically impossible to reconstruct a coherent narrative of the next hour. It seems that the garrison rushed out from various buildings to their alarm posts and made a determined charge upon the British, but in vain; a cannon was fired into the square from the roof of the south-western tower followed by a few scattered musketry shots. Lieutenant Nowlan of the 100th instantly forced open the door and disappeared in the darkness. Several shots rang out, and when his men reached the scene of conflict Nowlan was found stone dead with four bullet wounds and a bayonet thrust through his body. Beside him lay three American soldiers, two of them dying from sword cuts and the third disabled by a bullet from the pistol still tightly clenched in the dead officer's hand. Some of the inmates were killed by the exasperated grenadiers before they could be restrained.

Meanwhile Brevet Major Davis of the Regiment led his company, consisting of but 37 men, against the southern tower, which was at first resolutely defended. An incessant though random fire killed five and wounded two of his men in the first attack. Major Davis then retired his men to the shelter of a neighbouring storehouse until the firing ceased. Then seizing a prisoner he threatened him with instant death if he failed to guide him to the entrance to the tower. The prisoner yielded to the threat and Davis, immediately followed by his men, rushed forward a second time. The door was soon battered in and the men in the lower story ran upstairs, closely followed by their assailants, some of whom by the command of their officer had snatched brands from the wood fire to light them in their ascent. Others called aloud for scaling ladders and above the din could be heard the voice of Davis ordering his men to bayonet the garrison to the last man if they offered any resistance. Panic stricken the Americans begged for quarter and surrendered to the number of sixty-four men, having lost but one man in the brief struggle.

All resistance was now at an end and the Americans endeavoured to seek safety in flight. A crowd of fugitives from the barracks and mess-house attempted to make good their escape by the sally port, but were driven back by the grenadiers of the Royal Scots. Colonel Murray hastened to the spot and endeavoured to save the lives of the fugitives by ordering them to lie down, being wounded himself in the hand in his merciful effort. Dawn was now breaking and the drummers of the 100th made their way to the top of the main building and played "The British Grenadiers." The British flag broke out over the fort, where it was to continue to fly until the end of the war. More and more of the men clambered up and "the light-hearted Irish soldiers of the 100th were dancing on the flat roof of the barracks to the lively strains of 'St. Patrick's Day' when Sir Gordon Drummond rode through the gate."

The capture of Fort Niagara, which was almost entirely a 100th's achievement, was perhaps the most brilliantly successful action of the war. It deprived the Americans of one of their strongest positions ; it gave us a permanent footing in American territory, and threatened the whole line of the Niagara to Buffalo. It rivalled the operations of that Great War, which was to break out almost exactly a century later, in the explicit and minutely detailed orders which were issued to and thoroughly understood by all ranks. In view of the magnitude of the success the casualties of the victors were almost negligible, the total loss being but 1 officer (Lieutenant Nowlan of the 100th) and 5 men killed, and 2 officers and 3 men wounded; while on the American side 65 officers and men were killed, 2 officers and 12 other ranks were wounded and the prisoners amounted to 14 officers and 325 rank and file. Only about a score of the enemy effected their escape. The trophies of victory were immense. Twenty-seven guns were taken. The arsenal was found to contain upwards of 3,000 stands of arms and many rifles. Huge quantities of ordnance and commissariat stores fell into the hands of the victors.

There is always a tendency to judge of an operation not by the success achieved so much as by the amount of blood spilt in carrying it out. Such a criterion acts unfairly in the case of an attack based on the element of surprise, where the object is to get to close quarters at the earliest possible moment and to stifle opposition without delay. Such an operation was the night attack on Fort Niagara. It was a problem of immense hazard demanding exceptional staff work, highly trained officers, and brave and well-disciplined soldiers. These requisites were forthcoming. But the perfection of the arrangements and the valour of the troops are apt to be discounted by the very success in which they were employed ; and the storming of Fort Niagara in some narratives does not receive the recognition which is its due. It is, however, satisfactory to relate that the services of the 100th Regiment were recognized in the despatch forwarded by the commander of the operation to Lieutenant-General Drummond in which he states : " The highly gratifying but difficult duty remains of endeavouring to do justice to the bravery, intrepidity, and devotion of the 100th Regiment to the service of their country under that gallant officer, Lieutenant-Colonel Hamilton, to whom I feel highly indebted for his cordial assistance. Captain Martin, 100th Regiment, who executed the task allotted to him in the most intrepid manner, merits the greatest praise." The names of Lieutenant Dawson and Captain Fawcett were mentioned for their brilliant services, and an acknowledgment was made of the unwearied exertions of Acting-Quartermaster Pilkington.

The enemy were now seriously alarmed about the Niagara frontier, and on the 23rd December the American commander, Major-General Hall, fixed his headquarters at Batavia, about forty miles from Buffalo. Six days later he reviewed his troops, amounting to 2,000 men at the latter place. Meanwhile on the other side of the river Drummond was at Chippawa, whence he moved down to within a couple of miles from Fort Erie. From here the American position at Black Rock could be discerned, and Drummond determined to throw a force across the river and attack it. Accordingly on the night of the 30th Riall crossed the Niagara, having with him four companies of the 8th, 250 men of the 41st, the light companies of the 89th, and the grenadiers of the 100th Regiment, which, with 50 militia, made up a force of about 600 rank and file. The column, supplemented by 120 Indian warriors, landed without opposition about two miles below Black Rock. An American picquet was captured and the force seized the crossing of a stream which ran in front of the enemy's position, resisting several attempts made during the night to dislodge them. At dawn the Royal Scots and a detachment of the 19th Light Dragoons crossed the river with a view to landing above Black Rock and thus turn the enemy's position while Riall pinned them in front. Unfortunately, however, through an error on the part of the pilots, several of the boats grounded and the Royal Scots quickly had about fifty casualties. The advance of Riall's force, however, caused a favourable diversion, and after a short resistance the

Americans fled to Buffalo. To this town they were followed in close pursuit and after a slight resistance broke in all directions. The British captured 8 guns, a quantity of stores and three gun-boats. Only 130 prisoners were made " owing to the nimbleness of the American militia and the contiguity of the woods." In this operation the British casualties were 31 killed and 81 wounded, the number of casualties in the 100th Regiment—which was in reserve on the 31st—being 1 officer and 4 other ranks wounded. The officer was Captain Fawcett, who received a severe wound in the heel. After the war while Captain Fawcett was living at a Canadian boarding-house a guest endeavoured to raise a laugh by saying that " to have been shot in the heel Fawcett must have been running away." The reply of the latter was to raise his crutch and fell the humorist with it.

After the American side of the Niagara frontier had thus suffered retribution for the " frightfulness " of the enemy on the Canadian shore the British troops evacuated American soil with the exception of Fort Niagara. At that place, as well as at St. Davids, Burlington Heights and York, the centre division of the British Army went into winter quarters. There were, however, some outlying detachments for the 100th spent January and February at Bertie (with a company in Fort Erie) and later moved to Fort Niagara.

In 1814 the contest took on a sterner aspect. The end of the Peninsular War had set free large numbers of experienced British troops, which were now sent to the New World, and on the American side the experience gained by their soldiers made these opponents much more formidable than they had been in the earlier stages of the war. After some indecisive fighting in the east the Americans in July assumed the offensive on the Niagara line, and with nearly 5,000 men entered Canada again. At this time the British force in this region consisted of about 1,800 men, made up of the 1st Battalion of the Royal Scots, the 100th and 103rd Regiments, a troop of the 19th Light Dragoons, and a detachment of artillery.

THE 1st BATTALION

Portion of it was on detached duty at Burlington Heights; Fort Niagara; Fort George; Fort Mississaga, and Fort Erie, the garrison of the last-named post consisting of a few artillerymen and a company each from the 8th and 100th, the whole under the command of Major Buck of the former regiment. The invading army landed on either side of Fort Erie, which was, as is admitted even by American historians, in a defenceless condition. After a short engagement the fort was summoned to surrender and the garrison were made prisoners of war.

Having disposed of this British detachment the American commander, Major-General Brown, set his force in motion northwards with his right flank covered by the River Niagara. The main body of the British, under the immediate command of Lieutenant-Colonel Pearson, was now at Chippawa and consisted of 230 of the Royal Scots, 450 of the 100th Regiment, a troop of the 19th Light Dragoons, and a small detachment of artillery, amounting in all to 760 rank and file, to which number is to be added some 300 immobile militia just assembled and about the same number of Indians. The first intelligence of the landing of the invaders reached General Riall at Chippawa at about eight o'clock the same morning; and he immediately ordered that post to be reinforced by five companies of the Royal Scots. Even then his inferiority of force allowed him merely to reconnoitre the enemy's position, a service which was gallantly carried out by Colonel Pearson at the head of the flank companies of the 100th, a few militia and some Indians, the Americans being located on an eminence near Bertie. Riall was all for commencing an attack that evening, but was restrained by the non-arrival of the 8th Regiment which was hourly expected from York.

The initiative thus passed to the enemy, and on the morning of the 4th July the American army advanced towards Chippawa by the main road along the river bank. Flowing roughly parallel to the Chippawa Creek and about a mile and a half south of it is Street's Creek, and here the first collision took place. On its approach to

Street's Creek the leading American brigade struck against a British detachment consisting of the light companies of the Royal Scots and 100th with a few of the 19th Light Dragoons. The American brigadier, General Winfield Scott, immediately pinned the British in front while detaching a small force to make a turning movement against the British right. This threat, coupled with the heavy firing of the enemy's 18-pounders, compelled Pearson to retreat, but not before he had destroyed the bridge over the creek. This was repaired by the American pioneers, and the American army crossed the stream and went into camp with a strength of about 4,000 men and 9 guns. Riall had meanwhile stationed himself behind the Chippawa, and, having been joined during the morning of the 5th by 480 rank and file of the 8th Regiment determined to attack the Americans that afternoon. His force now consisted of 1,530 regulars, 300 militia without transport and but partially armed, and about the same number of Indians. His force, therefore, amounted to 2,130 men with two 24-pounders and a $5\frac{1}{2}$-inch howitzer.

At the appointed hour the British crossed the Chippawa and marched to the attack. On the extreme right were the Indians and some of the militia moving through the woods, which were skirted by the remainder of the militia and by the light companies of the Royal Scots and 100th under Lieutenant-Colonel Pearson. This flanking movement was attended with success, for, although the bulk of the Indians moved out too far, the threat thus exercised helped the operation and the Americans encountered broke and fled in every direction. Pearson now pursued vigorously, but the arrival of American supports compelled the retirement of the British right wing. Meanwhile Riall with his main body was confronting the American position. On his left he posted the 8th Regiment with his three guns; while the Royal Scots and 100th Regiment (less their light companies) directly fronted the enemy.

These two regiments were now ordered to charge.

The ground over which they had to pass was uneven and covered with long grass, which greatly impeded their progress. It was not, however, until the enemy's musketry, and a flanking fire from four of his guns, had caused a serious loss in the ranks of these brave regiments that the attempt was abandoned. It was now recognized that the enemy enjoyed an overwhelming superiority in numbers, and, accordingly, the British troops were ordered to retire upon Chippawa. The movement was carried out in perfect order, being splendidly covered by the wings consisting of the 8th Regiment from the left and Pearson's detachment (in which was the light company of the 100th) from the right. Riall's army then encamped once more on the left bank of the Chippawa.

In this engagement, known as the Battle of Street's Creek or Chippawa, the British losses were very severe. The killed amounted to 3 captains, 3 subalterns, 7 sergeants, and 135 rank and file. The wounded comprised 3 field officers (including the commanding officers of both the Royal Scots and the 100th), 5 captains, 18 subalterns, 18 sergeants, and 277 other ranks. Forty-six were missing. The 100th Regiment had lost nearly fifty per cent. of its personnel. Three subalterns, 3 sergeants, and 64 rank and file were killed; while the number of wounded was 134, including 9 officers. The dead officers were Lieutenant Gibbon, Ensign Rea and a subaltern shown as missing and killed, but whose name is not given, whilst the wounded were made up of the commanding officer, Lieutenant-Colonel the Marquis of Tweedale; Captain Sherrard; Captain Sleigh; Lieutenants Williams, Lyon, Valentine, and Fortune; Ensigns Clarke and Johnson and Adjutant Kingston. These figures will show that even a century before the Great War casualties of extreme severity could be and were incurred in but a few hours' fighting. In the case of the 100th Regiment its losses were so severe that it practically ceased to play an active part in the remainder of the war.

The Regiment was now reduced to a strength of 245 and was, in consequence, sent back to relieve some Canadian militia in Fort George and Fort Mississaga. It was due to this relief that the 100th missed playing a part in the Battle of Lundy's Lane on 25th July, the most hotly contested action of the war, in which out of 3,000 engaged the British had nearly 900 casualties, the strength and losses on the American side being very similar. The light companies of the Regiment took part in an unsuccessful attempt to regain Fort Erie in August, and in October a detachment of the 100th was engaged in a slight skirmish. Headquarters of the Regiment were during this period in Fort George, Fort Niagara, and Fort Mississaga. With the approach of November the British in this part of the theatre of war went into winter quarters, the 100th moving first to Kingston and thence to Montreal. Long before the Canadian snows had melted, the war was over and peace was signed.

The great victory of Waterloo removed for ever the danger of Napoleonic domination, and in the reaction which followed it was natural that sweeping reductions should have been made in the military budgets of Europe. England, alone of European nations, had seen the fight through from start to finish, but the cost had been heavy, and twenty years of war had left her with a national debt of staggering proportions for those days. The army was cut down, and on these occasions it is the regiments of recent growth which are offered as expiatory victims to economy. Amongst the doomed units was the 100th Prince Regent's County of Dublin Regiment, which now bore on its colours the honour " Niagara " to commemorate its distinguished services on the Canadian frontier. But, although it had won its laurels under this distinctive number, the bureaucratic mind endeavoured to rob it of its identity even when on the brink of the grave. With a fatuity almost inhuman the authorities juggled with the numbers of the regiments at the bottom of the list and the 100th actually became for some time the 99th of the line. But it is by the former designation that it will always be known. By this, another regiment, originally the New South Wales Corps and later the 102nd,

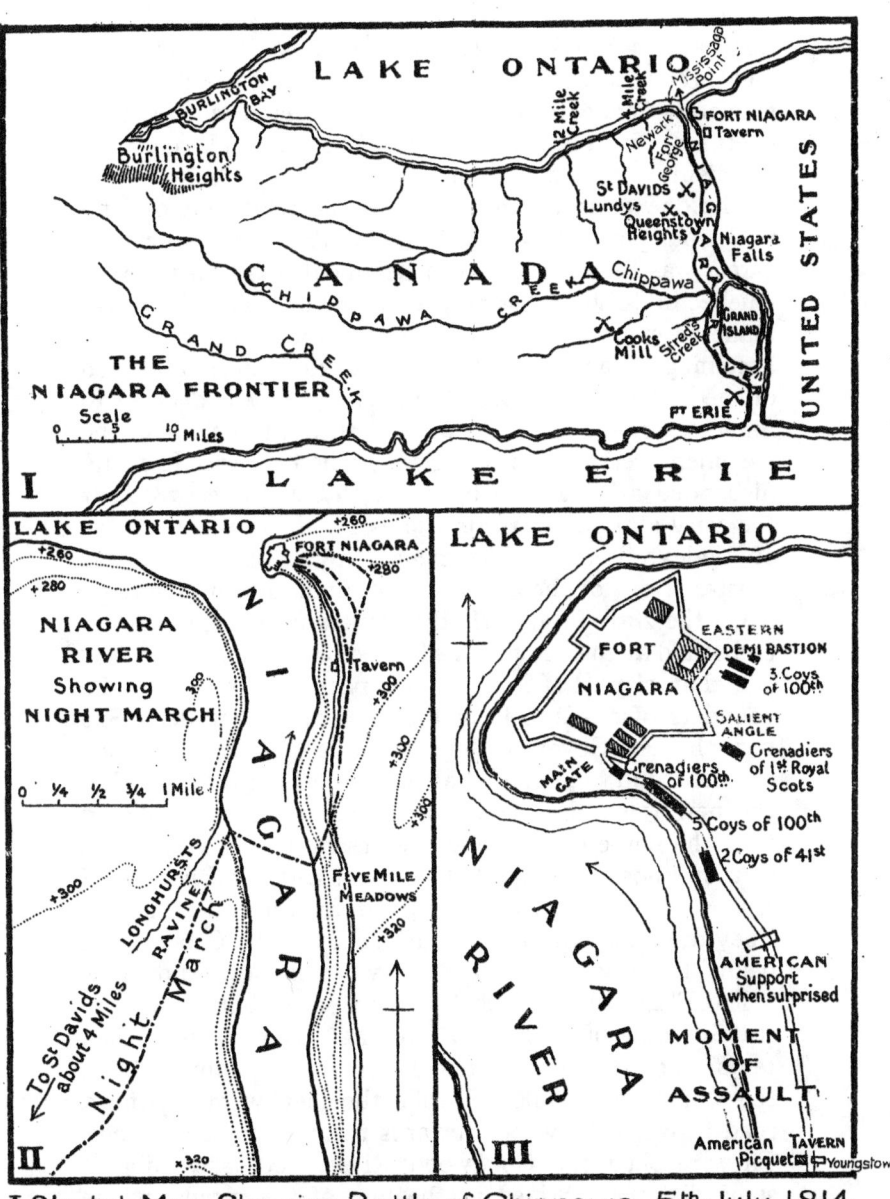

I, Sketch Map Shewing Battle of Chippawa 5th July 1814
II & III, Ditto Shewing the CAPTURE of FORT NIAGARA
18th-19th Dec. 1813.

succeeded to the title 100th Foot. It was disbanded at Chatham in March, 1818. This unit has no connexion whatever with the Leinster Regiment, and mention of it is merely made to assist future historians who will be confused by the "general post" system played with regiments with low numbers.

The one praiseworthy step was the allotment of land in various parts of Canada to the military veterans whose career was thus ended. The Regiment was broken up at Quebec in July, 1818, and a very liberal offer of land was made to every member of the corps on condition of his becoming an actual settler. About 300 officers and men of the Regiment accepted the offer and it was decided to found a settlement on the upper Ottawa, the cadre of the Regiment returning to England, where it was formally disbanded at Chatham on the 24th September, 1818, at the very station where its successor, the 1st The Prince of Wales's Leinster Regiment (Royal Canadians) was mustered out of the army over a hundred years later.

On the 28th July, 1818, the settlers from the old 100th embarked at Quebec *en route* for their new home. As they left that city H.M.S. *Iphigenia* passed them, amid the thunders of a salute from the guns of the citadel. She bore the new Governor-General of the Canadas, the Duke of Richmond, and the loyal soldier-settlers resolved that the new town they hoped to found in the west should bear the name of the King's representative. Travel was slow in those days, and it was not until the middle of August that the settlers arrived at their destination. They disembarked on the south shore of the Ottawa just below the Chandière Falls on what is now known as "The Flats," but which for many years bore the more stately name of Richmond Landing. Here they pitched tents, and here for the remainder of the summer dwelt the women and children while the men were cutting a road through the woods towards their permanent homes. They reached the Goodwood River, and, ascending it some distance, arrived at the foot of the rapids, where they decided to build their town. By this time the season was far advanced, and, before the women and children were brought down from the temporary settlement and housed for the winter, much suffering ensued. The colonists were greatly helped by the generosity of the Imperial Government, who supplied them liberally with tools and one year's rations free of charge. Under the able guidance of Lieutenant-Colonel Bourke, late of the 100th, the settlement steadily grew. Other settlers came in, chiefly retired officers and men from various regiments, and the military aspect of this little *colonia* was enhanced. From here the torch which the 100th Regiment had held high was passed to younger hands, for when forty years later the 100th or The Prince of Wales's Royal Canadian Regiment was raised in Canada many of the recruits who came forward were the grandsons of the veterans who served in the ranks of the old 100th Prince Regent's County of Dublin Regiment of Foot.

Continuity is as necessary in the history of a regiment as it is in genealogy. Cases have occurred where honours have been transmitted on no stronger ground than an identity of digits between an old, and disbanded, regiment and one which was later formed, and some ignorant critics have been inclined to assert that the honour " Niagara " is borne by the Leinster Regiment, through its 1st Battalion for no stronger reason. To this there is the reply that the nucleus of the Regiment (which was raised in Canada in 1858) was to be found in the descendants of the old 100th which was disbanded in that country in 1818. At the risk of anticipating the story which follows it may be stated that when a movement for the repatriation of the Royal Canadians was inaugurated in 1897 the first step was to bring to the notice of the Imperial authorities the existence of a great petition which had been signed in Canada for the purpose. A sub-committee was received by the Governor-General, the Earl of Aberdeen, at Ottawa, on 13th May, 1897. In the address to His Excellency occur the following words :—

" When a portion of the British forces was disbanded,

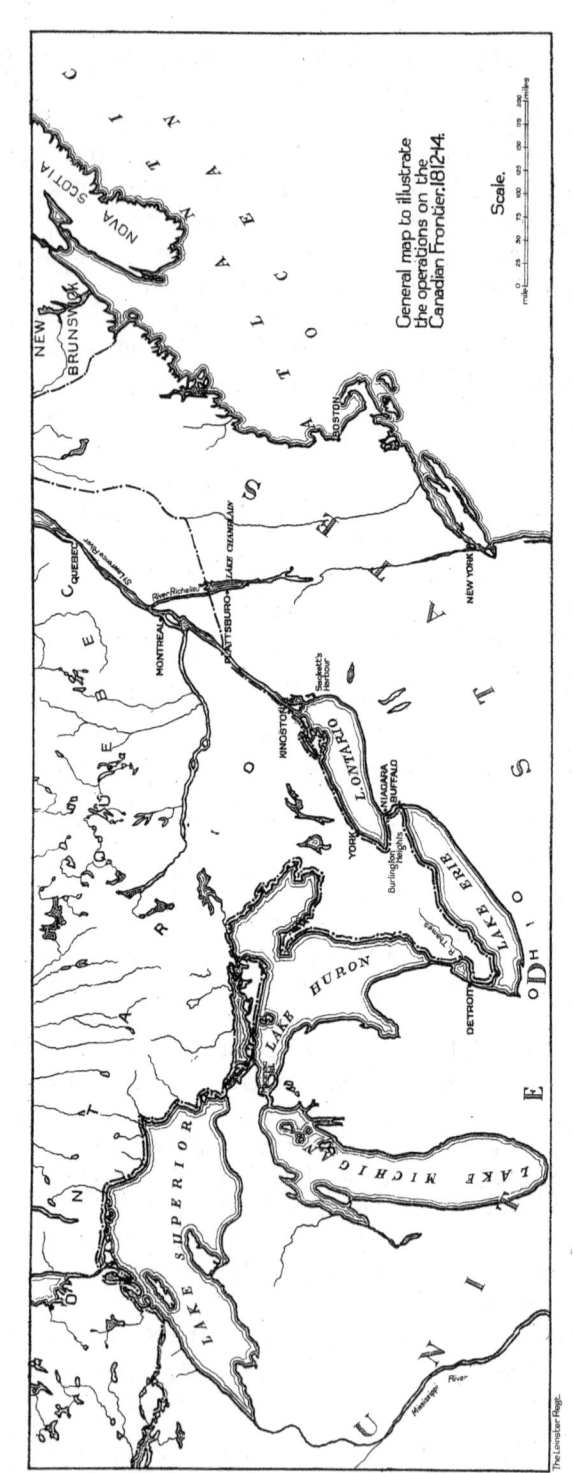

after the wars which agitated the world at the beginning of the century, the 100th Prince Regent's Regiment, which at that time was serving in Canada, was disbanded here in the year 1818, and the descendants of its members are now resident in our midst. When the forces were again increased during the Crimean War, followed by the Indian Mutiny, which it was feared would reach large proportions, His Excellency Sir Edmund Head, in 1858, then Governor-General of Canada, was authorized *to raise again for service the regiment whose ranks during the intervening period had never been filled.''*

Coming from a Canadian committee, whose interest would naturally have been, in this question of repatriation, to emphasize merely the Canadian aspect of the Regiment, this recognition of the British origin of the 100th is striking and conclusive.

CHAPTER IV

THE 100TH THE PRINCE OF WALES'S ROYAL CANADIAN REGIMENT — 1858–1859 — MONTREAL — QUEBEC — SHORNCLIFFE—ALDERSHOT.

A GENERATION now passes during which peace reigns over the world and during which the settlers from the old 100th are helping to build up a great Dominion. True to her inveterate habit England has been reducing her defences to a perilous minimum, and so, when suddenly she finds herself involved in a struggle in which four Great Powers are engaged, she is to a large extent unready. When the strain upon the resources of the British Army, caused by the Crimean War, and almost immediately afterwards by the Indian Mutiny, began to be realized by the numerous immigrants of British birth then settled in Canada there was a general feeling that an effort should be made to assist the mother country in her struggle against her foes. In a sparsely populated country, however, time is necessary to transform sentiment into action and negotiations had to take place through the Governor-General of British North America and the Home Government before permission could be obtained to raise troops in Canada for general service in the British Army.

It is not necessary to delve amongst the records of the Circumlocution Office of the period nor to reproduce the minutes of the Ranville-Ranvilles and Tite Barnacles of the time. Sufficient it is to say that in March, 1858, permission was given to raise in Canada an infantry regiment to be numbered the 100th and commissions were offered to gentlemen residing in Canada on the following conditions :—A major's commission to be given for raising 200 men ; a captain's for 80 men ; and a lieutenant's for 40. Recruiting began about the middle of March and in three months the complement was raised chiefly in Upper Canada. The physique of the men recruited was remarkable. Many of the men were of Herculean strength—these were chiefly the hardy lumber men from the forests and riverways, who from the nature of their former occupation were of enormous muscular development. A contemporary record remarks particularly on the " splendid fellows who came from the famous Richmond district—the descendants of the grand old veterans and settlers of 1812–1818." It is this connexion which provides the link between the 1st Leinster Regiment and the old 100th Prince Regent's County of Dublin Regiment and it is interesting to note that one of the recruits of the 100th Royal Canadians in 1858 was Milo Bourke son of Lieutenant-Colonel George Thaw Bourke " late of H.M. 100th Prince Regent's Regiment, and Richmond, County Carleton, Ontario." We have met Colonel Bourke's name before, in the description of the settlement founded by the disbanded veterans of the war of 1812.

Of those young Canadians who came forward with alacrity sixty-six years ago there is, so far as is known, but one survivor left to-day—Henry Gorman now a police magistrate at Sarnia, Ontario. It was the privilege of the author to get in touch with this veteran of 85 summers and there is now reproduced in his own words the story of the early days of the 100th The Prince of Wales's Royal Canadian Regiment.

To begin with I may say that I was born at Halifax, Nova Scotia, on 6th February, 1839, while my father was serving in the 23rd Royal Welsh Fusiliers, and spent the first eight years of my life in that regiment. On his discharge my father settled in London, Canada West, now Ontario. The Crimean War aroused the military inclinations of the young Canadians and a number of volunteer militia companies were organized, infantry, cavalry and artillery. In 1856 I joined the London

Volunteer Field Battery. The Indian Mutiny broke out in 1857. Early in 1858 a call was made by the Imperial Government, through the Canadian Government, for the enrolment of a battalion of infantry for the British Army, to be known as the 100th Regiment. The strength of the regiment was to be 12 companies of 100 men each, or a total of 1,200 men. Commissions in the regiment placed at the disposal of residents of Canada were:—One major, six captains, six lieutenants and six or eight ensigns. To qualify for these commissions the major had to recruit 200 men at his own expense; captains 80 men each, and lieutenants 40 men each. Ensigns were not required to furnish any specified number of men, but all, or nearly all of them assisted the senior officers in drumming up recruits. Toronto was the main receiving station for Western Canada, with London and Kingston as sub-stations. Montreal was headquarters for the Regiment and chief recruiting station for Canada East, with Quebec City as a sub-station. At the outset the mobilizing centre was at Montreal, with Colonel Rollo, Quartermaster-General for the forces in Canada, in command. Ensign Lee of the 17th Regiment was appointed lieutenant and adjutant, and Sergeants Taylor and Smith of the 17th were made sergeant-major and quartermaster-sergeant of the Regiment. As each company was formed non-commissioned officers of the 17th were placed in charge and instructed recruits and young non-commissioned officers in their duties and the routine of barrack-room life. They also acted as drill instructors. There was a considerable sprinkling of old soldiers among the newly enlisted men, who had served short terms in the regular army or in the old country militia regiments brought into service during the Crimean War. These were among the first to be promoted to non-commissioned rank.

In company with three other members of the London Field Battery I went to Toronto in April, 1858, to enlist in the 100th. To have done so in London might have been prevented by our parents who were in close touch with the recruiting staff in our home city. The terms of enlistment and service as set forth in printed proclamations were service for ten years, not exceeding twelve, pay 1s. a day for privates, 1s. 4d. for corporals, 1s. 10d. for sergeants and proportionate increase for colour-sergeants and staff sergeants. All recruits were to get a " free kit " and a bounty of three pounds sterling. In addition to this an extra bounty of three pounds was offered by officers who were recruiting their quotas to qualify for their commissions. Myself and three companions enlisted for Major Dunn. Knowing something of the tricks played on recruits and the way in which they were fleeced by the recruiting sergeants we applied to the captain in charge of the recruiting depot at Toronto, after enlistment, for Major Dunn's extra bounty and were assured that it would be paid after attestation. When that part of the enlistment routine had been complied with, we asked again for our bounty money and were put off with further excuses and finally at the end of four or five days were, with fifteen or sixteen others marched off to the railway station headed by the band of the Royal Canadian Rifles, whose headquarters were in Toronto, and entrained for Montreal, where the 100th was being mobilized. The recruiting staffs at Toronto, London and Kingston were all non-commissioned officers of the Royal Canadian Rifles, with a captain in charge.

We were joined at Kingston by another squad of recruits and arrived next morning in Montreal. Here we were greeted by a mob of hoodlums who jibed and jeered and pelted us with mud and snow slush. On arrival at the barracks we were taken in hand by non-commissioned officers of the 17th Regiment and posted to companies. Another doctor's examination had to be passed, after which we were taken on the strength of the new regiment. As soon as possible, after being approved as fit for service, my three comrades and I went before Colonel Rollo, our commanding officer, and complained of being deprived of our extra bounty money. We gave the colonel full particulars, with names of the two recruiting sergeants. The result was that in less than two weeks the money was paid to us. I am sure there were not many others who enlisted who received any of the extra bounty.

Early in May, 1858, practically all the men required to organize the twelve companies had arrived in Montreal. In Montreal we were stripped of every article of our civilian clothes by the non-commissioned officers in charge, who no doubt pocketed a good sized rake-off from the sales to old clothes men. Our stay in Montreal was a continuous scene of boisterous extravagance. The regular £3 bounty money was paid to the men after their arrival at headquarters and was freely spent under the guidance of the regular soldiers. There was not much time spent in barracks and the morning and afternoon drills were of brief duration. We scarcely knew how rations were obtained or paid for and our daily pay was seldom drawn. New arrivals kept the bounty money festivities in operation pretty well up to the time we left for Quebec. Before leaving Montreal my father came to see me and to get my discharge, if possible. On seeing me dressed in the old time pigeon-tailed coatee, he laughed heartily turned me around and said "My boy you look like a decorated cock sparrow." On applying for my discharge he was told that there was no authority for granting discharges in Canada and that he would have to wait until the Regiment arrived in England before anything could be done in that line. The necessary £20 to accompany the application was deposited with the paymaster, but I heard no more of it until months after the Regiment's arrival in England. I was very glad that my father's efforts to take me back to our home in London had failed, I did not like the idea of returning home and being subjected to the taunts of acquaintances that I turned tail on my comrades and had an attack of "cold feet."

The Regiment left Montreal for Quebec by steamboat early in May and was stationed in the Citadel barracks. The commissioned officers joined the Regiment there, including George Baron De Rottenburg, Lieutenant-

Colonel commanding. Baron De Rottenburg had been serving as Adjutant-General of militia in Canada. He was a British Army officer of experience, well posted in all matters connected with the command of a regiment in the field, a strict disciplinarian, with a kindly consideration for the lapses of young soldiers unused to army ways and etiquette and inclined to chafe at restrictions on their personal actions to which they were not accustomed. The major's commission was awarded to Alexander Dunn, V.C. Dunn was a Canadian, son of the Honourable William Dunn, receiver-general in the Canadian Government. He served through the Crimean campaign as a cornet or ensign in the 11th Hussars, and won his Victoria Cross during the memorable charge of the Light Brigade at Balaclava, when he was only 19 years of age. He was a splendid specimen of young Canadian manhood, 6 feet 2 inches in height, well proportioned and handsomely featured. He was an expert swordsman and pistol shot. The special act of bravery for which Dunn was awarded the Victoria Cross, as I remember reading it, was, that after the Light Brigade had charged through the Russian guns and were returning to their starting point they were pursued by the Russian cavalry that were in battle formation in rear of the guns. A troop sergeant-major, whose horse had been shot, was surrounded by three or four Russian lancers. Dunn went to the rescue of the sergeant-major and shot or sabred the Russians, took up the sergeant-major on his horse and carried him safely to the British lines.

Stricter discipline prevailed at Quebec. Colonel De Rottenburg and the other officers, aided by Sergeant-Major Taylor, took us in hand. It was not easy work to break the men into soldierly ways. They chafed at obeying rules regulating their conduct towards officers, especially. Saluting was very much disliked and blunt talk in answer to questions or remarks made by their superior officers were more frequent than otherwise. One incident in the company to which I belonged ever remained in my memory as a ludicrous sample of Canadian brusqueness and innocence of military etiquette. An ensign of the 39th Regiment, acting as subaltern of the day, visited the barrack-rooms at tea time. At the call of "Attention—Any complaints?" a big-boned Scots-Canadian named Kribs picked up the tin bucket in which the tea had been brought from the cookhouse and dipping his hand in it brought up a fist full of tea leaves which he thrust in the face of the astonished officer with the query: "Do you call that tea? I say it's nothing but beech leaves." Joe Smith, who had followed close on Kribs's heels, called the officer's attention to a piece of bread he had broken apart and in which there were traces of ash and pieces of a small nail and wanted to know if the officer thought that was fit stuff to give men to eat. The officer said: "The tea rations are not regimental issue and I have nothing to do with complaints about them." To this Smith promptly replied: "What the h—ll did you ask for then?" Joe was promptly sent to the guard room, much to his surprise, as he wasn't aware he had said anything out of the way.

The following is a complete list of the first officers of the Regiment. Those distinguished by an asterisk were Canadians, those by a double asterisk were also Upper Canada College boys, and those by a dagger were officers who were transferred to the Regiment from the permanent military staff here or from regiments then serving in this colony, the others joined the Regiment in England:—

Colonel—Major-General Viscount Melville; Lieutenant-Colonel— George de Rottenburg†, C.B.; Majors— I. H. C. Robertson, Brevet Lieutenant-Colonel; A. R. Dunn**, V.C.; Captains— T. M. L. Wegwelin, Brevet Major; R. B. Ingram, P. G. B. Lake, Henry Cooke, James Clary, Henry G. Browne, V.C., John Clarke*, T. W. W. Smythe*, George Macartney*, Chas. J. Clarke**, Richard C. Price*, G. P. Blake; Lieutenants—George B. Coulson, John Lee†, James Lamb, F. W. Benwell, Henry L. Nicholls, Joseph Dooly, Richard L. Bayliff, Jno. Fletcher*, Louis A. Casault*, L. C. A. L. De Bellefeuille*,

Phillip Derbishire*, Alfred E. Rykert**, Chas. H. Carriere*, Henry T. Duchesne*, Brown Wallis* ; Ensigns —C. McD. Moorson, Fred. Morris, John Gibbs Ridout**, Henry E. Davidson*, Charles A. Boulton**, T. H. Baldwin*, W. P. Clarke*. Paymaster—Joseph Hutchison. Quartermaster—George Grant. Surgeon—Wm. Barrett ; Assistant Surgeons—Thomas Liddard, Daniel Murray.

The mobilization of the Regiment was completed in Quebec and it embarked for England in June and July in three sections of four companies each, at intervals of a fortnight. The first section included the colonel and headquarters staff and the first four companies. It arrived on or about the 1st July at Liverpool.

While in Canada the men were clothed in uniforms of the Canadian Militia of 1837 ; some said of the war of 1812, when the Dublin 100th earned the battle honour of "Niagara," still borne on the colours of the Royal Canadian Regiment. That uniform consisted of a scarlet "coatee" or pigeon-tailed coat, plentifully ornamented across the breast and tails with white braid about half an inch wide, black trousers with small red stripe down the side and a woollen forage cap about double the size of the well-known collar box of more recent date, such as was in 1858 worn by the British Army. In the centre of the crown of this cap was a woollen ball about as large as a cricket ball, giving it an extra grotesque and ludicrous appearance. These uniforms had been in store since the war of 1812 or the rebellion of 1837. The coatee was further ornamented with shoulder epaulets, resembling the old time door knocker. As might be expected the cloth was rotten, and as a result of the rough and tumble usage that hundreds of young men thrown promiscuously together, as was the case in the formation of a new regiment, are sure to indulge in, the uniforms did not retain their original appearance very long. By the time the first lot reached England there was not a uniform in the Regiment complete in its furnishings. From many of them the coat tails had disappeared completely. reducing the coat to jacket dimensions. Many coats had but one tail, and, if the tails were complete on the coat, one or both epaulets were missing. The forage cap was converted into a variety of shapes to suit the fancies of the wearers. As for the trousers, many were the expedients resorted to in order to keep them sufficiently intact to make them wearable. No belts or arms of any description were served out to the men in Canada. The knapsack was a huge square affair nearly two feet wide and of equal depth. The haversacks were of equally generous proportions. We had no greatcoats. The knapsacks had been freshened up in appearance by a coating of tar paint. We put them on for the first time to march from the citadel barracks in Quebec to embark on the steamship. When we came to take them off they stuck to our backs without the aid of shoulder straps, and when removed left stripes of tar on our red coats, still further adding to the already disreputable appearance of that portion of our uniform.

We were a sight for the gods on landing at Liverpool. A mob of comically clad creatures like nothing that had been seen on the streets of that city within the memory of that generation of its citizens. Many were the inquiries as to who and what we were and from whence we came. In some way the impression prevailed that we were from the scenes of the slaughtered garrisons, women and children in India, and much sympathy was shown us by the Liverpudlians. They did not laugh at or deride us, that treat was reserved for our reception by the troops in camp at Shorncliffe. We certainly contributed to the gaiety of that camp. It was one continuous roar of boisterous laughter from the time we reached the camp grounds until we arrived at the lines assigned us. We were not annoyed at the loud voiced merriment of our newly met comrades. We knew we looked like caricatures of British soldiers and took it all in good part. Before the second section of the Regiment reached Shorncliffe, the first arrivals had discarded their antiquated outfit and were clothed in bright new uniforms of the regulation pattern of that day—red tunic with blue facings, red shell jacket, black trousers with red stripe for full dress, and blue serge trousers with red stripe, "collar box" forage cap for fatigue dress. With the tunic for full dress we wore a shako, with peak, a white pompon with red base rising from the Regiment's number plate on the front of the shako. The band wore white tunics and shell jackets; with these exceptions, the uniform was the same as that of the rest of the Regiment. Those who had arrived with the first lot could appreciate the figure they cut on arrival when they saw the second detachment of four companies march into camp, but the novelty and humour of it had worn off by the time the four remaining companies joined us.

The regular army officers gazetted to the 100th joined us at Shorncliffe. These officers did not understand some of the expressions used by Canadians. No. 1 Company to which I belonged was being served out with clothing. Brevet Major Wegwelin, commanding the company, seeing one of the men whose arms appeared to be full of uniform clothing loitering around the door of the quartermaster's stores asked him if he had not received all his clothing. The man replied "All but the pants, sir." "Pants, pants," said Wegwelin, "what are 'pants' Sergeant?" "Oh, sir," said the sergeant, "that is what these men call their trousers."

Fifty sergeants from the Brigade of Foot Guards were sent to Shorncliffe to drill the Regiment and when that was nearing completion the formation of a band was taken in hand. I could play a cornet tolerably well before I enlisted, but I had no desire to join the band, I enjoyed the drill and wanted to be a soldier in the ranks and make myself deserving of promotion. I therefore did not send in my name to the band president for membership in the band. Two of my old London Militia comrades, however, who had joined the band told the bandmaster that I could play a cornet. Two or three days after the band had been formed I was called to the orderly-room.

The colonel and band president were there and I was asked why I had not sent in my name for band duty. I told them I preferred to remain in the ranks, and that I did not think I would be of much or any use to the band. I was ordered to report to the bandmaster at once. I did so. Mr. Smalley, the bandmaster, questioned me as to what I played and put an instrument in my hands, set a piece of music before me and asked me if I could play that. It was a simple slow march and I replied " I guess so." The bandmaster jumped as if I had stuck a pin in him, turned to the sergeant and said : " Send that man to the guard-room. Did you hear the insulting reply he gave me ? " The sergeant, who had come from the 66th, had been long enough in the Regiment to know our peculiarities, said : " He didn't mean to insult you, sir, ' I guess so ' is a common expression among the men and means that they think so." It took some time for the bandmaster to cool down. On further acquaintance I became a prime favourite of his, and when he was leaving the Regiment a year later to take over the band of the 6th Royal Warwicks, he said to me as he was bidding me good-bye, " Gorman, I can say ' I guess so,' as well as any of you." I was surprised to find that he remembered the incident connected with our first meeting and I appreciated the humour of it.

The Guards drill-sergeants having completed their task of bringing the Regiment to a state of parade perfection, and the band being sufficiently advanced to play for a general's inspection and march past in slow and quick time as was then the custom, General Maunsell, in command of the camp, decided to inspect the Regiment. It was then late in December of 1858. An incident in which I figured to my sorrow and chagrin, occurred on the night before the inspection. I was in Sandgate when the bugles in camp sounded " First Post." I started for camp and at the foot of the road to camp I overtook Bandsman Allan, who was standing conversing with a couple of civilian friends. As I passed I called to him to hurry up. When I got to the band-room I asked for Corporal Miller, the orderly-corporal, to report myself present. Unfortunately Miller had indulged too freely at the canteen and was lying on his cot "dead to the world." I was told that all the men were present except Allan, and as I believed he was close behind me I put on my greatcoat and hurried out to parade with the orderly non-commissioned officers and answer for the band. "Last Post" was sounding. To the sergeant-major's query I reported the band "all present."

I had scarcely done so when Allan came running up, his white uniform quite conspicuous in the dark and reported himself to the sergeant-major. Result: I was taken to my room a prisoner by the regimental orderly-sergeant, who was instructed to send Corporal Miller to the sergeant-major. Miller was still in a stupor and could not be aroused, the orderly-sergeant so reported to the sergeant-major. He was then told to find Band-Sergeant Mahoney. Mahoney could not be found. He was not in camp and about 4 a.m. was seen entering the camp lines and placed under arrest. With the three leading players of the band under arrest the band was so seriously crippled that the bandmaster appealed to the adjutant to release us and we were ordered to get ready for parade. At the end of the inspection we were summoned to the orderly-room. Sergeant Mahoney and Corporal Miller were called in turn and each came out smiling, having been let off with a reprimand. Lance-Corporal Gorman was next to face the colonel. To my surprise the sergeant-major blamed me for not reporting the sergeant and corporal. I did not know what stories they had told to secure their acquittal and I could not bring myself to tell the whole truth of the matter, so said nothing. I was deprived of my stripe and confined to camp for seven days. How often it happens that the least culpable of a party of offenders has to bear the whole burden of punishment. I was so humiliated and indignant over the injustice and unfairness of the treatment I had received that I determined to apply for my discharge, the money for the same being still to my credit in the paymaster's books. When the seven days' confinement had been completed I was placed in orders again for lance-corporal and at the bandmaster's solicitation I withdrew my application for discharge, returned the money to my father and decided to remain in the Regiment a while longer.

At the inspection Kribs, of the tea leaves story, was corporal of pioneers. It was his and his men's first appearance on a full dress parade and he was totally ignorant as to what he ought to do. He applied to the bandsmen for instructions, they responded cheerfully. He was told that when the inspecting general and staff arrived at the head of the column he should have his command at open order, double distance. The words of command were " Grand Division rear rank two paces to the rear, March." Kribs followed instructions to the best of his ability. On the approach of the inspecting general's party Kribs called out " Grand Division, twa muckle spans to the rear, gang." None of the party apparently heard what Kribs said and the inspection of his " grand division " of twelve men passed off to his satisfaction. He came back to the band for further coaching. The flags marking the wheeling points were pointed out to him and he was instructed to wheel his men within the points with the command, " Grand Division left wheel," and on passing the general at the saluting point, " Grand Division, eyes right." It was here that the colonel caught on to what Kribs was saying, and when the column had returned to its original position the adjutant rode up to Kribs and wanted to know what he meant by such absurd words of command. When Kribs learned that the bandsmen had been making a goat of him he was furious and threatened to get even with the jokers.

The 11th Hussars arrived in camp late in the summer of 1858. Their befrogged blue tunics and scarlet overalls were in brilliant contrast to the plainer blue uniforms of the dragoon regiment that preceded them. On the roadway that divided their lines from ours, there was a sentry post connected with our regimental guard. On the morning following the day the hussars arrived, the sentry on that post was a man known throughout the Regiment as "Smiler" from the fact that a silly grin was constantly in evidence on his face. He was a half-wit and a sort of "butt" among his comrades. The hussars were getting ready for parade and there was much movement among them between the men's quarters and the stables. Smiler took the first of these gorgeously dressed men who approached his post for an officer of high rank and presented arms. The hussar appreciated the joke and passed it on to his comrades. One by one they passed at short intervals in front of Smiler, who paid them the full compliment to which he thought their rank entitled them. Wearied at last he ordered arms and stood at ease. He had scarcely done so when Colonel De Rottenburg rode up on his way from his quarters to the orderly-room; Smiler remained "at ease" paying no attention to the colonel. The latter called out: "Sentry, don't you know who I am?" Smiler, still standing at ease, his silly grin covering his face, said quite coolly "Yes, I know who you are all right." Colonel: "Then, why didn't you salute?" Smiler: "I have been saluting ever since I was posted here; I'm tired and I'm d——d if I will salute any more." Colonel, to his orderly: "Orderly, this man is a fool; tell the sergeant of the guard to have him relieved at once, and send him to the orderly-room." The result was that the doctor's attention was called to Smiler and in due time the latter was discharged as unfit for service.

Late in the same year the Royal City of Dublin Militia came from Aldershot and relieved the North Down Rifles, also a militia regiment. The embodied militia regiments had received numbers and the Dublins were wearing the numerals "100" on their caps when they arrived. Some confusion resulted from having two regiments in camp wearing the same number and a general order was issued requiring the Dublins to remove the numerals and replace them with a silver badge horseshoe shape bearing the words "Royal Dublin City." The Dublins did not take kindly to the change and showed their ill-feeling by picking quarrels with the Canadians, waylaying them on their return to camp, until it finally resulted in a riot between the two regiments. Matters had reached a critical stage when a little incident occurred in an alehouse in Sandgate that provided the spark to the combustible that caused the general explosion.

Canada was scarcely known, except as a place in America where wild animals, as the popular story books of the day recounted, were in great numbers and of undoubted ferocity. From the time the Canadians reached Shorncliffe, they were pestered with questions about the dangers of the forests and of personal thrilling encounters with its savage denizens, Indians and wild animals included. To maintain the reputation English fiction writers had given the land of the maple, many of our men were given to indulging their questioner's appetite for thrilling adventure by reciting imaginary adventures sufficiently startling to satisfy every demand. Three of the Dublins invited a Canadian to share a "pot" of ale with them, expecting to have their curiosity gratified with stories from the wild lands of America. The Canadian did his best to entertain them with exciting stories of Indians and bears, wolves and wild cats he was supposed to have met and conquered or from which he had escaped by a hair's-breadth. One of the Dublins, in the pause that marked the end of the Canadian's stock of sensational stories, asked if there was any game that a chap could hunt without danger of meeting the ferocious kind ? "Yes," said the Canadian, "near the settlements, wild pigeons, wild turkeys, ducks, and geese, quail, partridges, rabbits and hares are plentiful, affording good sport. There is a peculiarity about the Canadian hare, that while it is of the same brown colour in summer as in England, they turn white in winter to match the colour of the snow." The Dublins then rose in their wrath and wanted to know if the Canadian thought he could cram such an astounding lie as that down their throats! As it was in reality one of the few bits of actual truth he had uttered during the evening, he could not help laughing as he insisted on its absolute truthfulness, but this only increased the Dublin men's anger and convinced them that they were being humbugged. Indians, bears, wolves and perilous encounters with them were all right, for they had read of them in books, but brown hares turning white, to match the snow in winter, was too much.

They proceeded to satisfy their wrath by attacking the Canadian, then and there. Others joined in the *mêlée* and the battle spread from end to end of Sandgate. Both sides went to Sandgate next evening prepared for a real battle, sticks and waist belts were used and many were severely injured. Infantry picquets were powerless to clear the streets or separate the combatants and an armed party of the hussars was sent to the scene of the riot and succeeded in driving off the combatants. Commanding officers of the two regiments dealt in their own way with individuals who had been arrested for participating in the riot, but a more formal inquiry was held by order of the general in command of the camp. It was shown that the Dublins had earned a reputation at Aldershot and other places for quarrelling with other regiments and of pugnacity generally, while the Canadians had been on friendly terms with all corps in camp until the Dublins arrived. The blame for the riot was placed on the Dublins and as a penalty for their misconduct they were given an extra drill every day for a month.

In December, 1858, the officer commanding the 100th Regiment was informed by the Commander-in-Chief that on the 10th of the following month the Prince of Wales would visit Shorncliffe for the purpose of inspecting the Regiment and presenting it with its colours. This was felt by all ranks of the Regiment to be a very high compliment. His Royal Highness had just been gazetted to a colonelcy, but had as yet made no public appearance in any capacity, and his choosing this occasion for his first act was very greatly appreciated by officers and men. On the morning of the day fixed for the ceremony the Regiment was drawn up in line waiting for the Prince to arrive. This he did precisely at noon, and he was accompanied by the Duke of Cambridge, Major-General Viscount Melville and nearly all the officers of the Shorncliffe and headquarters staffs. He was received with a royal salute, the troops presenting arms, and the bands playing the National Anthem.

It is worthy of remark that the Prince's escort from the railway station to the camp was a troop of the 11th Hussars, the same regiment in which Major Dunn had, as a subaltern, fought so bravely and achieved such renown, and some of the very men who that day escorted the Prince had but very little more than four years previously followed Dunn in the glorious but fatal charge "into the Valley of Death." The Prince after acknowledging the salute rode slowly down to the ranks of the Regiment; he was followed by the Duke of Cambridge, who, one of the London papers of the time records, was "particularly struck with the fine body of men composing the 100th." The inspection over, the troops formed three sides of a square with the drums in the centre, upon which rested the colours. They were taken from there by Brevet Lieutenant-Colonel Robertson and Major Dunn and by them handed to the Prince. He in turn handed them to the two senior ensigns, C. M. Moorsom and J. G. Ridout, who with bended knee took them from his hands. In presenting the colours, His Royal Highness said: "Lord Melville, Colonel de Rottenburg and officers and men of the 100th Regiment, —It is most gratifying to me that, by the Queen's gracious permission, my first public act since I have had the honour of holding a commission in the British Army should be the presentation of colours to a regiment which is the spontaneous offering of the loyal and spirited Canadian people, and with which at their desire my name has been specially associated. The ceremonial on which we are now engaged possesses a peculiar significance and solemnity because, in confiding to you for the first time this emblem of military fidelity and valour, I not only recognize emphatically your enrolment into our national force, but celebrate an act which proclaims and strengthens the unity of the various parts of this vast empire under the sway of our common Sovereign. Although owing to my youth and inexperience I can but very imperfectly give expression to the sentiments which this occasion is calculated to awaken with reference to yourselves and the great and flourishing province of Canada, you may rest assured that I shall ever watch the progress and achievements of your gallant corps with deep interest, and that I heartily wish you all honour and success in the prosecution of the noble career on which you have entered."

Colonel de Rottenburg replied : " May it please your Royal Highness,—As the immediate commanding officer of your Royal Highness's Canadian Regiment, I tender my humble duty to your Royal Highness for the honour which you have done the Regiment this day in condescending to present its colours, and for the gracious terms in which you have addressed the officers and men. I assure your Royal Highness that we are deeply grateful for this act on the part of your Royal Highness. The great colony in which this Regiment was raised, amongst whose ranks hundreds of its sons are serving—and all who belong to it are more or less connected with Canada—will also feel most grateful for the honour which the first regiment raised in a colony for general service has received from your Royal Highness, and I assure you at the call of our Sovereign Canada would send ten such regiments as this one in defence of the Empire, should such an emergency ever arise requiring their services. The 100th Regiment has received its first colours in the most honourable manner such could be bestowed, namely, from the hands of the illustrious heir to the throne of this country. It rests with the Regiment to maintain their colours always with honour. I confidently assure your Royal Highness they will do so. If these colours are ever unfurled in the presence of an enemy, the officers and men of the 100th Regiment will be ready to shed their blood in the defence of their colours, of their Queen and of their country. I again humbly thank your Royal Highness for the honour you have done the Regiment."

These formalities being concluded, the Regiment re-formed line, then broke into open column of companies and marched past his Royal Highness, first in slow and then in quick time. After that they were dismissed to their quarters. On the conclusion of the parade the Prince lunched with the officers of the Regiment, afterwards returning to London. In the evening, in still further celebration of the day, the officers gave a grand ball which was attended by the whole of the youth, beauty and fashion of the county, and which passed off with great éclat.

About the end of March, 1859, the 100th went to Aldershot for instruction in field movements on a large scale not possible at Shorncliffe. A day or two after our arrival in camp the Regiment was greatly excited over an attempt of the military police to destroy its regimental dog. Dogs were forbidden in camp at Aldershot and it was the duty of the military police to capture and destroy all found running at large within the camp limits. when they were seen by some of our men endeavouring to rope the Regiment's pet, the alarm was given and the dog was taken from the police. The incident was of course reported to headquarters and the colonel of the 100th was called on to explain. He told the staff that the dog had accompanied the Regiment from Canada and that, if any further action were taken to destroy him, he could not possibly be responsible for what his men would do. It was arranged as a special favour that the dog would be permitted to stay with the Regiment, provided he was tied up and not allowed to run at large. He was accordingly secured with a rope in a stall in the officers' stable. Never before having been subjected to such treatment "Sam," as the dog was called, did not submit tamely to his confinement. Next day was a divisional field day in the Long Common. The whole infantry division, three brigades, was drawn up, ready to begin the day's movements. The 100th was in the centre of the 3rd Brigade on the left of the line. From the far end a dog could be seen trotting down the line, a yard or so of rope trailing behind him. It stopped not till it came to the 100th, taking up his usual position in front of the band. Sam, after the stable had been cleared of its occupants—horses and men—gnawed the rope that fastened him and made good his escape. He tracked the Regiment to the Long Common, where in the movements for forming up the division he lost the trail and by sight and scent, after traversing the front of twelve or more regiments, he found his own. Colonel de Rottenburg took the matter up again with headquarters and succeeded in getting Sam officially recognized as regimental dog of the 100th.

Sam's history may prove interesting. Lieutenant Fogo, of the 39th Regiment, bought him, a six months' old pup, in Quebec. It was a Newfoundland of the curly-coated variety, dense black. Fogo was returning to England on board the ship in which the first four companies were being carried over. The dog was placed in the care of a private in the 100th. When the ship arrived at Liverpool Fogo tried to coax or force the dog to go with him. Sam lay on the dock and refused to move, Mr. Fogo finally gave up the attempt and left the dog with the man who had cared for it on the voyage over. As he grew to maturity Sam developed an individuality peculiar to himself. He was no one man's dog. His home was with the main guard. He attended the quartermaster's store in the morning when rations were being served out and breakfasted bountifully on the raw beef scraps thrown to him. At 1 p.m. he called at the sergeants' mess for his meal, and in the evening he patronized the officers' mess kitchen. He took up his position with the Regiment on parade and after a while learned to walk in front of the band with the drum-major, but showed no familiarity with him, or with anyone else. In a garrison like Gibraltar, where each regiment in turn furnished a number of guards, Sam marched out with them and saw where each one was stationed. No party, great or small could leave without Sam being with it and seeing it back again. Sam returned to Canada with the Regiment in 1867 and died in Ottawa. His curly coat, I was told by old bandsmen I met who had been discharged, was tanned and made up as an apron for the big drummer to wear on special occasions.

Her Majesty Queen Victoria and the Prince Consort visited Aldershot twice while the Regiment was in camp and the 100th had the honour of furnishing a guard for the royal residence on each occasion. The Regiment's stay in Aldershot was brought to a close at the end of six weeks' training. This was an unusually brief term, due no doubt to the perfection attained in drill under the Guards' instructors, and the masterly manner in which Colonel de Rottenburg handled the Regiment in field movements. Orders to embark for foreign service at Portsmouth on two days' notice were joyfully received, and hopes ran high that India would be our destination. These, however, were not fulfilled.

So ends Mr. Gorman's vivid narrative of the early days of the Royal Canadians. It is a pleasure to be able to add to his story that when the Regiment left Shorncliffe it was given an uproarious send-off by its old antagonists the City of Dublin Militia.

CHAPTER V

THE 100TH ROYAL CANADIANS—GIBRALTAR, 1859–1863.

THE time had now come for the 100th to take its place on the roster for foreign service and Gibraltar was the station assigned to it. The Regiment left in two wings, the first to depart embarking at Portsmouth on the 7th May on board H.M.S. *Urgent*. Before disembarking at Gibraltar the men were visited by H.R.H. The Prince of Wales, who was at the time yachting in the Mediterranean with Prince Hohenlohe. The second division of the Regiment followed about a fortnight later and by the 4th June, 1859, the Regiment was united at Gibraltar where it occupied Windmill Hill and Buena Vista Barracks, its strength at this time being 30 officers and 823 other ranks.

At this time the Regiment had two depots one in Canada and the other at Parkhurst in the Isle of Wight, but during the stay of the Regiment in Gibraltar the depot in Canada was abolished on the score of expense. By this decision the 100th was fated gradually to lose its Canadian connection, a regrettable state of affairs. It must be remembered, however, that the Crimean War had only recently been concluded and the nation was now footing the bill; and the long era of peace which had preceded that struggle had made people forget that wars will occur and that they cost a great deal of money. Accordingly, the economy axe was at work, and to the bureaucratic mind it seemed an outrage that Imperial sentiment should be maintained if it were to cost a few thousands a year.

When the Regiment arrived at Gibraltar it was still under the command of Baron de Rottenburg who, however, retired during the stay of the 100th at the Rock and was succeeded by Major Dunn, V.C., late of the 11th Hussars. Alexander Roberts Dunn was the son of the Honourable John Henry Dunn for some years receiver-general of Upper Canada, and was born near Toronto in June, 1833, being educated at Harrow. In 1852 he was appointed cornet by purchase in the 11th Hussars and proceeded to the Crimea. There he took part in the memorable charge of the Light Brigade, during which he saved the life of Sergeant-Major Bently of his regiment by cutting down three Russian lancers, and afterwards cutting down a Russian hussar who was attacking Private Levett. For his gallant conduct on that memorable 25th October, 1854, Lieutenant Dunn, who was then but 21 years old, was subsequently awarded the Victoria Cross. He sold out early in 1855 but on the formation of the 100th in Canada in 1858 he was appointed major in the Regiment. When the Baron de Rottenburg retired on 25th June, 1861, Major Dunn succeeded to the command of the Regiment by purchase. The sum paid by him for the step was £10,000 an unusually high figure in an infantry regiment in those days and the amount furnishes a significant index of the prestige which was attached to the command of the 100th Regiment. The men were intensely proud of their youthful commanding officer—he was now 28 years old—and their devotion was testified in many ways. Often on his return from a short spell of leave a hundred or more men would assemble near his quarters to give him a rousing cheer on his return.

Apart even from the great prestige which came to the Regiment from its commanding officer it was distinguished amongst the garrison at the Rock in other ways. Literally it stood head and shoulders over the other regiments. It was composed of men of magnificent physique, the average height being something like 5 feet 11 inches—a statement which would be incredible were it not substantiated by unimpeachable evidence. Certainly in the size of the rank and file no Guards' regiment could touch it. The Regiment was noted for its *esprit de corps* and devotion to its officers. These were brought into contact with their men in an unusual degree for guard duties were very heavy and officers' guards were numerous. Half a century later Major-General Upton Prior would relate how the men of his guard would bring their coal to his fire so that he, a delicate youngster of 16 years, might not suffer.

From the numeral 100 which the men wore on their appointments the Regiment gained from the Spaniards the nickname *Cientos*, or *Cientopieses*, or Centipedes. Mention of the regimental number brings to mind a Horse Guards Letter dated 21st January, 1860, which stated that " Her Majesty has been graciously pleased to allow the officers of the 100th Regiment to wear the Prince of Wales's Plume above their number on their forage caps in consideration of the corps being designated The Prince of Wales's Royal Canadian Regiment." The regimental crest at this time—that is to say the Regiment's own private seal so to speak—was made up of the Prince of Wales's Plume, the Beaver, and Maple Leaves as follows :—In the centre of the crest was a beaver resting on a sandbank and facing to the left. Immediately underneath was the regimental number in Roman character—*i.e.*, C in gold. The beaver and the C were encircled by an oval shaped garter in red, edged with gold, and on this garter was inscribed in gilt black lettering the words " The Prince of Wales's Royal Canadian Regiment." On the top edge of the garter and intersecting it rested the plume which was surmounted by the Royal Crown. Encircling the garter, three-quarters of the way up each side, were sprigs of maple leaves. The whole crest rested on a background of royal blue.

A good many of the junior officers of the Regiment were Canadians, both French and English, and there was in consequence a little unpleasantness because the French Canadians would speak French at mess. Finally, one of the senior officers who had been brought into the

100th from another regiment complained to the commanding officer alleging that some of the Canadians were in the habit of conversing in French and the English officers imagined that they were the subject of unfavourable comment in the foreign tongue. Baron de Rottenburg, however, replied that Canadian gentlemen were unlikely to make disparaging remarks about their comrades, at the same time adding that he considered the ability to speak French a graceful accomplishment and that he recommended those who could not speak it to acquire the art as soon as possible.

Mention of this French element suggests the mention of another little known fact namely that there was a German element as well. In the story of the 2nd Battalion it will be related how disbanded German legionaries at the Cape volunteered for service during the Mutiny and were eventually amalgamated with the cadre of the 3rd Bombay Europeans. A fair number of the disbanded German Legion had, however, after the Crimea settled in Canada, and some of these enlisted in Canada when the 100th Regiment was raised in 1858 owing to the outbreak in the East.

Composed as it was of men of splendid physique it was natural that the 100th should have been well to the fore at sport during its stay at Gibraltar. Lacrosse, being essentially a Canadian game, was one of the special features of the Regiment. It turned out a very powerful team and many a time an appreciative crowd thronged the ground when the Royal Canadians had a match on. In rowing, too, the Regiment particularly excelled. The 2nd Battalion of the 6th Regiment ordered a new Clasper boat specially from England with which to lower the colours of the victorious sergeants of the 100th but were defeated after a terrific struggle. This led to a challenge from a crew of four Gibraltarian boatmen. Scores of natives had come out to see the *Cientos* beaten, but had to return disappointed after a contest Homeric—or rather Virgilian—in intensity. The Royal Canadians, who had at one time been well behind, overtook the leaders and were first past the post. After this the victors rested on their laurels for no crew was found to challenge them.

A bucket let down into the well of memory draws up some odd splashings of those Mediterranean days. There was the great alarm one night in 1859. A ship on fire. Out turned the garrison, fire picquets under arms, the Regiment in quarter column, the men all in their oldest clothes hoping to claim new kit by the magic words " damaged by fire." After about half an hour the discovery was made that the " fire " was a particularly rubicund harvest moon which had thoughtlessly risen behind a large vessel which then appeared to be bursting into red flames. However, the 100th had the satisfaction of being officially informed that they had been the smartest at turning out in the whole garrison. Other splashings are of guard duties. In the ranks were many well educated men, amongst them a young college graduate of poetic temperament. Once when on sentry-go he was visited by the officer of the day and asked, as usual, to repeat his orders. The reply was somewhat unconventional :

" Sir, my orders were to guard the shot and shell
Likewise the water in the well,
And all the shrubs and trees about
And challenge all when lights are out."

Startled by this rigmarole the officer blurted out : " Where the —— did you get those orders from ?" to which the young poet answered at once :—

" Sir, these were the orders I received
From the sentry I relieved."

It is not stated what happened next. A rhyming sentry late at night must have been rather a difficulty for Visiting Rounds.

There are, however, sadder memories. In 1860 Captain Coulson was drowned while sailing with Major Dunn in the latter's yacht. Captain Coulson had served with the 49th in the Crimea and had joined the 100th in 1858 as senior subaltern. Shortly afterwards a terrible thing happened. A private in a drunken fury shot at and killed another private, mistaking him for a sergeant against whom the assailant had a grievance. The murderer was one of the best men in the Regiment a fine, handsome soldier, clean and smart and of exceptional skill in his trade, that of a boiler maker. He had been detailed in garrison orders to repair the boiler of a disabled steamer in the bay and so well had he carried out his task that he was substantially rewarded by the captain. This proved his undoing. The few pounds went on drink and probably vile native liquor at that. Next came the murder and then the gallows on Windmill Hill parade ground.

Smuggling sometimes gave rise to alarms and excursions. There were smugglers who brought contraband from Spain to Gibraltar, and were called Spanish smugglers. *Per contra* there were smugglers who ran goods from the Rock to the mainland and these were called English smugglers. The two guilds had conflicting interests and when the rival organizations met accidentally in the middle of the night on the neutral ground there would be a certain liveliness in which shouts, screams, knives and fire-arms played a part. On these occasions sometimes the troops would be aroused and kept under arms for some time. The real smuggling excitement, however, was when our sentries would waylay one of the dogs carrying gin into Spain and great would be the celebration over a capture.

While at Gibraltar the musketry of the Regiment showed a steady improvement. From being at the foot of all the regiments of the Army in 1858—the Regiment not being exercised that year and therefore having no classification—the 100th soared up to 12th place in the year 1859-1860 and rose to 5th place in the following year, a position it retained in the following year. This was a fine record. Nevertheless in spite of the successes gained by the Regiment both in work and play Gibraltar was a station rather productive of *ennui* to both officers and men. The restricted life of a garrison town—and few garrisons could be more restricted than Gibraltar—was a sorry ending to the hopes of active service which had led to the enthusiastic formation of the Royal Canadians in 1858. For the officers there was very little society apart from the military, and rides in the country were confined to the celebrated Cork Woods and a few Spanish towns in the immediate neighbourhood. There was, however, a pack of hounds and a theatre. A certain amount of excitement was caused by the American Civil War and the occasional arrival of Federal or Confederate ships of war. The famous *Sumter* put in once and her captain dined or lunched with the officers of the Regiment. The Confederate officer was Captain—later Admiral—Semmes, who subsequently commanded the famous *Alabama.*

In his work " My Adventures Afloat," Admiral Semmes has left on record his impressions of Gibraltar while the 100th Regiment was there quartered, and the following little word picture may be of interest :—" The review of the troops which takes place, I believe, monthly is, *par excellence,* the grand spectacle of Gibraltar. I had the good fortune to witness one of these reviews and the spectacle dwells still vividly in my imagination. Drill of the soldiers, singly and in squads is the chief labour of the garrison. Skilful drill sergeants, for the most part young, active and intelligent men, having the port and bearing of gentlemen, are constantly at work, morning and afternoon, breaking in the raw material as it arrives, and rendering it fit to be moulded into the common mass. Company officers move their companies to and fro unceasingly lest the men should forget what the drill-sergeant has taught them. Battalion and regimental drills occur less frequently. These are the labours of the garrison. Now comes the pastime—viz., the monthly drill when the Governor turns out and inspects the troops. All is agog on the Rock of Gibraltar on review days. There is no end to the pipe-claying and polishing and burnishing in the different barracks on the morning of this day. The officers get out their new uniforms and the horses are groomed with more than military care. The citizens turn out as well as the military, and all the beauty and fashion of the town are grouped on the Alameda. On the occasion of the review which I witnessed, the troops—nearly all young, fine-looking men—presented indeed a splendid appearance. All the corps of the British Army were there represented save only the cavalry; and they were moved hither and thither at will; long lines of them now being tied into what seemed the most inextricable knots, and now united again, with an ease, grace and skill which called forth my constant admiration."

Although it had been a disappointment to the 100th Regiment to miss the chance of active service, at any rate the initial training at Shorncliffe under Guards' non-commissioned officers followed by four years' ceremonial work at Gibraltar gave birth to that reputation for drill which remained with the Battalion till the end.

During our first months at Gibraltar war had been in progress on the African side of the Straits between Spain and Morocco, caused by the encroachment of the Spaniards on the neutral ground at Ceuta, a Spanish fortified garrison and convict establishment. The smoke of battle could be seen, and with a favourable wind the sound of cannonading could be heard on Windmill Hill and furnished an attractive spectacle for our men stationed there. The Regiment went under canvas on the north front in June and remained there four months. Up to that time no opportunities had been given, either in England or on the Rock to indulge in athletic sports. A cricket club was formed, officers and men taking part in the games. Matches were arranged between regiments, but the 100th did not shine to any extent as cricketers. Those that way inclined took up foot racing, flat and hurdle, and the sergeants and the band each purchased a boat and spent their spare time rowing in the bay. At the annual garrison sports in 1859 the mile flat race was won by Private Charles Boyce, of the 100th; the following year and also in 1861 the mile flat was won by Sergeant Eli Clark of the 100th, and the half-mile hurdles fell to Private Belknap also of the 100th in 1861. Minor prizes, seconds and thirds were also won by 100th men both years.

The conclusion of the war between Spain and Morocco ended while we were in camp and a grand regatta was organized including the fleets of Spain, France and Britain that had been anchored in Gibraltar bay while the war was in progress—the British on the Gibraltar side and the Spanish and French on the Algeciras side. The military garrison also took part. The elimination contests between the rival navies ended in the British winning the two first places. In the military section the Royal Engineers, the 6th, 7th and 100th entered boats, that of the 100th being the sergeants' boat, a discarded navy ship's cutter, which was put into an approach to racing shape at short notice. There was no restriction as to the style of boats to be entered by the military. They were to be, like those of the navy, four-oared with coxswain. The course was from a point on the bay opposite our camp, to the judges' stand on the guardship *Samarang*, a distance of two miles straightaway. The 100th and the 7th boats headed the garrison elimination race after a neck and neck struggle for first place over the full course, which was won by the 100th. In the final contest the naval entries were left behind and again it was a fierce struggle from start to finish between the 7th and 100th, the latter winning by a scant half length. On this occasion Colonel de Rottenburg was among the naval and military officers, who witnessed the race from the deck of the *Samarang*. The winning crew insisted on rowing him to the camp. The Regiment to a man had assembled on the beach to watch the race, rushed into the water before the boat could land and took up the colonel and victorious crew, carrying them shoulder high in triumph to the shore. The names of the crew that proved the Canadians'

claim to a first place as oarsmen at that early day were :—
Sergeant McDonald, of Kingston, Canada, bow ; Sergeant
Henderson, of Toronto, Canada, No. 2 ; Sergeant
Hemphill, of Port Stanley, Canada, No. 3 ; Sergeant
Drummond, of Quebec, Canada, stroke ; Sergeant-Major
Rance, who tipped the scales at over 200 pounds was
coxswain.

Such official records as are available make mention
of the usual inspections and establishments that of
June, 1862, being fixed as follows :—1 colonel, 1 lieutenant-colonel, 2 majors, 12 captains, 14 lieutenants,
10 ensigns, 1 paymaster, 1 adjutant, 1 quartermaster, 1 surgeon, 1 assistant surgeon, 8 staff sergeants,
etc., 12 colour-sergeants, 38 sergeants, 1 drum-major,
24 drummers and fifers, 50 corporals and 850
privates, or 1,027 of all ranks. On the 28th September,
1862, Lieutenant-General Viscount Melville, K.C.B., was
transferred to the colonelcy of the 32nd Foot, being
succeeded by Major-General Sir Edward McArther as
colonel of the Regiment. The establishment of the
Regiment was reduced in April, 1863, the number of
privates being fixed at 640 for the service companies and
110 at the depot. On the 13th October the Regiment
embarked at Gibraltar on board H.M. Troopship *Orontes*
for conveyance to Malta, the strength being 20 officers,
801 other ranks, 68 women and 104 children.

CHAPTER VI

THE 100TH ROYAL CANADIANS—MALTA, 1863-1866.

IMAGINATION has never been a cardinal feature in the conclaves of Whitehall or Pall Mall and the actions of the War and Colonial Offices relative to the 100th Regiment are a case in point. Here was a regiment composed of virile and enthusiastic volunteers from a young country, burning with enthusiasm for active service and ready to make immense sacrifices for the motherland. Disappointed as they were by the suppression of the Indian Mutiny before their services could be utilized, the Royal Canadians might at any rate have found consolation in service in a region where fighting might be expected—as the Indian frontier, or at any rate in a country of wide spaces and freedom as South Africa. The clerkly and unimaginative pundits in London thought otherwise. From England the Royal Canadians were sent to Gibraltar where they were cooped up for four years, wearied by their incarceration in a fortress and condemned to forego the excitement of active service for the punctilious minutiæ of guard duties. That tour once over a change was obviously desirable. But a further spell of fortress duty was in store. The Royal Canadians were still to remain in the Mediterranean and merely to exchange a rock for a small island.

The dull monotony of garrison life at Gibraltar, so different from the stirring warlike scenes they had hoped to witness, had palled upon the men, and Authority, had it not been blind, must surely have discerned the fact. Many of the men had been bought out by their relatives and had returned to Canada. Others, having learned to speak Spanish married Spanish wives and disappeared into Spain. Desertions at one time had become frequent; the visits of American merchantmen making the " get away " easy by the connivance of the sailors. Then, the outbreak of the Civil War in the United States was a veritable magnet to the high spirited soldiers of the Royal Canadians. These depletions had been keenly felt by the colonel; he had referred to them feelingly on parade on more than one occasion and seemed to regard them as a reflection upon his command and a criticism upon his treatment of his men. Nothing could have been farther from the truth. The Baron de Rottenburg was well liked, his treatment of the soldiers had been mild and fatherly, rather than that of a martinet, and the officers and men respected and admired his talents. It is possible, however, that his action in selling out to Major Dunn had been prompted by the above considerations.

The move to Malta was, as will be understood, by no means popular although any station was welcome after over four years confinement at Gibraltar. That the 100th had suffered in no way as regards *moral* is shown by the report made by His Excellency Lieutenant-General Sir J. Gaspard Le Marchant after an inspection of the Regiment on the Floriana parade ground on 27th November, 1863. He " expressed his utmost satisfaction with regard to their excellent appearance and intelligence as a battalion, combined with the steady manner in which they performed their evolutions. His Excellency directs, as showing his sense of gratification, the immediate release of all defaulters of the Regiment." This report is typical of others received while on the island one of which may be quoted *verbatim*. It is dated 27th April, 1865, and runs as follows :—" The major-general commanding the 1st Brigade has much pleasure in expressing to Colonel Donovan his entire satisfaction at the result of his half-yearly inspection of the 100th Royal Canadian Regiment both as regards

1864] THE 1st BATTALION

their conduct in barracks and their clean and soldierlike appearance on parade."

The Regiment was at first stationed at Fort Ricasoli with two companies at St. Salvatore and one at Zabbas Gate. The year 1864 was a mournful one as regards the officers of the 100th. In January we lost Ensign Albert Grant Dunn a half brother of our colonel. Passionately devoted to sport he trained and rode his own horses, the enforced " sweating " bringing on a chill which caused his death. Lieutenant Ashford died of fever on 2nd July. He had a week or two earlier taken part in a rowing trial; it was a scorching hot afternoon at the end of June and at the end the rowers were streaming with perspiration. Some officers were met going to bathe and Lieutenant Ashford, in spite of their warning, insisted on joining them, a decision which cost him his life. In October we had to mourn the loss by death of Captain James Lamb. A distinguished officer, Lamb had been promoted from sergeant-major to ensign in the 50th for bravery in the field. He had been present at the Alma and Inkerman and had served throughout the whole of the siege of Sebastopol. In the same year, 1864, Lieutenant-Colonel Dunn exchanged with Lieutenant-Colonel Donovan of the 33rd. Death had our beloved commanding officer in view; four years later Colonel Dunn, while in command of his new regiment during the Abyssinian expedition, was accidentally shot while big game shooting. Thus fell at the early age of 35 Alexander Roberts Dunn a splendid specimen of a *beau sabreur.* He had, when little more than a boy, won the Victoria Cross in one of the great cavalry charges of history. One of the handsomest men in the army he had also the reputation of being one of the finest swordsmen and deadliest shots within it.

In the sixties polo and lawn tennis had not yet arrived so, naturally, rowing—for which the two harbours at Malta are so admirably fitted—occupied much of the surplus energy of the Royal Canadians. The officers won a grand victory in a gig race beating the crack crew of the officers of the Mediterranean Fleet. Another very sporting race was the result of a match made between Lieutenant Boulton of the Regiment and Captain Munn of the 2nd Battalion 7th Royal Fusiliers for an 18-oar race for £5 a side.

The race was rowed on 7th May, 1864, and was to be in 18-oar ship launches. The Regiment borrowed one from H.M.S. *Royal Oak* and, as it is the custom of the Royal Navy not to lend their boats without one of their own people in charge, the coxswain was taken over with the launch. Two " passengers " were also carried in the stern sheets one being a coach and the other an officer, Lieutenant J. B. Kersteman. The latter was detailed by Colonel Dunn " to see that the coxswain had fair play in case any of the crew should resent his language." The coxswain, to be quite frank, was exceedingly " old Navy," and spent his time throughout the race yelling " Row you beauties ; row you ———; oh ! row you ———," but as a matter of fact no " resentment " was shown at these well meant efforts. There is a picture extant of this race in which Lieutenant Kersteman is shown standing up like a stage "city-man" mutton chop whiskers and all, and there is an explanatory paragraph in an account to the effect " that officers going out of barracks in mufti had to wear tall hats and black coats." This alone was enough to colour the coxswain's vocabulary.

The Royal Canadians won very easily securing a lead early in the race and maintaining it comfortably till the end. The event had created quite a stir in the garrison and on board a pontoon moored at the winning post were the Governor and his daughters, the admiral of the squadron, two generals " and a great number of the brightest and best and bravest of the naval and military element of the island." One incident caused much favourable comment. Amid the deafening cheers of the spectators the winning crew " tossed oars "—they had carefully rehearsed the movement during the morning just " in case "—" there they stood, caps off, at attention grasping the oar with both hands in line with the chin, handle between the toes, turning the head slightly in the direction of the saluting point, if I may so term His Excellency the Governor. It was a demonstration of discipline which was much noticed and spoken of." It must have been a remarkable boatload with a crew which included "one Red Indian"—John Armstrong by name—an apoplectic bluejacket and a gentleman in top hat, frock coat and mutton chop whiskers. The men were given a tremendous reception on the *Royal Oak* and " when the coxswain got on board he could hardly speak he was so hoarse."

On the same day the officers were successful in a four-oar race alluded to above, but unfortunately the names of the other entrants are not forthcoming. A handsome silver cup was the trophy won and was engraved with the names of the crew as follows :—Lieutenant Prior, Lieutenant Ashford, Lieutenant Boulton, Ensign Fox (stroke), Captain Hutchinson (coxswain). The winners agreed that the cup should become the property of the officer remaining longest in the Regiment and it thus passed eventually to Captain H. H. Prior who presented it to the officers' mess in July, 1875.

It may be said that during the stay of the Regiment both at Malta and Gibraltar it was easily " cock " at rowing, no other ship, regiment, or corps carrying off so many prizes at regattas or matches as the Royal Canadians. Much of the success was due to Ensign Fox, who became later Colonel Fox the famous Inspector of Gymnastics, and a one time sergeant-instructor of musketry — E. D. Davies, who was a capable and enthusiastic coach. But it must not be forgotten that many of the men had been rafting and canoeing from their childhood and were thus at a great advantage as compared with the average English, Irish or Scots soldier of the line. It may be mentioned that the depot companies at Parkhurst kept up the credit of the Regiment in at least one big event at Cowes. The depot was of course not a depot in the later territorial sense but a depot battalion feeding five or six regiments. A greater honour than winning a boat race was the fact that the depot companies of the 100th for a time furnished the guard at Osborne.

During the years which the 100th spent at Malta, Italy was the scene of the fighting destined to bring about the union of the various portions of the country and to place her among the Great Powers of Europe. Garibaldi visited Malta on one occasion and there was much ill-feeling against him displayed by the ultramontane population, so much so that a few ultra-protestant members of the Regiment seem to have banded themselves unofficially for his protection, an action which later gave rise to a quite untrue legend that the 100th Regiment was formally assigned to the general as his bodyguard. During his brief stay Garibaldi held a daily levée at his hotel from nine in the morning till seven in the evening.

The Regiment was at Malta during a severe epidemic of cholera and suffered heavy loss. One morning alone two hundred men were down with the disease. More than half the Regiment was in hospital at once and the sights there were such as to leave a lasting impress on those who survived. Men were reduced to skeletons in a couple of days. The joints became loosened and it was possible to hear them creaking in their sockets as the patients tried to move. Some became delirious in their agony but fortunately the 100th were of tough physique and did not lose such a large proportion of their sick as other units did. There is on record a statement to the effect that the plague " was conveyed thither by pilgrims from Mecca," but this is somewhat difficult to understand and is perhaps due to a belief on the part of some journalist that Malta was populated by Mohammedans. What is more accurate is that the disease spread over Europe, including the United Kingdom. In Malta the inhabitants suffered frightfully and the 100th suffered considerably, many believed on account of being quartered at the time in Lower St. Elmo Barracks, " Hell Hole " as the men called it. After the Regiment went under canvas near Fort Manoel no more died. A lofty obelisk erected by the 100th outside the cemetery near Floriana commemorates the terrible visitation and records the names of the victims from the Royal Canadians.

In 1866 trouble broke out in Canada, and in the Regiment there quickly grew up a strong feeling that it should be sent to its native country to help in stamping out the rising there. Representations were accordingly made to authority and, as there was no other fortress where the Royal Canadians could be conveniently incarcerated, permission was given for its despatch to Canada. Accordingly on the 15th October, 1866, the Regiment bade good-bye to Malta embarking on the hired transport *Pennsylvania* under command of Lieutenant-Colonel William Campbell, its strength being 25 officers, 54 sergeants, 36 corporals, 20 drummers, 558 privates, 60 women and 89 children.

CHAPTER VII

THE 100TH ROYAL CANADIANS—CANADA, 1866–1868.

THE Regiment arrived "without casualties" at Quebec on 3rd November, 1866, where it was at once transferred to the river steamer *Quebec* for conveyance up the St. Lawrence to Montreal. That city was reached the following day and the Regiment, on landing, marched to College Street Barracks there to be quartered. It was now to be realized that the abolition of a depot in Canada had been somewhat premature for a draft of 126 rank and file which had reached Montreal a fortnight earlier had come *from England*. A detachment from this draft, 20 strong, had been sent to Ottawa under Ensign H. H. Prior, and it was now augmented to 200 by the despatch of two companies, the whole now being under the command of Captain Smythe. A "marching in" inspection by the major-general commanding took place at Montreal and before the end of the month regimental headquarters moved to Ottawa five companies remaining behind at Montreal under Major Cook. The disturbance in Canada which had led to the return of the 100th to its native country had apparently been squashed, and there is no mention in any record consulted as to the services of the Regiment having been required on the side of law and order.

In those days Imperial troops were normally stationed in Canada and there is mention made—in addition to the 100th Regiment—of artillery, a regiment of hussars and the 16th Regiment. Life there was enjoyable and the social aspect of a tour in Canada made the sojourn of a regiment there extremely pleasant, especially for the younger officers. There was a theatre at Ottawa and scarcely had headquarters of the Regiment arrived there before " the magnificent band of the Regiment was billed to play at a benefit of an actress at which ' Shakespeare's grand tragedy ' of *Othello* was to be presented." There is, too, an old newspaper cutting of the band playing at a grand gymnastic tournament at which " Henry Goodwin of the 100th, and James Drummond pupil," featured as a star turn in fencing and single stick. At the theatre the boxes and dress circle were 50 cents and private boxes a mere four dollars.

Eight years had elapsed since the formation of the Regiment and it was now back in the land of its birth. Nevertheless, it must be stated that brief though the period had been, these eight years seem to have completely changed the composition of the Regiment. The abolition of the depot in Canada, the disappointment of all ranks at missing active service, and the absurd selection of Gibraltar and Malta as stations had all tended to drain off the Canadian element. It is very significant that during the stay of the Regiment in Canada from 1866 to 1868 the Canadian title had almost entirely disappeared in official, semi-official or Press notices and publications. In a letter from Horse Guards of 25th April, 1868, on the inspection report—it may be mentioned that " His Royal Highness considers the same very satisfactory "—the Regiment is referred to as the " 100th Regiment " *tout court* and this, or " H.M. 100th Regiment," is the title used in every Press cutting extant. Even in the newspaper reports on the celebration of the first anniversary of Dominion Day the 100th Regiment is referred to merely as a unit of the British line. It is true that some verses appeared in the *Ottawa Citizen* of the 13th November, 1866, which opened with " Royal Canadians Welcome, Thrice welcome every man," and closed with the couplet " We give you hearty welcome to Canada again." These verses were probably productive of the warm welcome to the Regiment at Ottawa where " it was met by a torchlight procession and conducted to barracks in George Street, where it partook of a substantial repast provided by the good citizens of Ottawa."

But with the exception of this ode of welcome there is scarcely a reference to Royal Canadians to be found. The solitary exception appears to be a Horse Guards Letter of 18th September, 1868, where " the Corps named in the margin " is shown as " 100th P.W.R.C." At Ottawa there was, however, undoubtedly a great affection for the Regiment. In February, 1867, the citizens gave a ball to the officers (of the 100th Regiment as the *Montreal Gazette* puts it). " It was a magnificent affair. About two hundred ladies and gentlemen were present. The ladies were most numerous, about one-third (*sic*). The guests present were Colonel Campbell, Major Cook, 7 captains, 11 lieutenants, 8 ensigns, surgeon, assistant surgeon, and quartermaster. The ball was held in the spacious new dining hall of the Russell House, which was tastefully decorated under the superintendence of the gentleman usher of the Black Rod, Mr. Cambier, and the Secretary of the Committee, and Mr. Fraser Clerk of the County Court." A week later the officers (of the 100th Regiment again) returned the hospitality by another ball which " eclipsed anything given heretofore in this city in the magnificence of the decorations of the hall, the richness and taste of dress, and the sumptuousness of the supper." The band " of the 100th Regiment " was in attendance. It is certainly remarkable that in these journalistic eulogies there is not a word which would convey to the reader any hint of the Canadian connection of the Regiment ; although there is some months afterwards a reference in an account of a rifle meeting, reported in the *Ottawa Times*, to Captain T. W. W. Smythe of " 100th Prince of Wales's Royal Canadian Regiment."

On 12th June, 1867, headquarters of the Regiment returned from Ottawa to Montreal where it was soon, most appropriately, to take part in the ceremonies which marked the creation of the Dominion of Canada. There is a tendency to visualize Canada as having existed as a single vast country from time immemorial extending from Halifax to Vancouver and washed east and west by the Atlantic and Pacific Oceans. Nothing could be farther from the truth, and in the chapter dealing with the war of 1812-1814 some paragraphs were written to correct this error. Even when the 100th Regiment returned to the land of its birth in 1866 the expression Canada conveyed a signification widely different from that now associated with the name. Nova Scotia and New Brunswick were not Canada at all. A trading concern—the Hudson Bay Company—owned immense territories from part of which the province of Manitoba was to be created. British Columbia was not yet added to the country. Alberta and Saskatchewan were not created until the twentieth century. What constituted the real " Canada " as late as the beginning of 1867 was the union of the old Upper and Lower Provinces— Ontario and Quebec respectively—which had been joined in 1841 when a new constitution had been drawn up. Responsible government soon followed. But though Upper and Lower Canada were now united it still remained for these two provinces to be federated, first with the maritime province to the east and then with the immense territories west and north which had yet to be developed. The former was accomplished on 1st July, 1867, when the Dominion of Canada was created federating Ontario and Quebec with Nova Scotia and New Brunswick. At the inaugural ceremony the 100th Regiment took a prominent part and it is pleasant to be able to record that the Canadian connexion of the Regiment was emphasized. All ranks wore maple leaves, as symbolizing Canada, in their shakos. For many years afterwards Dominion Day was observed in the Regiment and long after all real connexion with Canada had ceased the colours were decorated and maple leaves worn every 1st July, the leaves being sent specially from Canada. Right down to the day of its disbandment the " Old Hundredth " always remembered the land of its birth.

Of the doings of the Regiment at Montreal there is little to chronicle. There is a paragraph in a Montreal newspaper of 1896—in an article on "The 100th Regiment"—to the effect " while quartered in Montreal between 1866 and 1868 serious internal trouble occurred in the Regiment and Major B. Van Straubenzee was detached from his old regiment, the 8th Foot, to take over the command from Colonel Cook and reorganize the Regiment which he successfully did." From other sources it is gleaned that "while the Regiment was quartered at Montreal and Ottawa a great many of the men took their discharge. When it returned to England it was a mere skeleton of a battalion. Thenceforth the 100th had little interest for Canadians." This is, however, to anticipate slightly. It was at Montreal that the 100th lost their regimental pet, the black Newfoundland dog called "Sam," who had joined the 100th as a puppy, in Quebec in 1858. He had served with the Regiment in England, Gibraltar and Malta and became a regular regimental institution being invariably present at guard mounting and orderly-room. Shortly before the Regiment left Malta Sam was in the markers' butt at Pembroke Camp during musketry and was struck by a bullet in the neck on leaving. The wound apparently healed but broke out again during the winter in Canada and on the 24th November, 1866, Sam breathed his last after eight and a half years' service with the Regiment. His death was much regretted; and as a memorial his skin was made into an apron for the big drummer.

In the spring of 1867 the Regiment was supplied with breach-loaders (converted Enfields, Snider pattern) this re-armament being due to the success which had attended the Prussian needle-gun in the Seven Weeks' War against Austria in the preceding year. It is curious—and depressing—to read of the Royal Canadians, while in Canada, receiving drafts from *England*, one being 185 of all ranks. The functionaries in the mother country who dealt with Imperial questions appear to have missed a splendid opportunity for cementing the Empire, and the treatment of the Royal Canadians is not what should have characterized two great departments like the

War and Colonial Offices. Rather it savours of those bloodless abstractions the Inland Revenue or the Board of Trade. However, the unreal situation of a Canadian regiment, while in Canada, receiving recruits from Lancashire and London was soon to be ended. On the 20th October, 1868, a telegram was "unexpectedly received" from the Horse Guards ordering the Regiment to be held in readiness for immediate embarkation for England. Four days later it was inspected by Major-General Bisset " who eulogized the Regiment on its good behaviour, clean and soldierlike appearance." Two companies and all the women and children were sent to Quebec where they embarked on the *Moravian* being joined there by the remainder of the Regiment from Montreal. On the 31st the Regiment left Canada, its strength being 2 field officers, 8 captains, 16 subalterns, 51 sergeants, 34 corporals, 15 drummers, 431 privates, 55 women and 66 children.

CHAPTER VIII

THE 100TH ROYAL CANADIANS—THE UNITED KINGDOM, 1869–1877.

AFTER a voyage of twelve days the *Moravian* steamed up the Clyde and the Regiment disembarked at Glasgow, headquarters and five companies marching to the Gallowgate Barracks while detachments of three and two companies proceeded by rail to Paisley and Ayr respectively. Within a few weeks the Depot companies under Captain G. Macartney joined headquarters and were amalgamated with the Regiment. The establishment of the Regiment was now laid down as follows :—There were 10 companies, 1 colonel, 1 lieutenant-colonel, 2 majors, 10 captains, 12 lieutenants, 8 ensigns, 1 paymaster, 1 adjutant, 1 quartermaster, 1 surgeon, 1 assistant surgeon, 9 warrant officers and staff-sergeants, 10 colour-sergeants, 30 sergeants, 1 drum-major, 1 bandmaster, 20 drummers and fifers, 40 corporals, and 560 privates, or a total of 709 of all ranks.

The Regiment stayed at Glasgow not quite a year and on the 9th September, 1869, the detachments from Ayr and Paisley were brought in and the Regiment moved to England. Its new station was to be Manchester and accordingly it embarked on H.M.S. *Himalaya* for conveyance to Liverpool arriving there on the 10th September and taking over quarters in Salford Barracks, Manchester, on the same day. Just one year was spent in this station and the records of the stay of the Regiment there are exceedingly scanty, there being little else chronicled than a couple of inspections and a similar number of changes in the establishment of the Regiment, the total of the rank and file being brought to 700 on the 24th August, 1870. This latter figure, it may be mentioned, was an advance of 200 privates over an establishment which had been laid down but three months earlier. But in that short space much had happened. France and Germany had rushed to war. Woerth, Spicheren, Borny, Mars-la-Tour and Gravelotte had been fought and won. Bazaine was shut up in Metz. The French Emperor had left the Army of the Rhine. England had begun to realize that a Regiment with 460 privates was not quite in keeping with the astounding events which were happening on the Continent.

The 100th was inspected by Major-General Sir John Garvock, K.C.B., on the 1st October, 1870. No extract is given from any of the inspection reports of those days and as regimental records usually make a point of inserting any laudatory remarks it is probable that the reports were not marked by any hyper-adulation. On the 18th another change took place but one involving only a short move; headquarters and three companies under the command of Lieutenant-Colonel John Campbell proceeded to Bury while five companies under Major Cook were stationed at Ashton, and a detachment of the remaining two companies went to Burnley. A point of some interest and one which foreshadowed future developments is the statement that the depot of the 109th Regiment was now attached to the headquarters of the 100th, this being the first record of the connexion between the two units which was later to be furthered by the linking of the pair, and later by their amalgamation to form the Leinster Regiment. The Franco-German War had by this time impressed upon England the necessity of setting her military house in order and a more intensified order of training was adopted. Service on detachment in Lancashire factory towns was hardly a suitable training for war so in the summer of 1871 the 100th was moved south to the more bracing military atmosphere of Aldershot, where it arrived on the 15th June, going into camp at Rushmoor Bottom.

A month later a change in command took place, Lieutenant-Colonel Campbell going on half-pay and being succeeded by Lieutenant-Colonel Hon. C. J. Addington; Major H. Cook was the senior officer of the right half battalion and Major W. W. Smythe of the left, the latter being one of the remaining Canadian officers. While the Regiment was at Aldershot Lieutenant-General Sir Hope Grant was in command of the division—" he had his photo took standing with the band and presented Bandsman Bob Quinn with a silver cornet for his ability as a cornet player." The brigadier was Major-General H. Parkes, his brigade-major being the present Duke of Connaught. In September the Regiment took part in " the autumnal manœuvres " returning to its tents at Rushmoor Bottom on the 22nd. A week later it marched into Aldershot and was quartered in what was then known as the centre block infantry barracks.

The stay of the Regiment at Aldershot seems to have been quite uneventful but it took part in at least one important ceremony. It proceeded to London by special train on 27th February, 1872, in connexion with the ceremony which marked the national thanksgiving for the recovery of the Prince of Wales—later King Edward VII—from a dangerous illness. In May the inevitable new establishment was issued—the War Office seems to have done little else in those days—by which the total for all ranks was fixed at 799. There were big manœuvres in August and the Regiment formed part of a Southern Army operating against a Northern one. At the conclusion of the manœuvres the Regiment marched to the Portsdown Hill Forts near Portsmouth, headquarters arriving at Fort Widley on 18th September, 1872.

When the Regiment arrived at Portsmouth there remained in it about 250 of the original Royal Canadians. These were men of impressive stature, and had Frederick the Great seen them he would have endeavoured to purchase them out of hand. Very few of them were under six feet in height; curiously enough there were no men of medium tallness for the few who were not six-footers were little men. The name of one of the latter is remembered in connexion with a little incident which throws an interesting light on soldiering in the seventies. Andrew Willing was a regular veteran in the Service and had just received his fourth good conduct badge, being the first man in the Regiment to do so. On the first commanding officer's parade on which he displayed it, he moved slightly in the ranks. Instantly a terrible voice roared out: "Stand steady *that young soldier*"—for to a commanding officer no old soldier could possibly be guilty of such a serious fault. The compiler may mention that when he joined the 2nd Battalion in 1894 he was informed by the present General Martin that when the latter was a young officer he once saw a soldier commit a similar enormity. There was for a moment a deathly silence and the commanding officer then exploded with "March that man to the guard-room." "Steady drill" *was* steady indeed in those days.

The clothing at the time consisted of a Glengarry cap, cloth tunic and shell jacket (both of brickdust red and not scarlet), a pair of so-called cloth trousers ("which, by the way, would stand alone they were so stiff"), a pair of serge trousers and two pairs of boots. The kit was much the same as at the present day but the recruit could have either two flannel or three cotton shirts. Hair brushes or tooth brushes were not issued. The equipment comprised a shako, leggings, knapsack ("an oblong box about 15 inches by 12 having two straps fastened to the inside top edge; these passed over your shoulder and hooked to the bottom inside edge. On top, reaching about halfway up the back of your head you carried your mess tin, and, lying flat on top of the box, two straps being passed round the whole, your greatcoat"). Waist-belt and ammunition pouches completed the ensemble. The rifle was the Snider and the bayonet was of triangular pattern.

The steady drill of those days was brought to perfection by non-commissioned officers who probably have no counterpart to-day and a few words may be given of the idiosyncrasies of Sergeant "Jimmy" Nolan said to be one of the smartest drills of his time. About thirty-five years of age, he was a small, thin, wiry man, with somewhat high cheek bones, hollow cheeks, full lips and a moustache that grew almost straight out of the lip, and when, as he often did, he protruded that lip, the moustache pointed straight like miniature porcupine quills. He was a very active little man and could run backwards as fast as his squad could run forward. As to drill, he was a monomaniac. After early morning parade he would come into the barrack-room where the bowls were placed in a line preparatory to being filled with coffee for breakfast, and prepare to dress them. Looking along the rank and holding his cane out parallel to the line, he would say in his best drill instructor voice : " Dress back numbers 4 and 6," of course, 4 and 6 paid no attention to him. " I say dress back numbers 4 and 6," this in a louder tone but with the same result ; " 4 and 6 you stupid men, dress back," and becoming exasperated by their non-compliance would dive at them with his cane and turn them over. The advent of the orderly-man with the coffee put an end to his drill for that meal, but every morning saw a repetition. Fences, palings, lines of stones, in fact anything standing in ranks came in for a muttered " Dress up number —— " or " Dress back number ——," and ducks waddling home as they do in a line one behind the other, would come in for correction, " Cover off number —— "—" Cover to the left you stupid man."

On the 19th June, 1873, headquarters marched into Portsmouth and took over quarters in the Cambridge Barracks, where they were soon joined by the detachments from the forts. A fortnight later the Regiment furnished a guard of honour at the dockyard on the occasion of the departure of the Shah of Persia from England. While at Portsmouth a tragic occurrence took place. Captain G. M. Fox with some officers of the Regiment and of the Royal Marines organized a boxing tournament at which one of the competitors was killed. The civil power intervened and all the officers concerned were put on their trial at the Winchester Assizes. A verdict of acquittal was the result, and on the return of the accused all the men of the Regiment turned up at Landport station and took the horses from the carriages drawing the officers in triumph to Cambridge Barracks.

There were some odd " characters " in the 100th at this time. There was Dan Butler, who invariably called himself—and was called by others—" The King of Ireland "; he had once been a sergeant but was " reduced for pulling an officer off his horse in Canada." Jack Morgan, " celebrated for having a conviction for drunkenness for every month of his service." John Bonet whose feet were so big that his boots could not be accommodated in his knapsack; while Jack Rhoner was noted for his immense hands and prodigiously strong grip. Paddy Halloran was a giant who was the only man able to shift, unaided, some of the targets then in use. Jim Welch the regimental quartermaster-sergeant, weighed over 20 stone. Jerry Potts, one of the cooks, was an enormously strong man who had " a way with him " with incapable subordinates; one " he seized with one hand by the back of the breeches and dropped him in a copper vat, saying ' Yer God darned winkle I'll boil you for my breakfast.'" There is a fine Elizabethan spaciousness about these old worthies. And amongst the non-commissioned officers " were some very fine men, gentlemen every one," amongst whom was Eli Clarke who gave six sons to the Regiment.

Associated with the stay of the Regiment in Portsmouth are some events which are worth recording. Scarlet—which had hitherto apparently been reserved for Guards and Royal Engineers—took the place of brick-red in the infantry of the line. The change was not at first popular as the new tunics soiled much more easily than the older pattern and sea water had an empurpling effect upon the former. Then, too, the old knapsack gave way to the valise equipment and "on the whole the change was an improvement." More important than either of these two occurrences was one due to the recent Franco-German War. In a later chapter—dealing with the 109th Regiment for this period—the reforms in the Army, thus brought about—*i.e.*, the abolition of purchase, the introduction of short service, and the "linked battalion" system will be found described at some length. Here it is necessary merely to state that in 1873 the 100th and 109th Regiments are shown in the Army List for the first time as constituting the "67th Brigade" with a common headquarters at Birr, the two Regiments being thus "linked" for the purpose of "feeding"—the home unit supplying drafts to the one abroad.

Having issued a further couple of establishments the War Office ordered the Regiment to Ireland and accordingly it embarked on the 5th May, 1874, on board the *Euphrates* for conveyance to Kingstown, the strength of the Regiment on embarkation being 19 officers, 43 staff-sergeants and sergeants, 44 corporals, 17 drummers, 475 privates, 65 women and 121 children.

The Regiment arrived safely at Kingstown on 7th May when headquarters and the right wing disembarked and marched to Richmond Barracks, Dublin. The next day the remainder of the Regiment disembarked and joined headquarters. The stay of the Regiment in Dublin was not of long duration for at the end of the summer it was split up into the numerous detachments which characterized soldiering in Ireland in those days. Headquarters and four companies under the command of Lieutenant-Colonel the Hon. C. J. Addington proceeded to Mullingar on the 16th September, detachments of one company being sent to Sligo, Boyle, Navan and Trim. The depot of the 109th seems to have been still attached to the 100th at this time and there was a very friendly feeling between the two. The Regiment was now in a good hunting country and made the most of its opportunities, seven or eight officers in pink usually turning out with the Westmeath Hounds, two officers of the 109th Depot, Captain Hempstead and Lieutenant Hoyes being always in the first flight. The 100th, during this tour, made the acquaintance of the Royal Meath Militia.

On the 31st March, 1875, a notification was received from the adjutant-general of the forces stating that Her Majesty the Queen had been graciously pleased to approve of the word " Niagara " being inscribed on the Regimental Colour, as formerly granted to the old Hundredth the Prince Regent's County of Dublin Regiment in commemoration of its distinguished conduct at the capture of Fort Niagara by assault on 13th December, 1813. Thus, the connexion between the two 100th Regiments now obtained official recognition, as, indeed, was due from the link formed by the descendants of the settlers from the 100th of Niagara days who enlisted in 1858 as described in an earlier chapter. It may be said here, however, that the honour " Niagara " includes a good deal more than the splendid capture of the fort of that name. It takes in also much hard fighting on the Niagara frontier in which the 100th was engaged. The honour is borne by several regiments who were not present at the capture of Fort Niagara at all but who like the 100th, took part in the various battles in that part of the theatre of war. For no regiment has the word " Niagara " such a wide significance as for the 100th.

In 1875 a new establishment was brought in by which the number of privates was fixed at 605, a figure which was raised to 780 in the following year, doubtless on account of an Indian tour being in prospect. In July 1875 the non-effectives, women and children moved to Kilkenny and on the 16th the Regiment proceeded to the Curragh for what was then called the " drill season." Here it remained just a month when it was distributed as follows :—Headquarters, with " H," " J," and " K "

Companies to Kilkenny; "C," "F," and "G" Companies to Waterford; "D" Company to Duncannon Fort; "B" Company to Carrick-on-Suir; "E" Company to Dungarvan; and "A" Company to Clonmel. Such was the system of detachments which then prevailed. In the spring of 1876 the detachments at Waterford, Dungarvan, Clonmel and Carrick-on-Suir moved to Dublin for duty and in June the whole Regiment embarked on the *Orontes* at Kingstown for Portsmouth whence it proceeded immediately by rail to Aldershot, encamping on the Church Plateau. Next month the Regiment marched to Blackheath in connexion with the mobilization " of the 2nd and 5th Army Corps " and returned to Aldershot on the 20th.

The year 1877 was marked by the outbreak of war between Russia and Turkey and it was doubtless this circumstance which led to the encampment of an army corps at Chobham. The Regiment camped there on the 9th July and next day took part in a great review before the Queen in Windsor Park; after which it marched back to Aldershot. The Regiment was now under orders for India and was inspected at Aldershot on 26th September; Colonel the Hon. C. J. Addington went on half-pay on the 29th and was succeeded by Lieutenant-Colonel H. Cook. For a moment it seemed as if the 100th was about to see active service. The situation in the Near East was disquieting and the threat of Russia against Constantinople was causing great disquiet in England. There was talk of sending troops and the writer has heard the late Colonel Glancy say that the baggage of the Regiment was actually on the barrack square labelled Gallipoli. Thirty-eight years were, however, to elapse before the Leinster Regiment set foot upon its shore.

CHAPTER IX

THE 100TH ROYAL CANADIANS—INDIA, 1877–1894.

THE Regiment, under the command of Lieutenant-Colonel H. Cook, embarked on H.M. Troopship *Jumna* at Portsmouth on the 5th and 6th October, 1877, with a strength of 19 officers and 692 other ranks. Bombay was reached on the 10th November and the Regiment proceeded by rail to Jullundur halting *en route* at Deolali, Khandwa, Sohagpore, Jubbulpore, Allahabad, Toondla and Umballa, the two wings of the Regiment uniting at Jullundur on the 21st. The depot under the command of Captain J. B. Kersteman had remained at Aldershot where it was attached to the 60th Rifles.

The *Jumna* was one of the old Lobster Pots, as those troopships were called which, manned by the Royal Navy and under Admiralty control, plied from Portsmouth to Bombay in the seventies and eighties of the last century. She and her sisters the *Serapis*, *Malabar*, *Euphrates* and *Crocodile* were veritable leviathans among the ships of forty years back, with their tall white sides and yellow funnels. But though of some 7,000 tons they can best be described as whited sepulchres. They combined a maximum of internal discomfort with a minimum of stability at sea. Even in moderate weather they nearly rolled their insides out. Their pace was leisurely—a solemn 9 or 10 knots—and a day's run of over 240 miles was a matter for congratulation. These vessels were officered as a rule by old lieutenants with no hope of promotion who were wont to vent their spleen on their soldier cargoes. Relations between the

Navy and Army were usually somewhat strained in these vessels. The accommodation was uncomfortable and old-time subalterns will carry to the grave a recollection of pandemonium, a small triangular space right aft in the lowest embowelment of the ship, surrounded by what were by courtesy called cabins—*i.e.*, dens separated from the central space merely by Venetian shutters which were removed soon after leaving England for the purpose of ventilation.

It was during the journey up country of the 100th that the first meeting with its linked battalion, the 109th, took place at Jubbulpore. Here the former took over some of the personnel of its link, and it was here apparently that the famous Indian mess table of the 109th was handed over to the officers of the 100th Regiment. Curiously enough no record of the transaction can be found. It has always been held by the officers of the 1st Battalion that the table was bought and duly paid for, but the tradition which has reigned in the 2nd Battalion ever since 1878 is that the table was transferred on the understanding that it could be reclaimed when the next Box and Cox movement of the two linked battalions might take place. This seems to be the more probable explanation, and if there had been a sale some memory of the amount which passed would almost certainly have been preserved.

In the following summer the Regiment went through a severe ordeal. The whole country round Jullundur was flooded, chiefly owing to the embankments built up for what was then known as the Scinde, Punjab and Delhi Railway. These massive erections ran for miles at right angles, more or less, to the flow of the main rivers from the north, and, this being an exceptionally rainy season, and there being a totally inadequate number of culverts and openings to let off the dammed-up waters, as a natural consequence the embankments and bridges were washed away, the country flooded and fever and cholera raged for months. The tablet in Jullundur Church to the memory of 88 men, women and children is testimony to the debt paid by the Regiment during the months of its stay in this place.

But the most trying part of our time in this cantonment was the fact that, while we were being decimated by fever and cholera, we were daily witnesses of the lucky corps passing through on their way to the Afghan campaign. Owing to the breaks in the railway many regiments and batteries had to halt temporarily, or at any rate were delayed, at the river crossings, and the unfortunate officers of the 100th were wont to ride to the temporary camps and sadly watch their more fortunate comrades bound for the front. Nothing more galling can be imagined than the disappointment of being so near the frontier and not being allowed to go on.

At Jullundur the younger officers took at once to polo, a game then in its infancy. Ponies were still cheap. In spite of the requirements of the army in Afghanistan Rs80 to 100 would buy a good animal. Even penniless subalterns had two or three ponies apiece. No wonder India was looked upon as the poor man's paradise in those days. The field battery commanded by a sporting major had tent-pegging weekly and in this the subalterns of the Regiment were always welcome to compete. There were other amenities, too, one being a large covered swimming bath where the younger officers would spend the greater part of the hot summer days not only in bathing but in learning Hindustani. " It was a quaint sight to watch the old Munshee, with his spectacles and a very dirty book, seated on a chair at one end of the bath, whilst we swam about, every now and then emerging from the water to talk to the old man and listen to his explanations and stories of some great king who lived centuries before the world." And those were the days of the faithful old bearer resolute to brave the most terrible difficulties in his master's service. On one occasion Lieutenant Willcocks was proudly bearing the Regimental Colour on a brigade ceremonial parade. The troops were drawn up in line with bayonets fixed in all the solemn panoply of those functions when an aged

H 2

Mohammedan was seen wildly waving a pocket handkerchief, and the venerable man, pursued by military police, rushed across the parade ground shouting " It is my master's handkerchief." He solemnly presented the article to the horrified officer and retired with the air of a man to whom duty was a sacred thing.

Some of the officers of the Regiment took advantage of the comparative proximity of the Himalayas to go shooting and brought back some fine heads, and what with cheap and abundant polo, tent-pegging and these expeditions, life in Jullundur was a pleasant one. Socially, too, things were lively though it may be said that the mess was perhaps too liberal in entertaining; " every guest night saw crowds of fellows—in fact, anyone who left cards—as guests, but it came hard on the subalterns, who in those days paid equally with seniors, and not by rank, as later on."

In December, 1878, the Regiment moved to Sialkot near the Kashmir frontier. While there the commanding officer exchanged with Colonel Barrett of the 19th, a circumstance which gave Fate an opportunity of playing a fiendish trick on two majors. In the 100th Major A. did not get on well with his commanding officer, Colonel Cook; and the situation was duplicated in the 19th where Major B. did not see eye to eye with Colonel Barrett. A. and B. had, therefore, after long correspondence and some expense effected an exchange. Soon to their horror, Colonels Cook and Barrett also got up a game of general post and the majors who had just begun to spread themselves in more genial atmospheres realized too late that *Plus on exchange plus c'est la même chose.*

At Sialkot the Regiment had again to experience the sickening disappointment of missing active service. It had been earmarked for the Afghan campaign while at Jullundur but, as has been related, severe sickness had robbed it of its chance; now at Sialkot disappointment came again. The first phase of the Afghan War of 1878 had ended with the signing of the Treaty of

Ganda-mak. The wiseacres had stated that India would now enjoy profound peace and most of the regiments and batteries had returned to their cantonments. Then came the news of the murderous attack on our Resident, Sir Louis Cavagnari, and his brave companions at Kabul in September, 1879. All eyes were turned once more to the north-west frontier and soon troops began to pour towards Peshawar, Kurram, and Kandahar. The Regiment, however, although from a contemporary record " in a very high state of efficiency, mostly composed of old soldiers " was once more left out. One young officer " had no intention this time of being left out of the campaign " and with frightful audacity sent a private telegram to Simla asking " to be sent on service in any capacity and on any pay or on no pay." It was a military crime of the most horrifying description and for three days the young officer thought of nothing but " usual channels," " arrest " and the various contingencies of a " severe reprimand." On the third day a telegram came to the Regiment directing this young officer to proceed to the front and to report himself at Peshawar. His name was James Willcocks.

In those days of small wars only a comparatively few regiments had a chance of active service ; war-experience was, therefore, by no means common and, as a corollary, was a tremendous professional asset for any officer. Consequently when a war did break out strings were pulled with immense vigour, and any regiment with influence or a " pull " moved heaven and earth to be in the " show." And then by the process known as the vicious circle such regiments and officers were all the more likely to be selected for the next campaign ; the expression " the Wolseley gang " was, indeed, applied to the small body of generals and staff officers who flitted from one small campaign to another to the exclusion of everyone else. This opinion of the writer's was at any rate shared by an officer of the 100th in 1879. " Long after sickness had gone and we had been moved to a more healthy station, and the second Afghan War dragged on, it became clear that there was no intention of sending the 100th to add one name to its colours ; and I vowed if ever I had a son he should go into a corps whose standards were thick with battle honours ; for there is no truer saying in such matters than ' To him that hath shall be given.' " Thirty-three years later Sir James Willcocks carried out his vow. James Lugard Willcocks entered the Black Watch in 1912, though, as a matter of fact, had he entered his father's old regiment he would have had as much fighting as he wanted. But that his father should have made such a vow and kept it for over thirty years is eloquent testimony to the existence of graft and pull in the seventies.

At Sialkot the 100th was short of officers as more than one managed to get to the front on transport or other duties. The sergeant-major, the drill-sergeant and many of the non-commissioned officers and men were Canadians but the only Canadian officer was apparently Major Smythe. Lieutenant Glancy was the adjutant and a very smart one. Sialkot is one of the hottest stations in India and in the hot weather of 1879 there were many deaths from heat apoplexy. Work generally started at 5 a.m. and finished by nine o'clock ; between that hour and 4.30 p.m. the men were not allowed out and they spent most of their time in sleep. There were very few Europeans in the station besides the military, but the few that were joined in all our sports. We played polo two or three times a week ; sometimes we had mounted paper chases ; there were racquets and lawn tennis and a little shooting, but it was poor. About this time the effect of the linked battalion system had begun to make itself felt, several subalterns being offered promotion into the 109th ; the linking was unpopular and at first all refused but when it was realized that the two regiments were certain to be amalgamated, two second lieutenants accepted the offer. As regards work, in the cold weather, " we had (strange to say for those days) one or two field days—quite good ones." Towards the end of 1880 orders were received that the

Regiment was to proceed by march route to Umballa to be there stationed.

The distance from Sialkot to Umballa, or Ambala as the modern purists spell it, is roughly 250 miles. The Regiment left the former station on 4th December, 1880, arriving at its destination on the first day of the New Year on which day Lieutenant-Colonel R. A. Barrett assumed command. Umballa differed from Sialkot in that it was a large garrison with the result that things were crowded and there were too many people wanting to play polo, racquets, etc. ; and although it was quite a good station there were many in the Regiment who preferred quieter ones. For a poor but honest infantry regiment the 100th had quite a useful polo team and it won the divisional tug-of-war " which was celebrated by a very big night in barracks." So far as is known this was the earliest tug-of-war success in the long series of triumphs which fell to both battalions of the Leinster Regiments. Black buck and bird shooting round Umballa were very good and the Regiment took a big share in it all.

During the hot weather part of the Battalion used to go to Solan, a small station, originally a musketry camp, halfway up the hill to Simla. The remainder would settle down to the hot weather routine at Umballa. The work was not hard and for most people was over at 8 a.m. having begun at six. Recruits had another parade in the evening, the term " recruit " being applied to any man who had come out in a draft, although he must have had at least two years' service. The idea was to see that the style and the finish of the Battalion was acquired but it is not difficult to see that it must have been secured at the cost of a considerable amount of discontent on the part of the victims.

From 15th April to 15th October was the leave season, when as many officers as possible went off, with one per company remaining, and a large number of men, women and children were sent to the hills. Summer was certainly an idle time. There were eight companies in the Battalion each nominally 100 strong. Battalion headquarters as a separate body did not exist. Clerks, storemen, etc., were scattered about in different companies and owed a divided allegiance, a bad system. Barrack square drill with markers out for every movement was the usual parade. Often the sergeant-major could be seen, even during an extended order advance, solemnly checking the intervals with a pace stick.

Khaki and Sam Browne belts were still unauthorized, though regiments that had been in Afghanistan used both. In the cold weather we wore red on all occasions, and in the hot weather, white. When it was decided to introduce khaki for hot weather use Government went the whole hog and we were ordered to dye our white drill suits under company arrangements. That meant each company engaging a dyer in the bazaar. The Battalion parade in this new kit was a joy. No two companies were dressed in the least alike; indeed, hardly any two suits in the same company matched, and after the first wash the effect was still more charming—if, indeed, variety be charming. Not only were all the suits streaky and of more diverse hues than ever, but hardly a single pair of trousers matched the jacket above them; indeed, legs of the same trousers and sleeves of the same coat sometimes differed. Captains and quartermasters lived troubled lives and commanding officer's parades were times of sorrow, so vitriolic were his comments. At last a Bombay firm managed to produce a yarn-dyed drill which would stand washing. The abolition of white as a walking out dress was very unpopular. The men could take no pride in themselves when dressed in bazaar-dyed abominations, and gave up walking out, loafed in barracks and the canteen and crime increased. Later, white was re-introduced as a walking out dress, and as usually happened in those days our first intimation of the step was a wire from some cotton mill asking for the regimental contract.

Although according to the standard of to-day a regiment was indifferently trained in the eighties, yet a battalion which had been a few years in India was as fine a body of men as any army could produce. Perhaps it was not a very temperate body, but at any rate the men could carry their liquor and turn out smartly at 6 a.m. after the heaviest bout. The commanding officer, Colonel Barrett, had served in the Crimea and the Mutiny, and was a fine soldier, very strict, rather hard, but very just. Always very well turned out yet he would sometimes carry an umbrella to shade his head when walking to the orderly-room. Majors were in those days stars of considerable magnitude in the military firmament. There were only two per battalion and both were mounted, the mud-crushing major commanding a company had yet to come. Promotion was very slow. Sam Denison, not a very senior captain in 1881, had been boots for seven long years. Fancy no promotion in that time! Captain T. V. Shepherd who had recently been promoted into us from the 109th had seventeen years' service as a subaltern. This long block naturally produced a run, which was further accelerated by many going to the Indian Staff Corps, so that some who joined in the early eighties got their companies in under six years.

It was while the Regiment was at Umballa that there took place the great upheaval by which regiments lost their numbers and to a great extent their identity. On 1st July, 1881, the new army organization came into force whereby the whole of the infantry of the line and the militia were formed into so-called territorial regiments. The 100th Prince of Wales's Royal Canadian Regiment now became the 1st Battalion of The Prince of Wales's Leinster Regiment (Royal Canadians) the 2nd Battalion being found by its "linked battalion," the 109th Bombay Infantry. The militia battalions were the King's County, Queen's County, and Royal Meath now called the 3rd, 4th, and 5th Battalions respectively. The depot of the Regiment was assigned to Birr. By an Army Order of 1st July the establishment of the 1st Leinster Regiment was fixed as follows:—
2 lieutenant-colonels, 4 majors, 4 captains, 16 lieutenants,

1 adjutant, 1 quartermaster, total, 28 officers ; 1 sergeant-major, 1 quartermaster-sergeant, 1 bandmaster, 1 sergeant-drummer, 1 paymaster-sergeant, 1 armourer-sergeant, 1 orderly-room sergeant, 1 hospital sergeant, 8 colour-sergeants, 1 sergeant-pioneer, 1 sergeant-instructor of musketry, 32 sergeants, 40 corporals, and 780 privates.

The whole question of the " territorialization " of the infantry will be dealt with in a later chapter namely that which treats of the 2nd Battalion during the year 1881 ; for inasmuch as the 109th was in the United Kingdom at the time and was thus more in touch with the depot and the militia battalions it will be more convenient to defer the discussion until then. Here it may be said that when the authorities were confronted with the extreme difficulty of finding a territorial common denominator for the 100th Prince of Wales's Royal Canadian Regiment and the 109th Bombay Infantry they telegraphed to India asking whether the 100th would be willing to drop the title " Royal Canadian." From nowhere except from a Government office could a query so inept have issued. The officers of the Royal Canadians refused to relinquish a title which had been conferred by Her Majesty and there thus came into being the clumsy, double-barrelled and contradictory title which the Leinster Regiment bore ever since that date. The 100th had, it is true, rather dropped the Canadian title for some years and the Regiment was apparently known as the 100th Regiment *tout court*. But anyone who knew anything about soldiers might have foreseen that the Regiment would have been up in arms at any attempt to filch from it an honourable designation. The result of the tactless action of the authorities was to revive the Canadian traditions and to give the Canadian sentiment of the 1st Leinster Regiment a new lease of life.

A great triumph was achieved by the Battalion in 1882 when it won the commander-in-chief's cup for musketry with a score of 681 points.

In November, 1883, the Battalion left Umballa by train for Fyzabad. In the records consulted there are several references to the usual inspections of the Battalion—or the Regiment as it was up to 1881—but there is an ominous absence of those eulogistic extracts which are invariably preserved in a Digest of Service. A change may now be noted. On 10th December, 1883, there is a reference to an inspection report dated Umballa 31st January in which the general officer commanding " expressed his satisfaction at the efficient state in which the Regiment was found, and has specially remarked its improved conduct " ; and a year later there is a report testifying to the efficient state of the Battalion and " the conduct of the men is also a subject on which the lieutenant-general is glad to remark favourably." As for life at Fyzabad one Indian station is, generally speaking, so like another that so far as sport and social life are concerned there is little to be said about Fyzabad which has not been said already about Sialkot and Umballa. There was the same polo ; " we stuck pig a lot," and " you could watch the pig-sticking from the roof of the mess." Another form of sport was killing muggers—*i.e.*, alligators in the river. In 1884 the Battalion won the commander-in-chief's cup for musketry a second time and to commemorate this happy event the officers presented a cup to the sergeants' mess and a shield to the men. During the stay of the Battalion at Fyzabad the reports upon it were of a most gratifying character. Curiously enough although the Battalion was third in order of merit in the musketry classification list of the battalions in India it was officially informed that this was " moderate," and " His Excellency hopes that next year the Battalion will attain a higher standard of efficiency." This curious document was signed by the adjutant-general in India on 4th September, 1886. But, three weeks later, the general officer commanding Oudh Division placed on record the following statement that " the 1st Battalion Leinster Regiment has been for some years one of the best shooting battalions in India.

It is well prepared for the field." Either the general musketry of the Army in India was woefully bad or the commander-in-chief confused the 1st Leinster Regiment with some other unit with a somewhat similar title.

Orders now came for the Battalion to move to Calcutta and on 1st October, 1886, a station order was published to the following effect : " The officer commanding at Fyzabad cannot permit the 1st Battalion Leinster Regiment to leave the station without placing on record his sense of the highly efficient state of the Battalion in every respect, and he desires to convey his best thanks to all ranks for their cheerful and prompt obedience to all orders. He much regrets their departure from Fyzabad, which station they have garrisoned since the 16th November, 1883, and he feels assured wherever they may be they will uphold the high reputation they have so well merited. Colonel Bartleman, in wishing the Regiment farewell, wishes Lieutenant-Colonel Collum, the officers and men of the Royal Canadians every success and prosperity." It will be noted that the station commander in his first official paragraph refers to the Battalion as the 1st Leinster Regiment, but his private good wishes are to the " Royal Canadians " the name which had now been resumed by the officers as a result of that " territorial " system introduced to eliminate it.

Calcutta was reached on the 5th October, 1886, and on the 9th January, 1887, Lieutenant-Colonel D. W. Mackinnon, an old 109th officer, arrived from England and assumed command. Early in February the Battalion was grieved to hear of a disaster to a party consisting of Lieutenant J. F. Stewart, Lance-Corporal McCormack, and Private Owens who were attacked and killed while on survey duty in the Chittagong hills. The party was about 24 miles from Rangemuttia on the British side of the frontier, and consisted of the three Europeans and a small detachment of native infantry. Lieutenant Stewart fought nobly and killed fourteen of the enemy, supposed to be from a warlike tribe called Pois. These hillmen looted the camp and took away the heads of the Europeans. A monument in the church at Fort William was, later, erected by the comrades of the dead men, to their memory.

On the 16th February the Battalion took part in the grand parade on the Maidan in honour of the Jubilee of Her Most Gracious Majesty Victoria the Queen Empress. Four days later the Battalion again paraded at Fort William for the purpose of receiving new colours in place of those presented by His Royal Highness The Prince of Wales at Shorncliffe in 1859. His Excellency the Earl of Dufferin, the Viceroy, and His Excellency Sir Frederick Roberts, V.C., commander-in-chief, were present. As the Earl of Dufferin had lately been Governor-General of the Dominion of Canada the honour conferred upon the Battalion by the Countess of Dufferin undertaking the presentation of the colours was greatly appreciated by officers and men. In presenting the colours Lady Dufferin said: "Colonel Mackinnon, officers, non-commissioned officers and men of the Royal Canadians, the Regiment to which you have the honour to belong sprang into existence in the hour of England's greatest need; it owed its birth to the loyal devotion of our Canadian fellow subjects, and its embodiment was one of the earliest indications given by our colonies of that determination which they have since so universally expressed to recognize and maintain the unity and common interests of the British Empire. I now entrust these colours to your guardianship fully believing that you will rally round them nobly and gallantly in whatever quarter of the world they will be displayed in defence of England's honour and the Queen's dominions."

Lieutenant-Colonel Mackinnon made a suitable reply and a lunch, with a ball in the evening, duly followed. It is a curious reflection on the new territorialization system that not one single word was uttered by the Countess of Dufferin upon either the Leinster or Irish connexion of the Battalion. Although every effort was being made by the authorities to suppress any titles which might overshadow the new " local " names—witness the long and futile struggle to call " The Queen's " and " The King's " the Royal West Surrey and Liverpool Regiment respectively—here at the formal presentation of colours the work of the territorialization committee was completely ignored. There is a certain piquancy in the fact that the Countess of Dufferin's speech was made in the presence of the highest military authority in India. The old colours were presented to and accepted by the Canadian Government, being placed in the House of Parliament, Ottawa.

The following officers were serving in the Battalion on the day the colours were presented :—

Lieutenant-Colonels : D. W. Mackinnon (commanding), L. J. Collum.

Majors : G. Poignand, J. Hart, H. H. Prior, A. C. Denison, J. G. Glancy.

Captains : A. G. Kaye, W. Seton, E. G. M. Short, J. Willcocks, A. K. Huddart, V. J. Garland.

Subalterns : G. Lamb, F. C. B. Lane, E. O. Wathen, M. J. Tighe, R. V. Davidson, T. St. C. Davidson, C. S. B. Evans-Lombe, E. de V. Wintle, A. H. Bingley, M. B. Roberts, N. H. C. Dickinson, G. T. D. Browne, C. Mitchell-Innes, G. T. Widdicombe, F. A. Kingston, E. A. E. Stevenson, H. O. R. Senior, J. W. B. Merewether.

Adjutant : Lieutenant J. Shakespear.

Quartermaster : Lieutenant A. Wilkin.

Although sport, as sport was known in up-country stations, was not to be had in Calcutta, the Battalion was not behind hand in local events. In 1887 Captain Short's " Odette " ridden by its owner, won the Calcutta Monsoon Skye Race and the goblet was presented to the officers' mess ; and in the same year the plate was augmented by a cup to commemorate what must be one of the most extraordinary tug-of-war triumphs on record.

The inscription on the cup tells its own tale :—
"This cup commemorates the famous Tug-of-War Match between the 1st Battalion Prince of Wales's Leinster Regiment R.C. (100th Foot) and the 2nd Battalion Sherwood Foresters (Derbyshire Regiment) (95th Foot), which was won by the 100th after a pull lasting fifty-seven minutes. Fort William, Calcutta, 1887."

In the year 4924 when this cup will be disinterred the successors to Lord Carnarvon and Mr. Howard Carter will stand amazed at this tribute to the stamina of the old British Army. Another sporting trophy in the officers' mess was a silver-mounted horse-hoof snuff box. This was the hoof of Major H. H. Prior's "Chatsworth," winner of the Grand Annual Hurdle Race and the Tally-Ho Plate, Calcutta; the Hastings' Plate, Cachar 1887 and many other races in India and Australia.

In 1888 the 1st Leinster Regiment won the commander-in-chief's prize for musketry for the third time, a magnificent record. The cup was presented by the commander-in-chief himself at Fort William in January, 1889. Tug-of-war, too, gave the Battalion an opportunity of showing its prowess, for at the St. Patrick's Day 1889 sports the team won the prize open to all the European troops in Bengal. Like all Irish regiments the Leinsters were always at their best when in a large station and a record from one who knew the 1st Battalion in those days states "the men were wonderfully smart in appearance and I think their summer uniform used to be the best fitting of any corps I have ever met." The band, at that time, was in a very high state of efficiency and made enormous sums by playing out. In another respect the Battalion also showed its efficiency; it made such good "soft drinks" with its soda-water plant and sold them at such a low price that the Calcutta firms complained and the powers that were put a stopper on outside sale by the Battalion.

Lieutenant-Colonel Campbell arrived from England on 30th March, 1889, and assumed command *vice*

Lieutenant-Colonel Mackinnon, retired, and in that year Captain Willcocks, D.S.O., gave up the adjutancy which he had held since 1887 on being posted as station staff officer at Agra, being succeeded by Lieutenant Merewether. Towards the end of the year the Battalion prepared to leave Calcutta for Agra, an advanced party and the married families entraining on the 13th December. Headquarters and six companies marched out of Fort William on 2nd January, 1890, and proceeded by rail to Bordwan. It is worth noting as showing what was feared of an Irish battalion in those days that the general officer commanding published an order "expressing himself as much pleased with the quiet and orderly manner in which the Battalion marched from Fort William." From Bordwan the Battalion marched to Agra arriving there on 21st March, 1890, having covered 748 miles in 72 days, a splendid performance of which any regiment might be proud.

Life at Agra was apparently uneventful and the records available for 1890 merely mention such purely regimental occurrences as that Lieutenant-Colonel Poignand returned to England to assume command of the 2nd Battalion, and that Lieutenant Merewether resigned the adjutancy in which he was succeeded by Captain Winton Seton. There were the usual inspections and a report dated 24th February, 1891, says that "the shooting is improving and there is a soldierlike spirit in the Battalion." The same document has a double-edged compliment contained in the words "the general officer commanding is very glad to be able to congratulate Colonel Campbell and all ranks under him on the improvement which has taken place in the conduct of the Battalion during the past year." In August Lieutenant-Colonel and Colonel J. H. Campbell retired on pension. He was succeeded by Lieutenant-Colonel G. Poignand who was now re-transferred from the 2nd Battalion.

While at Agra the Battalion went through precisely the same experience that both battalions of the Regiment were accustomed to undergo at a new station. Doubtless every Irish battalion has been in the same boat. The procedure invariably was that the staff would suffer considerable alarm at the prospect of the arrival of an Irish unit. There would be much examination of defaulters' sheets when the particular battalion arrived; much gloomy shaking of venerable heads and much grave talk about the " conduct of the battalion." Long before the unit moved the mists of suspicion would have cleared away. The authorities, in the most sporting way, would admit that they were wrong and that " there never was such a battalion," and so on.

That is just what happened at Agra. Before the Battalion arrived there had been the usual symptoms of panic. But Brigadier-General Gerald Morton knew a good regiment when he saw it and so at the inspection of the 1st Battalion on the 18th and 19th January, 1892, he addressed the Battalion in the following words : " The Battalion is as fine a one as I could wish to see. When I last knew the Regiment seven years ago in Fyzabad you were considered the best drilled regiment in the Oudh Division, and that amongst such crack corps as the Derbyshire Regiment and the Seaforth Highlanders. I am pleased to see you have lost none of your reputation in that capacity. I especially congratulate the Battalion on the excellent manner in which it performed the bayonet exercise. I have never seen it better done. Since the Battalion has been under my command its conduct has been all that can be desired—no serious crime. I have found out that the Regiment can march well and the men always seem as cheerful at the end of a long day's work as at the beginning. The only point I would like to see an improvement in is in shooting ; and I expect this because I know that at one time you were one of the best shooting regiments in India and that you have gained more than your share of the commander-in-chief's prizes. I will conclude by congratulating the lieutenant-colonel and the officers on the efficient state of the Battalion ; and if ever it is my good fortune to be on active service again I know there is no regiment I would rather take with me than the 1st Battalion Leinster Regiment."

This was good hearing and the reader may be referred to the same period of the narrative of the 2nd Battalion where in General Gregorie's farewell address to the 2nd Battalion at Aldershot in 1894 his final words were almost identical with those used by General Morton to the 1st Battalion at Agra.

To encourage military exercises and sports in which the Regiment had already secured a high reputation, Lieutenant-Colonel Poignand instituted a challenge shield in the 1st Battalion to be competed for annually by teams representing companies, and to be held by the victorious company for one year. The following competitions were decided on :—Cricket, football, tug-of-war, tent-pitching, physical drill, bayonet exercise and shooting. It must be confessed that the musketry of the Battalion had fallen away in a woeful manner. In the returns showing the result of the annual course executed by the British Army in India during the musketry year 1891–1892, out of 52 battalions exercised the 1st Leinsters were third from the bottom, being officially branded as "indifferent." No wonder that His Royal Highness "trusted that the greatest attention would be paid in future to this, the most important part of a soldier's training."

On 1st May, 1892, the first number of a regimental paper called the "Maple Leaf" was issued as "a monthly paper for the officers, non-commissioned officers and men of the 1st Battalion Leinster Regiment (Royal Canadians)." It was edited by Lieutenant and Quartermaster A. Wilkin, and printed and published by the Battalion printing press. Only those who have had something to do with regimental publications can appreciate the ability, indomitable perseverance, unbounded enthusiasm, and the compound of faith, hope, charity, courage and the Pauline trait of suffering fools gladly required of the editor of a regimental monthly. These qualities were not wanting to the staff of the "Maple Leaf," and in its honourable existence of eight years it held its head high amongst similar periodicals. Like all such publications it was sometimes severely gravelled for news and its opening number is distinguished by a report of the resignation of the public executioner in England " on account of some dispute with the medical authorities with regard to the length of drop to be given in particular instances." This paragraph, sandwiched in between a lengthy report of a performance of the Magpie Minstrels and a reproduction of the programme of a sergeants' dance, shows at any rate that the editor had sound views upon the necessity of a combination of grave and gay.

The tone of the " Maple Leaf " was predominantly—and at times passionately—Canadian right up to the end and here it may not be out of place to summarize the ebb and flow of Canadian sentiment which distinguished the 100th Regiment throughout its career. When the Regiment came to England in 1858 practically every man in the ranks was Canadian born and the people of Canada regarded the 100th as their regiment. Then, when the chance of active service passed away, and the Regiment was senselessly immured in Gibraltar and Malta, and the Canadian depot was abolished, feeling in Canada underwent a marked change, so much so that when the 100th returned to Canada in 1866, to be there stationed, it had become merely a British battalion of the line with a Canadian tradition. So far as can be judged from extant records this was, apparently, the sentiment which ruled in the Regiment itself from that date to 1881. In that year the creation of two battalion regiments with territorial titles revived the Canadian sentiment in the 100th to a remarkable degree and this feeling was probably most intense in 1898 when the repatriation scheme was put forward and the 100th was suddenly ordered to Halifax. How this idea failed to effect its object will be related in another chapter ; meanwhile it may be noted that the " Maple Leaf " exercised a twofold influence on the Regiment. It helped very much to consolidate the two battalions by its monthly record of the doings not only of the 1st but of the 2nd, on the other hand by its very strong Canadian bias and its continuous campaign for repatriation as a Canadian regiment it hindered the complete union of the two battalions as an Irish regiment.

Life in Agra was on the whole pleasant although the hot weather was very trying. There was a fair amount of polo, some shooting, and some excellent fishing—monsters of twenty-four pounds and twenty-six pounds being recorded. Major H. H. Prior won several successes with his stable on the local turf. The musketry of the Battalion was at a low ebb for in the classification for 1891-1892 the Battalion had 48 marksmen, 88 first, 374 second, and 396 third-class shots, an amazing record for a battalion that had thrice won the commander-in-chief's prize. During 1892 some circumstantial rumours were afloat that the Battalion was to move to Burmah; then the "shave" was Madras. The "Maple Leaf" was filled with long descriptions of these territories but as a matter of fact when the route came it was for Deesa and the Battalion moved there by rail, the last portion of the journey being by march—arriving at its new station on 9th December.

Deesa is one of the queerest spots in India for it is—or at any rate was in 1892—a small military cantonment dumped down in a howling desert. It is, however, within a few miles of the small and pleasant hill station of Mount Abu and became the terminus of a narrow-gauge railway from Palampur. Deesa is Deesa, and that is all. There is nothing to describe; everything is the same; the barracks are almost the only buildings; the club is merely a bit of one barrack; the drill grounds are the local parks; and one endless road—endless because it is circular and runs round the station—is the Rotten Row of the quaint little old-world place. There were, however, many compensations; the tiger and the sambhar roamed within easy reach, and a long day's camel ride brought one to some of the best sand grouse shooting in India. It could be distinctly warm at

Deesa and the thermometer has been known to touch 116° in the shade. From the point of view of health Deesa was the best station in Bombay having a decided immunity from cholera and enteric.

On the 15th December the commander-in-chief of the Presidency visited Deesa where he was received by a guard of honour from the Regiment. His Excellency was much impressed by the fine physique of the guard and said that it was the finest body of men he had ever seen in India.

Amidst various recollections of Deesa there stand out the phases of work and play usually associated with an Indian station. There was polo of course—but we read no longer of ponies at Rs80 to 100 and of subalterns with three in their stable; the inevitable competition had sent up prices and it was no longer a poor man's game; in fact India was rapidly ceasing to be the poor man's country. A pack of hounds belonging to Lieutenant Bell of the 14th Bombay Infantry gave good sport and it "made short work of a fox which had been bagged, on Thursday morning, 12th January, after a good run of twenty minutes." Sometimes the bagged fox refused to move, so, after his demolition by the hounds, his corpse was utilized to provide a drag. From April onwards the weather became very hot, temperature of 112° in the shade being common, but the nights were tolerably cool and by common consent it was not as bad as Agra. Mount Abu was a welcome change, as a hill station, and detachments were sent there to recuperate; there the rainfall in October, 1893, was prodigious, forty-two inches in four days, fifteen of which were registered in one day. The health of the Regiment was on the whole good but enteric took its toll and Captain V. J. Garland was thus lost to the 100th. Several gymkhanas took place, a regimental theatre was opened, and there were festivities at the opening of the railway from Palampur. On the 3rd September, 1893, Lieutenant H. J. Coningham rejoined headquarters from a long tour in Central Asia during which he had seen much of the Russian Army and had been received by General Kuropatkin. Lieutenant Coningham was always known thereafter by the honourable title of " Asiaticus."

Early in 1894 the Battalion took part in the rehearsal of the defence scheme at Bombay, on the conclusion of which it proceeded to Poona where it arrived on the 3rd March, 1894. Poona was a large station, with two British and several native regiments, scattered over a considerable area, a large native city and the country residence of the Governor of Bombay. There were a good club, gymkhana ground and racecourse and it was quite a society place, with many dances, etc. The Governor, Lord Harris, held levées and gave dinners and other entertainments to which some officers were always invited. The river was one of the chief attractions, there was a *bund* in Poona which dammed up the river and made good boating for several miles up stream. All kinds of boats could be obtained, sailing boats, racing eights, etc., and we used to get a boat just above the *bund*, row up to a place called Rosherville, where there was a country club and where refreshments could be obtained, and drive home in the evening. Sometimes we dined there and went home later. We had an eight on the river which rowed well under Captain Laughlin, there was a pack of hounds, which sometimes gave good sport, but the shooting in the district was poor. There is little to mention about the doings of the Battalion. At some sports in 1894 we were pulled over in the final of a tug-of-war by some garrison gunners but won several of the events. One company had a rather curious experience, it was marching back from a funeral and was struck by lightning but although several men were knocked down none was hurt. Lieutenant-Colonel Poignand retired and was succeeded by Lieutenant-Colonel H. H. Prior whose tenure of command was, however, over in 1894. The new commanding officer was Lieutenant-Colonel H. W. Trench who came from The Queen's and assumed command of the Battalion on 17th July, 1894.

Our long tour in India was now drawing to a close for in the programme of reliefs for the trooping season of 1894–1895 we were shown as for Tipperary. The Battalion left Poona on the 21st December, 1894, and sailed from Bombay on the 22nd.

CHAPTER X

THE 1ST BATTALION, 1894-1900—IRELAND—THE REPATRIATION QUESTION—HALIFAX.

THE Battalion came home in the *Dilwara*, commanded by Captain Mann, a hired transport. It was the first time the ship had carried troops, and the captain was glad to hear we had much baggage, being quite willing to take any baggage in excess of our allowance, for, as the ship usually carried a large cargo, she was likely to be somewhat top-heavy with only troops and their baggage on board. Extra ballast had been taken on board, but the ship rolled horribly on the voyage; later they fitted her with bilge keels which did much to lessen this. We had a rather unlucky voyage from the start, as on the first day out one of our men either jumped, or fell, overboard and was lost. The boat that went to pick him up thought that a shark must have got him, as we saw him swimming all right. On the second day a young officer, who was being sent home sick, died and was buried at sea, and on the third day one of our colour-sergeants fell down a hatchway and broke his arm. We spent Christmas Day at sea. The captain had taken some beer on board as a present for the men which was much appreciated.

Although there was a rough sea from the start we got to Port Said in fairly good time, but when we got outside the breakwater there we met a quite first-class gale. The wind was in the north-east, and delayed us so much that we were nearly a day late in arriving at Malta. This was unfortunate, as the 2nd Battalion, who were stationed at Gozo, had arranged to give us a dinner, etc., which we missed, as we did not arrive till the next day, and only stayed some hours. We had very rough weather till we arrived at the Straits of Gibraltar. The ship rolled about 40 degrees, many of the barriers round the men's quarters were carried away, and much damage was done to crockery, etc. Moving about was very difficult, and the only safe plan was to sit on the deck and hold on to something. Some ladies in the music room were shot off their seats and we found them rolling backwards and forwards on the floor and had some difficulty in getting them into a safe place. While passing Gib. things were a little better, but when we were sitting at dinner in something like a calm sea the ship gave a very heavy roll, and everything we could not catch was sent flying on to the deck. The gale then started worse than ever, the glass kept falling till it could hardly fall lower, the sky was black, it was almost dark, and it looked as if we were going to have a bad time of it. The captain, one could see, was a little anxious, and when we arrived off Queenstown in the middle of the night he brought the ship himself into the mouth of the harbour without waiting for a pilot. We arrived at Queenstown on the 13th January, 1895, and it was snowing; it was a Sunday, and no one came to meet us for some hours. On the whole, rather a chilling reception for a battalion which had been abroad for seventeen years and whose regimental march was "Come Back to Erin."

We arrived at Tipperary next day. The barracks at Tipperary were built on a plan which it was said had been prepared for barracks at Hong Kong. The officers' mess had many large French windows reaching down to the ground, and a veranda; the men's barracks were also light and airy, and everything would have been very nice in a hot climate, but they were certainly not suited to Tipperary in the winter. The battalion we relieved had left no coal, and on Sunday we could get none, so we were all very cold and rather miserable.

Those dreadful barracks will long live in the memory of those who inhabited them, for the remainder of the winter was exceptionally severe. A cold snap developed in January, and there were snow and frost until the end of

March—altogether an unpleasant experience for warriors just back from the burning East. Nevertheless we had quite a pleasant time at Tipperary. The hunting was very good; there was fair shooting; and a certain amount of golf. More than this, the people around were hospitable and friendly. As for the doings of the Battalion, there is little of importance to record, life being that of a " one-battalion " station in rather a military backwater. There were rifle meetings at the Curragh, where, however, the Battalion did not do more than average well; an inspection by Lord Roberts; and the usual sports on St. Patrick's Day and Dominion Day by which the Irish composition and Canadian traditions of the Battalion were symbolized. Three officers of the Battalion took unto themselves wives while at the station or shortly afterwards.

Of more serious import in a history was the despatch of 1 sergeant, 1 corporal, and 22 selected men to form part of a composite white battalion in an expedition to Kumasi, the detachment being commanded by Major Northcott of the Regiment. The detachment left on 26th November, 1895. Major Northcott was at the time serving at the War Office; but, being an old West India Regiment officer with Coast experience, he was selected for the command. The detachment performed its part well, but the expedition was a bloodless one, not a shot being fired throughout—much to the chagrin of the men. In May, 1897, a terrible tragedy cast a gloom over the Battalion. Lieutenant A. W. C. Sherwood was putting a squad of recruits through volley firing on the Ballyglass range. Having given the command " Cease fire," he moved in front of the squad, being at that moment accidentally shot. His condition was grave, and the local medical men advised the summoning of a specialist from Dublin. An operation was successfully performed, but after being two hours under the anæsthetic it was necessary to bring poor Sherwood to, and the remainder of the operation had to be gone through while he was conscious. He gradually became weaker and weaker and passed away on 22nd May, just 24 hours after the accident, at the age of 26 years and 10 months. He had served just over four years in the Regiment, and his straightforward and genial disposition, his thorough knowledge of his profession, and his many soldierly qualities had endeared " the Prussian " to all his comrades.

In September the Battalion moved by march route to Birr, a detachment of one company going on to Dublin, two of the day's marches of the latter being over 18 miles. It had been intended to send three companies to Dublin, but a sudden order to prepare a draft of 270 non-commissioned officers and men for the 2nd Battalion rendered this impossible. The Battalion arrived at Birr on 13th September, and was there received as an old friend with all the enthusiasm which a good county has for its own regiment. The detachment at Dublin was at first small, but later was increased to a half-battalion under Major Martin. It was stationed at Ship Street Barracks, and as it was a sort of extra guard to the Castle the officers were bidden to all the balls, State functions, etc., which took place there. There was no mess formed at the barracks, and the officers used to go to the Royal Hibernian United Service Club for their meals. There were several rumours that the whole Battalion was to be concentrated at Dublin, but though there were various false alarms, nothing came of them. The big draft left for Halifax to join the 2nd Battalion which had just arrived at that station from Bermuda, and the 1st Battalion settled down for another dozen years or so of service as the " home " or draft-finding battalion in the United Kingdom.

This idea was blown to the winds on the 5th April, 1898. About 7 p.m. on that evening Colonel Trench, the adjutant, Lieutenant Dugan, and a couple of other officers were sitting in the ante-room at Birr when a telegram arrived from the D.A.G. Dublin to the following effect :—

" Adjutant-General telegraphs : Hold 1st Leinster Regiment in readiness to embark for Halifax, Nova Scotia, about 24th instant. Detailed instructions to-morrow. Recruits at depot and battalion before March will embark. —Deputy Adjutant-General, Dublin."

Here was a bolt from the blue and a shock for the married officers especially who had settled down for a normal tour of service at Birr and who, not unreasonably, had counted on a home tour for the Battalion for another dozen years at least.

The explanation of this dramatic announcement is to be found, not in one single circumstance, but in a combination of things which shaped the destiny of the Battalion to a common end ; and these things were three :—the Diamond Jubilee of Queen Victoria in 1897 ; the outbreak of the Spanish American War ; and the ultra-Canadian tone which had always distinguished the Battalion magazine, the "Maple Leaf." To begin with, the Diamond Jubilee had led to an immense outburst of Imperial sentiment which, following the enthusiasm caused by the jubilee of ten years earlier, did more to bring home to the members of the Empire the greatness and unity of it than all the volumes of history which had been or ever could be written. To this feeling Canada had shown herself particularly responsive, and one form the sentiment took was a revival of interest in the Royal Canadians which for the past seventeen years had been the 1st Battalion of the Leinster Regiment. In anticipation of the Diamond Jubilee a committee had been formed at Ottawa in 1896 which had as its object the raising of petitions throughout Canada for " the repatriation of H.M. 100th Prince of Wales's Royal Canadian Regiment." Each petition was identical in wording, and after a brief summary of the raising of the 100th Regiment in 1858 went on to say :—

" AND WHEREAS, under a subsequent Royal Warrant on the 1st day of July, 1881, on the institution of the territorial system in her Majesty's army, the name, title and designation of the corps was changed to that of the Leinster Regiment, though at the earnest solicitation of the then officers of the regiment, the title of ' Royal Canadians ' was retained.

"AND WHEREAS, under the said new name, title and designation last above mentioned, to wit: The Leinster Regiment (Royal Canadians), the corps has served a further term of fifteen years with honour, fidelity and devotion to the crown in various Imperial garrisons in India and Ireland. Now this memorial prayeth that in view of the circumstances connected with the original formation of the regiment as a spontaneous offering from the loyal dependency of Canada to their Sovereign Lady, Queen Victoria, in the dark and ever memorable days of the great Mutiny in India, and as embodying the literal sense of the 'territorial system,' the loyal and devotional spirit of Her Majesty's Canadian subjects can be better and more appropriately recognized and honoured by having restored to the corps its original, much cherished number, title and designation of the 100th or Prince of Wales's Royal Canadian Regiment. The numerical predecessor of this regiment was disbanded in Canada in 1818 under the title of the 100th Prince Regent's Regiment, and to whose honour the present Royal Canadian Regiment became heir."

The memorial then went on to deal with questions of badges which were to include the Maple Leaf, the Beaver and the motto *Pro Patria*, and petitions for the formation of the recruiting depot in Canada. The Memorial Volume, comprising 225 Petitions in all, was on the 14th May, 1897, presented to the Governor-General of Canada, the Earl of Aberdeen, and the sub-committee entrusted with the task prayed that he would forward it to Field-Marshal H.R.H. the Prince of Wales. Summarizing the Memorial, it may be said that the then scheme of repatriation was confined to three main points: (1) The abolition of "Leinster" and the restoration of the old Canadian title; (2) details as to uniform of a Canadian nature; and (3) the establishment of *the* depot (not *a* depot) of the Regiment in Canada.

A careful examination of all the records available leaves no doubt of the fact that opinion in Canada had been shaped not a little by the tone of the "Maple Leaf" since its first issue some years earlier. It had always been enthusiastically Canadian in tone ; but a regimental paper is apt to voice the sentiments, not so much of its readers at large, as of the hard-working but usually extremely small staff of enthusiasts who conduct it. The officers of the 1st Leinster Regiment were extremely proud of their Canadian traditions ; they always spoke of the Battalion as the "Royal Canadians" ; for years they had their visiting cards so inscribed ; in 1887 they had sent their old colours to Ottawa. Still, sentiment is not necessarily concrete action. A man may be prodigiously vain of his Norman descent without wishing to give up Piccadilly and his club to settle down in Fécamp or Dieppe.

Further, it was inevitable that the union with the 109th Regiment and the conversion of the two units into an Irish regiment had not been without effect. The Regiment, in its total personnel, was overwhelmingly Irish as regards race. Of the officers serving in the 1st Battalion when the "bolt from the blue" arrived it is doubtful if any had ever been in Canada in their lives. Not more than two had joined the Battalion in the pre-Leinster days before 1881. The commanding officer, and one of the majors, had been brought in from English regiments, and of the remaining senior officers almost every one had either joined the 2nd Battalion originally or had done part of his service in it. Further, it is necessary to point out that in the long years from, say, 1869 to 1898 the Canadian traditions had been preserved more by the Regiment—or Battalion, as it became in 1881—than by the Dominion. In that period of nearly twenty years Canadian interest had almost entirely ceased, and consequently when the repatriation movement suddenly set in the 1st Leinster Regiment was not quite prepared for it.

The influence of the Spanish-American War was this : it was advisable to reinforce our garrison in the West Indies in view of the operations which were certain to develop in Cuba and Puerto Rico, and accordingly the

War Office thought they might kill two birds with one stone by hurrying the 2nd Battalion from Halifax to Jamaica and replacing it by the 1st Battalion from home. This would bring the old 100th to Canadian soil and would enable the authorities to see how recruiting for the 1st Battalion would "take on." Accordingly the latter embarked at Queenstown, sailing on the *Dilwara* on the 26th April, 1898, 19 officers and 643 other ranks, 55 women and 66 children. Lieutenant-Colonel H. W. Trench was in command; second-in-command, Major H. Martin; adjutant, Lieutenant F. R. Dugan; and quartermaster, Captain A. Wilkin.

After a rough and cold voyage the *Dilwara* safely reached Halifax on 4th May. We had looked forward to receiving a rousing reception on arrival; we were the Royal Canadians returning to the land of our birth; and the fact that the Battalion had been unexpectedly sent to Halifax to further the scheme of repatriation justified us in anticipating a welcome of unusual warmth. As we steamed up the harbour the band played the "Maple Leaf" with enthusiastic vigour, but, alas! the strains were wasted. There was the merest handful of people at the dock, and the handful was composed of two or three staff officers, a couple of our 2nd Battalion comrades and a few stevedores. Anything more unlike the greeting we had counted upon could not be imagined. It struck a chill in our hearts. Even the "Maple Leaf" in its first issue on Canadian soil had to remark, "There was not much of a crowd to witness our arrival: this was a bit disappointing." There is no doubt that the whole repatriation scheme was extremely badly stage-managed, and this incident killed any latent enthusiasm in the 1st Leinster Regiment for the scheme.

Next day we disembarked and marched up to the barracks just overlooking the harbour, where the 2nd Battalion was drawn up preparatory to embarking on the same ship for the West Indies. By an almost criminal failure to realize the importance of such an event as the parading of the two battalions of the Regiment on the same square no photograph was taken which might have commemorated such an historic event for all time. The real truth is that the 2nd Battalion felt rather aggrieved. Halifax, as a station, was purposely sandwiched between Bermuda and the West Indies, and the normal stay there was two years so as to give a battalion a spell of a healthy climate and a cheery station between two tours of semi-tropical or tropical islands. The 109th had, however, only been some seven months or so in Canada, and now they were being sent off to the heat and tedium of the West Indies just as they were beginning to enjoy their northern station. The officers had spent a great deal of money furnishing their mess, installing electric light, etc., and the married officers had settled down for a two years' stay at least. Now all this was to be upset; the 109th was to be hounded out of the only decent station on the Colonial tour; and it had to give place to its 1st Battalion, whom it not unnaturally looked on as cuckoos. The 1st Battalion, too, could not help feeling that the 2nd Battalion had rather taken the edge off the "Royal Canadian" enthusiasm which they had looked for; and this was true in the sense that the arrival seven months earlier of the 2nd Battalion had completely bewildered Canadian people who had not grappled with the anomalies and absurdities of the territorialization of regiments in 1881. Whatever may have been the theoretical merits of the repatriation scheme, it had these practical defects: it caused friction between the two battalions and it put the officers of both to no little expense. The essential weakness of the whole question was that the one lot of people who were never consulted in the whole business were the officers of the Regiment itself.

Although the system of writing this volume is to deal with the battalions of the Regiment in order of sequence, chronologically this chapter follows after Chapter XXIX. There a brief description of Halifax will be found and a short account of the doings of a battalion there in the winter months. The 1st Battalion carries on the story for the summer of 1898, to start with. It is a vulgar error to associate Canada with perpetual frost and snow; as a matter of fact the summers are hot, and while we were at Halifax the thermometer touched 98°. There was plenty of tennis and cricket; excellent fishing, and delightful sailing both on the harbour and the North-West Arm. And in more serious work the musketry camp on McNab's Island was extremely pleasant. From the social point of view we made friends slowly with the inhabitants, with whom the officers of the 2nd Battalion had been extremely popular and who, perhaps, at first were inclined to look upon us as usurpers. We had, on the other hand, great friends in the Navy, and many were the cheery nights on board ship or in the mess-room at Wellington Barracks, where the two Services fraternized and ragged. "Jacky" Fisher was the admiral, and under his regime there was no danger of dancing becoming a lost art. His flagship, the *Renown*, was known as the House of Lords from the fact that among its officers were six scions of the peerage. These cheery entertainments would have been productive of enormous mess bills had it not been for the amazing cheapness of food and liquor. "If memory serves aright, a small whisky and soda was about 5 cents or 2½d. *Eheu fugaces.*" Thus a bibulous old chronicler anent a bygone age of gold.

In the winter there were, of course, skating, ice-hockey, sleighing and tobogganing, and the Battalion went in for ice-hockey to a great extent. These sports brought the officers in touch with the inhabitants a good deal and, in more than one archive consulted, there is an allusion to a custom extremely popular with detrimental subalterns by which, "having settled on your particular charmer, it was customary to pair off for the season. There was no question of an engagement. It was quite customary to be asked out to dinner together, nor would there be any censorious criticism of little picnics *à deux*. This camaraderie as between sexes was very delightful and all to the good." We can quite believe it. But the most painstaking research has been unable to detect any allusion to the custom in records of the

K

2nd Battalion, apparently a more austere and monastic confraternity.

Meanwhile the question of the repatriation of the 100th was still under consideration. The War Office had replied cautiously to the original memorial by hinting that a decision must depend upon the success or otherwise of recruiting for the Battalion while it was in Canada. Recruiting, however, had been a complete failure, the real reason being that, roughly speaking, the pay of a private was one shilling a day while a dollar a day was a very ordinary wage in Canada. Other objections to the scheme gradually made themselves felt. As a body the officers of the 1st Battalion were not in favour of it, and on the Canadian side it was clear that Canada's regular regiment, the Royal Canadian Regiment of Infantry—and a very fine regiment, too—was not inclined to support a scheme which might have put it in the position of playing second fiddle. The whole truth is that times had changed. The Canada of 1898 was no longer the Canada of 1858. She had grown into a great self-governing Dominion with military forces and a military system of her own. The real connexion between Canada and the 100th Regiment was, and for long had been, a thing of the past. The sentiment remained, and remained till the end in that Regiment. But the French have a proverb " to go back is not to return." The 1st Leinster Regiment had gone back to Canada.

Solvitur pugnando. The South African War in which Canadian troops fought—as Canadian troops and not as a repatriated regiment, and in which they took to themselves the title of " Royal Canadians "—showed that Canada had her own military organization and had laid down the foundations of a great military tradition. This completely ended the repatriation scheme. This is, however, in anticipation of the course of events. All through the year 1899 the situation in South Africa had been one of unrest. The Transvaal, or South African Republic, was under a shadowy suzerainty of England; gold in enormous quantities had been discovered in it;

an immense influx of British settlers had been the result ; and the reactionary President Kruger had endeavoured to finance his country by severe taxation upon these while withholding political rights. Taxation without representation can have but one end. The British Government had no option but to interfere. Kruger replied with an ultimatum, and in October the Transvaal, supported by the Orange Free State, found itself at war with the greatest Empire the world had ever seen.

The war would be over in six weeks—so everyone, particularly people who had been in South Africa, said at once, and there was, therefore, very little chance of the Battalion having an opportunity of joining in. Things, however, happened, and a succession of British defeats kept us constantly on the *qui vive,* always expecting orders to go to the front. Till the end of December we kicked our heels in great impatience, our feelings being further exasperated by seeing Canadian contingents pass through. About the 28th December, 1899, we had returned from our usual Wednesday route march, the parade had been dismissed and the officers had sojourned to the anteroom when suddenly we heard the band playing " Soldiers of the Queen," and the next minute a subaltern rushed into the room and shouted out, " We are ordered to the Cape." We rushed out on to the square, and on the far side every man in barracks had turned out and was shouting and yelling like mad. We dashed across the square towards the orderly-room, where was Colonel Martin (who had by this succeeded to the command). As we passed through the men the cheering was redoubled, and all the time the band banged away for all it was worth. At the orderly-room we learnt that the whole Regiment was to be medically examined previous to being sent on active service.

On the following morning we found that the order emanated from the General, and it was only in case we should be sent to the Cape. Our depression was intense. All the same it was a thrilling experience, and it was delightful to witness the men's enthusiasm and to see staid old sergeants throwing their caps into the air.

The weeks dragged on, our hopes being alternately raised and dashed to the ground. It is to be feared we did not receive the news of the British reverses with that degree of sorrow which would have been becoming, as of course each reverse increased our chances of getting to the Cape. Then about 12th January a cable came from the War Office to Headquarters to prepare the 1st Leinsters for embarkation for England at an early date, to be relieved by the 6th Lancashire Fusiliers. At the same time the Colonel received a private cable saying the 6th Lancashire Fusiliers were leaving England on 15th January. The officers had just started dinner when the Colonel came in with this wire, and it was a curious thing that, directly he had given out the news, a boar's head which was hanging on the mess wall fell down with a crash. We naturally took this as a good omen.

At the end of the month we learnt the most alarming news that the 6th Lancashire Fusiliers, instead of being on the point of entering Halifax Harbour, were on their way to the Cape instead. The amount of bad language was wonderful, several people reaching dizzy and unheard-of heights in the way of damnatory phraseology. But at last definite orders came. The s.s. *Vancouver* was engaged to carry the Battalion to Liverpool, and the embarkation was to take place on the 25th March, 1900. The duties of the Garrison were to be taken over by the Provisional Battalion of Canadian Infantry, in course of formation. The following is a copy of the cablegram received from the War Office :—

" G.O.C., HALIFAX, N.S.

" Embark for home, 1st Leinster Regiment, steamer *Vancouver*, March 25th, except men unfit for active service or under following number of years of age, 20, who should be sent to 2nd Battalion Leinster Regiment under local arrangements. A report in numbers of latter to General, Barbados, and ascertain how many should be landed at Jamaica."

CHAPTER XI

THE 1ST BATTALION, 1900–1902—SOUTH AFRICA.

THE Battalion arrived in England about 5th April, 1900, and was sent to Aldershot, Marlborough Lines. There we got our Reserve men, who made our strength up to about 1,400, and the necessary stores, but had some difficulty in doing so, as it was Easter week. We were just a week in Aldershot and sailed from Southampton at 2 p.m. on 18th April in the hired transport *Dilwara*—an old friend, as we came home from India in her in 1894 and went to Halifax in her in 1898. Captain Mann, the chief officer, the purser and others had sailed with us on both former trips and all on board did all they could to help us. We stopped at St. Vincent, Cape Verde Islands, to coal on 26th April and the ship played the town at cricket. It was very hot and poor young Lieutenant Martin got a chill which on the 28th developed into pneumonia, and in spite of every care he died on 1st May and was buried at sea on the 2nd. He was a great favourite with everyone and his death was much felt by us all. Eight days later the *Dilwara* arrived at Cape Town but left again on the 12th, arriving at Port Elizabeth on the 13th. Here we landed and the first half battalion under Lieutenant-Colonel Martin left at midday on the 15th for Bloemfontein, where we arrived on the 17th, some of the men having travelled the last part of the way on the top of some coal trucks full of coal. No arrangements had been made for us and we marched up to the camp and then back to the station, where we slept on the floor of the waiting-room, etc. Next day the whole Battalion was located in the camp of the 6th Division under Major-General Kelly-Kenny. While at

Bloemfontein we attended the Queen's Birthday parade (and at the sports in the afternoon won the tug-of-war, physical drill and some other events), and the Proclamation of the Orange River Colony. We left for Winburg on 29th May by train, arriving on the 30th and on the 2nd June we started on the march to join our division. Two days later we arrived at Senekal, six days after the Guards' fight at Biddulphsberg. There were many wounded in the hospital and they were a horrid sight as the grass had taken light and many of them were horribly burned. On 8th June we started again, with a convoy nearly three miles long, for Klip Nek and we came under fire for the first time as the Boers sniped at the rearguard. Next day we joined part of our division at Hammonia, under Major-General Rundle.

The 8th Division was composed roughly as follows, and did not change much during the early part of the war :—

Commander : Major-General Sir Leslie Rundle.

    3 Battalions Imperial Yeomanry.
    Driscoll's Scouts.
    Tempest's Scouts.
    Manchester, Royal West Kent and Royal Scots Mounted Infantry.
    3 Batteries Royal Field Artillery.
    Detachment Royal Garrison Artillery.
    Pom-pom Section.
    Gun Section, with mounted troops.
    2 Sections Royal Engineers.

16th Brigade under Major-General Campbell.

    2nd Grenadier Guards.
    2nd Scots Guards.
    2nd East Yorkshire Regiment.
    1st Leinster Regiment.
    A Bearer Company.
    A Field Hospital.

17th Brigade under Major-General Boyes.
> 1st Worcestershire Regiment.
> 1st South Staffordshire Regiment.
> 2nd Manchester Regiment.
> 2nd Royal West Kent Regiment.
> A Bearer Company.
> A Field Hospital.

> An Ammunition Column.
> 6 Companies Army Service Corps.

Brabant's Colonial Division was with us for a considerable time, and various companies of yeomanry and batteries of artillery were attached from time to time.

When the 1st Battalion arrived at the front the war had passed into the second of the five phases into which it may be—if somewhat arbitrarily—divided. Phase one, that of the Boer invasion and the phase of the pitched battles had ended with the relief of Ladysmith on 28th February. The second phase, that of a constantly-waning organized resistance on the part of the Boers had now taken its place. Phases three, four and five may be described as transitional-guerilla; blockhouse-passive; and blockhouse-active respectively. Interest for the moment is now with phase two. The severest fighting was over. The Orange Free State existed no longer. And on the 5th June Lord Roberts's Army occupied the capital of the Transvaal practically without resistance. It had been anticipated that the occupation of both capitals would have brought hostilities to a close but this was not the case and the British were called upon to face two years of partisan warfare.

The duty of the 8th Division at this time was to keep the Boers from breaking south through the line Senekal—Klip Nek—Hammonia—Ficksburg, and it spent most of its time marching up and down this line and holding these places. It was broken up into parties of two or three battalions with some mounted troops and guns, our portion of the line being from Klip Nek to Hammonia, generally under General Rundle. We made this march many times and never knew when we went to bed whether we would be at Klip Nek or Hammonia next day as orders were always issued late at night and we started very early in the morning. The main force of the Boers, said to be about 10,000, seemed to be at Rooikranz about ten miles north of Klip Nek and most days we had some skirmishing with them and several times expected to be attacked. All the troops always stood to arms one hour before daybreak and as it was very cold at that hour it was rather a trial.

On the 23rd June the main portion of the division started on a tour towards Senekal, etc., leaving Colonel Martin at Klip Nek with our Battalion, 4 guns, Captain Browne and his yeomen and 100 mounted men of the Colonial Division. Our camp was in a hollow, and about two miles to the north there was a high plateau, almost precipitous towards our camp, but sloping gently towards the entrance to Rooikranz, where considerable numbers of Boers could often be seen entering or leaving the kranz. Major Stavert was in command on this plateau, with $3\frac{1}{2}$ companies and 2 guns and at first there was a good deal of firing at his picquets and few days passed without some sniping. The Boers apparently could not resist the temptation of firing at men trying to change their clothes or do some washing in some of the pools of water among the rocks of the plateau, and as we had no tents and this had to be done in the open a man without his clothes, or with little on, made a good target. As we always slept in our clothes, with our rifles at hand, and could often change nothing for more than a week at a time, and as the veldt seemed actually to swarm with vermin, we were all at times covered with these pests. A bath was an impossibility except at long intervals and so there was no means of getting entirely rid of them and it was a horrid experience.

The 8th Division, usually known as "The Starving Eighth," was, as a rule, very short of supplies except beef and mutton, and was nearly always on half rations or less.

At this date we, for a time, only got one biscuit or a little flour each day and had no sugar or salt and very little tea. We were supposed to be living on the country, according to General Rundle, but we were nearly starving as beef for breakfast, dinner and tea, without salt, eaten with some badly cooked flour, was not very palatable. Our cook invented some horrible porridge made of Indian corn, Kaffir meal and bran, which we used to eat with a squash of pumpkins, and we could sometimes buy something from one of the Boer farms. It was very cold at night and the water in a bucket froze almost solid and we had no tents, but no one seemed to suffer. We were all in the best of spirits, very good friends and I think rather enjoyed the experience. The Battalion remained at Klip Nek till 13th July, but the companies on the plateau were relieved by fresh ones under Major Seton, on 4th July.

Although the Orange Free State had been taken over by the British and renamed the Orange River Colony it was soon discovered that an active enemy will not lay down his arms for a mere proclamation. About the middle of June Lord Roberts planned a simple and systematic campaign. The towns and strategic points were to be strongly held while flying columns shepherded De Wet and his commandos and tried to enfold them. At the end of June four columns began to move. Each column was, so to speak, the head of a spear prodding the commandos towards the pen assigned to them. The Brandwater Basin into which the Boers retreated—taking with them President Steyn and the Free State Government, is a semi-circle formed by the Witteberg and Roodeberg mountains at the headwaters of two tributaries of the Caledon, the Little Caledon and the Brandwater. The river section marches with Basutoland and the mountain section is wild and with few paths or roads. The place was, therefore, really a prison and afforded but little scope for the chief asset of the Boers—mobility. De Wet quickly recognized the fact and broke out with 2,600 men and over 400 vehicles. By 27th July the greater part of 7,000 Boers were practically sealed up in the basin under Martin Prinsloo.

The British plan now was to use some columns from the south as beaters, supplemented by similar ones from the north. Amongst the former was Rundle's division in which was the 1st Battalion. On the 11th July a convoy arrived bringing us some much needed supplies and on the 13th the Klip Nek force started on this move, being ordered to move on Rooikranz, and we advanced to within about three miles of that place. We remained there watching the Boers till the 20th on which day we had orders to march to Hammonia, where we found General Rundle and a small portion of the division and were given some tents for the first time.

On 22nd July a force from the division, in which the Battalion was included, started to drive the Boers back slowly, and marched to Willow Grange. On the following day we kept on and drove the enemy still further back in conjunction with other columns. We fought all day on the 23rd and 24th, firing a large quantity of ammunition, without making a serious attack, as we did not want to hustle the Boers too much so as to give the other columns plenty of time to block all the passes and we wanted to allow the Boers to retire, which they did during the night of the 24th. On the 25th we followed them up, and the next day we marched to near Brindisi, about 20 miles. Just as we were settling down in camp General Rundle came to the Scots Guards and ourselves and asked each battalion to volunteer to send half a battalion another nine miles to Fouriesburg to protect 32 officers and 83 men who had been prisoners of the Boers and who were at that place under the care of Driscoll's Scouts, who had rescued them. We had only half a battalion as the other half was on baggage guard, but of course every man volunteered. We had a very rough march, much of it in the dark, crossing one wide spruit and arrived, with the pipers of the Scots Guards and our band playing, to find that General Rundle had already arrived with another company of mounted troops and that the late prisoners had turned out to welcome us, which they did most heartily. We had started at 6.30 a.m. and had marched about thirty miles. We were joined later by some of Hunter's force, which had come down from the north.

On the 27th we handed over Fouriesburg to some of Hunter's troops and followed the Boers; and on the 28th we started at 4.30 a.m., commenced fighting almost at once and fought all day. Some of General Clements's troops formed the advanced guard, some Wiltshires being on the right and some Royal Irish on the left. The Leinsters followed with the Scots Guards next and the Royal West Kents in rear. The advanced guard found the Boers holding a very strong position on Slapkranz on our left front. Slapkranz was a high kopje, almost perpendicular, facing our advance and sloping gradually towards the Boer laager in the rear. The edge towards us was covered with great boulders, which gave excellent cover to the Boers, while we had no cover from fire except some ant heaps, though the high grass gave some cover from view. The attack was made more difficult as on our right flank there was a perpendicular kopje with a narrow nek between the two, through which the road ran, so that we could not work round to the flank without coming under fire at close range. On the left the ground of our advance was almost as high as the Boer position but was separated from it by a somewhat deep ravine.

Our battalion was advancing in column of half companies at about ten paces interval and the men extended to one pace, and when we came into view the Boers opened fire with a field gun and one of the first shells landed right in the middle of the Battalion but fortunately did not explode. Our 5-inch gun at once replied and soon silenced the Boer gun. The advanced troops kept edging off to the flanks and when the Battalion had advanced a little farther, Colonel Harley, the chief staff officer of the 8th Division, who was commanding the attack, ordered two and a half companies of the Battalion under Major Stavert to support those on the right while the rest of the Battalion followed those on the left. By this move there was a large gap left in the centre which was afterwards filled by the Scots Guards. The troops on the right moved forward under a hot fire till they arrived near the narrow nek, where the advanced troops had halted in a small kraal, and as they could get no farther they remained there, under fire, till dark. Meanwhile the troops on the left advanced till they arrived at the ravine, which they could not cross under the hot fire, so they also continued to hold the ground they had gained. The Scots Guards came up in the centre and occupied a small hill between the two flank parties.

When it became dark the Boer fire ceased and we assembled our men and some food was sent up. Shortly afterwards Colonel Harley came up and gave orders that the Scots Guards and our companies on the right were to take the position during the night and we did so at 1 a.m. on the 29th without opposition as the Boers had retired. It was very cold and as we had no warm clothing with us we were nearly frozen. Our guns came up in the early morning and were trained on the Boer laager, which could be seen in the valley. General Prinsloo now came in and asked for terms but was told by General Hunter that he must surrender unconditionally. The next day the main body of the Boers in the basin laid down their arms at Slapkranz and the tangible result of the operations was that more than 4,000 Boers and 3 guns were taken.

After a couple of days rest we started to march on Harrismith, and on the 6th August we arrived at Wilge River Bridge, about six miles from Harrismith, reaching that town on the 10th. The greater part of the inhabitants of Harrismith were British and they had had a very bad time under Boer control so were very glad to see the division. They were getting very short of supplies so the arrival of the first train from Ladysmith on 9th August was a great event. It was also a pleasant event for the division as it meant the end of short rations for the present. By the time the division arrived at Harrismith we were a weird looking crowd, dirty, dusty, gaunt and hungry looking, with clothing in rags—some men wearing kilts made of a blanket, boots broken and some without soles, but wiry and wonderfully fit and, as usual, in the best of spirits. At Harrismith we got some clothing and good food, which, with the aid of much soap and water, soon worked wonders and although we were often on half rations after this, we were never again so short of supplies nor for so long a time.

We now started to clear the country, the Battalion with two guns and some yeomanry leaving for Cornelius River, a two days' march, where some Boers surrendered. On the 26th August we received orders to join our brigade at Bethlehem, ninety-three miles distant, through, to us, a quite unknown country and with at least one bad crossing over the Wilge River. We also knew that De Wet was somewhere near on our right flank and that he was getting busy. At the Wilge Drift we took ten hours to get over and killed eight oxen; the wagons had to be let down with a rope and the river was in flood. We arrived safely at Bethlehem on the 2nd September, and on the next day but one started another trek with the brigade to head off De Wet who was doing mischief in the south-west, arriving, after six days, back at Bethlehem, having trekked one hundred and eight miles. Two days later we were off again one hundred and twenty-three miles to Vrede. From there we crossed the Klip River into the Transvaal and arrived at Standerton on the 7th after a two days' march of thirty miles. Standerton was quite a good town, where we got good food and other things. On 9th October we were back again at Vrede. On all these treks there was some sniping nearly every day and some days quite a little fighting. On the 14th October the division left, leaving us to hold Vrede with 4 guns, 1 squadron yeomanry, 1 squadron mounted infantry, and some engineers.

At this time the idea was to hold all the towns, so that the Boers could not use them and we were five months shut up in Vrede, the nearest other troops being at Standerton, thirty miles distant through a rather difficult country infested by Boers. In the town were some good stores, kept by British, a British doctor (Dr. Bently) who did splendid work for us, a Boer parson, not a bad sort, a lot of Boer women and children, a bank, a large Boer kirk, and a small British church. Vrede was not an easy place to hold as like most South African towns it was in a hollow and all the surrounding hills had to be held, which necessitated holding a perimeter of about seven miles. On the east was a high ridge, close to the town, held by two companies, on the south an isolated kopje, about one mile from the town, held by two companies. On the west a lower ridge rose gradually for about three quarters of a mile from the town, then descended in two wide steps towards the Drakensberg Mountains which were distant about three miles. This was held by three companies, two of them forming the headquarters camp which, in addition to holding part of the line, was to render assistance to any of the other companies if required. On the north was the road to Standerton and this end of the town was held by one company.

On the 19th October we were attacked on all sides by Boers in some force about 1.30 a.m. One of De Wet's staff told us later that it was our horses they were after and that a shot from one of our guns killed five Boers. The attack lasted about an hour. The same week Lieutenant Browne of the Yeomanry was killed while we were wood-cutting, and on the 25th a yeoman was killed while riding out to our advanced post. On 5th November we had been much bothered by snipers so made a reconnaissance and burned a farm as a warning. About this time the Roman Catholic padre was invalided and sent in a convoy to Harrismith. We had now no chaplains so Major Stavert acted for the Church of England and Captain O'Shee for the Roman Catholic troops, and had to bury all who died or were killed. Service was held each Sunday in the British church at which Major Stavert read the service and Colonel Martin played the organ. These services were well attended.

THE 1st BATTALION

The convoy returned from Standerton on 16th November and left on the 18th, taking with it Captain Dickinson, who was sick. They left us a large amount of stores and we bought a large amount of supplies for our canteen. They also left us a patient with enteric which afterwards caused all the trouble. Up to this time we had been very comfortable and were enjoying the rest after marching more than eight hundred miles in a little over four months. Our camps had each a good water supply; they were kept beautifully clean and the tents moved at short intervals and everything was done to keep them right. The band played in the town, some of the subalterns played tennis, we had an officers' club, etc. But then the enteric began to spread and first one camp and then another was attacked. The headquarters camp was the last to be attacked and then 13 men went to hospital in one day. Over 400 officers and men got the fever and 2 officers and about 40 men of the garrison died at Vrede of it, and 1 officer two days after we left. We had two doctors, an army one and the doctor of the place, and they both worked nobly. There is no doubt the infection was carried by flies, they were in myriads and were all over everything. On 11th December Finlay died of dysentery and on the 28th Foulerton got enteric and died on 5th January, 1901. All this time the Boers were giving a lot of trouble.

On 16th January we had a race meeting. The Boers watched it from the hills and fired at the starters of the long distance race, which started outside our lines. We also had sports, a gymkhana, etc., about this time. Early in February General Campbell arrived with our brigade and left on the 12th for Standerton, after clearing out of the town everything likely to be useful to the Boers, and taking with him all our invalids, including several officers and all the Boer women and children. The garrison was thus reduced to about 12 officers and 500 men. The same month we received a copy of the following wire from General Rundle to General Campbell: " Have received your report *re* Colonel Martin and

Leinsters with greatest satisfaction. Please express to Colonel Martin and those under his command my regret at the hardships they had to undergo and my appreciation of the soldierlike spirit they had shown under them. It has been a great satisfaction to receive such a report from you of troops forming a portion of the 16th Brigade which has done so much to keep up the good name of the 8th Division." About this time we received another report of much less pleasant import, namely that De Wet, with 5,000 men and 7 guns was marching on Vrede, and on 26th February received the following message from General Campbell :—" General Rundle looks to you and your men, with every confidence in you being able to hold Vrede against any attack." We saw some of the Boer force in the distance but they did not attack. The brigade returned on the 5th March ; Lieutenant Scobell died the same day. On the 10th we all left for Standerton, leaving the town empty. There was much firing and it was very wet and we only marched twelve miles.

While on this trek we lost another officer, Lieutenant Leicester, and on the 14th we arrived at De Lange's Drift over the Wilge River and found it ten feet deep and impassable. We had now only 9 officers left in the Battalion including the quartermaster. We remained at the Drift till the 19th when some barrels arrived from Standerton and we crossed on rafts, etc., and reached Standerton on the 22nd. Three days later the brigade started to move in small parties to Ladysmith by train, and had all arrived by the 29th. At Ladysmith we could get everything, even ice, and we enjoyed our rest there very much.

Early in April the 16th Brigade started to march to Harrismith. The road up Van Reenan's Pass was very steep and the waggons had to be taken up by double teams. We arrived near Harrismith on 11th April. The idea now was to clear the country of everything that could be of use to the Boers and to destroy all mills, etc. Accordingly on 18th April a column under General Rundle, including three of our companies, under Major

Stavert, started for Bethlehem. There was some rather heavy firing each day and quite a little engagement on the 26th, several yeomen being killed, wounded, or missing on this march. On the 28th our companies had to take a hill to enable a mill to be burned. The hill was almost precipitous and a good height, but our companies took it in great style under a good deal of fire and were much complimented on their performance. The column now marched to Fouriesburg in two divisions, burning mills and collecting Boer property and at Fouriesburg small columns were sent out in all directions on the same duty. Our companies did much good work on these columns, were often under rather heavy fire and received much praise for their work.

On the 31st May an advanced column under Lieutenant-Colonel Reay of the Manchesters, including our companies, marched to Slapkranz, General Rundle following with the rest of the troops. Our companies occupied Slapkranz and took Surrender Hill and another kopje in great style under the fire of some 20 Boers, who were well placed. On 3rd June they had quite a little battle at a mill and fired 2,000 rounds before they drove out the Boers. The next day the force marched through the Golden Gate and during the next two days the going was terrible, down one long and very steep hill and up and down several others, with the road in very bad order; and the whole force had to help the waggons, making the road and letting the waggons down with ropes, etc. We now met the 16th Brigade at Eland's River Drift and on the 10th returned to Harrismith. The work done by the detachment was recognized in the following order:—
" The Lieutenant-General Commanding desires me to inform all ranks of the detachment Leinster Regiment how much he appreciates the manner in which they have carried out all the duties entrusted to them during the late operations. He particularly remarked the dashing manner in which they advanced up Surrender Hill as they could not tell that it was not strongly held by the enemy and he stated that it had been noticed by himself

and all his staff how well and cheerfully they worked at road-making, helping waggons, etc. Lieutenant-Colonel Reay desires me to thank the detachment for all their work while with his column and to say how proud he is to have had them under his command."

This trek resulted in the collection or destruction of :—

- 7000 tons of grain, flour or forage.
- 1400 cattle.
- 7100 sheep and goats.
- 1450 horses.
- 8300 rounds of S.A.A.
- 101 rounds gun ammunition.
- 75 packets dynamite.
- 25 rifles.
- 228 waggons and carts.
- 4 mills, innumerable ovens, ploughs, threshing machines, etc.
- 7 men and 260 women and children brought in.
- 53 Boers killed and wounded.

The detachment had marched about two hundred and eighty-four miles and there were few days on which it had not been under fire. The companies on this trek were "F," "G" and "B" under Legge, Raynsford and Butler-Kearney and they all worked splendidly.

For the next six or seven weeks the Battalion was engaged in clearing the Langenberg Range, in escorting convoys and in the general column work which now characterized the war. Large quantities of stores and thousands of cattle and horses were captured; a few Boers were killed or made prisoner and many Boer women and children were brought in. The division returned to Harrismith on 1st August and on 6th August there was a public holiday to celebrate the anniversary of its entry into the town. There were sports in the afternoon and the Leinsters won the tug-of-war after some good pulls with the Grenadiers and Scots Guards. Two days later we started on what was destined to be our last trek during the war. The brigade under General Campbell marched by Ratieff's Nek and the Brandwater

Basin to Brindisi, arriving on the 17th August. During the last three days the Boers were very active and there was much firing. Brindisi is situated at a ford on the Caledon River, on the way to Thlotsi in Basutoland, the river being the boundary. The Battalion was ordered to build a strong fort on a bluff overlooking the river and started work on the 21st. Next day a company was sent to hold the mill at the junction of the Brandwater and Caledon Rivers. They were attacked next morning by a considerable force of Boers, but drove them off. The blockhouse phase was now in progress and General Campbell's column started the construction of a line to Ratieff's Nek. The column worked in the basin, erecting blockhouses and forts and rounding up Boers till about 8th December, returning frequently to Brindisi for supplies, etc., and taking companies of our men to garrison the various forts and blockhouses as they were completed. By that date we were holding a line from Ratieff's Nek to the mill near the mouth of the Brandwater. We had three forts, Fort Maroney under Major White, just south of Ratieff's Nek, Fort Davidson near Fouriesburg, under Major Davidson, and Fort Campbell, our headquarters at Brindisi. These were linked together by a line of blockhouses, which were later joined together by a barbed wire fence. Each blockhouse had a garrison of about six men and the forts one or two companies, so the Battalion was spread out in a long thin line. The forts were places of some strength. Fort Campbell consisted of an inner and outer wall of stone, in all 1,400 yards long, 4 feet high and 4 feet thick, with a line of stone for head cover and surrounded by a barbed wire fence and some outlying blockhouses. In the centre was a square blockhouse of stone and lime, built by our men, two stories high, with a crenellated top and a turret on which we placed a flagstaff and flag. Forts Davidson and Maroney were smaller but also strong and well made.

While the column was in the basin and before the blockhouses were all joined by barbed wire, we had, on the whole, a peaceful time, though the Boers occasionally gave some trouble, firing on parts of the line and killing one of our cattle guards, etc. Before the fence was made they could pass between the blockhouses on a dark night and even after this could do so by cutting the wire, but later when this was made more difficult by running a piano wire along the fence, which alarmed the nearest blockhouses, they became very troublesome, fired on parts of the line frequently, made several halfhearted attacks on the forts, etc., and on the 7th April, 1902, with a considerable force, captured and destroyed three of our blockhouses, killing 3 men and wounding 14. It was a very dark night and as they could not get inside the blockhouses they got on the roof and fired through it, killing or wounding all the men inside. They then attacked a somewhat stronger blockhouse on Steinkamp Kop, in which were Captain Jones and the headquarters of his company, but were driven off with some loss.

About this time the division was broken up. General Rundle had gone to England in February and the command of the Harrismith District was given to General Brooke, while Colonel Kenyon-Slaney replaced General Campbell at Bethlehem. Nothing further of importance happened in the Battalion during the war. Peace was signed on 31st May and we heard of it on 1st June. A detachment under Brevet Major and Adjutant F. R. Dugan was sent to Cape Town to join the Coronation Contingent there embarking.

During the ten months we were on this blockhouse line we got our mails and supplies with fair regularity from Bloemfontein through Basutoland and lived in considerable comfort. We made a golf course at Brindisi and got some fishing in the Caledon River, we also got a little shooting at the mill but were occasionally fired at by the Boers while doing so. We were visited by civilians from Basutoland and Chief Jonathan presented Colonel Martin with a chief's dress. We played a golf match against civilians from Thlotsi under Mr. McGregor, the Commissioner, and defeated them. We were visited by columns trying to round up Boers and gave them what assistance we could, taking over their prisoners, etc.

On 23rd June the Battalion started in small parties for Bethlehem taking over blockhouses, etc., and were mostly collected there by the 1st July. On 9th August we had a coronation parade and sports, the Boers took part in these and we won the first and second in football, tug-of-war, etc., but the Boers pulled well. We started regular parades, working on the new drill book, and the commanding officer and some of us had some good days' shooting, the Boers being quite pleased to show us the best places. Early in September we started for Harrismith and arrived on 6th, our last trek. The Battalion had marched about 1,700 miles, and we were now to return to the United Kingdom. An advanced party of officers and their servants left for home on 12th September as there was not sufficient room on the troopship, sailing on the *Sicilian* on 15th September, and arriving at Southampton on 9th October. The Battalion followed about a week later.

During the war the staff and battalions of the 16th Brigade had worked very happily together on all occasions, but our chief friends were the Grenadier Guards, who worked with us on many treks, etc., and with whom we became very close friends. The following officers, amongst others, joined us during the war :—O'Shee, Currey and Finlay early in the war at Klip Nek, Davidson, Raynes, Riall and Irvine at Harrismith in 1901, Murphy, Dill, Massey, Dix, Scott and Cameron at Brindisi in 1902. The Battalion lost about 80 of all ranks. The officers were Foulerton, Leicester, Scobell and Finlay in South Africa, Martin on the voyage out, and Waudby at home, having been sent home sick. There is a handsome brass, with silver crest, etc., in St. Patrick's Cathedral, Dublin, to these officers and men, and a monument at Vrede to those who died there.

CHAPTER XII

The 1st Battalion 1902–1914—The United Kingdom—India.

THE Battalion arrived at Queenstown on 27th October, 1902, and at Fermoy on the 28th. Some of the officers had been sent home from South Africa in advance under Major Stavert, so the barracks were all ready for the Battalion. We were stationed in the Old Barracks and the Royal Irish in the New Barracks. It is said the barracks were both built at the same time so there seems no reason for the names. Colonel H. Martin's tenure of command expired in May, 1903, when he was succeeded by Lieutenant-Colonel T. Hope Stavert.

Fermoy was a good station with many hospitable people. In fact it may be said that for sport Fermoy was the best station in the British Isles. Many of the officers hunted with the United and the Duhallow packs; the Blackwater was the best of salmon rivers; there was fair shooting, and the boating on the river was a very pleasant amusement. The men were a little wild on first coming home as everyone wanted to stand them drinks, but they soon settled down and did very good work. We did our musketry at Kilworth, which was about three miles distant, and were camped there for some time in the summer; the season was a very wet one and the camp became a sort of bog. The Duke of Connaught, who commanded the troops in Ireland, came for the manœuvres and had a rather wet time. The last day of the manœuvres came to rather a premature conclusion as our Battalion and the Munsters who had been lent to the enemy, with a battery of artillery, made a flank march and succeeded in taking a position which enfiladed the whole line of defence on the Kilworth plateau. We led the advance which was quite a surprise to our enemy, and when we signalled our success to headquarters they decided that the manœuvres were at an end.

We were at Fermoy at the time of the Cork Exhibition ; our band played there for a week and gave great satisfaction which meant a considerable addition to our band fund as we refused to play for less than the other well-known bands which played there. King Edward VII came to Ireland and he paid a visit to the exhibition. We were taken to Cork for three or four days and we and other battalions lined the streets when His Majesty went to the exhibition in the morning and also when he returned in the afternoon. This was on a Saturday and the Duke of Connaught visited our camp on the Sunday and held a review of a large force on the racecourse on the Monday before the troops returned home. We found a guard of honour for King Edward at Waterford on the day he went to Lismore and His Majesty directed the officer in command to tell his commanding officer that the King had never seen a finer guard of honour. They were all big men who had been in South Africa and had two or more medals.

The Battalion made a rather fine march one day, they marched fourteen miles in three and a half hours, the last mile at the rate of four and a half miles per hour. It was a fine frosty day, the band was on furlough, the Battalion was not very strong and most of the men were Rundle's greyhounds—a name our division earned in South Africa. The commanding officer and Captain O'Shee marched in front and set the pace and the last mile was all down hill. It was while the Battalion was at Fermoy that it wore the new post-South African uniform for the first time, *i.e.* frock coat for officers, blue forage cap, and service dress ; the scarlet tunic and mess kit remaining as before but by this time the mess jacket had lost all its gold frippery and was worn with a rolled instead of a stand-up collar. In Association football the Battalion won the

Munster League Cup open to military and civilian teams in the province.

We moved to Shorncliffe via Waterford and Milford in the summer of 1904, and were stationed in the tin huts, the Queen's and South Lancashires being in the barracks. Brigadier-General Lomax was in command of the 10th Brigade and Major-General Grant of the Division, with headquarters at Dover. The Battalion did much good work at Shorncliffe doing musketry at Hythe and training on the hills between Folkestone and Dover. When we first went there we found several areas prohibited to the troops but we soon got on the right side of the farmers and they not only allowed the Battalion to go anywhere, but brought out milk which they sold or sometimes gave to the men. We were ordered to send a company to Hythe during a senior officers' course to show the different ways of distributing fire and any other exercises that were wanted, and the commandant was much pleased with the keenness of the men and their willingness during the course, which lasted a week, to turn out at any time and do anything they were asked.

The 10th Brigade went to Salisbury Plain for a month for manœuvres in 1904 and as the weather was fine we enjoyed the change to camp life. In 1905 we were in camp for three months, the first month at Arundel, the second at Worthing and the third at Parham. At Arundel we had the Queen's with us and did battalion training, and at Worthing and Parham we had the whole brigade and did brigade training. At Arundel the Duke of Norfolk was very good to the Battalion. The men were mostly Roman Catholics and attended his chapel and the Duke allowed them to enter the castle grounds whenever they liked and the officers to go over the castle itself at anytime, although he and the Duchess were living there at the time. The men and band joined in his procession on the feast of Corpus Christi. The Duke presented the Battalion with a cup in commemoration of this, and the Battalion in return presented his chapel with a statue. We were camped close to the town at

Worthing and it was not so pleasant as there were many trippers. At Parham the brigade gave a garden party with a combined band concert; we asked a large number of people and it was a great success.

It was while riding back from a field day near Parham that General Lomax told the commanding officer that he had just received the bad news that he was to lose the Battalion from his brigade and that we were under orders for Aldershot. The general had always been very fond of the Battalion, and he thanked it for all its good work while under his command and said he was very sorry we were leaving it. In 1905 the Battalion began its great sequence of successes in tug-of-war and bayonet fighting by pulling off every team and individual event at the Bronze Medal Tournament held at Shorncliffe besides winning many prizes at the District Rifle Meeting.

The Battalion arrived in the Aldershot Command during the relief season of 1905-1906 and, with the South Lancashires, was stationed at Blackdown about seven miles from Aldershot. We were in the 2nd Brigade of the 1st Division; the brigade was commanded by Brigadier-General Alderson, the division by Major-General A. Paget and the corps by Sir John French. Later Sir Henry Rawlinson succeeded General Alderson and General Grierson became our divisional commander.

The disadvantage of being at Blackdown was that in all operations that took place at Aldershot or near it we had to march seven miles before they began and another seven after they ended, and if the operations were long it made a hard day for the Battalion; but as we had succeeded in making the men rather proud of their marching powers no man ever fell out unless he was sick. The advantages of Blackdown were that it was close to a rifle range, and, from the officer's point of view, that the people who lived at Frimley, Camberley etc. called on the mess and invited the officers to dinners and other entertainments. Blackdown had, therefore, a social atmosphere which was always notably absent in Aldershot itself. The Battalion worked very well at Aldershot and gained much praise from all the staff and when General Alderson gave over command of the brigade he wrote a letter thanking all ranks for their good work, while under his command. General Grierson was an old friend of the Battalion. He had a great admiration for our fifes and drums and several times asked for them to play for him ; when the Battalion at the Aldershot Tournament won all the prizes for the tugs-of-war, and all except a third prize for recruits in bayonet fighting he was almost as pleased as we were ourselves.

The 1st Division under our commanding officer did a three days' march to Chichester and after being joined by the generals and their staffs, who had been doing a staff tour, carried out divisional manœuvres over the Downs for some days. These manœuvres are described in one narrative as " same as 1909 and 1910 but not so fatuous."

Aldershot was a very pleasant station under Sir John French, for, although there was plenty of hard work, everyone was trying to help everyone else and the generals and their staffs were as ready as anyone to help even the most junior officer, and if possible without finding fault. The result was that the work was generally well done and was both instructive and interesting. The Battalion, it may be said, came out from the test at Aldershot with flying colours. Both in training and in sport it achieved a very high reputation. It was informed that it was the best battalion in the command and that, in the event of a brigade being despatched on active service from Aldershot, the 1st Leinster Regiment would be the first unit to be selected. The record of successes gained in shooting, physical drill, and bayonet exercises and other competitions during 1908 was phenomenal. A pamphlet was published regimentally to chronicle these victories and there were many days when the Frimley ridges " resounded to the strains of 'Jackets Green' and 'Brian Boru' playing in winning teams." In the Evelyn Wood Competition " B " Company (Captain M. F. Fox) tied for first place in the preliminary and was second in the final; at the Aldershot Command Rifle Meeting the officers won the challenge cup, and the men won second and third for teams of privates. Captain Fox won the open revolver competition. The successes in bayonet fighting fill a whole page. In tug-of-war the Battalion carried almost everything before it, and in boxing held its own. The Battalion dramatic club produced several plays including "H.M.S. *Pinafore.*" These, and other successes, show the spirit which animated the Battalion. Give an Irish regiment a big station and it will always come out near the top.

During the stay of the Battalion in Aldershot Lieutenant-Colonel T. St. C. Davidson, D.S.O. succeeded to the command and Lieutenant J. G. Dill was appointed adjutant *vice* Captain R. A. H. Orpen-Palmer whose tenure of office had expired. The strenuous but pleasant days of the Aldershot Command came to an end in the relief season of 1908-1909, the Battalion being then assigned to Devonport.

The Battalion moved into North Raglan Barracks on arrival at Devonport. These barracks were about the worst ever erected by the barrack department, which is saying a good deal. Old, dirty, sunless and unkempt they lacked even the amenities of civilization and there was not even a lavatory in the officers' mess. A pantry was fitted up with a tin basin, and at luncheon time fatigue men would attend with cans of hot water to enable officers and their guests to sit down clean handed to their mid-day meal. At this time the sailor people at Devonport resided in naval barracks which reminded one of the Ritz or Cecil and rather emphasized the slatternly decay of the military quarters.

Save for these disgusting barracks and for the fact that the climate of Plymouth and Devonport was extremely relaxing in summer our new station was very pleasant indeed. Practically every kind of sport could be had; there was a great deal of social life; and the place was cheap, a feature which appealed to the married officers. A drawback, however, was the constant movement caused by the necessities of training. Musketry, company and battalion training, not to mention brigade and divisional training and manœuvres, implied a great deal of shifting, and for months kept the Battalion divided. Field firing, and sometimes training were done at Willsworthy camp on Dartmoor. It meant a march of twenty-two miles and a climb of over one thousand feet, but the Battalion laughed at the distance and the change to the " moor " was always appreciated *provided it did not rain*. Dartmoor rain was something to be remembered and compared with it a tropical downpour was simply a perspiration.

It was while the Battalion was at Devonport that its second regimental paper was born. The Journal of the Leinster Regiment, or as it was called later, the *Leinsters' Magazine* owed its success to the ability and demoniac energy of its editor, Captain R. F. Legge, assisted by Captain R. M. Raynsford as its sub-editor. It struck a completely new note in regimental journalism by subordinating regimental intelligence to general articles grave and gay, and, speaking with that impartiality which only the lapse of years can ensure, the opinion may be hazarded that neither before nor since has the *Leinsters' Magazine* had a serious rival. It enlisted some distinguished outside writers, including the present Lord Rawlinson, Hilaire Belloc, C. B. Fry, the late Frank Richardson, Stephen Gwynn, Major Drury, L. S. Amery, Aliph Cheem, Saki, and many others. It was splendidly illustrated, turned out in Messrs. Gale & Polden's very best style, and the amount of advertisements was the despair of rival regimental journals. It made a feature in each issue of humorous verse and was the only regimental paper which ever published a comic opera on the subject of manœuvres. Alas! when the Battalion was ordered abroad the editor got a home job and the inevitable upheaval caused by the change to India killed the magazine which perished after just two years' brilliant existence.

The autumn manœuvres of 1909 are worthy of record

as being almost the last during which steam mechanical transport was used. The manœuvres *per se* were extremely strenuous, but were rendered positive martyrdom by the inefficiency of the crazy traction engines on which the troops relied. Rations and kits were invariably hours late in arriving. The engines broke down, ran amok down hills, and ditched themselves on every conceivable opportunity. The whole mimic campaign was like a nightmare and in actual hardship probably exceeded even the Retreat from Mons. But it is a striking tribute to the Army Service Corps that although the whole of Wiltshire and the Thames Valley rang with blasphemy over the rotten *matériel* not a reproachful word was ever uttered against the personnel of that corps which well earned a few years later the soubriquet of " Royal."

On these manœuvres on one occasion the 8th Brigade (in which was the 1st Leinster Regiment) marched sixty-six miles in three consecutive days. Not a single man fell out in the Battalion, and the greater the hardships caused by the non-arrival of blankets or food the cheerier every member of the Battalion became. But bivouacking, cold, hungry and tired, in sopping fields in late September produced the finest curses that the present writer has ever heard. There were big manœuvres in 1910, too, but no memory remains of indifferent transport. Possibly petrol had come in by that time.

On 6th May, 1910, His Majesty King Edward VII died and the Battalion took part in the great funeral procession through London on the 20th. We entrained at Devonport about midnight on the 19th, reached London, after a crowded journey, early next morning and marched to Hyde Park where we breakfasted and dressed in a temporary camp. We were in the streets by 8 a.m. our position being on the west side of Park Lane just by Stanhope Gate, where we stood for just five hours. After the ceremony we marched back to the camp and after a few hours' rest proceeded to Paddington, arriving back at Plymouth at midnight after a very tiring twenty-four hours. The first public act of the late King had been to present colours to the Battalion, as Prince of Wales, just 52 years before, and it was fitting that the 100th Regiment should have taken part in the monarch's last journey through his capital.

When the programme of reliefs came out early in 1911 it was notified that in the forthcoming trooping season the Battalion was to proceed to India, and that the 2nd Battalion would return home. Thus the stay of the 100th at Devonport came to an end after nearly three years, and happy years, in one of the best stations in England.

It may be mentioned here that it was at Devonport that the regimental colours of blue and green were adopted by the Regiment, in lieu of the red, blue, green and white which were apparently an attempt to amalgamate the old red and blue of the 100th with the red and white of the 109th, with green "thrown in" for Ireland. This combination had been introduced by the 1st Battalion but had never been popular in the 2nd, some of the officers of which could never be got to adopt it even in spite of some pressure from above. The blending of dark blue and green, however, gave a quiet combination, symbolizing the Royal title and the Irish composition of the Regiment, and was adopted by the two battalions practically *nem. con.*

On 29th September, 1911, the Battalion embarked at Devonport on the hired transport *Dongola*, the "Innocents Abroad" as unkind people called us owing to the fact that, with the exception of Major Dugan, none of us had any previous experience of India. Before we had been long at sea we had gained another soubriquet "The Lovesick Leinsters" due to the presence of three brides and to the fact that quite obviously two other officers had left their hearts behind them. The ship was rather crowded but we had a good voyage, stopping only at Port Said. We passed through the Canal to the accompaniment of a starry night with a glorious full moon, and "The Lovesick Leinsters" became more lovesick than ever. On 19th October we arrived at Bombay and the following morning " the officers' wives were torn from the arms of their sorrowing husbands and sent literally into the blue." It is a relief to learn that this was merely a " Q " arrangement for sparing the ladies the discomfort of the troop train which left the Victoria terminus the same evening.

The troop train arrived at Bareilly about 7 a.m. on the 23rd. Bareilly is a really pleasant looking spot and subsequent experiences did not belie our first impressions. The Battalion marched to its canvas home on the Maidan, a beautiful grassy plain stretching for miles. The tents had been pitched for us by the Worcesters, a real friendly act. The married officers and their families were also in tents—bungalows in the cantonments being scarce. It is wonderful what a charming home can be made with tents in India, during that most delightful season, the Indian cold weather. The wives and families of the men after a brief stay at the rest camp went straight on to Ranikhet, under charge of Lieutenant Finlay. Ranikhet adjoins Chaubatia, our hot-weather station-to-be. A few days later the draft from the 2nd Battalion arrived, with Lieutenants Greville, Small, McLean and Westmacott.

November was spent in settling down and finding our feet. We bought our experiences, especially in the mess, dearly; so much so that Captain Raynsford was induced to write his famous book " Officer's Requirements in India " for the benefit of future innocents. Major-General Forbes Macbean commanded the brigade, with Major Glasgow of the Royal Sussex Regiment as his brigade major. Besides the Worcesters, who were in the infantry barracks, there were the King's Own Scottish Borderers under canvas alongside of us, a battery of field gunners; and of the Indian Army, the 17th Cavalry and 16th Rajputs, soon to be joined by a battalion of Gurkhas from Almora, who came down to Bareilly for their annual training. In December there took place King George V's Coronation Durbar at Delhi, when His Majesty announced the change of the capital from Calcutta to Delhi. The King's Own Scottish Borderers were under orders to attend, when at the eleventh hour one of their men went sick with cholera and their orders were cancelled, and we were ordered to go in their place. Durzies worked all night at the men's uniform. At the eleventh and a half hour *our* orders were cancelled and a regiment nearer Delhi was ordered to go instead. Sir James Willcocks, commanding the Northern Army, sent an invitation to the officers' mess, asking to his camp at Delhi any officers who were able to be present and some half dozen departed for Delhi and had a delightful experience.

Our first Christmas in India was very cheery, dances, dinners, week-end shoots, polo, tennis, together with one of the pleasantest clubs in India. On New Year's Eve it was brought home to us that we had a Scotch regiment alongside of us.

The New Year opened with a slight outbreak of smallpox in the Battalion, the colonel being one of the victims and we were in quarantine for a short space. With many good jhils in the neighbourhood and keen shikaris in the Battalion, such as Mather, Scott, Westmacott and Murray, there were many good bags of duck and snipe. The "Bareilly Week" was held in February, some excellent racing, a polo tournament—in which we were too much of beginners to compete—and the usual dinners and dances, a really good show. The following month the Battalion moved to Chaubatia by train to Kathgodam, thence by easy uphill marches to the very foothills of the Himalayas. The scenery along the road was wonderful. Thickly-wooded hillsides covered with a tangle of jungle vegetation, deep valleys whose sides were often terraced and cultivated, dried-up beds of mountain torrents, through all this the ever-rising road twisted and turned and crept around the spurs of the hills. Soon these hills became of a more formidable nature and the road pursued a tortuous course over long upward stretches followed by equally lengthy descents. Sometimes the corners are terrific. One looks ahead, the road apparently stops and there is nothing but empty space in front, but on reaching the ominous spot one finds the road has doubled back almost on its tracks around the most precipitous of turns. Tonga wallahs pass us in both directions driving their one-horse and two-horse tongas at a reckless gallop, utterly regardless of the terrors of the road. We passed the spot where a man-eating tiger had been shot a few days before. His last victim was a luckless syce, who had been leading two horses. The tiger did not eat him up then and there and on returning the following night to finish his meal he found one of the forest-rangers waiting for him and this worthy shot him dead, thus earning the Rs500 Government reward and Rs250 from the Coolie Company.

Ranikhet, some six thousand feet above sea level, is a charming spot, something like Branksome Park at Bournemouth, except that all the roads are very steep, but not too steep for driving. It has all the social amenities of a hill station, many bungalows, a good club, polo ground and a few shops. Chaubatia, the best part of a thousand feet higher, consists of the bungalows for one battalion with the usual accessories in the way of a church, hospital, etc. and nothing else. From Ranikhet it is reached by a fairly easily graded cart road but most of the traffic goes up and down the precipitous bridle path.

The officers' mess at Chaubatia at the very crest of the hill is probably the highest officers' mess in the world and looks straight on to the eternal snows. One gazes from the mess windows on to the Kumaon hills, rising in successive ridges and gradually giving place to the Himalayas, one gigantic semi-circle of snow-capped monsters, stretching for about two hundred miles from the eastern to the western horizon. From the mess the distance to these mountains is about fifty miles, but in this clear hill atmosphere they stand out with amazing clearness and rather give the effect of colossal stage scenery. At their base is usually a certain amount of mist so that, from the snow line upwards, they appear like a vision in

M

the air which might vanish into space at any moment. In the evening they are often practically obscured by clouds which are frequently dissipated with a strange suddenness as the sun is setting, as if Nature had rung up her stage-curtain in order to give mortals a final glimpse before nightfall of one of her most magnificent spectacles. In the daytime little fleecy clouds clustering around the snowy summits of the mountains, but not thick enough to hide them entirely from view, give an almost fairy-like, unreal picture-book appearance to the scene. In the centre towers Nanda Devi, 25,693 feet high, a height which is only surpassed by three other mountains in the world.

Training in Chaubatia called for considerable ingenuity for the only piece of flat ground was the barrack square and all the rest was precipitous khud-side, for the most part thickly wooded. Climbing up and down the hills in the rarefied atmosphere was severe work, and made one puff and blow like a grampus. All social happenings took place at Ranikhet to which everybody migrated each afternoon on foot, or on a pony, or in a dandy or driving down the cart road. Our officers' mess and sergeants' mess at Chaubatia had, however, their own tennis courts. By May musketry was in full swing. The range was quite close at hand situated down the ridge of a spur; the atmosphere in these mountainous regions made for eminently erratic shooting. At the end of the month high wind, showers, thunder, lightning and a quite cold temperature in the evenings heralded the approach of the monsoon. Company training involved a week's stay at Majkhali camp, some twelve miles along the road to Almora, where the ground admitted of something in the way of ordinary training. On 3rd June the King's birthday was celebrated throughout India and we had a parade on the barrack square. The monsoon made a brief appearance but seemed to think better of it and a spell of hot weather ensued, bringing with it a pest in the shape of innumerable sandflies. On 17th June there was a big fancy dress ball at Ranikhet to which the Battalion officers went in force, headed by Lieutenant-Colonel White as a blue pierrot.

In July the monsoon starts in earnest. Towards evening the air would fill with dust; deep, sustained growls of thunder reverberated through the mountains, and the heavens became strangely dark. Then about dinner-time came heavy rain, making a furious uproar on the tin roofs of the bungalows, and accompanied by the vivid prolonged flashes of lightning, such as one never sees at home. Sometimes the whole sky seemed one blaze of light. The heavy rain gave a dark, green tinge to the parched hill-sides which looked very beautiful and stood out with a vivid distinctness after the showers.

On 17th July a ball was given at the Ranikhet Club by the bachelors of the station. Returning by dandy in the small hours of the morning was a romantic experience with the winds whispering in the pine trees like the waves beating on a shore. The voice of the tree frog is now heard in the land with maddening iteration. Actually, as a matter of fact, its wings are responsible for the strange rattling noise. Over three inches of rain fell on 3rd August. The end of the month saw amateur theatricals at the club, to wit "The Arabian Nights," in which Mrs. Raynsford and Lieutenant Meredith took part, also Lieutenant Deane. On 13th September inspection of the Battalion by Major-General Forbes Macbean. Chakor shooting in progress. Following the birds up and down the sides of the khuds is " phenomenously hard work (*sic*), and the bags were small, but the birds when you do get them are most delicious eating."

On 1st October " G " Company under Captain Raynsford left Chaubatia as advanced party *en route* for Bareilly. They passed General Pilcher, commanding the Meerut Division on 2nd October, who asked a few questions and then dashed on. They arrived at Bareilly on the evening of 5th October, and on the following day started on their job of pitching over two hundred Indian pattern tents and marquees for the Battalion. On 13th October Captain Weldon who was to take over the adjutancy from Captain Jones, arrived at Bareilly from home. By the 24th October the Battalion was concentrated at Bareilly and four days later Battalion training started. " Up at 6 a.m. every morning. Very unpleasant." Manœuvres followed on 9th November and lasted till 16th December.

The year 1913 opened with preparations for the ceremony of the presentation of new colours. The club was handed over to us for the colour ball. The scheme of decoration for the ball-room consisted of white Corinthian pillars on a white muslin background and in between festoons of muslin in the regimental colours. At one end of the ball-room an alcove, leading out on to the veranda, was formed to hold a pile of drums and the new colours. At the other end a pillared doorway was formed; the band to play outside this on the back veranda. The scheme was somewhat severe but extraordinarily effective. Lieutenant G. Orpen-Palmer was the designer, and the pillars, made of lath and plaster, were made under the orders of Lieutenant Farley, R.E. The ladies of the Regiment worked with intense enthusiasm at the beautifying of the ball-room and its precincts.

On 4th February Lieutenant-General Sir James Willcocks, K.C.S.I., K.C.M.G., C.B., D.S.O., presented new colours to his old Battalion on the Maidan.

The parade was witnessed by a large number of people including many visitors from out-stations. General Willcocks was accompanied by his complete staff, and at the flag-staff were Generals Pilcher and Forbes Macbean. After receiving the general salute General Willcocks inspected the Regiment, and the preliminary ceremony of trooping the old colours for the last time was at once proceeded with. This ceremony, always an impressive one, was rendered doubly so by the fine band of the Battalion. Before the old colours, which had been in use for twenty-six years, were cased for the last time, they were marched round the Regiment to the familiar strains of " Auld Lang Syne." The ceremony of consecrating the new colours next followed. This was performed by the Bishop of Lucknow and the Roman Catholic Archbishop of Simla. The colours were then handed to the two senior subalterns by General Willcocks, who then addressed the Battalion as follows :—

" Lieutenant-Colonel White, officers, non-commissioned officers and men of the 1st Battalion, Prince of Wales's Leinster Regiment, Royal Canadians. Any officer who can stand before his old regiment to present them with colours must indeed deem himself a fortunate man. For twenty-two years I had the honour of being enrolled in this Battalion, and now to-day falls to me the distinction of handing over to your care the emblems which are so rightly cherished and treasured by the soldiers of every army.

" The colours of a regiment stir the imagination and call up all the higher feelings of proper pride and self-sacrifice, and it is such feelings, I firmly believe, which actuate those who realize that there can be no nobler calling on earth than that of the soldier who deems life itself as nothing in comparison with his duty to his King and the necessity of maintaining the honour of his country's flag. If the sight of the colours can awake such feelings in us, then surely there can be no greater treasure for us to possess and guard.

" The Regiments numbered 100th have in the past served in many lands and with much distinction. In the wars against Hyder Ali and Tippoo Sahib the Regiment was four years continuously in the field and lost 39 officers and 1,200 men killed, wounded and died of disease. At Niagara in 1813 (which is borne on your colours) the Regiment behaved with distinguished gallantry. To quote the words of General Drummond ' the highly gratifying but difficult duty remains of endeavouring to do justice to the bravery, intrepidity and devotion of the 100th Regiment to their country.'

" The first public act of His Royal Highness the Prince of Wales (afterwards King Edward VII) was to present colours to this Battalion and those colours it was often my privilege and honour to carry.

"In South Africa, in 1900, the Battalion formed part of the 8th Division, and took part in the operations ending in the surrender of Prinsloo with 4,200 men. During the war the Battalion lost 5 officers and 74 non-commissioned officers and men killed in action or died of wounds, disease etc. besides 2 officers and 39 non-commissioned officers and men wounded.

"In these days it does not fall to the lot of all corps to add battle honours to their colours, but it does rest with them to keep themselves ever ready for war should such come, and no greater incentive to this can there be than to treasure and keep green the memory of those deeds which are emblazoned on your standards.

"Irishmen have ever been amongst the staunchest and bravest soldiers of the Crown, and I am indeed proud to-day to commit to the care of my comrades of the Leinster Regiment these colours, which under all circumstances and in all climes you will guard with honour, on which, when opportunity offers, you will inscribe new names, and which I know you will never allow to be tarnished."

Colonel White, D.S.O., commanding the Battalion, replied as follows :—

"On behalf of the Battalion it is my privilege to command, I have to thank you for the honour you have done us in coming here to-day to present our new colours. As an old officer of the Regiment, I think it is singularly appropriate that this presentation is being made by you, and I am sure all ranks appreciate it at the hands of so distinguished a soldier and old brother officer. The old colours to which we have just said farewell have served their time and are being placed in St. Patrick's Cathedral, Dublin, over the memorial which is erected there to the memory of those officers and men of the Battalion who fell during the South African War. I cannot imagine a more suitable resting place for them than this to mark the memory of those who fought under them and gave

Photo] [Langfier

GENERAL SIR JAMES WILLCOCKS, G.C.B., G.C.M.G., K.C.S.I., D.S.O.
Late 100th Regiment

their lives for their King and country. The new colours which you have just presented have yet to justify existence, but I have no hesitation in saying that we are willing to a man to do under them what we have done under the old ones, to keep them flying for the honour of the Regiment and the glory of the British Army, whether in this country or in any other where duty calls us to fight for our King and country. I think, Sir, you will have no cause to regret having entrusted them to our care."

After the new colours had been saluted the Battalion marched past. Then the Battalion formed quarter column and General Willcocks again personally addressed the Battalion in which he had served some twenty-two years, congratulating it on its splendid display that morning, and assuring it of his interest in its welfare and expressing his great pride that to him should have fallen the honour of presenting the new colours. The Battalion replied by giving three hearty cheers to their old comrade. The whole proceedings passed off without a hitch of any sort, and it was the universal opinion of all present that for impressiveness and precision the ceremony had never been surpassed and seldom equalled.

The parade was an overwhelming success, a success for which perhaps chief credit should be given to Captain and Adjutant H. W. Weldon. There was not a single hitch, not a man fell out during the long periods of standing to attention, and the whole ceremony was carried out with a mathematical exactitude and finish which delighted Sir James Willcocks and the four other generals who were present.

The colour ball the same night was a brilliant success and was kept up until 4 a.m. with a tremendous éclat and vivacity. Everybody from Sir James and Lady Willcocks downwards simply let themselves go and went wild with enthusiasm.

On 6th February there was a large official dinner at the mess and afterwards everybody went to a ball given by the sergeants which was as successful as everything else had been. Sir James Willcocks had to leave by the night train for Agra and as he paid his farewells said : " The Leinsters do everything well."

After all this junketting the historian is not surprised to find the entry " 13th and 14th February. Brigade field firing. Tremendously heavy work over fearfully sandy soil." However, the Bareilly week soon came and on the 18th there was the first night of the three-act comedy " The Passport," which was a roaring success. Leinsters in the caste were Captain Raynsford, Mr. G. Orpen-Palmer, Mr. A. J. M. Pemberton, Mr. J. V. Meredith and Sergeant Tector. The brigade sports took place on 6th March, which the Leinsters won easily. Result : Leinsters 6 events, 4th Worcesters 2, 2nd Leicesters (who had recently taken the place of the King's Own Scottish Borderers) 2, and the Royal Field Artillery nil. From this date until September there is nothing of any moment to relate, events being very similar to last year. In October Lieutenant-Colonel White returned from leave at home and brought with him a bride. The Battalion was under orders to go to Fyzabad.

The Battalion did not leave for Fyzabad until 28th November and so got a taste of what a hill station is like during the cold weather. It froze every night, and was pretty cold during the day, too cold to play tennis. The whole place seemed absolutely dead. At this time of the year the views of the Himalayas are perfectly wonderful, but man cannot live on views alone.

The Battalion, moving by half-battalions, arrived in Fyzabad during the first week of December. Pretty cantonments with the River Dogra winding along their outskirts, and a nice cosy little club but rather an air of lifelessness about the whole place, and it was of course very much smaller than Bareilly. The rooms in the officers' mess bungalow were colossal. The men's bungalows were of the usual hot-weather station type. The 4th Cavalry stationed here was being relieved in a few days time by the 12th Cavalry from Allahabad.

The Native Infantry regiment was the 9th Bhopal Infantry. Both prior to our arrival and immediately on our arrival we started practising for the trooping of the colours in celebration of the centenary of the storming of Fort Niagara, and the parade duly took place on 19th December, 1913. It was a great success everything being done in perfect style, but unfortunately there were very few people to witness it. The salute was taken by Colonel Wintle, commanding 12th Cavalry, as senior officer of the garrison. Curiously enough he had done his attachment to a British regiment, on being posted to the Indian Army, with the 1st Leinsters, and actually joined them at Fyzabad. His photo as a subaltern figures in the regimental album. After the parade practically all the sahib log of Fyzabad came to lunch. Champagne flowing, and all merry. The most eminent guest was Lieutenant-General Wylde, Royal Marines, who was at Fyzabad on leave. He said he had seen a lot of trooping of the colours, but had never seen it better done. This coming from a member of the Royal Marines who are unsurpassed in drill, was high praise.

When 1914 dawned the 1st Battalion had long ceased to be "Innocents Abroad," and no longer confused roti and rupees and knew a shroff from a sahib. After the bracing atmosphere of a hill station and the excitement of colour balls and Niagara centenaries life in mere cantonments probably felt a bit flat. A member of the Battalion appealed to for "copy" concerning Fyzabad and 1914 has written: "I can remember nothing of what happened, in fact there was nothing to remember." Let us leave these emancipated griffs to their brandy pani and curry bat and follow the fortunes of the 2nd Battalion.

CHAPTER XIII

THE EARLIER 109TH REGIMENTS.

THE earliest record of a regiment bearing the title of 109th Foot dates from the period of the Seven Years' War. In 1761 the proposal of Captain John Nairne of the 1st Foot, son of the third Baron Nairne, a Jacobite who took an active part in the '45, for raising a corps of infantry without any expense to the Government was approved. Orders for raising the Regiment were issued in October of that year, Nairne being appointed to command it with the rank of major commandant (dated 13th October, 1761) which rank he held until the Regiment was disbanded. Recruiting for the corps being forbidden in the Highlands, the Regiment was raised principally in Hertfordshire and Middlesex, a draft of six men and one drummer being transferred from the 14th Foot for the purpose of assisting in raising the men and disciplining the recruits. The Regiment was stationed at Harrow, Royston and Wisbech until March when it was sent to Aylesbury; over two hundred men being drafted out in February and March for other regiments serving abroad.

In April, 1762, the Regiment, which had formerly been known as the Battalion of London Volunteers, was ordered to be placed upon the establishment as the 109th Foot, dating from 25th December, 1761, with an establishment of four companies of seventy privates each. A fifth company (Pountenay's Independent Company) reduced to the same establishment, was added from 25th April, 1762. Originally it had been intended to raise a regiment of six companies of one hundred privates. A sixth company was, however, added to the Regiment later in the year. This company (Manby's) originally known as the Independent Company of London Volunteers, was principally stationed in Essex. It did not join the Regiment at Belleisle, but was sent in December, 1762, to Bristol, where it was employed in guarding French prisoners of war and was ordered to be disbanded there in April, 1763.

At the end of May the Regiment (still stationed at Aylesbury) was ordered to hold itself in readiness to embark for Belleisle, which had been captured from the French in the previous year, to relieve the garrison there ; and in June it marched to Portsmouth where it embarked for Belleisle. The Regiment remained in garrison there until the Peace of 1763, under which treaty Belleisle was handed back to France, when it was ordered home for disbandment. It accordingly sailed for Portsmouth in May of that year and marched from thence to Bristol where it was disbanded on the 10th June. The colours were given by Nairne to the Duke of Atholl, and are preserved at Blair Castle.

A generation later the terrible outbreak of the French Revolution caused every nation to set its house in order, to withstand the fury of the elements. To an unmilitary nation like England the first step necessary was to increase her land forces, and, consequently, many extra battalions and some new regiments were raised of which latter one received the distinguishing number 109. The history of that unit will now be told, but here it will not be out of place to remark that, save for identity of numeration, this old 109th has no direct connexion with the later regiment of that number, which was eventually to become the 2nd Battalion of the Leinster Regiment. This statement is unlikely to lead to contention since the 109th Regiment of the end of the eighteenth century enjoyed a career so ephemeral as to afford it no chance of garnering renown. Nevertheless, sentiment alone would lead any regiment to take a special interest in any bygone corps which had been known by the same identifying number, and to the 2nd Leinster

Regiment that old 109th, like the still earlier one of 1761, is, if not a direct ancestor, at anyrate a family connexion.

Even so late as 1792 the barrack accommodation in Great Britain sufficed for a mere 20,000 men with the result that a large part of the army was constantly in camps or billets. Further, the whole military system resembled far more that of the Middle Ages than of the present day. The manner in which regiments were raised is a case in point. The Crown would contract with a distinguished soldier, or gentleman of high position, who undertook to raise the men, receiving a certain sum as bounty money for each recruit ; and for the maintenance of the regiment the colonel received an annual sum sufficient to cover the pay of the men and the expenses of clothing and recruiting. The colonel was given a " beating order," without which no enlistment was legal and was responsible for maintaining his regiment at full strength. Hence rose that branch of bureaucracy, the " muster masters," whose duty it was to muster regiments and check the numbers. These " muster parades " survived for over a century—and perhaps still exist—although the writer's last recollection of one is of 1894, and by that date this old time parade had come to be regarded as merely an excellent opportunity of inspecting the men's greatcoats. The cardinal feature of a muster parade was that *every one* in the unit who could stand on two legs had to attend. And so from every hole and lair, from every job and employ, would creep to the unaccustomed drill ground unknown warriors—the sergeant-cook, the battalion postman, the officers' mess sergeant, queer old pioneers, shoemakers, the colonel's servant (*rara avis in campo*), the armourer-sergeant, the orderly room personnel—all greatcoated and blinking like bats in the unaccustomed light, but, by their presence, refuting any legend that the commanding officer was obtaining money by false pretences. This is, however, getting away from Revolutionary years. The point to remember is that in those days the colonel was a contractor no less than a commanding officer, the soldier being raised, paid and clothed by him.

The 109th or Aberdeenshire Regiment was raised by letter of service granted, on 2nd April, 1794, to Colonel Alexander Hay of Rannes, then on the half-pay of the late 104th Foot. Having kissed the King's hand he immediately left London for Aberdeen to levy the corps, about which much interest was being taken in the county. Already a meeting, held at Aberdeen, under the auspices of Mr. Leith of Freefield had voted Colonel Hay its most cordial support, while on 17th April a large and enthusiastic assembly of noblemen, gentlemen, freeholders, and commissioners of supply passed unanimous resolutions of countenance and confidence, appointing a working committee and offering a substantial bounty to volunteers for the Aberdeenshire Battalion. This offer Colonel Hay handsomely declined, stating that the King had given him the regiment on such liberal terms that the pecuniary aid of friends was quite unnecessary. Some idea of what those terms were may be gathered from the fact that the new levy bounties were found to be so prejudicial to the manning of the Fleet that an army order was issued limiting their amount to fifteen guineas for general service recruits, and ten guineas for fencibles, and this at a time when navy bounties stood somewhere about twenty-five guineas for seamen and twenty guineas for landsmen. Every effort was made to beat up recruits.

The recruiting parties made a brilliant show parading the Castlegate in the tasteful uniform of the regiment, while it was claimed that the adoption of trousers for the kilt was calculated to give extra comfort to the soldiers. In the end of April a general meeting of the county, with Sir William Forbes of Craigievar as chairman, voted Colonel Hay its best acknowledgments for the manner in which he was conducting the recruiting service, for enlisting none but likely lads, for having prohibited his recruiting parties from using any improper device to obtain men, and for preventing interference with the many other parties then recruiting for His Majesty's Service.

The following is an example of the devices referred to :—

Five pounds bounty and 100 pounds to be raffled for among twenty recruits ; the winner to be paid on the spot with power to purchase his discharge for twenty pounds. The record adds that at a certain centre in Ireland " the dice box is constantly at work."

Recruiting for the 109th went on briskly. The colonel was so popular that one market day as many as eighteen men joined him in Aberdeen. Mr. Skeen of Skeen brought a large contingent drawn from his own estates, and obtained at Rood Fair, Montrose, where he had liberally regaled all and sundry at the Market Cross. The Earl of Aberdeen was at Tarland to help on the work, and, punch being distributed in great abundance in the street, a number of very fine young men were enlisted.

The Regiment was complete by the beginning of September. The first muster roll, on a large sheet of vellum, embraces the period " from letter of service, 2nd April, to the 4th September, 1794, being the day preceding the establishment," and contains the names of 23 officers and 718 non-commissioned officers and men. The senior major was Erskine Fraser of Woodhill, whose monument as " sometime lieutenant-colonel of the late 109th Regiment of Foot " is in Oldmachar Cathedral. Five hundred of the men are said to have belonged to the city and county of Aberdeen, and all of them were of excellent physique. The 109th was inspected and passed at Aberdeen by General Sir Hector Munro, K.B., commanding the forces on 5th September, 1794, when, after a very successful parade, the colours gifted by the county were presented. Dinners and balls followed in rapid succession, and the officers were given the freedom of the city. The strength was ordered to be augmented to 1,000 men, and Colonel Hay promised to pardon all deserters who immediately surrendered.

The Regiment did not long remain in Aberdeen. Marching by divisions by the end of September it was concentrated at Dundee, while orders were received to proceed to Burntisland and embark for Southampton, which was reached on 26th October. The best wishes of the town and county accompanied the Battalion, and its good behaviour on the line of march amply justified the most sanguine expectations regarding it. The next move was to Jersey, whence the 109th returned in July 1795 to join a force—fixed at twenty-nine regiments—assembling on Nursling Common, Southampton, under General Sir Ralph Abercrombie, for a descent on the West Indies. And now all unexpectedly came an order to draft the 109th into the depleted 53rd, then also on Nursling Common. In vain did Colonel Hay protest that this was being done in flagrant violation of his letter of service—that if the regiment were disbanded it should be disbanded in Aberdeenshire and the men not drafted into or disposed among other corps. Similar protestations were made in the House of Commons by General Macleod and others, but all to no purpose. In the debate Mr. Allardyce of Dunottar certainly did not strengthen the case by declaring that he had no complaints from Aberdeen.

Eighteen officers were transferred to the 53rd in the *Gazette* of 12th September, 1795, and the 109th Aberdeenshire Regiment ceased to exist. In those days there were some 118 numbered regiments of Foot, with several others numbered or with territorial titles, many being as ephemeral as the 109th. Thus passed away a predecessor of the 2nd Leinster Regiment, the 109th Aberdeenshire Regiment of Foot. More than half a century was to elapse before this number once again made its appearance in the Army List. But before that comes to be narrated it will be necessary to launch upon the history of a remarkable political, civil, commercial and military institution—the Honourable East India Company.

CHAPTER XIV

THE EAST INDIA COMPANY

EVERY schoolboy knows who imprisoned Montezuma and who strangled Atahualpa. The words are Macaulay's but even his authority cannot lend them veracity, for the present writer even in advancing eld can hazard but a wide solution as to the perpetrators of these tyrannical occurrences. But Lord Macaulay was less incorrect when, referring in the same paragraph to the growth of the East India Company, he declared that every Englishman who takes any interest in any part of history will be curious to know how a handful of his countrymen, separated from their homes by an immense ocean, subjugated in the course of a few years, one of the greatest Empires of the world.

What was known as the India Company sprang into existence in the first year of the seventeenth century. In December, 1600, the Indian Adventurers were formed into a chartered company with a monopoly, so far as England was concerned, in Eastern trade, and with the full intention of disputing that trade with two nations—the Portuguese and Dutch—who had already made good their position in the East. At first the trade though very lucrative was small, and conflicts with the Dutch and Portuguese tended to a state of permanent hostilities. Events in Europe, however, practically destroyed the rivalry of the latter, and the stress even of Dutch competition greatly decreased. Leases from native princes enabled the foundation of Madras and Calcutta to be taken in hand, and the island of Bombay, which Catherine of Braganza brought in her dowry to Charles II, was, later, handed over to the Company. Repeated extensions of its privileges were granted, and the three settlements grew to separate presidencies, to become, later, Bengal, Madras and Bombay.

The territorial growth of the Company was, however, at first but slow. After a hundred and forty years of existence it was still merely a trading corporation. Its territory consisted of a few square miles, for which rent was paid to the native governments. Its troops were scarcely numerous enough to man the batteries of three or four ill-constructed forts, which had been erected for the protection of the warehouses. Such natives as formed part of these diminutive garrisons had not been disciplined on European lines and were armed with swords and shields or bows and arrows. The European subordinates of the Company were in no sense civil servants with administrative and judicial functions but clerks and tallymen, miserably paid, though able at times to amass fortunes by trading on their own account.

What really shook this association of pedlars from its lethargy was the necessity of struggling for its existence against the French. A French East India Company had been established under Louis XIV, and in 1744 when the two companies first came into active competition two men of great genius were at the head of the French presidencies—Labourdonnais at Mauritius and Dupleix in Pondicherry. Here Providence intervened on the side of the English Company in bringing to India a young civilian, Robert Clive, whose military genius, as told later in this chapter, turned the scale decisively in favour of the English Company.

So long as the Company's chief business had been trade it had been left to manage its own affairs, but after Clive's brilliant victory at Plassey, and the subsequent final overthrow of the French in 1761, it was felt that the British Government should be in a position of exercising some control over the new and vast territories acquired. Lord North's Regulating Act in 1773 effected something in this direction. Next followed Pitt's India Bill of 1784, which created the Board of Control as a department of the English Government to exercise political, military and financial superintendence over the British possessions in India. From this date the direction of Indian policy passed definitely from the Company to the Governor-General in India and the ministry in London. Further control was given the Board in 1833 over the Company's commercial transactions, but its property was secured on the Indian possessions and its annual dividends of ten guineas per £100 stock were made a charge on the Indian revenue. Henceforth the Honourable East India Company ceased to be a trading concern and exercised only administrative functions. Such arrangement was obviously anomalous and unsatisfactory for, shorn though it was of its commercial privileges the Company had yet its directors and stockholders and the flag of this quasi-mercantile corporation flew over India from Cape Comorin to Kashmir and from Bombay to Pegu.

So much for the political and territorial expansion of the Company, but it is obvious that such expansion could have come about only by the possession of armed forces. This was the case. Ever since its inception the East India Company had maintained an army, or the nucleus of an army, which increased in size *pari passu* with the growth of area and responsibility. But, although for convenience the title " army " is used, it must be pointed out that, historically, the Indian army grew up in three distinct divisions, the Bengal, Madras and Bombay armies. This separation was the natural result of the original foundation of separate factories and settlements in India; and each retains, even to the present day, some of its old identity.

In the two former presidencies for many years the armed forces consisted chiefly of small armed guards over factories and warehouses, and in Bengal for long the English traders were restricted by the native princes to a military establishment of an ensign and 30 men.

Even by 1683 the Bengal "army" consisted merely of 250 men, all Europeans for it was not until years later that natives were first enlisted. A similar handful was quartered in Madras. In these tiny forces was, however, concealed the germ of the great Indian army, priority being granted by historians to the little force in Bengal, and this claim being recognized in the numbering after 1858 of the 1st Royal Bengal Fusiliers as the 101st of the Line, i.e., the first in order of the Regiments (101st—109th inclusive) then transferred from the Company to the Crown.

With the Bombay army the 2nd Leinster Regiment, originally the 3rd Bombay European Regiment, is more concerned. The origin of the Bombay army is in sharp contradistinction to that of the armies of Bengal and Madras, for whereas the latter grew from the accretion of small bands of armed watchmen and peons, the army of Bombay was built on the foundation of a royal regiment. When Charles II wedded the infanta of Portugal, Catherine of Braganza, she brought as her married portion both Tangier and the island of Bombay. For the defence of these newly acquired possessions two regiments were raised—the latter being the Bombay Regiment of Europeans formed in 1662. The Government of that period was singularly dense on the subject of overseas policy. In 1668 the island of Bombay was transferred to the East India Company, and with the island went the regiment. Sixteen years later, on the ground of expense, Tangier was abandoned to the Moors; but as it was impossible to transfer the Tangier Regiment, as had happened in the case of Bombay, it remained in the service of the Crown. A curious result of this action of the then Government was revealed nearly two centuries later. The Tangier, or Queen's Regiment (so called from Queen Catherine) was, and had been for nearly 200 years, the 2nd Regiment of the Line. After 1858, however, the Bombay Regiment became the 103rd, and, in the linking, and territorialization which followed later, actually became the junior battalion of the junior regiment of the whole of H.M.'s infantry. There is much that is anomalous in this happening and not a little which appears unjust. The history of the old Bombay Regiment can be read in an admirable work whose apt title " Crown and Company " testifies to the origin and subsequent transfer of the Bombay Regiment of Europeans. The 3rd Bombay European Regiment always regarded itself as sprung from the loins of that distinguished corps and it was natural that in 1881 it should have desired a permanent union with it, as will be related in another chapter.

The first harvest of military glory garnered by the Indian Army was due mainly to the forces in Madras, and the Madras Army owed its distinction to the genius of Robert Clive who landed as a young civilian cadet in the Company's service in 1744. From his first visit dates the renown of the English arms in the East. As Macaulay well says "Till he appeared, his countrymen were despised as mere pedlars, while the French were revered as a people formed for victory and command." A collision between the two European Powers in India had already been brought about, not by any Eastern question, but by a cause as remote as the Austrian succession. England had sided with Maria Theresa ; France had espoused the cause of Frederick the Great. The war had encircled the globe and in it " black men fought on the coast of Coromandel and red men scalped each other by the Great Lakes of North America."

The " coast of Coromandel " is Macaulay's picturesque periphrasis for Madras and there success crowned the efforts of the French. In 1746 the town of Madras was captured by them. When peace came it was restored to the English ; but though peace existed between the French and English Crowns there arose between the rival companies a contest in which the prize was nothing less than the dominion of India. That country was now in a state of dissolution. The Mogul Empire was crumbling. " A succession of nominal sovereigns, sunk in indolence and debauchery, sauntered away life in secluded palaces, chewing bang, fondling concubines and listening to buffoons." How the anarchy and strife throughout Hindostan were to end no man could tell. But there was one Frenchman who saw that it was possible to found a European Empire on the ruins of the Mogul monarchy—Dupleix.

Dupleix saw clearly that the greatest force which the Indian princes could bring into the field would be no match for a small body of well-trained and disciplined Europeans; he saw also that the natives of India might, under European commanders, be formed into effective armies. The sepoy army, originally born in the brain of another Frenchman, was really made effective by Dupleix though it is just to say that the presidency of Bombay had already begun, in a tentative manner, to train native soldiers, and in 1747 actually sent some to Madras. Nevertheless the English Company made but a feeble attempt to cope with the brilliant efforts of its rival, and it was due to the valour and military genius of an obscure young English civilian that the tide of fortune suddenly turned.

At Arcot Clive commanded 200 English soldiers and 300 sepoys " armed and disciplined after the European fashion "—Dupleix's weapon turned against himself. The English had now the measure of the French, and in 1757 at Plassey—one of the decisive battles of the world, though Creasy knew it not—Clive with 1,100 European soldiers, 2,100 sepoys and 10 field pieces defeated the Nawab Suraj-ud-dowlah with 50,000 men, 53 guns and some French artillery. Three years later Coote secured at Wandewash in Madras the greatest victory ever gained over the French in India. Thus the English had beaten the French at their own game. Dupleix had foreseen how India could be won; but the English had beaten him in the training and disciplining of a sepoy army. A new factor had now been introduced into the organization of the fighting forces of the Company. H.M.'s 39th Regiment had arrived in India, taken part in the battle of Plassey, and later commemorated the fact by the proud motto *Primus in Indis* borne till this day. The army of the East India Company had now taken on the shape it was to maintain for just one hundred years for, after 1757, it was composed of royal troops (lent to the Company); its own European regiments; and sepoy soldiers.

From this date the military power of the Company rapidly increased. Three King's regiments quickly followed the 39th, and in each presidency the army increased in size. In 1796 a general reorganization took place. Hitherto the officers in each presidency had been borne on general lists according to branches of service. These lists were now broken up and cadres of regiments formed, while higher commands were distributed between the royal and Company's officers. Further augmentations took place consequent on the great extension of British supremacy, and in 1798 the sepoy infantry in India numbered 122 battalions and in 1808 the strength of the armies of the Honourable East India Company were as follows :—

	British.	Native.	Total.
Bengal	7,000	57,000	64,000
Madras	11,000	53,000	64,000
Bombay	6,500	20,000	26,500
Totals	24,500	130,000	154,500

The first half of the nineteenth century was filled with war and annexations, and the army was steadily increased. Horse artillery was formed and the artillery in general was greatly augmented. Irregular cavalry was raised in Bengal and Bombay, and recruited from a better class of troopers who found their own horses and equipment. Local forces were raised in various parts from time to time the most important being in the Punjab after the annexation of that territory in 1849. Another kind of force which had been gradually formed was that called "contingents" raised by the protected native states. The officering and recruiting of the three armies were in all respects similar. The officers were mainly supplied by the Company's military at Addiscombe in Surrey (founded in 1809) and by direct appointments, the latter applying to cavalry and infantry while the artillery and engineer cadets were trained in the college. The depot of the Company came to be at Warley in Essex.

The year 1853 is one of interest to the Regiment for the East India Company then decided to increase its European troops by a third infantry regiment in each presidency. These were to be brought on establishment on 15th November, 1853, and were to consist of 1 colonel, 2 lieutenant-colonels, 2 majors, 12 captains, 20 lieutenants, 10 ensigns and 920 other ranks. By Bombay General Orders of 1st December, 1853, the new regiment in that presidency was to be entitled the 3rd Bombay European Regiment and the existing 1st Bombay Europeans (Fusiliers) and 2nd Bombay Europeans (Light Infantry) were each to furnish as nucleus 2 sergeants, 2 corporals, 1 sergeant for promotion to colour-sergeant, 10 corporals for promotion to sergeants, 10 lance-corporals or privates for promotion to corporals, 2 drummers or buglers and 50 privates. The first officers were Lieutenant-Colonel Commandant H. Cracklow, promoted from the Line; Lieutenant-Colonel J. E. Hume, promoted from the 10th Native Infantry; and Lieutenant-Colonel G. Le G. Jacob, promoted from the 2nd Grenadiers Native Infantry.

Thus began the real life of the Regiment, which, later as the 109th Foot and later still as the 2nd Leinster Regiment, was for seventy years to serve in four quarters of the globe till the fatal day of disbandment in 1922. Fortune smiled upon it at its birth, for of the three Bombay European Regiments only one—the 3rd—was to share in the brilliant campaign which, within a few years, saved India for the British; and, ere its death, Fortune granted that its colours should be flown within the territory of the greatest military Power in Europe.

With this accession of strength the army of the Company reached the following figures :—

	BRITISH*				NATIVE				
	Cavalry	Artillery	Infantry	Total	Cavalry †	Artillery	Sappers and Miners	Infantry †	Total
Bengal ...	1,366	3,063	17,003	21,432	19,288	4,734	1,497	112,052	137,57
Madras ...	639	2,128	5,941	8,708	3,202	2,407	1,270	42,373	49,2
Bombay ...	681	1,578	7,101	9,360	8,433	1,997	637	33,861	44,92
Local Forces etc.	—	—	—	—	6,796	2,118	—	23,640	32,55
Ditto ...	—	—	—	—	—	—	—	Unclassified	7,75
Military Police	—	—	—	—	—	—	—	—	38,97
Totals ...	2,686	6,769	30,045	39,500	37,719	11,256	3,404	211,926	311,03

* Including Company's European troops.
† Including irregulars, etc., not shown in Local Forces, etc.

Grand Total, British and Native Troops, 350,538.

The 3rd Bombay European Regiment spent its early years in Poona and it was doubtless from its popularity at that station that the nickname " Poona Pets " was bestowed upon it, another nickname being the " Bombay Lilywhites " from the scrupulously clean appearance of the white facings of the Regiment. Poona was a good station very frequented during the rains—" that season of damp, mildew and sociability " as a contemporary chronicler puts it. " Here are a number of people congregated together professedly for the purpose of holiday making ; the civilian is relieved from his district wanderings, the merchant from his toils and cares of business, and even the military man enjoys some relaxation from the usual routine of daily parades. The consequences are obvious, the younger officers especially having nothing on earth to do start off directly after breakfast on a round of visits, indefatigably collecting and carrying on the news collected at each house, until the most marvellous knowledge of everybody's affairs is obtained." The same satirist comments sourly on the extravagance displayed in the mess of the Company's regiment there quartered and leaves the reader with the impression that life in Poona in the '50's of last century was a round of scandal, extravagance, manœuvring mammas (with bachelor civilians as the quarry), re-unions, private parties, "many gay balls given by the different regiments," private theatricals, and "junior officers of regiments shackled by heavy mess expenditure." Soon, however, these good days were to end and the 3rd Bombay Europeans were to be called upon to prove their mettle in the field.

CHAPTER XV

The Outbreak of the Indian Mutiny.

IN the beginning of the year 1857 peace reigned throughout the length and breadth of India. The East India Company had fared on since its formation in 1600, from small beginnings and through many a disastrous day, until it had come to be the undisputed ruler of two-thirds of the Indian Peninsula, and to exercise a real if undefined control over most of the remainder of that immense tract of country. The vigorous administration of Dalhousie had consolidated and strengthened British power; his extensive reforms had stabilized the system of government; and the annexations which took place under his regime had added vast areas to the possessions of the Company. There were some, however, who, surveying the political heavens, were not deceived by the sunshine and the calm. Among them was Lord Canning, who succeeded Dalhousie in 1856. At a banquet given by the directors of the East India Company, a few months before his departure, he voiced his doubts in a memorable phrase: " We must not forget that in the sky of India, serene as it is, a small cloud may arise, at first no bigger than a man's hand, but which, growing larger and larger, may at last threaten to burst and overwhelm us with ruin."

There were indeed many circumstances connected with the India of that day sufficient to justify presentiment in the mind of a prudent administrator of Canning's stamp. The East India Company itself was an anomaly. It had ceased to be a commercial organization and now exercised merely administrative functions. Such exercise was, however, indefinite and unreal for the direction of Indian policy had long passed from the Company to the Governor-General in India and the ministry in London. Pitt's India Bill of 1784 had created the Board of Control, as a department of the English Government to exercise political, military and financial superintendence over the British possessions in India. Nevertheless the changes in the scope and status of the Honourable East India Company though drastic had been gradual; and anomalous though its position was, the Company with its long history and traditions had come to be accepted as a permanent feature of English empire. It was not a trading company. It was distinct from the Crown. Looking back to-day it is difficult to realize a state of things where immense dominions, a vast army, and a navy, were, even in theory, governed by directors in the City with their traditions of ledgers and warrants, of manifests and scrip. It is as if in our time the administration of South Africa and the conduct of the great Boer War had been in the hands of the Worshipful Company of Fishmongers or Horners.

Briefly, what had been merely an association of merchant adventurers, timidly establishing factories on the coast line of Hindostan, had become the nominal ruler of provinces an emperor might have envied. Of the three major divisions of India Lower Bengal was as large as France. Bombay equalled Germany. Madras exceeded the United Kingdom in extent. Over and above these immense areas there was the Punjab, as large as Italy; the North-Western Provinces and Oudh almost equalled Norway; while the Native States in the aggregate contained an area not less than France, Germany and the United Kingdom combined. Over this vast conglomeration of territory John Company, directly or indirectly, ruled. Obviously, and in the nature of things, such a position was not likely to endure.

In an earlier chapter the growth of the great army of the Company has been sketched, and here it is necessary merely to give such figures and data as will elucidate the military position in 1857. At the close of Lord

Dalhousie's administration British India was held by some 233,000 Native and 45,000 British troops—roughly a proportion of 5 to 1. It was already clear to many of the men who knew India best that this was a dangerous state of things, and in the year of the Mutiny the proportion was more perilous still. Two British cavalry regiments had been withdrawn for service in the Crimea and had not been replaced, and four infantry regiments were absent with the Expeditionary Force in Persia. When the Mutiny broke out the relative numbers were 257,000 Native to 36,000 British soldiers. Actually, as well as relatively to the British troops—whether of Crown or Company—the sepoy army was an enormous force; and distinct from its master the East India Company in race, religion and character. The soldiers of that army may be regarded as divisible into Hindus and Mohammedans—the former patient and obedient but bound in the prejudices of caste; the latter restless, fanatical, imbued with the pride of a conquering race, and ready for any adventure that might come to hand.

The fidelity of this sepoy army was an article of faith in the board room of Leadenhall Street. That the sepoy would be true to his salt was there an axiom. Self-interest alone, it was urged, would prompt him to such course, and Macaulay in 1840 had written that, of all masters, the East India Company alone would not leave the native soldier to die of hunger in a ditch when he had ceased to be useful. The history of the Company's army was long. It had proud traditions. Trained and led by British officers it had taken a distinguished part in every Indian battle from Assaye to Gujerat. The glories of Arcot and of Plassey played around its bayonets. Its history was that of British India. Nevertheless, the record of the sepoy army was marred by incidents which might have convinced its masters that its loyalty could be over-estimated. Seven years after Plassey the senior regiment in the Company's service broke out in unprovoked rebellion; and thirty of its ringleaders were blown from guns in the presence of their comrades. In

1806 there was a serious mutiny at Vellore which was stamped out only by the prompt action of the English commandant at Arcot. In 1824 several regiments at Barrackpore refused to march when ordered on service to Burma. Offered the alternative of consenting to march or laying down their arms, they refused to do either. British guns opened fire at once. The regiments fled in panic, the surviving ringleaders were hanged, the most guilty regiment was disbanded, and its name erased from the Army List. In 1844 a succession of mutinies took place. The disasters of the Afghan War had shaken faith in British prestige; no less than seven native regiments broke out in open mutiny over real and fancied grievances. This time the old stern measures were not adopted to stamp out disobedience. Ten years earlier corporal punishment had been abolished in spite of the vehement protests of native officers, who prophesied that now the native army would no longer fear its masters and that mutiny would ensue. The view was shared by thoughtful Englishmen on the spot. Lord Ellenborough often stated that a general mutiny was the real danger to India. His warning was solemnly repeated by Sir Charles Napier. General Jacob went so far as to declare in *The Times* that mutiny was the normal condition of the army of Bengal.

A feature of the military system of the Company was the division of its armed forces into three separate armies of Bengal, Madras and Bombay. The discipline of the Bengal Army was bad. For many years prior to the great outbreak the Bengal sepoy had shewn an insubordinate spirit. The regimental officers had deteriorated. In various ways the Bengal Army differed from those of the other presidencies and in a manner which did not add to its military worth. It was peculiarly affected by the rigour of caste. The effeminate Bengali shrank from entering its ranks; and, recruited almost exclusively from the warlike population of the north-west, the Bengal Native Army was mainly composed of high caste men, brave in danger but averse from the performance of the humbler duties of a soldier. In the regiments of Madras and Bombay on the other hand men of different races met and fraternized and were more generally useful and amenable to control; and in those presidencies native opinion condoned the performance of services which would have shocked the scrupulous ritualists in Bengal. In the Bengal Army the code of caste counted for far more than the authority of military rank; it was no uncommon sight to see a low caste native officer, off parade, crouching in abject submission before the Brahmin recruit he was supposed to command. Such subservience to the dictates of religion was fatal to discipline. In the Bengal regiments sentries relieved each other when and how they pleased, and it was no uncommon occurrence for men to quit the ranks, while on the march, and scour the country round for plunder. In the words of Holmes, the historian of the Mutiny, it was a marvel how the troops of Bengal preserved even the semblance of an army.

In another respect the armies of Bengal and Madras differed widely from one another. The Madras sepoy was almost always a married man whose wife and children lived in the lines of his regiment. The Bengal sepoy was usually married too, but his wife and family lived in his own village. To the Madras sepoy the regiment was his home, the greater part of his interests lay there, and he was less liable to be moved by outside influences. The Bengal sepoy, on the other hand, was necessarily more in touch with the countryside and more liable, in consequence, to be influenced by native and anti-British sentiment. These social conditions tended to tranquillity and contentment amongst the Madras sepoys and to turbulence and unrest amongst the soldiers of Bengal. And though the effect of these conditions must not be pressed too far it is an historical fact that while nearly the whole of the Bengal Army mutinied the army of Madras remained staunchly loyal to its British rulers.

An ill-disciplined army is ever an army of grievances and to this rule the Bengal Army of 1857 was no exception. Some grievances were, however, real, for there were genuine causes for discontent with the British rule, which specially affected the class from which the Bengal sepoy was drawn. Chief among these was Dalhousie's policy of annexation, particularly of Oudh—the chief recruiting ground of the Bengal Army. This inflamed the natural patriotism of the Bengal soldier; and the religious opinions of Hindus were outraged by well-meant, but drastic social reforms. The Brahmins were offended by the prohibition of *suttee* and female infanticide, the execution of Brahmins for capital offences, the remarriage of widows and the spread of Western education and missionary effort. Owing to the system by which the Indian *sowar* provided his own horse and provender in return for a monthly wage the Indian cavalry were in debt, almost to a man, and therefore favoured any attempt to upset the existing regime. Another grievance came into prominence in 1856. It was necessary to relieve some Bengal regiments in Pegu. The overland route was impassable; there remained only passage oversea. The bulk of the Bengal Army was prohibited by the iron dictates of caste from crossing the black water. Exasperated by the absurdity of the situation Canning resolved to be master of his army. He introduced enlistment for General Service by which no recruit would be accepted unless willing to proceed wherever his services might be required. High caste striplings at once shrank from entering the service. But this was not all. Old sepoys now whispered to each other that the oath, voluntarily taken by new recruits, would be made binding on their services.

Where even Governors-General were providing sources of discontent it was not likely that the financial authorities would refrain from using their sting. As far back as 1828 the policy of " retrenchment " had been in the air. Cutting one's throat according to one's cloth was the order of the day and reduction of the officers' allowances of the Madras Army, though a gross injustice, at any rate reduced the debit side of the Leadenhall Street ledgers.

The officers contented themselves with a temperate but ineffectual protest ; and the sepoys, noting the futility of their efforts, despised their weakened authority. Since then another case, directly affecting the pay of the sepoys, had constantly arisen. When troops were sent into non-British territory for warlike or other operations an allowance was made to the native soldier to cover the increased cost of food and other incidental expenses. So soon as the operations were successful the usual outcry was made by the purse-holders of the East India Company against the great expense of the Native Army. The financial authorities would respond by suggesting that the occupied country should be proclaimed British territory forthwith. This would be done, and the stroke of the pen required for this territorial fiction would automatically deprive the troops of their extra pay, although the expenses they had to meet had suffered no corresponding diminution. Other instances could be cited but one will be sufficient to reveal the spirit which animated the military financial branch. When the 15th Bengal Infantry mutinied, the adjutant, at the risk of his life, tried to recall them to their duty. Some shots were fired and the adjutant's horse was killed under him. Compensation was applied for but this was refused on the grounds that, as the regiment had mutinied, it no longer existed and the necessity for the ex-adjutant to maintain a charger had therefore disappeared. Shortly before the Mutiny an ill-judged parsimony had dictated another measure, namely, that sepoys declared unfit for foreign service should no longer be allowed, as had been their right, to retire on pension but be utilized for the performance of cantonment duty.

In an army like that of Bengal, lacking in discipline and sullen with real and fancied grievances, it was easy for a feeling to spread that the star of the Company was on the wane and that there was truth in the old prophecy that the British would rule in India a bare century from Plassey. That battle had been fought in 1757 ; and now on the eve of its hundredth anniversary bazaar rumours of British reverses in the Crimea and in Persia increased the temptations for a rising against the dominant race. Merely a spark was required to set this mass of inflammatory material in full blaze and this was applied by an act of incredible folly on the part of the military authorities.

In 1857 the army in India was armed with a rifle described, indifferently, by historians of the Mutiny as the Minié or Enfield. The discrepancy is immaterial; probably the troops were at the time exchanging one pattern for the other; the important point is that both were muzzle-loaders. The ball ammunition was carried in rounds; but, differing from the cartridge of modern days, the propellant—black powder—was enclosed, not in a metal case, but in a paper bag affixed to the bullet and terminating in a stout " twist " at the lower end. For the double purpose of keeping the powder free from damp, and to facilitate the insertion of the bullet in the barrel, the paper envelope containing the powder, and the bullet itself, were coated with a lubricant of animal fat.

As it is doubtful whether one reader in a hundred has ever had to use a muzzle-loading rifle and as it was this question of loading which shook the whole of India, the operation is worth describing in detail. The essential point is that the soldier had to employ both knees and two hands, and even then a further effort was required. One hand held the cartridge, the rifle being meanwhile gripped between the knees, and the other hand was held, hollowed, to receive the powder which had to be poured loose into the barrel and then rammed home before the bullet was inserted. With both the soldier's hands already in use the bag or envelope, containing the powder, obviously required some other means to perforate it. This was supplied by the soldier's teeth. The end of the bag or envelope was bitten off, the powder then poured into the hollowed hand, and the operation of loading proceeded. Equally obvious is the fact that in biting the cartridge the soldier's lips must come in contact with the lubricating grease.

What any given cartridge was actually greased with is an open question, but it is clear that no attempt had been made to exclude the fat of cows or pigs—one animal a subject of veneration to the Hindu, the other an abomination to the disciples of Mahomet. To one soldier the use of the greased cartridge was sacrilegious and profane, to his comrade it was horrible defilement. A gross outrage had thus been perpetrated on the religious feelings of both Hindu and Mohammedan sepoys, and in the minds of both was the fixed idea that the Company intended to issue these cartridges for the sole purpose of destroying their caste and stamping out their religion.

So soon as the authorities realized the feelings of the soldiers they gave permission to the sepoys to use what fat they liked for greasing the cartridges. But it was too late. The Bengal Army was ripe for disorder. A series of minor mutinies occurred early in the year, culminating in a serious outbreak at Meerut on the 3rd May, 1857. Here the native regiments burned some bungalows and murdered their officers. The mutineers then made for Delhi unpursued by the British troops at Meerut, who were commanded by a general in his dotage. The seizure of the ancient Mogul capital with the great arsenal inside it was an immense moral and material asset to the rebels, more mutinies followed and the British were now faced with the task of saving India.

The narrative so far has been but introductory, to lead up to the great Central Indian campaign in which the 3rd Bombay Europeans performed their part; and it is merely necessary, from that point of view, to summarize the operations which preceded it. The military record of the war known generally as the Indian Mutiny divides itself naturally into two sharply defined sectors as regards time—the campaigns of 1857 and 1858 respectively, and these can be further split up into Northern and Southern operations. The first year consisted mainly of Northern operations, and these were focussed round the three centres of Delhi, Lucknow and Cawnpore. On the 8th June, just four weeks after it had been seized by the mutineers, a British force arrived before Delhi and laid siege to the city. Cawnpore and Lucknow were shortly afterwards invested by the rebels. The garrison of the former place was massacred on 27th June when embarking under promise of safe conduct and a further massacre of women and children took place on 15th July. The following day a relieving force under Havelock reached Cawnpore and moved on to the relief of Lucknow; but after a series of severe actions was forced to fall back on Cawnpore once again. A month later came the definite turn of the tide; Delhi was captured by assault on the 14th September and was completely occupied by British troops on the 20th. Five days later came the first relief of Lucknow by Havelock who remained with the Residency garrison. Meanwhile the new Commander-in-Chief, Sir Colin Campbell, had reached India and on the 27th October he left Calcutta for the front. The second relief of Lucknow soon followed, the garrison being successfully withdrawn. Thereafter ensued a kind of general interregnum, each side husbanding its strength and increasing its resources for the long and final struggle.

CHAPTER XVI

THE 3RD BOMBAY EUROPEANS—CENTRAL INDIA.

ALTHOUGH the close of the year had brought welcome and dearly won success to the British Army, the situation in India was as yet far from reassuring. Whole armies were still against us and entire kingdoms in insurrection. Oudh had still to be reduced to subjection; the evacuation of Lucknow furnished the rebels with a valuable rallying point; the ancient province of Behar in the north-west of Bengal was in revolt; in the vast country of Rohilcund the Khan of Bareilly held sway; in Central India the authority not only of the Company, but of the two friendly Mahratta chiefs Scindia and Holkar, had almost vanished; the Rani of Jhansi, to become known as "the best man on the side of the enemy," was in open rebellion. Nevertheless the campaign had come gradually to assume a different aspect and one favourable to the British. Exactly as proved to be the case in South Africa forty years later, the opening phase of the Mutiny threw the British largely on the defensive. Up to the beginning of 1858 the chief difficulty had been to protect isolated communities of the white race from revolted troops and other insurgents. The offensive was practicable only in rare cases, such as the attack on Delhi; the protection of cantonments and residencies was the chief concern. Now, however, the arrival of reinforcements turned the scale. By 1858 troops had been hurried from England or detained *en route* to China, and units from Mauritius, South Africa and Burma swelled the total. The British could now look forward to a vigorous policy of attack by which the rebel bands might be broken up, the ringleaders brought to justice, and the country restored to an orderly state.

In the closing months of 1857 a plan of campaign had been drawn up to effect this object with the augmented forces which would soon be to hand. Sir Colin Campbell was to proceed with the subjugation of the vast area between the Jumna and the Himalayas ; and, to obviate the risk of his being attacked by the formidable rebel contingent at Gwalior, a Bombay force was to march through the heart of Hindustan, restore order and distract the attention of the insurgents. This Central India Field Force was to be based on Mhow and was to be supported on its left by the Rajputana Field Force and on its right by a force brought up from Madras. The prime duty of the Central India Field Force—here it may be said that the 3rd Bombay European Regiment marched out of Poona on the 1st October, 1857, to take its place in it —was to capture Jhansi, the rebel stronghold of Central India. Thereafter it was to march to Calpee on the Jumna, where it was if possible to gain touch with the force under Sir Colin Campbell. As for the Madras column on the right it was to start from Jubbulpore and, marching across Bundelcund, was to make for Banda near the Jumna some ninety-five miles north-west of Allahabad.

The command of the Central India Force was given to Major-General Sir Hugh Rose, a brilliant, impulsive and daring soldier, then in his fifty-seventh year. Entering the Army in 1820 Rose received his first commission in the old 93rd and, on obtaining his majority, was appointed to the 92nd Gordon Highlanders with whom he served eleven years. In 1840 he was attached to Omar Pasha's Brigade in Syria in the operations against the Sultan's rebellious vassal Mehemet Ali, diplomatic service in Syria and Constantinople followed, and when war broke out with Russia in 1854 Rose was appointed commissioner at French General Headquarters in the Crimea with the rank of brigadier-general. In the Crimean War Rose gave proof of extraordinary intrepidity and daring, his name being submitted for the Victoria Cross for gallant conduct on three separate occasions ; but he was debarred by a regulation which expressly excluded general officers from this decoration. When the news of the Mutiny reached England the Duke of Cambridge gave Major-General Sir Hugh Rose the command of the Poona Division of the Bombay Army. Landing in India, for the first time, on the 19th September, 1857, Sir Hugh two months later assumed command of the Central India Field Force. A diplomat, a man of the world, a daring soldier, a strict military disciplinarian and a *beau sabreur* Sir Hugh Rose was to breathe new life into the Indian war. Devoid of the exaggerated cautiousness which gained for Colin Campbell the nickname of " Old *Khubadar* " from his soldiers, and immune from the lethargy which so often characterized Anglo-Indian generals, Rose possessed a range of character eminently adapted for the conduct of a campaign which was to throw many other operations of the Mutiny comparatively in the shade.

Sir Hugh Rose's force consisted of two mixed brigades, the whole amounting to some 4,500 men of whom the bulk were Native troops. He had many difficulties to contend with on assuming command. Supplies were and would be scarce, and there was very little transport. The batteries of artillery were incomplete in men and horses and the siege artillery was quite inadequate for the work which lay before it. Rose, however, was not the man to brook delay, and thanks to his energy and determination his force was ready and equipped in an astonishingly brief period. Now he was to shew a readiness to undertake responsibility and to diverge from the plan of campaign laid down for him to follow. In the town of Saugor, 120 miles from Sehore, a small force of Europeans was at the mercy of a thousand Bengal sepoys and about a hundred irregular cavalry ; these troops had so far behaved well but it was inadvisable, in the existing circumstances, to pin undue faith in their loyalty. Orders had consequently been issued for the relief of Saugor

Composition of Central India Field Force.

1st Brigade (Mhow).

Cavalry:
1 squadron H.M. 14th Light Dragoons.
1 troop 3rd Bombay Light Cavalry.
2 regiments Hyderabad Contingent.

Artillery:
3 batteries Field Artillery.

Engineers:
Detachment of 21st Company Royal Engineers.

Infantry:
2 companies H.M. 86th Regiment (later, whole regiment).
25th Bombay Native Infantry.
1 regiment Hyderabad Contingent.

2nd Brigade (Sehore).

Cavalry:
14th Light Dragoons (less 1 squadron).
3rd Bombay Light Cavalry (less 1 troop).
1 regiment Hyderabad Contingent.

Artillery:
1 battery Horse Artillery.
2 batteries Field Artillery.
Siege Train.

Engineers:
1 company Madras Sappers.
Detachment Bombay Sappers.

Infantry:
3rd Bombay European Regiment.
24th Bombay Native Infantry.
1 regiment Hyderabad Contingent.

and the task had been assigned to the Madras column which, as already stated, was to move northwards from Jubbulpore on the right of the Central India Field Force. Sir Hugh Rose, however, realized that the Madras column could not possibly carry out its task for at least two months, and he accordingly decided to march with a portion of his force to relieve the place. The 2nd Brigade, being the nearest to Saugor, was selected and the siege train was to accompany it. Meanwhile the 1st Brigade was to march up the Grand Trunk Road from Mhow and eventually reunite with the 2nd under the walls of Jhansi. In accordance with this plan the 1st Brigade marched out of Mhow on the 10th January, 1858, and six days later the 2nd Brigade, with Sir Hugh Rose at its head, left Sehore. It was a hazardous experiment in the circumstances for this right column to diverge out of its line of march, as far as Saugor, but Sir Hugh Rose rightly concluded that a bold course was necessary to deal with what might be a menace to the right flank of the 2nd Brigade.

It was while waiting at Sehore that the 3rd Bombay Europeans experienced, in a gruesome and unusual form, their first taste of war. There was a long list of rebels under guard in Sehore and these were brought to trial before a military court. No fewer than one hundred and forty-nine were found guilty, and those being days when the gloves were off, the culprits were sentenced to death by being shot. The duty of carrying out the extreme sentence of the law fell to the 3rd Europeans. A long trench was dug, and at evening just as the sun was setting the prisoners were brought out and ranged in one long line just in front of the trench. On the signal being given 150 of the 3rd Europeans opened fire and from the shambles only one rebel escaped. Ere the execution was well over the Indian darkness had come on and an officers' guard from the Regiment had to be posted over the horrid line of dead. So ended the debt against this rebellious contingent and few regiments can have had a grimmer initiation than the 3rd Bombay Europeans

On leaving Sehore on the 16th January the 2nd Brigade passed over a rich plateau, and, after ascending a range of hills saw below them the beautiful city of Bhopal. An astute and up-to-date old lady, the Begum of Bhopal welcomed the British force, furnished it with supplies, and placed at the disposal of Sir Hugh Rose 600 or 700 of her own troops. The Begum's capital was prosperous looking and well kept and her territory was a model principality; she even kept a private steamer on a large lake near the city—an unusual sight, to say the least of it, in the middle of India in 1857. On leaving Bhopal the country became very difficult and it was a severe task to transport the heavy guns of the siege train through jungle and nullahs and over rough ground and hills. Sir Hugh Rose now learned that the rebels had determined to defend the strong position of Rathghur in order to prevent the relief of Saugor. On the morning of the 24th the British force arrived before the former place and after some brisk skirmishing the enemy withdrew into their stronghold. The following day Sir Hugh Rose and his chief engineer, escorted by a small force of the 3rd Light Cavalry and 3rd Europeans, made a complete reconnaissance of the position with a view to its attack and capture.

The position was sufficiently formidable. The fort was situated on the spur of a long high hill. The west and south faces were almost perpendicular the rock being scarped and rendered stronger by a deep rapid river running close beneath. The north face looked along the densely jungled hill, and was strengthened by a deep ditch some twenty feet wide; the east face overlooked the town and the Saugor Road; on this face was the gateway, flanked by several square and round bastions. To the north side the wall was strengthened by an outwork looking like a second wall. Along each face were strong bastions commanding various points, and also at the four angles. Approach from the west and south was practically impossible and a matter of the utmost difficulty from the east or town side. Sir Hugh Rose now ordered an investment, as close as the great perimeter, the hills, the thick jungle and the deep and difficult river would allow. The south-west face was confided to the Bhopal force as this faced Bhopal territory. On the north and north-east were the 3rd Bombay Light Cavalry and the cavalry of the Hyderabad Contingent. The remainder of the force—including the 3rd Bombay Europeans—occupied the plain across which runs the Saugor Road.

Sir Hugh Rose decided to breach the eastern face with artillery and early on the morning of the 26th the 3rd Bombay Europeans, followed by howitzers, mortars and field guns, arrived at the jungle which lay at the foot of an open plateau where the breaching batteries were to be posted. A guide was procured to lead the force through the jungle but when well in the dense undergrowth the 3rd Bombay Europeans found themselves in the midst of fire. Before, behind and on both sides the jungle grass was ablaze, and, what with the heat of the sun and from the flames, " we were pretty nearly roasted." At this juncture the guide frankly acknowledged that he had lost his way—so like a guide—and there was nothing to be done but to fall back, and to do so quickly. Fortunately, however, the path was discovered and the force emerged at the ascent to the plateau. So rugged and steep was the slope that progress save in single file was impossible and the order " sappers to the front " was given so that a road might be made for the guns. These were man-handled up with incredible exertion, and under a galling fire from the enemy who, however, were soon being dealt with by a 6-pounder and some $5\frac{1}{2}$-inch mortars. In the afternoon two 18-pounders with elephant draught were brought up part of the hill, but so steep was the ascent in places that these mighty beasts quietly but firmly refused to go any further. What elephants failed to do the men of the 3rd Bombay Europeans could and would achieve. Anticipating the prowess in tug-of-war which was to distinguish their successors of the 2nd Leinster Regiment the Europeans unhooked the elephants and quickly had the guns in position.

The 28th January was the critical day of the siege. The enemy had been completely driven into the fort by the above operations which for convenience may be described as the right attack to distinguish it from a similar attempt on the left, also directed against the eastern face. By 8 a.m. on the 28th the sand-bag batteries of the left attack were completed and two 18-pounders and an 8-inch howitzer opened fire with considerable effect. Soon, however, a diversion occurred which threatened to be serious. From the thick jungle in rear of the British appeared a large body of armed rebels who advanced with flying colours intent on the relief of the place. These, however, were quickly dealt with and driven off and the attempt to raise the siege was thus defeated. Meanwhile artillery fire from besieged and besiegers went on all day. Every quarter of an hour the British pieces sent their projectiles into the fort. By 10 p.m. a breach appeared which seemed practicable. Everyone was convinced that the assault would take place next day, and the troops waited through the clear, cold moonlight night for the expected signal to advance.

When dawn broke the fort was strangely silent, and, curious to ascertain the reason, a couple of officers scrambled down the ditch and crept into the breach. Not a soul was to be seen in the fort. Meanwhile the 3rd Bombay Europeans had been excited witnesses of the movements of the pair and as soon as they disappeared in the breach the Regiment immediately rushed in a body down into the ditch. The commanding officer, Colonel Liddell, was furious at such irregular conduct and sent orders for the immediate return of the Regiment and for the two officers—a young gunner subaltern and a surgeon—to be placed in arrest. Not even the terrors of military command could, however, restrain the 3rd Europeans. They poured into the fort, and though the enemy had fled some stragglers remained who were quickly dealt with. Some grisly relics indicating atrocities on white women were discovered; but the Regiment in spite of this treated the women and numerous children of the rebels who were left there with the humanity which was to be expected from their discipline and faith. The words are those of Sir Hugh Rose himself who thus testified to the conduct of the Regiment in the first action of its career. How the garrison had escaped was at first a mystery, but investigation of a precipitous path, where no foothold could be seen, solved the problem. One or two mangled bodies at the foot told their tale. Some 500 rebels had thus made good their exit from the fort, had crossed a ford over the river near the Bhopal camp, and forced their way through the Bhopal lines into the jungle.

On the 30th January the sappers and miners occupied the fort and set about demolishing the defences. Meanwhile, during the forenoon spies brought in word that the rebels had taken up a fresh position about twelve miles off and posted themselves in a small fort. The place was Barodia on the left bank of the Beena—a strong village with a *gurrie* or small fort and surrounded by dense jungle on all sides. Hugh Rose was not the man to grant a defeated enemy time to recover breath and he at once decided to lead a detachment of the 2nd Brigade in person against Barodia. The force was a mixed column of the three arms with some sappers, the 3rd Europeans being the only complete unit in it. At midday on the 31st this column left Rathghur and, after a trying march, arrived at its objective. As it approached the River Beena the enemy were observed on the left well concealed by long grass and nullahs. The guns were immediately ordered into action and the 3rd Europeans advanced in skirmishing order on the flanks. The enemy meanwhile had opened a heavy rifle fire and our guns replied with round shot and grape—the range being too small for the effective use of shrapnel—while the 3rd Europeans maintained a steady discharge of musketry which kept down but did not completely check the fire of the enemy. The resistance of the enemy was most obstinate and the long and trying march, the heat and the thick jungle were taking the sting out of the attack.

Sir Hugh Rose saw that the moment had come for vigorous measures. He sent an order to Colonel Liddell directing him to charge the enemy's position with his regiment. The 3rd Europeans responded with alacrity and gallantly drove the rebels from the thick jungle and nullahs, although the Afghans and Pathan mercenaries fought with their accustomed courage, several of them, even when dying, springing from the ground and inflicting terrible wounds with their broadswords. The Regiment immediately took possession of the bank of the river commanding the ford to Barodia, which now for the first time became visible.

The charge of the 3rd Europeans brought about a rapid transformation in the fortunes of the day. The river line was now lost to the enemy, and Sir Hugh Rose immediately turned the advantage to account. He sent some troops of Native cavalry across the ford, protected by the 3rd Europeans, with orders for them to push on through the jungle and fall upon the enemy in the open beyond, while he himself, with a troop of the 14th Light Dragoons and four horse artillery guns, followed closely in rear. Behind these again came the rest of the force. The movement was completely successful; the Native cavalry charged and broke the enemy centre; and when the enemy fell back behind their guns to a strong position protected by jungle and a nullah our guns opened fire upon them. The rebels then retreated into the village and the jungle; the former was quickly seized and the little fort occupied by the 3rd Europeans but the bulk of the survivors fled into the jungle and made good their escape. It was inadvisable to attempt to follow them up as the camp at Rathghur with the siege train and a large quantity of stores, protected but by a small force, might easily be attacked. Sir Hugh, therefore, allowed his troops, who had been on duty for five days, but a brief halt and marched back by night to Rathghur which was reached at 2 a.m. on the 31st, after the column had been marching or fighting for fifteen hours.

Thus ended the action at Barodia, one which had cost

the rebels dear. Their losses according to their own statement were between four and five hundred; their ablest military leader was killed and the Rajah of Banpore was wounded. On the British side the casualties were 23, of which two were killed, one quarter of the wounded being from the 3rd Europeans. As shewing how closely the forces were engaged it may be mentioned that from the small staff attached to Sir Hugh Rose one officer was killed and four more wounded. Of the units engaged one was selected for mention by the commander in his despatch—the 3rd Europeans, of whom he wrote:—
" Although very young and now for the first time in the field the 3rd Europeans have qualified themselves for a career of honour; and Lieutenant-Colonel Liddell is sure to lead the way."

Though the escape of the mutineers was to be regretted, by the fall of Rathghur three most desirable objects were effected. The relief of Saugor was now feasible and the place was entered on 3rd February; the road from Indore was once more opened; and an immense quantity of supplies fell into the hands of the victors. Their casualties had been slight only 5 killed and 39 wounded, of which number 1 and 11 respectively were from the ranks of the 3rd Bombay Europeans. The operations of Rathghur will always be of interest to the 2nd Leinster Regiment as being the first action in which the Battalion was engaged. Fifteen names were mentioned in Sir Hugh Rose's official despatches upon the operations, 14 officers and 1 private. Included in the former were the names of Lieutenant-Colonel Liddell, and Captain Campbell; the private was Private Davies of the 3rd Bombay European Regiment.

Although Sir Hugh Rose had done much towards clearing off the rebels who threatened the advance of his right brigade on Jhansi there was still another menace to be dealt with. To the east about twenty miles away was the strong fortress of Garrakota perched on elevated ground and washed on three sides by the Sonar River and a tributary stream. Here the mutinous 51st and 52nd

Regiments of the Bengal Army, aided by large bodies of other rebels had ensconced themselves and preyed upon the countryside. Their stronghold was a formidable one and so well built were the works that, when it was besieged by a British force of 11,000 men with 28 siege guns in the Pindari War of 1818, no breach was made in the massive walls and the garrison had been allowed to march out with the honours of war. Rose, however, decided to tackle it at once and detailed a flying column of which the 3rd Europeans formed a part.

On 9th February the column started. The going was rough, through heavy jungle and it was only after a very fatiguing march of about 25 miles that the fort was sighted. Only one long rest had been allowed the troops—" to breakfast and hang a few more rebels." The day was well nigh spent when the column halted ; marching through the jungle, skirmishing, halting and stalking the enemy were most trying to the troops ; the heat had been almost unendurable ; and the constant checks overpowered many of the men.

As usual Sir Hugh Rose made an immediate and personal reconnaissance, and despite the darkness quickly resolved to drive the enemy from their position. The horse artillery batteries came into action and opened a brisk fire. But the mutinous sepoys were brave and hardy soldiers and, with bugles sounding the charge, they bore down upon the guns. The 3rd Europeans awaited the onrush steadily and drove back the attackers. The mutineers, however, quickly reformed and advanced with unabated vigour only to be beaten back once more and forced to retire within the fort. During the night a breaching battery was placed in position and all through the following day a 24-pounder howitzer was at work, in the end silencing the enemy's guns. At dawn on the 13th the enemy could be seen creeping from the fort and the 3rd Europeans were sent forward at once but when they entered the stronghold it was deserted. The cavalry with a couple of horse artillery guns were now sent in pursuit and after a rapid ride of twenty-five miles the rebels were overtaken and charged by the mounted troops, a great number of the fugitives being killed or captured. The flying column now withdrew and on the 17th February rejoined the 2nd Brigade at Saugor.

Now ensued a delay tantalizing indeed to a temperament as ardent as that of Sir Hugh Rose. He was eager to move on to Jhansi without respite. Convinced that the soundest plan was to strike another blow at the rebels before they had recovered their *moral* he was above all things anxious promptly to follow up his previous successes. But the supply and transport were inadequate for the long march north. With his usual energy Rose set about collecting transport and provisions; and sheep, goats, oxen, grain and flour, large supplies of tea, and soda water for the sick and wounded were collected with all possible speed. The siege train, too, was supplied with a large amount of ammunition and strengthened by the addition of other heavy guns, howitzers and large mortars. Many more elephants were obtained and particular attention was devoted to the ordnance and engineer parks.

The 3rd Europeans utilized the brief period of rest to change " their relaxing and highly injurious uniform " for one more suitable to the season and the country. In common with all the regiments, both of Crown and Company, they wore in India the thick red and blue uniform used at the time in England and other temperate climates. The system was highly injurious, and indeed the excessive mortality of British troops in India in those days was attributed in a great degree, by a medical writer, to the system by which European troops were year after year exposed to the effect of a tropical climate " trussed up in uniform suited only for England and the Polar regions." By some means or other the 3rd Europeans now obtained large supplies of stone-coloured cotton from which they fashioned for themselves blouses and trousers, and dyed their puggarees the same shade. The new kit seems to have been a complete novelty at the time and it is tempting to believe that the 3rd Europeans were the pioneers of the reform of dress in India and that they were the first

British regiment ever to fight in khaki. The new dress had two great advantages; it rendered the wearers of it almost invisible at a distance of about half a mile, but of far more service was the fact that the men could now bear considerably more fatigue with comparative comfort. Certain it is that the 3rd Europeans were so able to stand the terrific heat of the hot weather of 1858 as to gain for themselves the nickname of " Brassheads " throughout the army.

The Regiment, however, did not limit its activities to dress reform. There were creature comforts to be considered. The officers' mess laid in large stocks of beer, soda-water and wine. The Parsee shopkeepers at Saugor proved " invaluable friends," and if their friendship was purchased at a pretty stiff price they were positively philanthropic compared with the " business as usual " villains further north. The brief period of rest at Saugor came as a welcome interlude on the eve of a long and trying march north and everyone determined to make the most of it. The band played every evening. A few evening parties were got up. There was a picnic to the beautiful lake near the fort; there was actually a " ball " —at which five ladies were present; but of these, alas! " only two could waltz "; there was " music and feasting in all due order." Every anniversary was celebrated in the messes with wine and song—birthdays first, but these fitted in awkwardly; then promotion dates; then " dates of receipt of gratuity for service wounds," and when this desperate expedient was exhausted a wide catholicity ordained that " any other memorable occasion " must be well and duly honoured. Soon, however,—and all well knew it—these scenes would give place to roughing it, the night bivouac in the jungle, the hurried cup of tea and hard biscuit before the midnight march, and hard fighting in scorching weather and wasted country. The end to these good days came at two o'clock on the morning of the 27th, when the camp was roused and the 2nd Brigade of the Central India Field Force moved off over a belt of hills on its long march north.

P

CHAPTER XVII

THE 3RD BOMBAY EUROPEANS—CENTRAL INDIA (*Contd.*).

BRIEF as had been the period of rest enjoyed by the 2nd Brigade at Saugor it had been sufficient to allow the rebels to recover their *moral*; and they took advantage of the enforced delay to occupy certain forts and difficult passes which barred the way to Jhansi. Sir Hugh Rose was eager to reduce that powerful fortress and the importance of doing so had been emphasized in a letter from Sir Colin Campbell's chief of staff. Rose, however, required no spurring, and he had already resolved to settle the question of the passes without loss of time. These were three in number, Narut, Dhamoni and Mundinpur, of which the first named was the most difficult, and the enemy thinking that the British must endeavour to pass through it had increased its natural difficulties by barricading the roads with abatis and parapets of boulders. The Rajah of Banpore, an enterprising and courageous prince, defended this position with 8,000 to 10,000 men. The next most difficult pass was Dhamoni. Very little was known of the Pass of Mundinpur, about twenty miles from Narut, but a vague official map stated that it was "good for guns." Sir Hugh Rose had the pass reconnoitred and, acting on the report sent back, decided to make his main effort here while making a serious feint against the Pass of Narut. The 3rd Bombay Europeans were included in the main effort against Mundinpur and the story now turns to the doings of that force.

For five or six miles the column marched along the foot of a long range of hills and then began to enter upon the almost pathless route to the Mundinpur Pass. As the troops moved silently on to a horseshoe shaped plateau, with hills densely clad with jungle on both sides, a heavy artillery and infantry fire was opened upon the advanced guard. Quick as thought the officer with the artillery of the advanced guard galloped his guns into action, but before he could unlimber came under a very heavy musketry fire at short range. The fire was extremely hot, as rapid and hot as Sir Hugh Rose, with his experience of Syria and the Crimea, had ever witnessed—as he wrote later. The general himself had a spur shot off and his favourite charger wounded. Men were now dropping fast and Sir Hugh Rose instantly ordered a hundred of the infantry of the Hyderabad Contingent to charge into a glen which flanked the pass, and at the same time sent a company of the 3rd Europeans against the front. Not giving the enemy time to breathe he now directed a staff officer to take two more companies of the 3rd Europeans and to storm the heights. The companies rushed up the almost precipitous slopes and, quickly extending, drove the enemy from the first to the second line of hills. Meanwhile Lieutenant-Colonel Liddell had come up with the remainder of the Regiment, and Sir Hugh Rose at once sent him ahead to support the companies of the 3rd Europeans already in action and to drive the enemy successively from all the hills commanding the pass. This movement was skilfully performed and gained for the commanding officer another mention in despatches. By this success the day was won. The main body of the enemy, repulsed in flank and front, fell back to the village of Mundinpur situated at the end of a large lake along which ran the road to the pass. Behind the strong masonry dam the enemy had posted some guns which played on the 3rd Europeans as they advanced, but a few rounds from our artillery settled matters. Thus the Pass of Mundinpur was won; the British had got in rear of the enemy's strong line of defence; and the Pass of Narut considered by them as impregnable had been turned. Four men of the 3rd Europeans had been wounded in the action.

Then followed a march, through deserted country, and devoid of any incidents of battle. On the 9th March the 2nd Brigade started for Banpore. On the way some natives were met who stated that they had come from Chanderi, to the west, and had left the town on account of the fighting there taking place. This was good news for it shewed that the 1st Brigade was attacking the strong fortress there and that the union of the two wings of the Central India Field Force was now in sight. As the 3rd Europeans marched into their camping ground opposite Banpore they heard the sound of very heavy firing at regular intervals from the west ; this came from Chanderi and was the sound of the siege guns of the 1st Brigade in action against the place. While searching the deserted palace of the Rajah of Banpore Dr. Brown discovered in the piles of loot some of his own property—a camphor-wood box, instruments and some letters. Dr. Brown had been in the Gwalior Contingent and was stationed at Lalitpur when the Mutiny broke out ; forced to fly he had, with many others, made his way to Saugor where he had remained for nearly eight months till that place was relieved by the 2nd Brigade. He was now doing duty with the 3rd Europeans waiting an opportunity of being sent to Calcutta for passage to England to recruit his shattered health.

By this time the heat was becoming intense. Every day seemed hotter than the preceding one ; the marches began to tell upon the troops and cattle ; and the whole countryside was seared and barren. The roads were thick with dust, the wells almost dry, the trees—naked of leaves—gave no shade. The winds began to blow as if from the infernal regions, scorching up every pore of the body and making the eyes feel as if blistered. In the tents the thermometer stood at 110°. The chairs one sat on felt as if they had been baked ; tables and tent poles were too hot to touch without necessity. Cold water was a luxury. One cold drink in the evening was the dominant thought of all ; the necessity of having one's beer cooled became " one of the great and momentous objects of our existence." Each bottle was carefully enveloped in a wet cloth and either hung up in a breeze or assiduously fanned by a native servant. So great was the heat that many of the officers adopted the same process for themselves; they had their hair cropped to the bone and would frequently pour water on their skulls and, allowing it to evaporate, would thus gain some relief.

In these conditions the River Betwa was reached and on arrival it was found to be fordable with a gravel bottom. The whole of the 2nd Brigade crossed the river on the 17th of March, St. Patrick's Day, and encamped on the left or northern bank. On the same day the 1st Brigade to the west captured the strong fort of Chanderi, the 86th Royal County Downs fighting in a manner worthy of their reputation and of the day. Touch had now been gained between the two brigades and an important feature of the campaign had been brought about; the 1st and 2nd Brigades were about to unite under the walls of Jhansi. It is curious to note how Sir Hugh Rose's strategy anticipated that employed by von Moltke eight years later in the decisive campaign against Austria; there was the same concentric advance of two wings from a wide front with concentration on or near the ultimate battlefield; and the forcing of the passes by the 2nd Brigade is similar to the passage of the Crown Prince's army through the mountains. The same conditions, it may be mentioned, were reproduced in the advance of the Japanese into Manchuria in 1904. The comparisons must, of course, not be pressed too far; but the undoubted similarity which exists between the campaigns of Jhansi, Königgrätz, and Liao-yang will be of interest to those who maintain that strategy is eternal.

At 2 a.m. on the 21st March, 1858, the 2nd Brigade of the Central India Field Force marched upon Jhansi and arrived before the city about seven o'clock. The 3rd Europeans piled arms on the right of the road and gazed upon their immediate goal, the guilty city whose capture was to crown their long and arduous march.

The sight was a formidable one. Due north, dominating the landscape, or rising like an island from a sea of plain, was an immense granite rock crowned by the fort of Jhansi. The fort was massive, with walls of solid masonry in thickness from sixteen to twenty feet. The extensive and elaborate outworks of the same solid construction had front and flanking embrasures for artillery, as well as loopholes, of which there were in places five tiers, for musketry fire. On that side which faced the watchers were four strong looking bastions or towers, and overtopping these a tall white turret from which floated the red standard of the Rani. Along the east face of the fort were other towers overlooking the city which crouched north, east and in part to the south beneath the shadow of the stronghold. The city itself was surrounded by a fortified and massive wall some four and a half miles in circumference, from six to twelve feet thick, and varying in height from eighteen to thirty feet, with flanking batteries armed with artillery and with loopholes, and a banquette for infantry. The steepness of the rock on which stood the fort protected the place from the west, and the south face was protected by flanking fire from the city wall which, springing from the centre of the south side of the rock, ran due south terminating in a high mound. This mound was fortified by a strong circular bastion for five guns round part of which ran a ditch of solid masonry twelve feet deep, and fifteen feet across. On this strong point the 3rd Europeans could behold parties of the enemy feverishly working—not without good reason, for the mound commanded any possible approach from this quarter. Further to the east, along the city wall at a salient angle was another battery commanding the road by which the 3rd Europeans had marched. Two other bastions overlooked other points, and every tower of the fort had its guns pointing east, south and west. Between the city and where the 3rd Europeans stood lay the ruined British cantonments and beyond them, still nearer the city, were tamarind groves and temples with their gardens. It was in one of these, nine months earlier that the massacre of English men, women and children had taken place.

Even when the 1st Brigade should come to hand the total force at Sir Hugh Rose's disposal would be far too small to permit of a regular investment of the city; nevertheless he set about isolating the place as far as possible by utilizing his cavalry and some guns to form seven flying camps to cut off entrance into, or exit from, the fortress. Meanwhile it was clear that an attack upon Jhansi would present very serious difficulties. The fort could only be breached from the south but that face was protected by flanking fire from the city wall and mound. The city, therefore, must be taken before the fort, and as the mound was the key to the city its capture or demolition was first essential. On the 22nd March some hours after darkness had set in a battery was placed in position against the eastern wall to form subsequently what was known as the Right Attack; it was here that the 3rd Europeans were employed. During the night a mortar battery was thrown up by a little temple and heavy guns were placed in batteries on the rocky ridge about three hundred yards from the wall. When morning broke the enemy opened fire from the fort and from two or three batteries on the city wall; the Right Attack was not yet in a position to reply but by the evening of the 24th four batteries were in position and at daylight on the 25th they came into action and the bombardment of Jhansi began.

On the same day a siege train of the 1st Brigade arrived and steps were quickly taken to erect batteries for the Left Attack from a position south of the fort. The pieces employed in both these attacks were by no means contemptible in size, there being a 10-inch howitzer, an 8-inch howitzer, and several 10-inch mortars, the transport of which through the heart of Central India had been a fine achievement. Two 18-pounders were also used to dismantle the defences of the fort. On the morning of the 26th the guns of the Left Attack opened fire and did great execution against the fort, the mortars especially causing immense havoc. A prisoner had given away the position of a rebel magazine and this was blown up by our fire. The bombardment was now in full swing, right and left, and for eight days it endured, the enemy stubbornly maintaining the fight, their guns being admirably controlled by a Bengal artilleryman who could be plainly seen through a telescope directing the fire. Enemy guns were silenced but the damage was always swiftly repaired and the guns once more put in fighting condition. In places the parapets were swept away, but quickly native women would be at work repairing them. On the side of the attackers riflemen were posted to fire at the parapets; all the batteries had embrasures and loopholes protected by sandbags; and the snipers occupied also various advanced positions behind boulders of granite, cottage walls and temples, killing and wounding considerable numbers of the enemy. Nevertheless the rebels put up a most determined resistance; notwithstanding the damage done to the fort and to the wall their vigilance and determination to resist never abated; on the contrary, danger lent them fresh courage. It was now the hottest season of the year but the British gunners and riflemen stuck nobly to their task. The heat was terrible. All day from sunset to sunrise it was endured. Not a morsel of shade was to be had. And this among great boulders of granite, heated as with an internal fire, from which they never cooled and from which radiated a blinding glare all day long.

During the midday heat the enemy's guns were usually silent but in the afternoon a tremendous fire would be opened which severely tried the besiegers. In the cool of the evening a touch of romance was sometimes added to the scene, when the Rani of Jhansi accompanied by her ladies in rich attire, could be descried visiting the batteries of her soldiers. Once a bombardier of one of the breaching guns reported excitedly to Sir Hugh Rose that the queen and her ladies were covered by his gun, and asked permission to fire upon them. To the old *beau sabreur*, however, the proposal was distasteful and he replied that " such kind of warfare was not approved."

So well were the besieging batteries served that by the 30th March the gunners had dismantled many of the defences of the fort and city or disabled the enemy's guns; and a breach had been made in the city wall near the mound. Ammunition was, however, now beginning to run short, and the general made arrangements for the storming of Jhansi at the earliest possible opportunity. Moved by the representations of the senior artillery and engineer officers who thought that the breach was difficult and probably mined Sir Hugh Rose decided to have recourse to escalade, a risky expedient as he fully realized. Before, however, the matter could be put to the test a new peril had to be met.

For some time past Sir Hugh Rose had been receiving information to the effect that Tantia Topi, a relative of the notorious Nana Sahib, was assembling an army estimated at 20,000 to 25,000 men with 20 or 30 guns for the relief of Jhansi. With a view to securing early information of any possible advance of this force Sir Hugh had caused a signal station to be erected on one of the hills east of Jhansi which commanded an extensive view of the country north and east. During the afternoon of the 31st an aide-de-camp galloped up to Sir Hugh with the news that flags on the signal station denoted the approach of a large hostile force from the north. Imperturbable as usual the general rode off as if nothing had happened; nevertheless the situation was one of desperate gravity. His force was chained to a fortress garrisoned by 11,000 desperate men; now, behind that little force had appeared a relieving army 20,000 strong; made up of the fine Gwalior Contingent which had fought against Colin Campbell at Cawnpore and commanded by Tantia Topi the ablest general the Mutiny had produced. The force commanded by Sir Hugh Rose was far outmatched, so far as numbers were concerned, by either of those of the enemy; together, the garrison of Jhansi and Tantia Topi's relieving army outnumbered the Central India Field Force by about ten to one. Withdrawal was of course not to be thought of, and was indeed a physical impossibility. The only hope lay in preventing the garrison from making a sortie and at the same time, by taking every available man and gun, to make a desperate attempt to beat back the army of relief. This was the decision taken by Sir Hugh Rose. Meanwhile news of the impending danger had flown round the British camps, but was discounted by the fact that the morrow would be the 1st April. Many were convinced that the story was some humorist's attempt to observe the traditions of All Fools' Day.

Unfortunately, the news was true, and the force which the general was able to withdraw from the operations against the fortress was almost pathetically inadequate in numbers. Some 1,400 to 1,500 were all he could scrape together, and of these only some 500 were European infantry. The latter were drawn almost equally from H.M. 86th Regiment and the 3rd Bombay Europeans, the exact figures being 208 and 226 respectively from those units. No time had, fortunately, been lost in making these dispositions; indeed the 2nd Brigade had the evening before struck camp and moved out to a position commanding fords over the Betwa. Realizing, however, that the soundest strategy would be to lure the enemy on Sir Hugh Rose withdrew the brigade leaving merely outposts to observe the river. The ruse was successful, for during the evening of the 31st March Tantia Topi crossed the Betwa and took up a position in rear of the 2nd Brigade in which were the 3rd Europeans.

The scene was an extraordinary one. The 3rd Europeans found that they had now really two fronts—the fortress which they were preparing to take by storm and the relieving army now but a short distance away. Tantia Topi's troops lit great fires and could plainly be seen preparing their evening meal. All this was of course in full view of Jhansi and the garrison shouted with joy and fired a salvo as a salute. All night long tom-toms and bugles " went on at a Bedlam pace " and the rebel sharpshooters on the city wall kept up a hot fire for hours. And all night our batteries added to the din throwing shot and shell into the city; the camp fires of both sides burned, and so close were our pickets to those of the enemy that the latter would taunt our men threatening that on the morrow they would be sent to hell for "What is the handful before us to our thousands?"

The little British force had been drawn up in two lines, but the second, shortly after midnight, was sent off to the north to deal with an outflanking attempt by the enemy. This left but one line to deal with the main enemy advance. This line had its flanks protected by cavalry, with a few field and horse artillery guns; while the centre was formed by the 3rd Europeans, the 24th Bombay Native Infantry, and three heavy pieces. Between 4 and 5 a.m. while it was still dark the British picquets fell back upon the main body, and as dawn broke dense masses of rebel infantry accompanied by numerous batteries and hundreds of cavalry were seen pouring over a knoll with colours waving and drums beating. Then began the roar of heavy guns and field artillery, answered by those of the enemy, and from both lines a storm of rifle fire broke forth. Thick clouds of smoke now covered the plain but through them vast numbers of the enemy could be seen moving to outflank the left of the British line. At this juncture Sir Hugh Rose acted with the utmost promptitude, ordering the artillery on both flanks to advance outwards so as to bring enfilade fire upon the enemy. The guns on the right were the Eagle Troop of the Royal Horse Artillery and as it moved diagonally to take ground to the right a round shot broke the wheel of one of the guns, the mishap being greeted by a loud yell of triumph from the enemy. The other guns of the troop were, however, quickly in action as were those upon the left, and as the enemy began to waver under their fire the general ordered the 14th Light Dragoons to charge upon both flanks. Sir Hugh Rose himself rode at the head of Captain Need's troop which charged upon the left. Both attacks succeeded, throwing the whole of the enemy's first line into confusion and forcing it to retire. Then the infantry, taking advantage of the confusion, dashed forward with the bayonet and completed the rout.

At once Sir Hugh Rose moved forward all his cavalry and artillery in pursuit. Soon six of the enemy's guns were found; but, leaving these for the infantry who were following up in rear, the mounted troops kept after the rebels who were scattering in every direction. Many of the enemy, however, preserving their resolution and courage gathered in masses in ravines and nullahs and fought desperately to the end. Some of the skirmishers of the 3rd Europeans now came up, led by Lieutenant Armstrong, and reached a nullah held by a band of rebels who were inflicting heavy casualties. Roaring out " Who'll follow Bill Armstrong ? " the officer rushed down the nullah, followed immediately by the men, and in a moment the whole rebel band was bayoneted though not without loss on our side. It was here that a sergeant of horse artillery, after cutting down ten of the enemy, had been hewn in pieces by other rebels attacking him from behind. The rebel who had cut him down then ran " like a mad dog " amongst the 3rd Europeans till one of them shot him dead.

Lieutenant Armstrong was really Postmaster of the Central India Field Force; but what ordering of Providence relegated him to such a humdrum appointment is a mystery. He was constitutionally unable to keep out of a fight if one was going on anywhere near the field post office. Sir Hugh Rose was a strict disciplinarian with stern views as to an officer sticking to his own job, but he knew and respected a brave man when he saw him. He mentions Armstrong's dashing exploit in his despatch adding—not without dryness, " this officer is Postmaster of the Force but his zeal always leads him into action where he does good service on those occasions which require bold decision."

The battle was now practically over. The second line of Sir Hugh Rose's force which had been detached to the left to deal with an outflanking attack had been completely successful. Tantia Topi, seeing his front line broken and his right flank turned, determined to retreat across the Betwa. He caused the jungle to be set on fire and fell back rapidly covered by his guns. It now became a regular cavalry and horse artillery battle and in the pursuit all the enemy's guns, some twenty in number, were taken. By evening the rebel army of 20,000 men had been beaten and dispersed, a thousand of them lay dead upon the field, and the little victorious force was on its way back to camp. Considering the sum of the success achieved the losses on the British side were small—81, of whom 15 had been killed. In the 3rd Bombay Europeans two men had been killed and two non-commissioned officers and a private wounded.

CHAPTER XVIII

The 3rd Bombay Europeans—Central India (Continued)—The Storming of Jhansi.

IN Central India there was no such thing as withdrawing into rest areas; there was no fattening for the kill; and no elaborate system of training with life-size replicas of the objective to be gained. In 1858 the troops simply proceeded from one operation to another, and a long day's fighting under a burning sun against immensely superior numbers of the enemy was merely an interlude in the real task in hand, the storming of the fortress.

The assault was fixed for the morning of the 3rd April and the order to attack was communicated secretly to commanding officers. The business was to consist of two distinct but co-ordinated operations. On the left the Left Attack was to storm the breach at the mound with its main body, while a detachment was to escalade the Rocket Tower—and the low curtain immediately right of it—which was situated between the mound and the south face of the fort. The Right Attack was to carry out its mission entirely by escalade its objective being the city wall right and left of the Orcha Gate, the escalading force being for the purpose divided into two columns, with a reserve of 100 men. In each case—both in the Right and Left Attack—the initial capture of the city wall was entrusted to European troops, in the former to the 3rd Bombay Europeans and in the latter to H.M. 86th Regiment. That is so far as the infantry were concerned. In both attacks the engineers, true to their noble traditions of pride of place in the storming of a fortress, did magnificent service in the forefront of the fight.

About two o'clock on the morning of the 3rd April the 3rd Europeans were quietly roused and ordered to prepare for immediate assault. An hour later the Regiment moved off from its camp in two columns, the right under Lieutenant-Colonel Liddell, the left commanded by Captain Robison, a hundred men remaining as a reserve under the orders of the commander of the 2nd Brigade. In dead silence the columns moved to the positions marked out for them whence operations should begin. The moon was very bright; too light indeed for the work which was to depend for much of its success upon surprise; and the Regiment waited in suspense, for dawn was fast approaching. At last three guns were heard upon the western side—the preconcerted signal. Immediately the order to advance was given in a whisper. The ladders were hoisted on the shoulders of the sappers who moved off preceded by covering parties from the 3rd Europeans and Hyderabad Infantry.

So soon as the covering parties drew near the wall the enemy's bugles sounded and at once a fire of indescribable fierceness opened on them both from the wall itself and from those towers of the fort which commanded this portion of the front. For a time it seemed a veritable sheet of fire out of which burst a storm of bullets, rockets and round shot. The columns, loudly cheering, doubled across the intervening space, under this fire, but when the wall was reached and the ladders planted the resistance of the enemy increased. The crash of musketry, with the roar of the guns and the hissing and bursting of rockets and infernal machines, seemed like pandemonium let loose, and the rebels hurled down stones, blocks of wood and even trees on the heads of the stormers below.

The portion of the wall to be escaladed by the 3rd Europeans was the highest in the whole *enceinte*, the rampart here being some 25 to 30 feet from the ground. And now a serious discovery was made. Some of the ladders were found to be too short. In the confusion which followed many of the stormers fell and the living were forced to seek such shelter as could be found immediately at hand. The chief engineer of the Right Attack proceeded in hot haste to the brigadier to ask for reinforcements and was given the hundred of the 3rd Europeans, till then with the reserve, who apparently had with them a reserve of ladders as well. The stormers thus reinforced returned to the assault with alacrity and once more rushed for the wall. Up one ladder dashed Lieutenant Dick of the Bombay Engineers calling on the 3rd Europeans to follow. He fell from the wall bayoneted and shot dead. But now with the crush of men crowding on the ladders these proved unequal to the strain. Lieutenant Meiklejohn another engineer officer and a man of the 3rd Europeans reached the summit of the wall when the ladder broke from the weight upon it and, left alone upon the wall, they were literally cut to pieces. Other ladders, too, collapsed. In Captain Robison's left column one gave way while Corporal Hand and Privates Rogers and Archibald of the Grenadier Company; Private Drummond of No. 1; and Private Doran of No. 3 Company, were fighting most gallantly at the top. In the right column Lieutenant-Colonel Liddell found his ladders of no use and for a moment essayed to force a way through the wall. Calling Lieutenant Goodfellow of the Bombay Engineers to him he ordered that officer to try a bag of powder at the postern. Assisted by a few native sappers the gallant young officer carried it to the postern gate, fired it and out flew the door in fragments. The 3rd Europeans rushed through the cloud of smoke to force an entrance, but without success; the gateway was filled with huge blocks of masonry and stone.

The Right Attack had now, owing to the failure of the ladders, been brought for the moment to a standstill, and the 3rd Europeans were withdrawn from the heavy fire to which they were thus unnecessarily exposed. The movement was made with great precision and coolness, and Ensign Newport, assisted by Corporal Hand and Private Gillman, carried off the body of Lieutenant Fox of the Madras Sappers and Miners, through the hottest of the fire. But just at this time victorious shouts were heard upon the left. These were from the 86th Regiment of the Left Attack, who without difficulty or loss had forced the breach and by dashing gallantry had escaladed the wall hard by the Rocket Tower. An engineer officer reported the passage of the breach to Captain Robison who it will be remembered was commanding the left column of the 3rd Europeans in the Right Attack. That officer at once doubled round with some of his column to the breach, where he effected an entrance and, with the 86th Regiment, cleared the ramparts so as to enable the remainder of the 3rd Europeans to scale the wall. It is clear, however, from the evidence of an eye-witness of the Right Attack that Lieutenant-Colonel Liddell's column on the right had already forced its way to the ramparts. Describing the situation of the 3rd Europeans of that column at the moment the shouts of victory were heard upon the left he says that "in streams from some eight ladders they at length gained a footing upon the ramparts dealing death among the enemy, who still contested every point of the attack in overwhelming numbers." The same writer—Surgeon Lowe of the 2nd Brigade—also mentions the two streams of stormers meeting on the wall when "the air resounded with yells and huzzas of victory." The two tributary streams which now formed one attacking flood through the city were the 86th Regiment (reinforced by Captain Robison's men of the 3rd Europeans who had doubled round to the breach) on the one hand; and, on the other, the right column of the 3rd Europeans, under Lieutenant-Colonel Liddell which had now gained the top.

The Postmaster of the Central India Field Force had taken a day off to enjoy the pleasure of being in the thick of things at the Betwa and might now be expected to deal with accumulated arrears of work. But with the escalade of a fortress going on just outside his office not all the peremptory provisions of the Standing Orders of the Central India Field Force nor all the postal regulations in Asia could keep Lieutenant Armstrong at his desk.

In the darkness of the assembly and preliminary march he seems to have escaped observation, but later when the 100 Europeans from the reserve were sent up the officer in command met a *dhooli* being carried back. Enquiring of the soldier in charge as to the occupant he was told " Sure it's poor Mr. Armstrong, he's gone at last." The officer passed on, but a moment later he heard a great commotion behind and on looking back saw a figure covered with blood and dirt emerge violently from the *dhooli* and with blood curdling oaths in Hindi and English proceed to belabour the native bearers for all he was worth. It was Bill Armstrong who had slipped into one of the columns, taken part in the first abortive rush, had been blow up and then hit on the head with a brick. Imagining probably that he was being taken back to the field post office he shewed considerable resentment at this curtailment of his liberty. Sir Hugh Rose, after this, seems to have abandoned all hope of securing an efficient postal service for his force and started recommending Armstrong for the Victoria Cross instead. This he did three times. They were a well matched pair, Major-General Sir Hugh Rose and Lieutenant Armstrong —each thrice recommended for this high distinction from which each was debarred by what seems unnecessary red tape.

So soon as the 3rd Europeans had scaled the city wall they pushed on quickly towards the palace which was also the goal of the Left Attack which had entered by the breach, and by escalade at the Rocket Tower. It was while fighting their way through the streets that the 3rd Europeans were discovered by Sir Hugh Rose who, anxious at having received no news of the Right Attack, had moved rapidly along the ramparts from the breach until he came across the Regiment in the south-eastern portion of the city. Street fighting of a savage kind was now in progress, and the rebels kept up a deadly fire from some of the houses. Soon the houses on both sides of the street were ablaze, and the heat, both from the sun and the flames, was appalling. The assailants burst

open the doors ; the contest was furious, but it was short.
Heaps of dead lay in the streets which were red with
blood and in the struggle many of the 3rd Europeans
fell. So the way was won to the palace where the
Regiment joined with the 86th which had fought its
way from the breach and the Rocket Tower. The gateway to the palace was immediately commanded by the
fort into which the enemy had fled and from which they
kept up a murderous fire ; and now the rebels blew up
some powder in the palace from which several of the
3rd Europeans suffered agonizing wounds.

Once in the palace the wearied soldiers sought a brief
rest. Some threw themselves exhausted on the ground ;
others wrapped two or three puggarees round their heads
as a protection against the heat ; the wounded lay
groaning from their wounds or the burns caused by the
explosion. Sir Hugh Rose now issued orders for a line
to be taken up across the city and through the palace
and the 3rd Europeans moved out accordingly to the
north-east. When the movement was completed the
right flank of the Regiment rested on the Banaghong
gate and their left on the palace, part of the Regiment
being in the building itself. The 86th Regiment likewise held a portion of the palace and continued the line
thence to the mound. A great wedge of British troops
had thus been thrust into Jhansi, the apex being the
palace and the base that portion of the city wall between
the mound and the Banaghong gate. The two regiments
at once occupied with picquets commanding houses to
their front and for hours the work of clearing the buildings
went on.

Now, in the palace it was found that forty or fifty
Afghan troopers, the chosen bodyguard of the Rani,
were occupying the stables, and a force consisting of the
Grenadier Company of the 3rd Europeans and some of the
86th was sent to deal with them. The British soldiers
rushed in under a heavy fire and immediately a bloody
hand-to-hand struggle ensued from which many of the
86th and 3rd Europeans came staggering out with

frightful wounds. Driven from the stables by the bayonet the Afghans retreated behind the houses, still firing or slashing with their swords held in both hands till they were overcome. A party of them, in a room off the stables which was on fire, held out till they were half burnt; their clothes in flames they rushed out hacking at their assailants and guarding their heads with their shields. In the end all the Afghans were killed but not without casualties on our side, and here fell wounded Captain Sandwith of the Regiment who "commanded with spirit the Europeans on this occasion."

In this fighting the soldiers of the 86th and the 3rd Europeans captured the Rani's standard, the colours of her bodyguard, three kettle-drums, some horses and a silken Union Jack which had been given to the grandfather of the Rani's husband with permission to have it carried before him—a reward for fidelity awarded to no other Indian prince. Now when it was discovered the soldiers clamoured to Sir Hugh Rose for permission to hoist it. The general at once consented; and the adjutant of the 86th raced to the top of the palace running up the flag under a furious fire from the fort. Meanwhile Sir Hugh Rose had been informed that a body of 400 rebels were endeavouring to escape through the investing line, but had been driven back and were holding out on a rocky hill west of the fort. A force was at once sent from the camps of the two brigades and the rebels were cut up. Here the Rani's father was wounded; taken prisoner a few days later he was hanged in the garden where British women and children had been slain.

All next day fighting in the streets went on and the Central India Field Force lost many men, but eventually a combined movement of the troops wrested the whole of the city from the enemy; the arsenal and two magazines being gained in this operation. The fort, however, still remained but on the morning of the 5th its guns were silent. Lieutenant Baigrie of the 3rd Europeans moved cautiously up to the fort gate, and to his surprise found it open. He then crept from gate to gate peering everywhere but seeing no one, and in a few minutes found himself in possession of the fort of Jhansi. Detachments from the 86th and 3rd Europeans were immediately sent forward and entered the stronghold.

The signal station at this time was flying a signal " enemy escaping to the north-east " and all available cavalry were at once sent in pursuit. The night before the Rani's horse had been brought into the fort ditch. She had been let down from a window of her turret and accompanied by 300 Afghans and 25 troopers she made her escape. The cavalry came up with the Rani and her escort some twenty miles out and a hot chase ensued, a subaltern running her to view until he fell from his horse severely wounded and his quarry escaped. The Rani's flight had been the signal for a general retreat of the rebels. The outskirts of the city were scoured by cavalry and infantry of the Central India Field Force; in one patrol a party of the 14th Light Dragoons killed 200. The rebels, who were chiefly Afghans and Pathans, sold their lives as dearly as they could, fighting desperately to the last. A band of forty desperadoes barricaded themselves in a spacious house and resisted the attacking infantry. Even when siege pieces were brought into action the rebels continued to resist in the passages and vaults, but in the end they were exterminated to a man and the last flickering flame of rebel effort was stamped out.

Thus ended the storm of Jhansi. The capture of the fortress is universally regarded as one of the most brilliant feats in the Mutiny campaigns. The Central India Field Force had been contending against an enemy more than double its number, posted behind a strong rampart or in a massive fort—an enemy who, when the city wall had been surmounted, fought desperately from house to house and later in the outskirts of the city beyond the wall. The strain upon the attackers had been enormous. The investing cavalry had been continuously on duty for seventeen days; the men never took off their clothes; and the horses remained saddled up and bridled all night long. A handful of infantry in broad daylight scaled the lofty walls and after four days of fighting captured the city—and all this under a terrible Indian sun which struck down many men, and in spite of an attempted relief by a powerful rebel army. In killed alone the rebels lost over 5,000, and 35 guns fell into British hands. The casualties on the victor's side amounted to some 320 of whom 68 perished. In the 3rd Europeans 12 were killed and 42 wounded. A survey of the casualty rolls shews that the Regiment even in 1858 was very largely Irish in composition, such names as Doran, Feeney, Nolan, McGuinness, Murphy (three of them), Brady, Roach, Conroy, Moriarty, Byrne, McEvoy, etc., telling of connexion with the Emerald Isle. Five officers of the Regiment were awarded a mention—Lieutenant-Colonel Liddell, Captain Sandwith, Captain Robison, Lieutenant Park, and Ensign Newport, and the names of eight non-commissioned officers and men were brought to the Major-General's notice by the commander of the 2nd Brigade. In his despatch Sir Hugh Rose expressly exonerates the 3rd Bombay Europeans from all blame for the initial check in the escalade and states that the Regiment "did its duty as it has always done."

CHAPTER XIX

The 3rd Bombay Europeans—Central India (*Continued*).

ALTHOUGH the capture of Jhansi and the slaughter of over 5,000 of its garrison was a memorable achievement there was still much for the Central India Field Force to do. Its goal was the Jumna, where it was to get in touch with Sir Colin Campbell's force operating beyond that river, and on the right bank of the Jumna was the well-fortified arsenal of Calpee, full of arms and ammunition and still in rebel hands. It was of prime necessity to capture that strategic point and Sir Hugh Rose was not the man unduly to delay, but a further advance was for the moment impossible. Food, transport and ammunition were lacking, and for nearly three weeks Sir Hugh had perforce to remain at Jhansi collecting these essentials. Finally on the 25th April he set out for the Jumna but the 3rd Europeans were not destined as a Regiment to share in the remainder of the campaign. Even at the expense of crippling the Central India Field Force it was imperative to leave a mixed force at Jhansi so as to prevent it once more forming a rallying point for the mutineers. Of this force the headquarter wing of the 3rd Europeans formed a part and the whole was placed under Lieutenant-Colonel Liddell, the commanding officer of the Regiment, "one of the best of my superior officers," to use Sir Hugh Rose's own words.

Meanwhile the left wing marched on with Rose over depressing flat country where the wells were almost dry and the water filthy. The heat became more and more oppressive and the cattle began to emaciate and die. A speedy arrival at Calpee was now a paramount necessity for it was quite evident that unless the troops could gain the shelter of buildings during the day, and be sure of an adequate supply of water, the sun would prove a deadlier enemy than even the rebels. Tantia Topi realized this to the full. Leaving merely a small garrison at Calpee he had marched with the remainder to Koonch where he proposed to dispute the road from Jhansi to the Jumna. Koonch was surrounded by woods, gardens and temples with high walls and these were supplemented by entrenchments which Tantia Topi had caused to be thrown up, his policy being to compel the British force to expose itself to the blaze of the Indian sun in its efforts against the place. Against another commander such a policy might have had its effect and cautious operations against Koonch might have worn down the attackers. To a man of Sir Hugh Rose's stamp the action of Tantia Topi was merely an extra inducement to go all out for a rapid victory.

Acting on his usual principle that nothing was so likely to disconcert the rebels as an attack on a flank with a threat against their line of retreat Sir Hugh Rose decided to make a long flank march to his left; but before doing this had to deal with an obstruction in that quarter. This was the strong fort of Lohari held by about 500 rebels and situated some six or seven miles from his left flank. The general now sent a force under Major Gall of the 14th Light Dragoons, and consisting of the wing of the 3rd Europeans, some artillery and light dragoons to take it. But the fort was too strong to batter down with field artillery, so the 3rd Europeans prepared to storm it while the dragoons formed a ring round it to prevent the escape of the garrison. A curious incident now occurred. Major Gall "wished to lead the men into the fort, but was pulled back by some of the 3rd Europeans, having first received some ugly blows on the head with stones." It is not mentioned who threw the stones but the sentence —an extract from a letter of an officer of another unit in the action—seems to infer that they came from the 3rd Europeans. If so, the reason is not difficult to understand. The 3rd Europeans had with persistence and bravery made their way up to the third and inner door of the fort, and in the final rush wanted nothing better than to be led by their own officers.

The initial advance had been made by two companies under as good a leader as there was in India—Bill Armstrong. Whether he had been permanently relieved of his duties as Postmaster of the Force, or was simply having another day off is not clear; but at any rate there he was at Lohari at the head of two companies, about to storm a fort—and what more could a Postmaster want? Taking advantage of a sort of guard house which afforded some cover the leading company forced two outer doors leading to the fort but was held up by a difficult double gate with a small postern at an angle. The gate must first of all be demolished and here the ingenuity of a young sapper officer—Lieutenant Bonus—was equal to the test. Procuring a blacksmith's bellows from the village he filled it with powder, laid it against the gate and the explosion blew out the entrance to the fort.

Before the smoke had cleared away the 3rd Europeans burst in, the first man through being a bugler, Private Whirlpool, who just forestalled two officers, Newport and Donne. Now appeared a lane leading to the fort proper and either side of this lane was fitted with scaffolding lined by rebel swordsmen. The bugler was cut down at once and immediately the two officers stood over him and tried to get him away but both fell slashed with sword cuts. However, the remainder of the 3rd Europeans were pressing on from behind and in a moment had swept their way into the fort. Then there was desperate work. Every male in the fort was put to death. One rebel who endeavoured to escape with his wife, finding salvation impossible, smote off the woman's head with one blow and then cut his own throat. Thus the fort of Lohari was won by an operation in which " the 3rd Europeans particularly distinguished themselves."

Whirlpool, when he was brought out, was found to have received no less than nineteen wounds. "Take care, lads" he said when they put him into a *dhooli* " and don't shake my head, or else it'll come off." Sir Hugh Rose saw Private Whirlpool when visiting the hospital and was so struck with the story of his gallantry that he promised if the bugler survived to recommend him for the Victoria Cross. Whirlpool pulled through and lived to wear the Cross for many years. Sir Hugh Rose always thought that the name Whirlpool was assumed and afterwards learnt that the man was a son of Mr. Conker the postmaster of Dundalk. When the general was later in command in Ireland the parents came to thank him for his kindness to their son who was then in New South Wales where he ultimately died. There must be some martial magic compounded in post offices whether at home or in the field; in the 3rd Europeans the son of a country postmaster won the Cross and the chief postal official in the Central India Field Force was recommended for it three times.

In the evening orders were issued to march on Koonch about nine miles away. The men were worn out by their exertions in the frightful heat; many fell out and had to be carried in *dhoolies*. Shortly after daybreak on the 7th the left of Sir Hugh Rose's force was on the north-west of Koonch in rear of the fort and town, his right was in front of the village of Oomree, while the centre—in which was the wing of the 3rd Europeans and some of the 71st Regiment who had now joined the force—was astride the Jhansi road. After the troops had rested the artillery opened fire and the infantry prepared to storm the fort. A wing of the 86th Regiment and the 25th Bombay Native Infantry were thrown into skirmishing order supported by detachments of artillery and cavalry, the remainder of the attacking force being formed into a second line. The promptitude of Sir Hugh Rose and the gallantry of the 86th cut the rebel line in two. The enemy seeing their defence thus broken retired in masses towards Calpee for some time preserving admirable order;

but so fierce was the cavalry pursuit that the rebels eventually became a helpless mass losing in the retreat some 600 men and 15 guns.

Through some misunderstanding, apparently, the British centre was kept back with the result that the wing of the 3rd Europeans although it was engaged in the opening stages had no opportunity of intervening with effect at the close. But they suffered to the full the terrible conditions in which the battle was fought. The temperature rose to 115° in the shade. Men of the 71st and the 3rd Europeans dropped in numbers struck down by the sun. While the action was going on *dhooli* after *dhooli* was brought into the field hospital with officers and men from the front suffering from sunstroke ; some dead, others prostrated, some laughing and sobbing in delirium. The dreadful heat paralysed everyone. Eleven were thus killed outright. Four times had Sir Hugh Rose to dismount, unable to remain in the saddle in the blazing sun ; four times his doctor poured water over him, gave him restoratives and set him on his horse again. That is how the dandy of Pall Mall and London drawing rooms fought his way from Indore to the Jumna.

It will be remembered that the Central India Field Force was to be supported by the Rajputana Field Force on the left and a Madras column starting from Jubbulpore on the right. The former had been co-operating strategically for some time but the Madras column was not in a position to render any aid in the advance on Calpee and the tactical operations against the fortress had to be carried out by the Central India Field Force alone. For a moment the rebels, disconcerted by their defeat at Koonch and furious at the precipitate flight of Tantia Topi, had decided not to contest Calpee ; but the fiery energy of the Rani of Jhansi and the moral effect of the presence of a nephew of Nana Sahib encouraged the insurgents to hold the stronghold to the last. Calpee was indeed a formidable obstacle. It stood on a steep and lofty rock springing from the southern bank of the Jumna and was protected in front by no less than five lines of defence—a chain of ravines, the tower, eighty-four temples of solid masonry, and, on the outside, a line of entrenchments. Confident that the British would advance along the main road the rebels had fortified it but Sir Hugh Rose had no intention of fulfilling their expectations. He had learned that a force under Colonel Maxwell had been detached by Sir Colin Campbell to co-operate with him and received information that this force was on the northern bank of the Jumna opposite Galowlee about six miles south-east of Calpee. Rose accordingly struck off the main road and marched for Galowlee which he reached on the 15th May, a manœuvre which placed him in position to turn the defences of Calpee and virtually effected a union with Sir Colin Campbell's army. Some delay had been caused in moving the force on a broad front owing to difficulty as regards water and the 2nd Brigade was, therefore, somewhat in rear. On the 15th its rearguard, in which were about 100 of the 3rd Europeans under Lieutenant Mackintosh, was smartly attacked by about 5,000 sepoys of whom nearly a quarter were cavalry. The Regiment did good service in this action and the long train of baggage was got safely through, Ensign Mackintosh being mentioned in despatches for his good work on this occasion.

The troops were now fearfully exhausted. Sickness was rife. The 2nd Brigade in the affair just described had marched upwards of *twenty miles* in the sun. Scores of dead animals were passed which had dropped dead from the heat; but there was no decomposition going on, they were drying up like mummies. Even the Native Infantry, trussed up like everyone else—except the 3rd Europeans—in red cloth coats, fell out by dozens and lay gasping in any morsel of shade. Roughly half of the field force was incapacitated; all were more or less ailing. In one regiment of Native Infantry of 400 men 200 fell out in one day from the effects of the sun. The rebel leaders knowing what their opponents were suffering issued an order that the European infidels were never to be attacked before ten o'clock in the morning.

Out of 36 men of the 14th Light Dragoons forming part of a forage escort seventeen collapsed after only two hours' exposure to the sun. The hospital tents, where the temperature ranged from 109° to 117° and seldom fell below 100° at night, were crowded. On the 19th May there were 310 Europeans in hospital. During the week 21 had died of sunstroke. There was scarcely an officer on the staff fit for duty. The Superintending Surgeon reported officially that if the operations against Calpee were to be protracted the whole force might be stricken down. Yet " these noble soldiers, whose successes were never chequered by a reverse, with a discipline which was as enduring as their courage, never proffered one complaint. They fell in their ranks struck down by the sun and exhausted by fatigue; but they would not increase the anxieties of their general or belie their devotion by a complaint." It was a hard school in which the old 3rd Bombay Europeans learned their trade of war but at least they received a generous meed of praise from the master.

The battle which led to the fall of Calpee is difficult to disentangle from the involved and belated despatch in which Sir Hugh Rose eventually reported it; but the course of operations will be readily understood if in the first place a map is referred to and in the second place four facts be borne in mind. These facts are: Sir Hugh Rose intended to take the initiative so as not to expose his troops to the sun longer than was absolutely necessary but was forestalled by the rebels who advanced against him. Secondly, his army lay between the river near Galowlee and the Calpee-Jhansi Road, the right flank being posted perpendicularly to the Jumna and facing some blind ravines; and it was here that the wing of the 3rd Europeans was posted. Thirdly, the proposed operations against the fortress were to be supported by artillery fire from batteries erected by Colonel Maxwell on the northern bank. And fourthly, some reinforcements consisting of some companies of the 88th Regiment, a camel corps and some Sikh infantry had been transferred from Colonel Maxwell's detachment to the Central India Field Force.

Sir Hugh Rose intended to deliver his blow on the 23rd May, but two days earlier spies brought him word that the rebels had determined to attack him the following morning, and had sworn on the sacred waters of the Jumna to destroy the British force or die. Accordingly on the morning of the 22nd a large force was observed marching across the plain as though to turn the British left. Shortly afterwards some rebel guns opened fire upon the centre and a brisk artillery duel went on for some time. So far there was no sign of life in the ravines opposite the 3rd Europeans on the right; but Sir Hugh with the intuition of a born commander divined that the advance of the enemy so far was largely a feint against his left and centre and that the main effort would be delivered against his right flank. The quickest way to ascertain whether this was really so was to send a force to explore the ravines running down to the Jumna and a company of the 3rd Europeans was sent forward for the purpose. Hugh Rose's conjecture was well founded; the ravines proved to be a veritable hornet's nest; immediately a roar of artillery and rifle fire broke out and the ravines were enveloped in fire and smoke. Next, the enemy roused from his lair pressed forward out of the ravines making a serious attack on the British right flank.

Battle was now joined all along the line. Feints and real thrusts were all one. There was a determined attack against the centre but Rose could meet that. There was vigorous movement against the left but that wing was intact. The weight of the rebel onslaught was clearly against the right and soon the British fire in that quarter became ominously fainter. Sir Hugh Rose was now about to anticipate the tactical skill—heaven extolled—of General Foch over half a century later at the Marne, a judicious transfer of force from one flank to the other, not at the enemy's bidding but in his own good time. The key of the position was now in danger and Hugh Rose at once took the mounted infantry from the left—Camel Corps it is called but the more modern term expresses its function better—and rode rapidly at its head to the right flank. On reaching the foot of some rising ground the mounted infantry—men of the 80th and Rifle Brigade—dismounted and, led by their commander and Sir Hugh Rose himself, went up the rise at the double and in perfect order.

Volleys of musketry came over the crest and killed or wounded every horse, except one, of Rose's staff. On the mounted infantry went and on topping the rise witnessed a disconcerting sight. The rebels, wild with native drugs and fury, were pouring across a small strip of level ground against the guns. The brigadier was on foot bidding the gunners draw their swords and defend their guns to the last ; round the brigadier were lying forty men struck down by the terrible sun. No sound of musketry came from the British side ; an inferior brand of ammunition had just been issued, the cone of the bullet was in some cases merely blown off and the shell lodging in the barrel " leaded " the gun. The skirmishers weakened by death, wounds, sunstroke and abominable ammunition had been pressed back by overwhelming numbers. Rose saw it was time for cold steel. Without allowing the mounted infantry to draw breath he led them forward with the bayonet. The 86th, the 3rd Europeans and the 25th Native Infantry with a yell threw themselves into the charge and streamed forward. The advance was taken up by the whole line. Everywhere the enemy was in retreat. Rebel infantry, cavalry and guns, all mingled together, streamed over the heights, up and down the ravines and along the high road to Calpee, pursued by our mounted troops and guns till man and beast could go no further and could do no more.

When darkness fell the wearied victors lay down in eager expectation of the morrow hoping that in a few hours Calpee would be theirs. A brief rest was, however, imperative. The day had been a fearful drain upon their physical strength. The enemy had fought with a vigour and a tactical skill such as he had never so far displayed. The burning heat had been unbearable. The thermometer had risen during the battle to 118° in the shade. The awful suffocating winds and torrid sun, which the men had to endure all day long without time to eat or drink, had made fighting a matter of almost unsurpassed difficulty. Every soul had suffered—officers and men had fainted away or dropped down as if struck by lightning in the delirium of unconsciousness. Sir Hugh Rose had had his fifth sunstroke; his chief of staff was ill; the quartermaster-general was worn out; the senior chaplain had gone mad. Yet all these sufferings were borne without complaint, and " in the cool of the evening " (somewhere about 100°) the indomitable soldiers speculated on the capture of the morrow.

Day had not dawned when the camp was struck but through the darkness could be seen the flashes from Maxwell's batteries. The force moved forward in two columns, one by the ravines along the river bank, the other by the Calpee road. A few rounds were fired from a masked battery in the nullahs but these rebel guns were soon silenced, limbered up and disappeared. A short halt to allow the two columns to get abreast; the advance was sounded; and on went the noble Central India Field Force and Calpee was in its hands. Sir Hugh Rose had fulfilled his instructions to the letter. Jhansi had been taken; Central India had been cleared; the Jumna had been reached; and communication with Sir Colin Campbell was effected.

In this battle three officers of the 3rd Europeans received a mention. Ensign Mackintosh for his good work already mentioned on rearguard on the 17th May; Ensign Trueman for great steadiness and gallantry when the picquets of the Regiment were attacked during the battle itself; and Lieutenant Baigrie for devotion to duty —he was acting A.Q.M.G.—although badly wounded. This officer charged with the mounted infantry and his horse was killed under him.

Thus closed a campaign than which none more brilliant

has occurred in Indian warfare. Historians with hardly a dissentient voice have extolled it in no measured terms. Prichard calls it one of the most brilliant achievements that the military history of any country in ancient or modern times has recorded. Forrest declares that it has a high title to be regarded as one of the great achievements recorded in the annals of war. Fortescue writes of the extraordinary campaign wherein Rose marched from Indore and fought his way without a check to the Jumna. These pæans of praise are justified. In five months Rose had beaten the enemy in thirteen general actions and sieges, and under a burning sun had captured some of the strongest forts in India. With a small force, but a tithe of that with which Campbell confronted an enemy scarcely more formidable he had marched in one career of conquest unchequered by reverse.

Instructions had been conveyed to Sir Hugh Rose that after the capture of Calpee the Central India Field Force was to be broken up and its units distributed as garrisons for Jhansi and Gwalior. Steps were at once taken for this end, and on June 1st, 1858, Sir Hugh Rose issued his farewell order in which he paid a glowing tribute to his troops. He thanked them with all sincerity for their devotion, bravery and discipline—that discipline of Christian soldiers which had brought them triumphant from the shores of Western India to the waters of the Jumna. "Soldiers!" he wrote, "you have marched more than a thousand miles and taken more than a hundred guns; you have forced your way through mountain passes and intricate jungles, and over rivers; you have captured the strongest forts and beaten the enemy, no matter what the odds, wherever you met him; you have restored extensive districts to the Government and peace and order now reign where before, for twelve months, were tyranny and rebellion; you have done all this and never had a check."

Sir Hugh Rose was now about to proceed on sick leave to Bombay but, before he could start, intelligence came which upset his plans and caused a sensation throughout

India hardly less than that caused by the first outbreak of the Mutiny. The rebel army under Tantia Topi and the Rani of Jhansi had attacked the loyal Maharajah Scindia nine miles from Gwalior whereupon that prince's troops, with the exception of his bodyguard, had gone over *en masse* to the enemy. Rose immediately offered to take command of the force ordered to recapture the fortress. The offer was gratefully accepted and the Central India Field Force was once more upon the move.

The short but decisive campaign which now ensued may be rapidly summarized, for the wing of the 3rd Europeans played but a subsidiary part in it. The wing was left to form part of the garrison of Calpee pending relief by troops from Bengal, and though, a few days later, it moved to Gwalior its services were not called upon for operations of an active nature. It arrived at the cantonments of Morar four miles from Gwalior on the morning of the 18th June just too late to take part in the fight for that important strategical point; and was then left as part of a mixed force at Morar to protect the place, to aid in the investment of Gwalior, and to be prepared to pursue the enemy when Gwalior should be stormed. Gwalior fell on the 20th June and the pursuit of the rebels fell naturally to the mounted troops. The worst enemy the 3rd Europeans was called upon to meet in this brief campaign was the sun; so fierce was the heat that in an officer's tent a thermometer burst at 130 degrees.

The capture of Gwalior was the crowning stroke of the Central Indian campaign, and practically put an end to the Mutiny, though the work of stamping out the embers went on for many months. The Rani of Jhansi had been killed in the operations round Gwalior, and though Tantia Topi was still at large he was eventually laid by the heels and executed in April, 1859. Meanwhile the 3rd Bombay Europeans had been marching down country to resume peace soldiering and on the 8th May they went into quarters at Mhow.

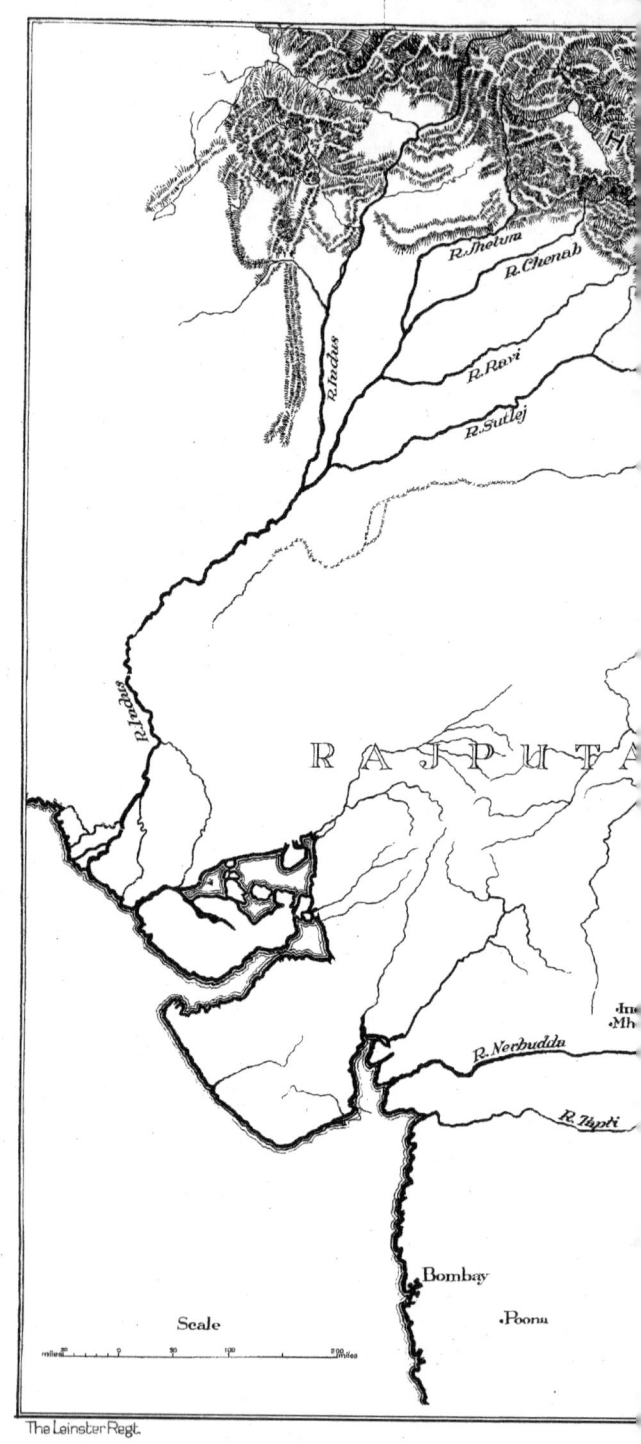

Campaign under Sir Hugh Rose, 1858.

NOTE:—The position of Lohari relative to Koonch is as described in pp. 232-234, and not as shewn on map.

CHAPTER XX

THE 109TH BOMBAY INFANTRY.

BEFORE the smouldering embers of the Mutiny were finally extinguished an event had occurred which marked the close of the crucial period of the struggle and the restoration of British supremacy. The Mutiny sealed the fate of the East India Company. After a career of just over two and a half centuries it was plain to thinking men that this great institution had outlived its usefulness. Its existence was an anomaly. And in England all political parties agreed in saddling it with the blame for the great upheaval in the East. The Company was therefore abolished ; and Queen Victoria became virtually Empress of India though it was nearly twenty years before the title was formally assumed. On the 1st November, 1858, a proclamation was read in every station in India explaining the principles in accordance with which the Imperial functions were henceforth to be exercised. It declared that the government of India had been assumed by the Queen ; that Lord Canning was to be the first viceroy ; that all officers who had been in the service of the Honourable East India Company were confirmed in their appointments ; that all treaties made with native princes would be faithfully observed ; that the Queen desired no extension of territory ; that she promised full religious toleration to her new subjects ; that an amnesty was offered to all rebels who had not directly taken part in the murder of Europeans ; and that Her Majesty would always labour for the prosperity of her newly acquired dominions.

As for the measures of military re-organization rendered necessary by this change in the state of affairs a Royal Commission, assembled in England, recommended the abolition of the local European army of the Company and its amalgamation with the so-called "Queen's Army." This proposal was accepted and the European troops of the late East India Company, numbering according to various sources from 14,000 to 24,000 men ceased to have a separate existence. The artillery became Royal Artillery, three newly raised cavalry regiments became the 19th, 20th and 21st Hussars, and the infantry, whose existence covered an era of two centuries, were eventually formed into regiments of the line and numbered from 101 to 109. This transference of the Company's Europeans was not unattended with disturbance. The men resented what they regarded as a breach of faith on the part of the Government and objected to being made a "make weight" as they called it to suit the convenience of politicians. In some cases a spirit of active insubordination was displayed which, weakly handled by the authorities, grew into the so-called "White Mutiny."

The 3rd Bombay Europeans were at Mhow when the proclamation was issued, transferring the British rule in India from the hands of the East India Company to the Crown. The non-commissioned officers and men of the Regiment were asked to transfer to the Queen's service. This request gave rise to a considerable amount of discussion among the rank and file, and finally they gave a practically unanimous answer that they would transfer provided they were given a spell of leave in England and a fresh bounty. The authorities apparently did not see their way to granting these conditions, and nothing more was said for some time, until one day, at the conclusion of a battalion parade, the commanding officer again read out the conditions of transfer to the men, adding, "There will be no tickets for the canteen to-day, and beer will be issued free." This, as may be imagined, was a very popular announcement, and before long the majority of the men were in the canteen, drinking heartily of the free beer, and expressing sentiments of the utmost loyalty towards the Queen, and determination to transfer to her service under any conditions, or none at all, for that matter. The next morning the canteen was again free, and the same loyal sentiments and determination to transfer were expressed with even greater vehemence. When the battalion had drunk itself into a sufficient state of cheerfulness, the men were invited to step into their various company offices and sign their names to their transfer in the presence of their officers, and a certain number did so.

Next morning there was a very different scene. The canteen was closed, and the roysterers were confronted with their own signatures, unable to deny them, and yet with very little, if any, recollection of having written them. Many, more cautious, had, however, contented themselves with a modest pint or two, kept sober, and steadfastly refused to sign anything, and were consequently now able to claim their discharge and free passage home to England. These were sent down to Bombay and shipped home, with a number of discharged men, in a sailing transport. This turned out to be a rotten, leaky old tub, which took five months to perform the voyage, while the food and water served out was so bad and scanty that the men believed it was the intention of the authorities to poison them all on the way home as a punishment for not having agreed to transfer.

The blunders on the part of those in authority when added to the casualties from wounds and sickness in a strenuous campaign reduced the 3rd Bombay European Regiment to a mere skeleton. At Mhow it lost nearly 600 men, sent to England for discharge. This left the Regiment a mere cadre though reinforcements were soon available from an unexpected source—the German Legion.

The German Legion had come into being during the Crimean War. In 1855 the situation had become serious; war had been going on for some months, and there was a very great shortage of men for the necessary reinforcements. But to such a depth of unwarlike sloth had England sunk in the long era of peace which succeeded Waterloo that the Government was in despair as to how to raise the necessary men. Voluntary recruiting was totally insufficient and the very idea of universal service would have scared every minister in the Cabinet. Men, however, had to be found and about this time Lord Palmerston writing to Lord Panmure, Secretary of State for War, used these despairing words : " We are 40,000 men short of the numbers voted by Parliament. We must resort to every possible means and every possible quarter to complete our force. Let us get as many German and Swiss as we can, let us get men from Halifax, let us enlist Italians, and let us forthwith increase our bounty without raising the standard. Do not let departmental or official or professional prejudice and habits stand in our way ; we must override all such obstacles. We *must* have troops. War cannot be carried on without troops ; we have asked Parliament for a certain amount of force, and we have pledged ourselves to the opinion that such a number is necessary. We shall disgrace ourselves if we do not make every effort to raise that amount." To such abject impotence had fallen the Power which for over twenty years had withstood the energy and genius of Napoleon himself.

The Government of the day was strenuously urged by the Press to raise a Legion in America. *The Times*, in a leader, was enthusiastic as to this grand opportunity. It said that the troops so raised would be mostly men of German origin, formed of emigrants to the States ; that they had been inured to military discipline, and possessed a practical knowledge of arms ; and, further, being generally of mature age and vigour, it seemed likely that they would supply the class of troops the country then was in need of. The Thunderer ended up a powerful article with the following extraordinary words : " If the Americans can show us the way to take Sebastopol, we should be quite ready to learn, and give them every credit for the lesson."

The Duke of Cambridge was the first to make any practical and tangible offer to raise these foreign troops. In April, 1855, having then but recently returned from the Crimea, he wrote to Lord Panmure, proposing the idea of the Foreign Legion, and at the same time offered to train it himself, and to command it at the front. Curiously enough he was strongly of opinion that it should take the form of cavalry, although the immediate military problem was the reduction of a great fortress. The project soon assumed a corporate shape. Recruiting commenced in May, 1855. Depots were formed at Heligoland, Shorncliffe and Haslar, and training centres at Aldershot, Colchester, Hythe, Tarlingham and Brown Down. Recruiting continued on to 31st March, 1856, and during that period 441 officers, 539 non-commissioned officers and 8,702 other ranks joined the colours. There was in addition a receiving depot at Niagara in Canada, which provided a large body of men and forwarded the recruits to Halifax as they came up. The original terms of their enlistment was for the duration of the war; recruits were not to be under 5 ft. 2 in. in height, nor over thirty-five years of age. Concurrently with the formation of the German Legion, the task of forming the Swiss and Italian contingents was taken in hand. The uniform was the ordinary red tunic, black or grey trousers, white belts and heavy fur cap or helmet served out to all ranks after the first Crimean winter. Queen Victoria displayed a deep interest in these fellow-countrymen of her husband and desired that their name should be changed from the "Foreign" to that of the "German" Legion. "I am sure," she writes, "that this will have a good effect in Germany and help the recruiting; the German papers have been taunting them with not being allowed to bear their own names."

The Duke of Cambridge was appointed Colonel-in-Chief, and the first detachment, 2,000 strong, under Brigadier-General Woolridge, left Southampton for the seat of war in October, 1855, consisting of Jäger and Light Infantry battalions. General Simpson, the commander-in-chief, was informed that they should be attached to his Light Cavalry Division; in any case the German and Swiss levies were to be kept apart, and it was thought that the Swiss might be more likely to fraternise with the

Highlanders than any other corps. The contingent, under the command of Colonel Kinloch, landed at Scutari in November, and was much admired by all the officers who saw it. But though originally meant as a reinforcement for the Light Division in the Crimea, the units had arrived so late in the year that it was found impossible to hut them all there conveniently; they were therefore landed at Scutari, whilst a camp was found for the Swiss at Smyrna. The strength of the British German Legion at the seat of war early in 1856 was 138 officers and 3,615 men, and consisted of the 1st Jäger Battalion and the 1st, 2nd and 3rd German Light Infantry. These were the only representatives of the Legion that ever went overseas, though the total force included the 1st and 2nd Light Dragoons, the 1st to 5th Light Infantry and the 1st, 2nd and 3rd Jäger Battalions. The names of many English officers occur in the musty pay rolls of the Legion; at least six of the infantry battalions had British commanding officers, whilst almost without exception their adjutants came from the Regular Army.

From early in the year until March, 1856, there is almost complete silence in official documents as to the activities of the German Legion, and beyond the fact that 173 of the Legion had died at Scutari, probably from Crimean fever, which was very prevalent that winter, there is no mention which is worthy of record. Peace was now in the air, and both the Queen and Lord Panmure were concerned as to the ultimate disposal of the Legion. So deeply did she feel for these mercenaries of German birth that almost before hostilities had been concluded Her Majesty was writing to the Secretary of State for War : " As the Queen fears [*sic*] Peace seems now pretty certain to be concluded she is very anxious to impress upon Lord Panmure the question of the German Legion; she trusts there is no doubt they will be provided for in the Colonies as these poor men have many of them lost their nationality, and the Queen is certain that it would be very bad policy to act ungenerously towards them." Reverting again to the subject on the very same day she says: "It must not be forgotten they have gone to very great expense, and probably will find themselves in a very painful position in their own country for having ventured to enter the Queen's service. If, therefore, they were not considered or treated with generosity the effect on the Continent would be most mischievous as regards this country."

Although the men of the British German Legion who had entered into the service of Great Britain were entitled by the terms of their enlistment to receive a gratuity at the close of the war, and to be sent to their country of origin at the public expense, it was found that public opinion abroad was very antagonistic towards them, and that there was a strong probability the men might not meet with a favourable reception in their own homes. In this position of affairs it was suggested that the members of the Legion should be established as military settlers at the Cape of Good Hope. The scheme provided that officers and men who volunteered for the purpose should be settled on land in suitable stations along the borders of Kaffraria, where a large area was lying derelict as a result of one of the greatest delusions in history. The Amaxosa tribe of Kaffirs had been defeated by the British and, in their hour of humiliation, there arose a native Joan of Arc who told of supernatural messages, by obeying which her countrymen would triumph over the hated white men. The celestial orders were that all cattle and grain should be destroyed which the placated divinities would then replace by myriads of kine and unexampled harvests. The deluded natives carried out the behests only too faithfully. The appointed day dawned which was to usher in the terrestrial paradise. But no paradise appeared. The sun rose and sank and the expected miracle did not come to pass. The starving Amaxosa now sought the aid of the British but in spite of every effort thousands perished miserably. The depopulated country was then peopled by European settlers among whom were members of the late German Legion. The terms on which these were granted land were that they should preserve their military training and be liable to any military service when called upon, and further that they should assemble every seven years for a limited period of training.

Towards the end of November, 1856, the first contingent, 1,000 strong, left Southampton in the transports *Culloden* and *Sultana* arriving at Cape Town on the 28th January, 1857; a further contingent sailed very shortly afterwards, raising the total number to 2,351 officers and men, 378 women and 178 children. They were in the first place quartered at East London, and the Governor in reporting their arrival took great exception to the paucity in numbers of the females accompanying the party. He warned the Government that there might be great restlessness and even immorality, and he went so far as to say that on this account alone they would as a military force be quite useless to the colony. Later he modified his opinion, writing that the settlers were taking up their vocations, that their conduct was satisfactory, and that the experiment of sending them out would no doubt prove a successful one. The men were now divided into three regiments, with distinct districts in Kaffraria; and at the same time some transferred voluntarily to the Frontier Military Police, where they were a great success. It is worthy of note that in all papers dealing with these emigrants, particular stress is laid on the fact that they were very musical, a national characteristic of the German in every quarter of the world. All villages and settlements were given German names, such as Berlin, Frankfort, Potsdam, etc., and many of these became familiar to British ears in the South African War.

Save for an inevitable percentage of ne'er-do-wells and desperadoes the members of the German Legion were a valuable asset to Cape Colony. They were industrious and sober, while the military discipline to which they had been accustomed rendered them peculiarly suitable for frontier protection. Many of them were high principled men who, rather than submit to the stifling autocracy of reactionary Austria—then the dominant state in Germany

—had emigrated to America where their countrymen showed themselves good citizens. These be it re-membered were the days before 1866, when Prussia came to the front with her dazzling army, and before 1870 when her brain was turned by the intoxication of the stupendous successes over France. Sober, hardworking, courteous and contemplative the typical German of the middle of the nineteenth century was as different from the Hun we so lately knew as a crusader is from a costermonger. Many of them were strongly imbued with the military spirit and on the outbreak of the Indian Mutiny over a thousand ex-Legionaries in South Africa volunteered for service in the East. A battalion was raised and landed at Calcutta; but, as in the Crimea, they arrived too late to take any striking part in the campaign although, again as in the Crimea, there were severe casualties from cholera and fever. It was these members of the German Legion who were now offered the chance of volunteering for the British service.

Five hundred and sixty non-commissioned officers and men from the Jäger Corps—as the German battalion was called—responded to the call for volunteers and left Poona for Karachi, arriving at the latter station on the 25th January, 1860, pending the arrival of the 3rd Bombay European Regiment at that station. This was not long delayed, for in less than a month the 3rd Bombay Europeans arrived and the remnant of the Regiment was at once amalgamated with the men from the Jäger Corps. Towards the end of the year a detachment of three companies proceeded by sea to Hyderabad to relieve a similar detachment of the 64th Regiment, remaining there a twelvemonth till relieved itself by a detachment of the 4th King's Own.

Technically the Regiment was still the 3rd Bombay Europeans but on the 7th May, 1861, orders were received that the 3rd Bombay Europeans were to become a battalion of the line under the title of the 109th Bombay Infantry and the non-commissioned officers and men, both of the old regiment and the Jäger Corps, were asked to volunteer for the new unit and to undertake the consequent liability of general service. Practically all accepted, over 770 coming forward, and on the 30th July, 1862, the 109th was formally enrolled as a regiment of the Line. The feelings of these European regiments of the Honourable East India Company for the master they served were deep and enduring and as the 3rd Bombay Europeans were the last regiment to be raised by the Company there was a general wish that permission might be granted to bear on the appointments of the 109th the crest of the Company. The application reached the Heralds' College in due course ; but owing to the political necessity for emphasizing the disappearance of the Company and the supremacy of the Crown the application was not favoured. Now when nearly three-quarters of a century have elapsed, and the Regiment is no more, the question has been revived, and the Lion holding a Globe has been included in the crest of the Regimental Dinner Club, the connexion of the two regular battalions of the Leinster Regiment with Canada and India respectively being thus symbolized by the Maple Leaves and the Company's Lion.

Order having now been restored in India the 109th settled down to the duties and recreations of peace soldiering at Karachi. Of the German officers of the Jäger Corps most had returned to their farms at the Cape but Major Wohlfahrt, Captain Schmid, as well as Lieutenants O. Schmidt (the adjutant) and Luckhardt and Dr. Brink, remained in the British service.

The officers' dress was at this time precisely what it had been in the Mutiny, i.e. duty dress was a red shell jacket with white duck trousers and a forage cap, either with a white quilted cover or with puggaree and tail. At social functions where uniform was required a blue frock coat with a double row of brass buttons was worn. The swords had black leather scabbards with brass mountings and the full dress red tunics—seldom worn—had leather stocks, and cuffs and tails similar to those worn by Guards regiments of to-day. With the tunic were worn a crimson sash, white gloves and dark blue pantaloons with a red stripe. In 1861 the Regiment went into khaki and helmets, the colour being obtained by dipping the white cotton clothing into the company coppers filled with a boiling decoction of berberry bark and water. As the resulting tint depended on the strength of each company's brew uniformity was impossible and the kit was discontinued for ceremonial the Regiment being clothed in white the following year, the scarlet and blue being retained for the cold season. The officers now substituted a red serge with white facings for the blue frock coat.

The men were armed with the long muzzle loading Enfield rifle with long triangular-section bayonet, while the sergeants had a shorter rifle of the same pattern and sword bayonet. A sword bayonet with saw back was carried by the pioneers. The accoutrements were a cartouche box and belt worn over the left shoulder, the box resting on the base of the spine and kept in place by the bayonet belt round the waist, which also carried a pouch for twenty rounds. The percussion cap pouch was attached to the cartouche belt and worn on the centre of the chest. A knapsack with great coat attached, canteen, haversack and water bottle completed the kit. The head-dress was a helmet with puggaree, or a round forage cap carrying a worsted ball on top.

Karachi was a fair sized garrison, the 109th having as companions the 64th, later replaced by the 4th King's Own, and the 1st Baloochis. Life was pleasant in this northern station, the various bands playing regularly at "Scandal Point" and picnics were a feature of the garrison life of those days. Drives in the evening to "eat the air" to Ghizri and Clifton were the usual relief after the "long, long Indian day," the chief amusement at the former place being the turning of turtles during the season when they came to lay their eggs in the sand at night. We had our own theatre with an ambitious repertoire, and put on a burlesque called "Dido," and the dramas "Faust" and "Der Freischütz." There was considerable histrionic talent amongst the officers, and the

Germans in the ranks provided some excellent scene painters so that the performances were well above the level of the usual regimental theatricals. There was also a race course where frequent race meetings were held, as well as gymkhanas and cricket matches, the Regiment more than holding its own in the latter game. Polo had not yet come into being as an army sport. The Regiment had in those days two bands, brass and string until the latter was discontinued in 1867 by order of the authorities. The musical talent of the Germans was a great asset, and in time the 109th earned the reputation of having the best band, the best cricket team, and the best theatrical company in the length and breadth of Hindostan.

The Colonel of the Regiment was General Sir William Wyllie, K.C.B., who was however transferred to the 103rd Royal Bombay Fusiliers in 1873 when he was succeeded by General Mark Kerr Atherley. In actual command was Lieutenant-Colonel C. S. Whitehill who had belonged to the old 3rd Bombay Europeans and on whom devolved the honour of forming the 109th of the Line. It was while the Regiment was at Karachi that some officers were sent to the 20th Depot Battalion at Cork to form the two extra draft-finding companies required. The Regiment in those days consisted of ten companies designated by numerals the alphabetical nomenclature not being adopted till later. Lieutenant-Colonel Whitehill retired in October, 1864, and was succeeded by Major Maude. Amongst the officers of, or attached to, the Regiment one name deserves mention—Dr. Palaeologus, familiarly known as " The last King of the Greeks." Towards the end of the month of October, 1864, the first draft of recruits arrived from Cork in Messrs. Green's ship *Agamemnon*, and it is interesting to note that in mid-ocean she spoke one of the Confederate commerce destroyers. The *Agamemnon* arrived after a voyage of 93 days from Gravesend.

In accordance with Horse Guards G.O. No. 834 dated 3rd September, 1863, the 109th Bombay Infantry was permitted to wear the scroll with the honour

"Central India" on the Regimental Colour by command of His Royal Highness the Commander-in-Chief and in recognition of its services during the campaign with the Central India Field Force under Sir Hugh Rose, afterwards Lord Strathnairn.

Towards the end of the year orders were received that headquarters and six companies were to proceed to Aden the remaining four companies being ordered to Hyderabad, Scinde, there to relieve the 95th Regiment. The Regiment was inspected by the major-general commanding, who on the 6th November, 1864, published the following appreciation of the 109th. " On the departure of H.M.'s 109th Foot from Karachi to Aden in the course of relief the Major-General commanding the Sind Division desires to place on record his sentiments as to the conduct and military qualifications of that Regiment during the time it has been under his command. It has performed its garrison duties with attention and steadiness strictly according to H.M.'s Regulations. All its parades and evolutions are marked by great facility of movement and a perfect knowledge of the principles of military formation. In a word every man conveys the impression to a spectator of being a well drilled soldier. The arms and equipments are of the best description. The rifles and belts are new and the clothing nearly so. The Regiment is also particularly well shod. All the departments are perfect and in excellent working condition. The Band which must not be left out in the catalogue and which has given so much delight to the community of Karachi is second to none in excellence. The conduct of the men in quarters is orderly, quiet and soldierlike, and tinctured with a fine military *esprit de corps* and tone. The Major-General considers the departure of the 109th Foot from Karachi as a great loss to the Sind Command. They are a most powerful body of troops. He bids them farewell and cordially hopes that they will enjoy themselves in their new station."

With their record of service in the field and this eloquent testimony to their discipline and efficiency in peace the officers, non-commissioned officers and men of the 109th Bombay Infantry could well feel that they had upheld the great military traditions of the Honourable East India Company and could look forward to meriting similar praise in the Royal Army. Apart from its military efficiency the Regiment had gained great popularity socially in Karachi, and before its departure 750 non-commissioned officers and men were entertained at a banquet given by the European residents. During November headquarters and seven companies left in three separate ships for Aden, the remaining three companies under command of Major Brown proceeding to Hyderabad.

CHAPTER XXI

THE 109TH REGIMENT—ADEN, 1864-1866.

THE Regiment arrived complete by the 13th November, 1864, and settled down for a two years' tour at Aden, its companions in garrison being two batteries of artillery and the 1st Bombay Grenadiers who had also a detachment on Perim Island. The idea of sending a battalion for two years to Aden was in the nature of an experiment, the question being whether an old salted Indian regiment or one fresh from home could stand the climate better. For this experiment the 109th represented the Indian unit and the 1st Battalion of the 2nd Queen's the regiment from home. It may be said here that the salted Indian regiment emerged victorious from the trial and thenceforth the system was inaugurated by which Aden was garrisoned by a unit which was finishing its Indian tour instead of by one on its way to the East. The stay at Aden was, however, reduced to one year.

Headquarters and two companies were in the Crater, where the native town was, some five miles east of the landing place. Two companies were at the Isthmus, guarding the approach from the land side, and the remainder of the Regiment was at Steamer Point. One of our first duties was to build the rifle butts outside the Isthmus fortifications, during which process we were guarded by an Arab with a matchlock from raids by his compatriots. As a further preventive against such attacks the Isthmus detachment used solemnly to man the ramparts once a week and fire volleys towards the distant hills, just to show the lurking Arabs what they might expect if they tried any nonsense. The rifle butts having been finished we turned our attention to a more congenial task, the construction of a regimental theatre. This was erected in the Crater close to the officers' mess and in it during our stay at Aden we produced many burlesques and farces.

Aden had many drawbacks but at any rate it was on the great highway to the East, and when a distinguished visitor passed through there was always some break in the ordinary garrison routine. In April, 1865, the Duke of Brabant landed during his voyage to the East and the Regiment supplied a guard of honour. A visit of still greater interest was that, a week later, of General Sir Hugh Rose on his way home on the completion of his tenure of the post of Commander-in-Chief in India. Sir Hugh was entertained to dinner by General Raines, the commander of the garrison, and when the talk turned on the great events of the Mutiny Sir Hugh Rose spoke in high terms of the dash and gallantry displayed by the 109th (then the 3rd Bombay Europeans) in the Central Indian campaign. The Regiment found the guard of honour and the officer in command of it was bidden, as is customary, to the banquet. When he rose to rejoin his command Sir Hugh Rose remarked to his host "There goes a man I have recommended three times for the Victoria Cross." The officer referred to was Major Armstrong who had served during the Mutiny on the staff of the Central India Field Force. His duties being connected with the postal service of the force failed to give him sufficient opportunity for his fighting spirit, so he compromised by leaving his official work whenever an action was imminent and resuming his old place as commander of the Grenadier company. His gallant services have been described elsewhere in this volume and it is only necessary to say here that he was technically disqualified from the award of the Cross. He received a brevet majority and died on the 27th November, 1865, at Alexandria while on his way home to England on leave, his death being a great blow to the Regiment.

The scourge of soldiering east of Suez, cholera, took

its toll of the Regiment in 1865. On the 12th May it broke out in the Isthmus originating, so it was thought, from the decomposing bodies of millions of fish cast up on the sands. The epidemic spread to the Crater, and the troops there and at the Isthmus were at once moved out into the open, those from the Isthmus being once more guarded by the old matchlock-armed Arab. As is so often the case with cholera the outbreak was curiously local, one particular corner of the barracks at the Isthmus and the adjoining corner of the married quarters yielding most of the victims. The epidemic continued for two months during which the Regiment lost about a hundred men, women and children. Amongst the victims was Dr. Nicholas Carter who died from heat apoplexy brought on by incessant hard work, deeply regretted by all ranks.

The tedium of garrison life at Aden was now to be relieved by the excitement of active service. In November, 1865, the Fudhli Arabs, a tribe occupying the territory north-east of Aden, became very troublesome attacking our allies the Abdhalis to the north of us, and cutting off the supply of fresh provisions and water from Aden. All remonstrances by the Resident, Colonel Merewether, were in vain and the Arabs replied by a challenge to us to come out and fight. This message could not be ignored and it was decided to take effective measures to bring the recalcitrants to book. Accordingly on the 22nd December, 1865, an expeditionary force moved out composed as follows :—

 2 Companies 109th Regiment.
 2 Companies 1st Bombay Grenadiers.
 2 6-prs. and 2 small howitzers Royal Artillery, drawn by bullocks.

This force marched out at 5 a.m. and moved to Sheikh Othman at the head of the Isthmus, where we learnt that the Fudhlis were encamped some twelve miles off to the north. After a hasty breakfast we started once again, all the baggage being left behind, the country traversed being a mass of hillocks, sand, and bushes which rendered reconnaissance difficult. The 1st Grenadiers were now thrown forward as skirmishers, the 109th following in support and the guns behind the centre; and in this formation the march was continued for some six miles when the 109th took the lead. The conditions were trying in the extreme. The heat was intense and the burning sand made marching absolutely painful, the men suffering most, for their boots were so uncomfortable that many walked in their socks. Then about 3 p.m. the enemy were sighted to the left front and, by the smell of burning matches of their matchlocks soon followed by the swish of bullets overhead, we knew that they meant business. The right of our line seemed to have struck the centre of their camp, for there was a small glade in the sandhills down which a mass of men and camels could be seen. When Colonel Woolcombe R.A., the commander of our force, learnt this he ordered up the guns which quickly came into action causing hurried movement on the part of the enemy. The Fudhlis did not seem to mind our rifle fire and replied readily, if too high; but the guns were a different matter and the shells at once caused considerable confusion. The order for a general advance was now given to the British force and this was the signal for a hurried retreat on the part of the enemy who fled having lost, according to native reports, some 160 to 170 men. On our side there were six men wounded of whom one was in the 109th. As showing the different tactical conditions which prevailed in 1865 as compared with the present day it may be mentioned that the order for the general advance was given when we were only about 100 yards from the enemy. We attributed the smallness of our casualty list to the fact that we were at the time probably just out of effective range of the Arab muskets. Up to 90 yards the Arabs could shoot very well if they loaded their matchlocks properly but over that range their marksmanship was indifferent. In all, the Arabs must have had some fifteen hundred on the field, all of whom were mounted on horses or camels and were armed with matchlocks, swords, knives and spears.

Even though they were armed with muzzle loaders

the British impressed the Arab by the rapidity of their fire. The Fudhli prisoners declared that they could not stand " the guns that fired twice." Those of the present day who are inclined to think that firing with the old Enfield was a leisurely operation will be interested in the following episode. When the one wounded man of the 109th went down, bowled over by a bullet fired by an Arab on a camel, his comrade shot the camel and before the rider could take to his legs he was bowled over too, a matter of seconds. It was a neat and well managed little fight but how any of the officers of the Regiment survived is a mystery, for they were dressed all in white and wore a crimson sash across the left shoulder. To stand up in that kit opposite more than a thousand Arabs only a hundred yards off, even though they were armed only with matchlocks, made one realize the unsuitable nature of the uniform.

After this success we continued our march some three miles till we came to Dhurub where we bivouacked for the night the baggage coming in about midnight, and in the morning pitched our tents awaiting the arrival of General Raines who came up with another company of the Regiment and assumed command of the whole force. We then returned to Sheik Othman arriving there on Christmas Day. Here we stayed three days collecting camels for the further advance of our increased force, the route which we had to traverse being a three days' march through a waterless country.

At last we started following the line of the sea shore, doing 18 miles a day, then turning a little into the sand-hills again till we came to the neighbourhood of Almodra where we heard that the Fudhlis were awaiting us at the further side of a broad nullah and had three guns with them. The next morning a direct attack combined with a turning movement on their left drove them out of the grain fields that lined their bank of the nullah, and again they fled leaving the guns behind them. These pieces were old ship's guns which they had evidently salved from some wreck. This time the Fudhlis fell back to their chief town Ussallah and they now requested a parley. This was granted and the Fudhlis received orders to " come in " before the end of three days. This peremptory injunction was, however, not to the liking of the enemy who spent the days of grace in removing all their goods and then vanished to the hills leaving nothing behind except three old women down with smallpox. In consequence of this action of the Fudhlis orders were given to destroy Ussallah and these instructions were duly carried out, the fort being blown up. We then proceeded to the forts of El Khor a day's march to the north-west which offered but little resistance and were soon destroyed.

All opposition having now ceased we returned to Aden after having been out for three weeks and having penetrated some seventy-five miles into country never previously visited by Europeans. We had, however, not yet finished with the Fudhli for in March, 1865, we heard that the Sultan had called all the neighbouring chiefs together and informed them that as it had been revealed to him that he had but a short time to live he proposed to ensure a strong claim on Paradise by taking Aden and putting the whole garrison to the sword. The assembled chiefs, however, for their part, decided that a claim on Paradise was dearly bought at the price of immediate defeat and death and declined to have anything to do with the enterprise.

To put an end to any further trouble the British Resident decided that the time had come to destroy the remaining forts at Shugra where the Sultan had taken up his abode. The Armstrong guns were got out again and 200 men of the 109th, formed into three companies under Captains Forbes and Beville and Lieutenant Mordaunt, the whole under the command of Captain Schmid, embarked in H.M.S. *Penguin* and H.M. Indian Navy ship *Victoria*. We then proceeded down the coast to Shugra Bunder where we disembarked under a heavy but ill-directed fire from the sand dunes. That night we bivouacked at Shugra Bunder (incidentally being nearly eaten alive by bugs) and next day advanced towards the forts, the sailors rendering invaluable assistance in helping to drag the 6-pounders. The forts were found unoccupied but our guns were brought into action against some of the enemy who could be seen lurking in the hills; and, having blown up the stronghold, we marched back to the coast. The main body now re-embarked leaving one company to fire the place and while this was being carried out the son of the Fudhli came in and was received by the O.C. British force. The Arabs had by now recognized the futility of further resistance and terms were soon arranged. The last company of the 109th then re-embarked for Aden and so far as we were concerned the Fudhli episode was at an end.

In those days the slave trade was actively carried on by Arab dhows, and our East India Squadron was busily engaged in suppressing the traffic, the various gunboats constantly bringing in mobs of slaves which they had taken off captured Arab vessels. We were allowed to have " liberated slaves " provided we guaranteed to train them and gave a formal receipt for them. Some of us tried the experiment but as the individuals usually liberated themselves after a few days' good feeding the system was discontinued. We had about this time some interesting visitors passing through, Sir Samuel and Lady Baker stopping at Aden on their way back from their great Nile discoveries. Another interesting visitor was the great John Roberts on his way to a billiard tour in Australia. The champion took on our best player and heavily defeated him though using, himself, an umbrella to his opponent's cue.

On the 23rd January, 1866, the 109th Regiment received its first Colours as a regiment of the Queen's Army. The ceremony was performed by Mrs. Raines, wife of the G.O.C. the garrison and was followed by a dinner given by the officers of the Regiment. In his speech at the dinner General Raines gave an admirable résumé of the work done by the 3rd Bombay Europeans during the Mutiny repeating the commendation he had recently heard from the lips of Sir Hugh Rose himself. " Quite lately," said

General Raines, "when Sir Hugh Rose passed through Aden on his way home I was greatly gratified to hear him speak in the highest terms of the dash, the gallantry, and good service performed by the 3rd Europeans not only throughout the operation but especially in this particular battle of the Betwa when he told me he had endeavoured to secure the Victoria Cross for a captain of the corps (now Major Armstrong) for his conspicuous individual bravery." Later in his speech General Raines spoke of the courage of the Regiment and the goodwill and splendid spirit which pervaded all ranks during the recent operations in the interior. These Colours presented at Aden in 1866 were carried by the Regiment for just over half a century in Asia, Europe, America, and Africa. The old Mutiny Colours were sent to Bombay Cathedral but were lost sight of until discovered in the Arsenal nearly thirty years later. Reclaimed in 1895 by the 2nd Leinster Regiment, they remained with the Battalion until disbandment when they were sent to—and this time installed in—Bombay Cathedral, 56 years after the original mission. Things are done methodically in the Army.

The rest of the year 1866 passed quietly enough. Colonel Maude went home on sick leave and as Major Wolfahrt had died at Pau in 1863 the command devolved on Major A. A. P. Browne who came for the purpose from the detachment still in India. The great recreation was to visit the various steamers as they came in, in search of old friends and to glean news of the outer world. The French line the *Messagerie Impériale* was a boon to us as in these vessels were carried brandies and wines in the wood straight from Bordeaux; brandy, for in those days whisky had not been adopted as the basis of the service peg. We went in a good deal for rowing in the harbour, played a deal of cricket, kept up the reputation of the Regiment in theatricals and bathed a good deal in the sea. Everything, however, was hampered by the conditions of climate. Sometimes the heat was terrific and there was a certain amount of heat apoplexy. On one occasion an officer had to go round barracks at 10 a.m.

but both he and the officer detailed to take his place were knocked over, and it was not until a third officer had been despatched that the duty was carried out. Sand storms were also a nuisance and we had one of such magnitude as to make the daily sand storm seem a mere trifle. Rain was of course a rarity but once during our stay it came down very hard producing a curious result, for after a day or two the sides of the Crater came out in green. Where the vegetation came from was a mystery for previous to the downpour not a vestige of plant life could be seen in the Crater.

In the beginning of November, 1866, orders were received for the Regiment to hold itself in readiness for a move to India and on the 14th of that month we were relieved by the 1st Battalion of the 2nd Queen's Regiment and embarked on the steamer *Coromandel* and the sailing transport *Albert Victor*.

CHAPTER XXII

THE 109TH REGIMENT—INDIA 1867–1874.

HEADQUARTERS and the bulk of the Regiment were in the sailing ship which was towed by the *Coromandel* but before half of the voyage was completed the steamer displayed a blackboard on which was displayed the message that coal was running short and that the *Albert Victor* would be cast off and must " proceed independently." The latter vessel had a slow trip working along the coast until it fell in with the Indian Navy ship *Auckland*, which towed it into Bombay Harbour, a month out from Aden. From Bombay the reunited companies moved to Poona where they were quartered in Wanouri Barracks, though even yet the whole Regiment was not together, for although the detachment from Hyderabad had come in another had to be detailed for Parandhur.

There are lucky and unlucky regiments—luck being bound up, be it understood, with the question of active service. A lucky regiment happens to be at the right spot and at the right time and comes in for a campaign ; the unlucky regiment is ever at a distant and peaceful station just at the moment when a " show " begins. So far in its short life the 109th had been fortunate. As the 3rd Bombay Europeans it had played an important part in the most brilliant campaign in Indian History ; and while at Aden it had further experience of active service though of a minor nature. And now while at Poona it was apparently about to take part in another war. The situation in Abyssinia called for sharp action by the British Government. King Theodore, although he had been friendly with the British, became irritated over the non-reply to a letter forwarded by him to the Foreign Office and made prisoners of the British Consul and two gentlemen of his suite. Remonstrances having failed England decided to send a force to Abyssinia to bring King Theodore to book, and on the 2nd January, 1867, the 109th were overjoyed to hear that they were to proceed to Abyssinia early the following month. There were at Poona at that time in addition to ourselves the 45th and 96th Regiments, and the 14th and 24th Bombay Native Infantry with artillery at Kirkee. Inspections and frequent drills were now the order of the day and we were constantly taken out and exercised in new forms of light infantry tactics which were most interesting. We temporarily exchanged our old Enfields for Snider breech-loaders and the new tactics were practised in order to discover the best formation in which to advance so as to take the fullest advantage of the increased volume of fire assured by the new weapon.

On the 18th January, 1867, we were inspected by Major-General M. W. Smith C.B. Those old time inspection reports throw an interesting sidelight upon the importance of minutiæ of interior economy and precision of drill in the minds of mid-Victorian martinets. The inspecting officer goes in his report to the one serious blot on the Regiment—some of the defaulter books are insecurely bound ; and, next, the surgeon of the Regiment is to be called upon to submit a memorandum upon some question of "Persuasion Tickets." These important matters having been dealt with a reference is made to "Parade and Drill." The general remarks that more attention must be paid to the position of the chin at the "Cap," when loading. Also, when the Regiment is drawn up in Review Order " the band must not play more than 8 bars of the Salute ; the drums on the right played too long and the Big Drum, being on the right, is contrary to custom." In Marching Order the Regiment turned out " very clean and in good order "—as it always continued to do down to the black day of disbandment.

The Books were "in very good order"; but those wretched defaulter sheets still weigh on the general's mind for exception is made of one or two companies' defaulter books "the sheets of which are loose." Then follows the significant hint "This must be rectified." The bayonet exercise in quick time "might have been performed more together and as one man," the idea of a man in a hand-to-hand, life-and-death struggle fighting on his own being of course out of the question. In drill the "officers called out by the brigadier acquitted themselves remarkably well" but there was "still room for improvement in sword exercise." The whole question of the fighting efficiency of the Regiment as regards musketry and fire discipline is considered towards the end of the report and is dismissed with the brief criticism "Ball firing good" and a few lines about skirmishing, picquet duty, regimental schools and the advance in Review Order which was "Very Good" conclude the document. The brigadier stated that he would make a good report on the state of the Regiment and that he was particularly impressed by the knowledge of the officers and non-commissioned officers in company drill and skirmishing.

The 109th had therefore satisfied the Higher Powers in spite of those loosely bound defaulter books. It is easy to smile at the excessive interest displayed in these sheets and at the solemn dictum on the exact position of the Big Drum, which was "not according to custom"—an extremely serious matter in the Old Army. But let it never be forgotten that it was this close scrutiny over matters of minute detail which was at the bottom of the grand discipline of the Regular Army. Reformers have again and again scoffed at ceremonial and close order barrack square drill but those who served in France will remember how "steady drill" was often practised after long operations by both Battalions, and how the Guards when they had been withdrawn into second line at the close of the bloody First Battle of Ypres paraded the shattered remnants and practised Trooping the Colour. After South Africa there was a parrot cry for " initiative, more initiative " but soldiers, who knew better than stunt journalists, never wavered in their belief that prompt unhesitating obedience to orders and attention to detail were the very groundwork of the training of the British Army.

Whether it was those loose defaulter books or not the fact remains that the luck of the Regiment changed, for not only did it not go to Abyssinia but for thirty-six years it had to " stand and wait " until its entry into the final phases of the South African War. It was at the end of May that we were informed that we were earmarked to proceed to Mooltan in the autumn and as we would thus form part of the Bengal Command our chances of active service vanished, the troops for the expedition being detailed from Bombay. It was a great disappointment for the Regiment—which was still the 109th Bombay Infantry—though it was to some extent mitigated by a speech made to us on parade by Sir Robert Napier the commander-in-chief of the Bombay Army who informed us that he had personally applied for the Regiment to form part of the force he was to take to Abyssinia. It should be mentioned, too, that Colonel Merewether the Resident of Aden who was well known for his splendid services on the frontier between 1847 to 1862, volunteered to compel the release of the British prisoners if he were given a force consisting of the 109th, the Scinde Horse (his own old regiment) and the two Baluchi regiments in garrison. The delay in sending the expedition was hard luck upon us as it enabled the people who kept the roster of reliefs to take us for Mooltan. We heard afterwards that the Regiment was officially reported to be suffering from scurvy contracted at Aden. This was, however, the first we had ever heard of the affliction.

So there was nothing to do but to keep a cheerful countenance in our disappointment and to plunge into the gaieties of garrison life at Poona. The rains and the Poona " season " now began and as we had seen only one decent downpour in two and a half years we would have welcomed the Flood itself. There was a good deal of amusement at Poona. The band of the Regiment played at Wanouri every Wednesday evening and proved a very great attraction to the residents, while the troupe of German singers from the Regiment was a unique feature. There were also balls, cricket matches, races, gymkhanas, picnics and theatricals; for the last named we put on a burlesque called "Kenilworth" in the Assembly Rooms lent us on the strict injunction that we did not put a single nail into a wall.

There is a reference to a flogging parade while the Regiment was at Poona and the fact that mention is made of it shews that this horrible punishment had become a comparative rarity by this time. The maximum number of lashes had been reduced to 50, a contrast indeed to the frightful punishments of 1000 lashes—and more—of far off days. The degrading system still lingered on and it was not until about 1879 that it was finally abolished.

On the 11th October, 1867, the mess was broken up and on the 28th the Regiment left Poona for its new station, marching down the ghauts and embarking on the P. & O. steamers *Sultan* and *Salsette*. Karachi was reached on the 3rd November and the Regiment went under canvas temporarily. We had now a new commanding officer Lieutenant-Colonel A. A. P. Browne who had succeeded to the command on the retirement of Colonel Maude on the 27th August.

Mooltan is situated some 500 miles up the Indus and the Regiment accordingly embarked on the 18th November in the steamer *Frere* which towed two flats. The journey was pleasant though slow, for we tied up at the bank each evening. We had been led to suppose that we would get some fine shooting along the right bank on our way up but those officers who pushed out in search of game after the flotilla tied up for the night had but poor sport. At last we came to the country of pig and parah (the sentence seems almost an extract from Xenophon's *Anabasis*) and a number of us determined to try our luck, leaving the steamer in the morning and marching overland to rejoin it in the evening. Fortune, however, frowned upon our zeal. Only one of our party even saw a pig and he had nothing but a shot gun with him at the time. And when we arrived at the next stage on the river after a long and tiring day's tramp it was to see the steamer's smoke six miles ahead. Eventually we arrived at Mooltan on the 12th December, 1867, less a detachment of 100 rank and file left behind attached to the 33rd Regiment under orders for Abyssinia. Headquarters went into cantonments, one company garrisoned the fort and two companies were sent on detachment to Dera Ismail Khan. The depot for feeding the Regiment with recruits was now at Chatham.

Mooltan was a sporting station in which the garrison besides the 109th consisted of a battery of Field Artillery, the 15th Bengal Cavalry and the 45th Rattray's Sikhs. Colonel Browne and some other enthusiasts started a pack of foxhounds which afforded considerable sport, and the officers of the 5th Fusiliers and, after them, of the 85th King's Light Infantry used to come down from Lahore to join in the gymkhanas and sports. Of course we had our regimental theatre, turning a disused barrack room into one and here for the first time ladies took part in the pieces we played. There was a racquet court too and a Mall, with actually a row of trees, and a cricket ground in front of a big Parsee-owned shop where we used to meet in the evenings. The great drawback to Mooltan, however, was the heat. We had felt the heat severely in Aden, especially as we had no punkahs there, but at Mooltan many of us had no punkahs either and at night we would sleep in the compounds as far away from the heated houses as we could get. The first duty of the orderly officer in the morning was to clear away the women and children with their beds from the roadway. We lost many men from heat apoplexy; and the troubles of a stage manager in India of those days will be appreciated when it is stated that in one night three members of the cast died from heat stroke.

The three years of the stay of the 109th in Mooltan

passed without any outstanding incident. We just missed one it is true—the blowing up sky high of the company in the fort, when some coolies, clearing away the bricks caused by the demolition of the fort in 1849, put their picks into *chatis* found to contain enough powder to blow part of the fort to smithereens. The cold weather was filled up with the usual frivolities of garrison life, while during the hot weather those who could not afford a trip to the hills simply existed as best they could. In those days the authorities had not grasped the fact that to keep troops in the plains in the hot weather as the normal procedure was an appalling waste in man power ; and as an instance of the inefficiency of the system it may be mentioned that out of a draft of 40 fine young soldiers who came out at the beginning of the hot weather of 1868, by the end of the year only six were doing duty the remainder having either died or been invalided to the hills.

The year 1870 was one full of interest in army circles for the startling successes gained by the Germans in the Franco-German War showed clearly that a new era in warfare had dawned. Immense numbers and a super-efficiency in staff work were recognized to be essential factors for success, and there was now a tendency to take things more seriously and an intensive form of training reigned for a time, though oddly enough in a farewell speech to the Regiment by the general officer commanding the Mooltan Brigade there is no allusion to the new state of things in the military world. The Regiment was now under orders for Roorki and Delhi and in a final inspection on the 18th November, 1870, General Kaye expressed himself as highly pleased with the drill, discipline, interior economy and general good conduct of the Regiment during the whole time it had formed part of the Mooltan Brigade. He commented on the very small number of serious crimes that had occurred, and noticed that no general court-martial had been held in the Regiment for four years. He concluded by thanking the officers, non-commissioned officers and men " for the credit that was reflected on him by the good behaviour of the Regiment while in his brigade."

It is somewhat difficult to fathom the depths of self-complacency which filled the soul of a general who could talk of " the credit brought upon himself " by the absence of crime at a time when the whole of Europe was convulsed. The greatest military Power in the world had gone down in the dust. The whole of the French army was either dead, wounded or captured; the French Emperor was a prisoner; the French capital was besieged. Never since the Babylonian captivity had there been such a national disaster and Prussia had set a standard of war efficiency which other Powers must adopt or perish. One would expect to find in the records of the Regiment a grave warning from Authority as to the urgent need in these circumstances of super-efficiency in manœuvre and fire discipline; but in those days the shadow of defaulter sheets blinded the eyes of those in command. The whole balance of power in Europe might be shattered, a small state might suddenly leap into prominence as the greatest military Power on the Continent—the union of Germany so long desired might now be taken as an accomplished fact; yet to one Anglo-Indian mind these trifles were not worth mentioning when compared with the " credit brought upon himself " by the absence of general courts-martial for four years in the 109th Regiment of the Line.

As for the move of the Regiment on the 22nd November, 1870, the right half battalion under the command of Major Schmid left for Delhi and two days later the left half and headquarters proceeded to Roorki. As the Regiment was detained at Mean Meer the two half battalions reunited for a short time leaving for Umballa on the 29th November arriving there on the following day. Then on the 19th December the two wings of the Regiment left for their destinations arriving at Delhi and Roorki on the 20th and 22nd respectively.

The effect of the war in Europe was shewn by the revival of training and the Regiment took part in various

T

camps of exercise besides undergoing instruction of a nature rather more intensive than had been the case before the Franco-German War. At headquarters there was a course of " shelter trench drill " for which practice " great praise was given to the Regiment by the Right Honourable the Commander-in-Chief " ; while as regards the right wing at Delhi under the command of Major A. W. Lucas the companies were constantly exercised in outposts and picquets and there was a series of operations of company versus company in the region round Delhi. These latter exercises were the forerunners of those " Company Marches " which came into being some years after the South African War and were then thought to be something absolutely original. An important step in the arming of the Regiment took place on the 11th October, 1871, when the Snider breech-loading rifle was issued.

On the 20th December Regimental headquarters with " F " and " G " Companies and the Band and Drums marched from Roorki to the camp of exercise near Delhi, where they were joined by " A " and " C " Companies from the latter place and by " E " and " H " Companies who were on detachment at Futteghur, the two remaining companies of the Regiment, " B " and " D," continuing to garrison Fort Delhi. The Regiment formed part of the 2nd Brigade of the 2nd Division and took part in all the manœuvres and field operations which took place while the force was assembled. The camp of exercise was broken up on the 1st February, 1872, when the two wings of the Regiment returned to Roorki and Delhi. These manœuvres brought about an important order *re* dress which was due to the Regiment. On the march from Delhi to the camp of exercise the officers of the left wing of the Regiment—taking a leaf from the book of experiences of the old 3rd Bombay Europeans—dyed their white helmet covers, and the officers of the companies which came from Roorki did the same. The result was that the 109th were able to lie concealed in nullahs during operations and to spring out upon the unsuspecting enemy at the last moment. So successful was this early attempt at camouflage that the British regiments were immediately ordered to dye their helmet covers dust colour, and for the remainder of the operations if we wanted to find their whereabouts it was only necessary to search for a strip of sand in the broken ground, cultivation or jungle.

During these years the Regiment worthily maintained its reputation in sport. The wing at Delhi kept a bobbery pack and under Major Lucas used to scour the ground miles round the city. A note in an old diary is to the effect that "among the men are some excellent *shikarris.*" Lieutenant Alec Hoyes won the Khader Cup, and Lieutenant D. W. Mackinnon, while on leave, played with success for the Gentlemen of the North versus Gentlemen of the South at Manchester. A brilliant success for the Regiment came when a non-commissioned officer won the Commander-in-Chief's shooting prize. The news was contained in a telegram to Colonel Browne from the Military Secretary on the 25th February, 1872, to the following effect, "Lord Napier of Magdala congratulates your Regiment on having in it Corporal Kidd, the best individual shot of the three thousand men who competed for His Excellency's prize."

On the 4th December, 1871, Lieutenant William Holden Webb was appointed adjutant *vice* Lieutenant Oscar Schmidt who vacated the adjutancy on promotion. The latter officer, who came from the old German Legion, had been adjutant for nine years and the zeal, tact and ability he had displayed in his office called forth a highly eulogistic battalion order from the commanding officer Lieutenant-Colonel A. A. P. Browne.

Of the remainder of the stay of the Regiment in Roorki and Delhi the official records of the Regiment have not much of importance to chronicle. There was an outbreak of cholera in Roorki in 1872 on the conclusion of which the Right Honourable the Commander-in-Chief was pleased to place upon record his appreciation of the very prompt and energetic measures adopted by Surgeon

Major R. Thornton of H.M.'s 109th Regiment in concert with the cantonment magistrate. An unusual entry is the brief report of a civil action taken by the Regiment. When moving down country in November, 1870, some property of the Regiment, which was being conveyed by rail, was destroyed by fire and the officers took an action against the railway company. The suit, however, was dismissed with costs by the Chief Court of the Punjab, and as this verdict was not given until the 16th March, 1873, it is probable that the costs had by that date amounted to a fair sum.

On the 17th April Major A. W. Lucas assumed command of the Regiment temporarily *vice* Lieutenant-Colonel Browne, on leave, and towards the end of the year orders were received directing the Regiment to hold itself in readiness for transfer to Dinapore on conclusion of the cold weather camp of exercise which began on the 28th November. On the 30th December General Travers on relinquishing the command of the division was pleased to convey his appreciation of the state of the Regiment, testifying especially to the improvement in musketry and to the " Good conduct of the soldiers which testifies to their cheerful recognition of a discipline temperately and judiciously administered." The report from which the above is an extract drew later the following gratifying testimony from the highest authority: " His Royal Highness the Commander-in-Chief has been pleased to record the following remarks ' The Corps is in a most satisfactory state of efficiency.' "

The Regiment left the camp of exercise on the conclusion of the manœuvres on the 3rd January, 1874, and marched to Roorki and on the following day it moved by march route down the Grand Trunk Road towards Cawnpore. Here it may be left for the moment while a brief survey is made of the changes—revolutionary changes as some of them were thought at the time to be—which were now taking place in Her Majesty's Army.

CHAPTER XXIII

THE 109TH REGIMENT—INDIA, 1874-1877.

THE military events which had recently taken place in France had been of such a striking and marvellous character as to excite in the minds of Englishmen a settled purpose to review their military institutions and to place them on a basis of security. Two lessons had already been suggested by the victories of Prussia over Denmark in 1864, and over Austria and her South German allies in 1866. These were the paramount necessity of arming infantry with a breech-loading rifle and the vital importance of a system of expansion by which, within a few days, an army could muster a force at least twice as large as its peace establishment. As regards the breech-loader, as a temporary expedient the Snider rifle had been adopted in the British Army. It was undoubtedly superior to the famous Prussian needle gun though possibly not to the Chassepot with which the French fought in 1870, but it had this advantage that the conversion of the existing Enfield rifles into rifles on the Snider system was a comparatively simple matter. A more perfect weapon had, however, been designed in the Martini-Henry to which reference will be made later.

In addition to the necessity for a system of expansion Prussia had shewed the world that astounding victories depend on super-excellent training of staff and regimental officers. The whole system, therefore, of the entry, education, and advancement of officers in Her Majesty's Army received an earnest attention in England, and in this era of army reform another question came to the fore—the best method of maintaining our foreign service battalions in the highest state of efficiency as regards personnel. Before, however, these questions had been decided circumstances arose which almost led to the disappearance of the 109th Regiment. In October, 1869, the Government of India, having fallen into financial difficulties, requested the Home Government to withdraw a number of regiments from India, but Mr. Cardwell was strongly of opinion that if economy were essential such local European regiments as had been raised only in recent times should come under the axe. Such a policy, if adopted, would necessarily have implied the disbandment of the 109th, but fortunately a scheme was adopted by which the infantry battalions in India were reduced from twelve companies to the home establishment of ten companies, and the depot companies were attached to a regiment at home. By this method the newly raised regiments of the late Honourable East India Company escaped extinction.

Prussia's method of expanding an army had produced a great sensation in England in the '60's of the nineteenth century but as a matter of fact it was no new thing. After the crushing disaster of Jena in 1806 Napoleon had imposed upon the defeated Prussia the condition that her army was henceforth not to exceed 42,000 men, but the genius of Scharnhorst had hit upon the method of passing men quickly through the ranks and then, after this short term of intensive training, allowing them to disappear into an invisible but highly efficient reserve. The success of the experiment was striking, for at Leipzig, a bare seven years after Jena, Prussia with a standing army of nominally 42,000 men had in reality over 150,000 trained to arms. It needed, however, the lapse of half a century, and the sight of two more successes in 1864 and 1866, before England moved in the same direction. In those days the British soldier enlisted for 21 years; there was thus a "long service" professional army but no reserve. The Army Enlistment Act of 1870 was the first step, the term of engagement of an enlisted soldier being then fixed at twelve years of which only a portion was to be passed with the colours and the remainder in the reserve; the period now fixed for the infantry being six years in each, and it was calculated that in course of time a reserve of 60,000 men would be thus created available for service in any portion of the globe. This Act was destined to have most far reaching consequences. For the first time in English history a measure was adopted by which an army, small in peace, might be at once converted into a large and effective army for the purposes of war. Before the Act received the Royal assent war broke out between France and Germany, and the lessons of that struggle must have converted almost every opponent to the measure. There were of course still many old military die-hards still unconvinced, and many were the gloomy prophecies and dark hints as to the inefficacy of "boy soldiers" made by those whose service had been passed with old bearded privates in their forties—and looking sixty if a day.

A still more far-reaching reform—at any rate so far as the officers of the army were concerned—was the abolition of purchase.

The sale and purchase of commissions appear to have come into existence as far back as the creation of a standing army and the evils it gave rise to had in some cases exercised an extraordinary influence. Writing to General Craig from the Low Countries in 1794 Sir Hew Dalrymple throws an illuminating sidelight upon the frightful inefficiency brought about by the system, and although it would be false assumption to say that such evils were always connected with the purchase system his words are worth quoting. "We are," he says, "the most undisciplined, the most ignorant, the worst provided army that ever took the field. . . . There is not a young man in the army that cares one farthing whether his commanding officer, his brigadier, or the commander-in-chief himself approves his conduct or not. His promotion depends not on their smiles or frowns—his friends can give him a thousand pounds with which he goes to the auction room in Charles Street and in a fortnight he becomes a Captain. Out of the fifteen regiments of cavalry and twenty-six of infantry which we have here, twenty-one are literally commanded by boys or idiots. ... You will hardly be surprised when I repeat that we have no discipline, that we are naked and unprovided of everything that depends on the regiments themselves, that we do not know how to post a piquet or to instruct a sentinel in his duty; and as to moving! God forbid we should attempt it within three miles of the enemy. ... As to plundering it is beyond anything that I believe ever disgraced an army; and yet I think we do all we can to prevent it—that is with the little assistance the ignorant boys or idiots alluded to above can give us."

Many of the more flagrant evils due to purchase had doubtless disappeared by the middle of the nineteenth century, but even in 1854 a Royal Commission reported that under purchase there was little inducement for officers to acquire proficiency in the science of war or to study the military progress of other nations. Provided only an officer had ready money available he was able to look forward with confidence to the attainment of high military rank. "While the subaltern who has not the means to buy advancement may serve during all the best years of his life in distant stations and in deadly climates, yet he must be prepared to see his juniors pass over him, for he will find that knowledge of military science and attention to regimental duties do not avail him, unless he is able to buy the rank to which his qualifications entitle him." Such a system naturally led to many incongruities. In one regiment the senior lieutenant had more service than any one of ten of the captains. In another the commanding officer had joined the service two years after the senior subaltern. And a few years earlier there was in a regiment serving in India a captain of forty-seven years' service who had fought at Waterloo at which time not a single officer of the regiment, except the lieutenant-colonel, was born. That the necessity for the possession of ready money was very real can be realized by an examination of prices called for, these being swollen by a figure known as the " over regulation " price, the tendering and acceptance of which, though illegal, had long been winked at. Thus the usual price of a company in a line regiment was £2,400 and nearly three times that amount was paid for a lieutenant-colonelcy.

The necessity for highly trained officers was brought home to the public by the Franco-German War. The German officers were known to be highly trained and the German army had scored an astonishing series of successes; the French officers had been trained on the lines of North African warfare and the French army had gone down in crushing and unredeemed disaster. It was natural, therefore, that public opinion in England should grow restive about a system of the appointment of officers which not only led to startling incongruities but was unique among the armies of the world. The matter was brought before Parliament, and, although a fierce opposition was encountered in the House of Lords, the Queen on the advice of her Ministers signed a Royal Warrant abolishing purchase as from the 1st November, 1871.

The effect of this ordinance though very great was not universal in the Army. Purchase did not prevail in the artillery or the engineers. In the regiments recently taken over from the Honourable East India Company nominally it had no existence, but as a matter of fact the officers used to subscribe privately to a fund the purpose of which was to bribe the commanding officer to go. Further, with the transfers and exchanges, which in the normal course of events came about, it followed that in the Regiment there were two classes of officers—those who had purchased their commissions and those who had not. As the former now were not allowed to sell their commissions they cherished a grievance against the Government as having defrauded them of a just right. To the argument that in lieu they had now a statutory right to a pension they would reply, and not without reason, that the same right was enjoyed by those officers who had received their commissions without the expenditure of sixpence. Many who read these lines will remember the post-prandial diatribes of these old warriors. The system of purchase had of course its grotesque features but not more grotesque than that abominable injustice in the Great War when young civilians in uniform, masquerading as majors, would come out to command professional officers who had joined the service before the newcomers were weaned. At least one such case occurred in the 1st Battalion.

A more far reaching effect was brought about by what was known as the " Linked Battalion System," the introduction of which was necessitated by the amount of foreign service, both in peace and war, peculiar to the British Army. It had long been evident that when any regiment consisting of a single battalion was serving abroad it had to have a depot in the United Kingdom. Four-company depots had been tried and these gave considerable satisfaction, but were abolished because they were too large and too expensive for mere depot purposes. On the other hand, were the depot to be increased to the size of a battalion it would be useful not only for training but as a fighting unit itself and regimental *esprit de corps* would be stimulated. The experience of the Crimean War shewed up in strong relief the inefficiency of mere depots as a reserve for units in the field, and indeed by 1857 the advantages of a double battalion system were so obvious that second battalions were added to the first twenty-five regiments of the line and an additional battalion to both the 60th Rifles and the Rifle Brigade.

It was now decided to complete the reorganization of the remaining single battalion regiments by transforming them into regiments of two " links. " Normally one regiment would be abroad and one at home, the latter acting as a feeder to the former to supply its casualties in officers and men. Recruits were to be enlisted for the two " links " and would be available for service in either of them. The linking together of single battalion regiments in pairs was, however, a problem of considerable difficulty and delicacy, and there were many factors to be taken into consideration. Some regiments had a nominal connexion with particular counties while in some cases this nominal connexion was complicated by the fact that the same regiment had a much more real recruiting connexion with another county. Then there were susceptibilities upon such minor matters as dress and facings, and on such major issues as history and tradition to be considered. Admittedly the task of the committee charged with the duty of finding links was a most difficult one and the duty was on the whole carried out with care and judgment. The existence of a unit with the unique distinction of being the sole regiment in the army to have a colonial title, besides being the only infantry regiment with the double honour of " Prince of Wales's " and " Royal " made the task of linking the Prince of Wales's Royal Canadian Regiment a distinctly delicate one. The decision arrived at was to link it with the junior regiment of the line the 109th Bombay Infantry. All linked regiments were finally fused in 1881 and the consideration of the whole localization of regiments is deferred until that year is reached. All that is necessary now to state is that this particular linking was extremely unpopular with both the regiments concerned.

This necessary if somewhat tedious digression has left the 109th Regiment plodding along the Grand Trunk Road toward Cawnpore. The march was a pleasant one; we were generally under canvas by 9 a.m., and after breakfast many of us would go off in search of black buck, wild geese, duck, teal and snipe, not returning to camp till just in time to dress for mess. The longest day's march was one of twenty-eight miles into Alighur when only one man fell out. It was a memorable march, for the last mile was covered at the double the striking up of the drums for the final stage causing an attack by swarms of bees from the bushes which lined the roadway.

The horses of the mounted officers, so soon as they had received the attention of the attackers, broke into a wild gallop, followed by the Regiment, many of the officers and men becoming "casualties."

We arrived at Cawnpore on the 3rd February, 1874, and after a short stay there proceeded by rail to our new station Dinapore. A battery of artillery and the 2nd Native Infantry were our companions in the garrison and we had detachments at Chunar and Hazaribagh. Before these detachments were sent out, and after the arrival of our detachment from Delhi, the strength of the Regiment at headquarters on the 14th March, 1874, was 892 of all ranks. A fortnight later the Regiment was inspected by Major-General Sir James Brind commanding the Allahabad Division who expressed himself as highly pleased with the appearance and drill of the corps.

In 1875 the Prince of Wales—later King Edward VII—arrived in India on a tour throughout the dependency. The 109th Regiment had the honour of acting as a guard of honour to His Royal Highness, and headquarters and the right half battalion strength 450 rank and file left by rail for Calcutta on the 17th December arriving two days later. The troops were encamped on the Maidan and remained in Calcutta until the Investiture of the Star of India, which took place on the 1st January, 1876, proceeding thence to Bankipore where they were rejoined by the remainder of the Regiment from Dinapore. Here we received the Prince of Wales whose visit was viewed with some concern by the authorities owing to native unrest but everything passed off very well, the most prominent agitators being bidden to an entertainment and feast—at the local gaol. On the day of the Prince's arrival he was graciously pleased to accept as a gift from the sergeants of the Regiment a fine panther which was formally presented to him by Sergeant-Major W. Affleck. The Regiment then returned to Dinapore on the 6th January, 1876, and was much gratified to receive the following day a tribute to its work at Calcutta in

Presidency Orders, which ran as follows :—" Brigadier-General Hume thanks sincerely the officers of the staff, commanding officers and men of corps and detachments that composed the garrison of Calcutta during the visit of H.R.H. the Prince of Wales for their cordial co-operation in carrying out the numerous and heavy duties devolving on them which have been performed in the most satisfactory manner."

Back in Dinapore the Regiment threw itself into the usual station gaieties, and here the meticulous historian pauses to comment on two items of sport. Polo is now mentioned for the first time and there is a reference to a new recreation called " lawn tennis " (men in pork pie caps and mutton chop whiskers, standing ankle deep in grass, gazing at a concave net, and armed with weapons which looked qualified for admission as urgent cases to an orthopædic hospital for bats). In addition to these new features there were the usual racquets, cricket matches and theatricals, badminton, dances and band evenings. Once a year there were the great fair and race meeting at Sonapore to which we always sent our band. The officers had an encampment there, and for a week racing, cricket matches and dances were the order of the day and night. Over and above this we had the excitement of a miniature deluge, two great floods occurring during our stay at Dinapore, over fifty miles of country to the south being under water. At any rate both officers and men were able to get a good deal of boating, boats being purchased in Calcutta and hurriedly sent up country.

A great chapter in the history of India was now to be opened in which it was fitting that the 109th, as the last of the Regiments of the old East India Company, should be represented. The conduct of foreign affairs by the Prime Minister of the day, Mr. Disraeli, had been marked by a wise and statesmanlike outlook as regards the Eastern possessions of England ; he was always inclined to support Turkey and to ensure her the possession of Constantinople so as to keep back Russia from attaining a menacing position on England's highway to the East ; and on his own responsibility he purchased for England a controlling number of shares in the Suez canal, recently opened. It was Disraeli, too, who sent the Prince of Wales " to shoot tigers in India," inaugurating the happy policy by which the heir to the throne is nowadays allowed to view Indian conditions at first hand. As if upon the impulse of the transaction of the purchase of the Suez Canal shares Disraeli opened the next session of Parliament with a bill to confer upon Queen Victoria the title of Empress of India. The measure was by no means enthusiastically received. An imperial title was an innovation to a people whose knowledge of the history of their country was founded largely on " The Kings and Queens of England," and for a thing to be not only new but " un-English " meant in those ultra-conservative days that " it simply couldn't be done." Besides, the title of Emperor had either a foreign, or a disastrous, or a Roman Catholic significance. The shoddiness and tinsel of the Second Empire in France had been consumed in the crucible of Sedan ; the ill-fated Maximilian in Mexico had staged a farce which ended in tragedy ; and the newly created " German Emperor " vaguely suggested the title of " Cæsar " and was strongly reminiscent of " The Holy Roman Empire," associations which were by no means to the taste either of the rising democracy of England or of Macaulay's race of " country squires fat with Staffordshire ale." Disraeli, however, carried the day and on the 1st January, 1877, the 109th Regiment marched to Bankipore and was present at the reading of the proclamation announcing the assumption of the title of " Empress of India " by Her Majesty.

Just six months later the 109th Regiment was to receive proof that it was no longer an Indian but a " Queen's " Regiment, for under orders dated Simla 31st May, 1877, it was directed to hold itself in readiness for a move to the United Kingdom. It left Dinapore at the beginning of 1877 in two detachments, headquarters under Lieutenant-Colonel A. A. P. Browne proceeding to the rest camp at Jubbulpore. Here took place the first meeting of the

109th with its linked battalion the 100th Prince of Wales's Royal Canadian Regiment, the latter newly arrived and on its way up country. This being the affiliated regiment under the new scheme of things the 109th handed over a certain number of men under the new regulations, and it was here, apparently, that the transfer of the famous blackwood table belonging to the officers' mess of the 109th to the officers of the 100th took place. This splendid and massive piece of furniture—fit both as regards dimensions and appearance for a royal banquet—was popularly supposed to have been the identical table on which were laid the dead bodies of the officers of the 24th Regiment after Chillianwallah, but this theory has not been confirmed by research. The table remained with the 100th ever after, and on the disbandment of the Leinster Regiment was handed over to the Army Council for safe custody.

The 109th moved down to Bombay embarking in two detachments. Headquarters of the Regiment, Colonel A. A. P. Browne commanding, strength 2 field officers, 4 captains, 4 subalterns and 2 staff, 409 N.C.Os., rank and file, 21 women and 43 children embarked on board H.M. troopship *Crocodile* on the 21st and 22nd November, 1877. The Regiment had recently been re-armed with Martini-Henry rifles in place of the Sniders, now returned to store, and was the first armed body to pass through the Suez canal, the reason for the retention on board of the rifles being that it was considered probable that England would have to intervene in the Russo-Turkish War. British policy at the time was expressed in the famous " Jingo " song declaring that " The Russians shall not have Constantinople " (the last word being ideal vocally for the throaty-baritoned patriotism of the " halls.") An Indian contingent was actually brought to Malta and the 109th were informed that they would " receive orders " at that port of call. No orders were, however, forthcoming and the *Crocodile* arrived safely at Portsmouth the day after Christmas. Meanwhile the remainder of the Regiment " B " and " H " Companies, under the command of

Major A. W. Lucas, strength 1 field officer, 2 captains, 2 subalterns and 1 staff with 117 other ranks, 15 women and 29 children had embarked on the *Malabar* and arrived at Portsmouth on the 7th January, 1878. It is significant of the higher mortality in trooping of those days that the regimental records note with satisfaction that " only one death occurred on the voyage."

CHAPTER XXIV

THE 109TH REGIMENT—ENGLAND 1878–1882.

THE Regiment proceeded on disembarkation to Gosport occupying three of the forts there, and shortly afterwards a change was made in the infantry head-dress of the army by which the 109th Regiment was of course affected. The Franco-German War had had the effect of extolling everything German, with a corresponding depreciation of anything French, with the result that the Frenchy looking shako had to give way to a modification of the German *pickelhaube*. From those Gosport days there dates, therefore, the helmet with spike and chain, which despite its unsuitability continued the full dress head-dress until the disbandment of the Regiment. About the same time, apparently, a new valise equipment was issued to the infantry regiments of the army.

The Russo-Turkish War, in spite of the stubborn resistance of Osman Pasha at Plevna, had resulted in a series of brilliant successes for the Russians who were in 1878 almost at the gates of Constantinople. Considerable alarm was felt in England at the possibility of a Russian menace to our route to India, and owing to the serious state of affairs the British Government decided to place a large portion of the army on a war footing. Orders were, therefore, at once issued calling out the 1st Class Army Reserve and the reserve men of militia regiments who in those days were liable to recall for active service. In that year militia battalions did not form an integral part of Territorial regiments—indeed the territorialization of the infantry did not become an accomplished fact till three years later—but an indication was given as to the future territorial connexion of the 109th Regiment by the fact that 306 men from the King's County, Queen's County and Royal Meath Militias joined for duty in April, 1878. These reservists were drilled and equipped, and remained with the Regiment until the end of July when, as there was no longer any probability of their services being required, they were sent back to Ireland. These Irishmen behaved extremely well while with the Regiment but on one occasion while crossing to Portsmouth, apparently to re-embark, they were met by reservists of other regiments who had occupied all the public-houses on the route and were busily engaged in handing out free beer. A contemporary record makes the grim reference "The result was chaos."

The expression "Territorial" as applied to regiments which became associated with cities, counties, provinces and larger portions of the United Kingdom had of course a signification completely different from that which attaches to the term to-day. "Territorial" regiments in those days were simply the *regular* regiments of the line as apart from the King's Royal Rifle Corps and the Rifle Brigade which had no particular association with any definite portion of the United Kingdom.

Some changes in the headquarters of the Regiment took place while it was at Gosport. Lieutenant and Adjutant W. H. Webb retired with a gratuity and was succeeded in the adjutancy by Lieutenant E. W. Murphy whose only son, then unborn, was forty years later to meet his death in France while gallantly commanding his father's old battalion. Lieutenant Simpson the instructor of musketry was transferred to the School of Musketry at Hythe. Musketry returns and figures, even in the memory of many now serving, were far from being considered the last word in human veracity, and in a eulogy on Lieutenant Simpson it is interesting to note that "he always carried out his duties in a strictly upright and honourable manner." A cynic might explain that this unusual rectitude accounts for the next sentence in the panegyric, "The Regiment has not been what is called a good shooting regiment."

A more important change occurred when Colonel Browne retired and was succeeded in command by Lieutenant-Colonel A. Schmid on the 13th July, 1878. The new commanding officer had in his younger days served in the Prussian Army and had taken part in the war with Denmark in 1848, when Prussia burnt her fingers badly in a war in which, as Moltke wrote later, "Prussia fought with but one weapon and the Danes with two," the reference being to the possession by the Danes of a fleet. Later A. Schmid had joined the German Legion and from it had volunteered for service with the 3rd Bombay European Regiment after the Mutiny. A fine soldier Captain Schmid was seconded for the staff in 1871 entering the Adjutant-General's Department in India, subsequently rising to be A.A.G. at Lucknow.

It is difficult now to realize that less than fifty years ago there was a British regiment of the line largely composed of Germans, yet it is an historical if half forgotten fact. In the 109th, even a score of years after amalgamation with the German Legion, there was an unmistakably German atmosphere about the Regiment. The commanding officer was a German, the orderly-room sergeant was a German, and so were the assistant orderly room clerk and the C.O.'s personal orderly. In one company the captain, the colour-sergeant and the company storeman were all Germans, and they had many compatriots amongst the rank and file of the Regiment. It must not, however, be assumed that these Germans in any way resembled the unspeakable Hun to whom we were later to be introduced; the words of a British private who lived and soldiered with them in those days are worth quoting:—" They were clean, smart, honest, sober and for the most part simple God-fearing men who were not ashamed to kneel at their cots in the barrack room night and morning and offer their prayers to God. During the writer's long service those old Germans were the only soldiers he ever saw kneeling regularly in prayer in the barrack room. Also they were loyal to the Queen, and to the country to which they had willingly given their services. It was impossible not to like these men."

Yet these old Teutons had a tender spot in their hearts for the ungrateful Fatherland which had driven them into exile. It was forbidden in the Regiment to talk German; but German songs were not proscribed and it was to a knowledge of German and an ear for music that one young British soldier owed his first step on the ladder of promotion. In January, 1879, James Duffield was a young soldier, so young in fact that his total service amounted to no more than two days. James Duffield on that second day was sitting alone on a six foot form gazing pensively into the barrack room fire. He knew a few songs and, moved doubtless by the German atmosphere, lifted up his voice in *Die Wacht am Rhein*. The solitary songster was soon startled to find a tense audience behind him, and a voice of thunder roared out " Hoch, Hoch " and then instantly demanded " Vere you learn zat song ? Vere you come from ? " The lungs which belched out these words were those of Colour-Sergeant Kalbitzer, a splendid old non-commissioned officer, who without waiting for a reply, dashed from the room and soon returned with a batch of fellow-countrymen. The military canary was urged to pipe again and the room rang with ecstatic " *kolossals* " and " *wunderbars* " and James Duffield concluded that soldiering in the 109th was very pleasant indeed.

The next morning James Duffield was formally warned for the orderly-room. He had now three days' service; but even the most lion-hearted young soldier will quail at a summons to " the mat " so early in his career. James Duffield could look any lion in the face but he quailed and quailed badly that morning, and he kept on quailing during the following preliminary investigation of his case :—

Captain Schmidt (O.C. Company) : " What you vant vis zis man ? "

Colour-Sergeant Kalbitzer : " I vant him made lance-corporal at vonce."

Captain Schmidt : " Very well."

Not knowing whether he was on his head or his heels, or whether he was British or German, or whether that blue streak in the distance was the Solent or the Rhine Private Duffield found himself on the mat.

C.O. : " Vell, vat is zis case ? "

Captain Schmidt : " My colour-sergeant wants this man made a lance-corporal at once. I recommend him. He is a ver gut man."

C.O. : " Vat service has he, adjutant ? "

Adjutant (Lieutenant Murphy, dispassionately) : " Three days, Sir."

C.O. : " Let his name be again submitted when he is dismished drill."

James Duffield worked hard at the goose step, and, when dismissed, found himself a lance-corporal the next day, and the day after that saw himself in orders for a cushy job. Soldiering and song were a rare combination so thought James Duffield in those sunny days.

But alas ! in a weak moment Corporal Duffield—as he soon became—volunteered for a draft to India. He arrived at the linked battalion, the 100th Foot. Most unfortunately he had forgotten to include any French-Canadian ditties in his repertoire and he was now in a unit where *Die Wacht am Rhein* cut no ice at all. And this is what happened on his first commanding officer's parade :—

C.O. (In a voice of thunder) : " Sergeant-major who's that d——d fool of a corporal who can't slope arms ? "

Sergeant-Major (in the acid tone utilized by sergeant-majors when referring to backsliders of the ' other battalion ') : " Corporal Duffield, Sir. Last draft, Sir."

C.O. : " Duffer by name and duffer by nature. Send him to third-class drill sergeant-major."

The unhappy corporal endured intense mental and physical suffering but it is pleasing to record that his displacement from the ladder of promotion was but temporary. Many an old retired officer, glowering over his cocktail in some Die-hard club at Bedford or at Bath, will remember his days on the square at Aldershot under the eagle eye of Sergeant-Major Duffield; and will recall many instances of those little kindnesses later by which a considerate quartermaster can alleviate the hardships of barracks or of camp.

The Regiment moved from the Gosport forts to Portsmouth at the end of August, 1878, and took up quarters at Cambridge Barracks. A few weeks later the commander-in-chief, the Duke of Cambridge, came down to inspect and a field day—or "sham fight" as it was called in those days,—was arranged for His Royal Highness. The special idea involved an attack on Fort Fareham and the Regiment came in for considerable praise for its part in the operations. Several Press correspondents watched the battle and the following is an extract from an account which appeared in *The Times*: "The advance of the 109th Regiment was one of the prettiest sights of the engagement and was very skilfully carried out, every available cover being taken advantage of. A deep ditch which ran at right angles with the beleaguered fort enabled a body of skirmishers to turn a hedge behind which some Royal Marines (the enemy) were posted and to send them flying in the open where, however, they maintained the struggle for a short time under circumstances which would have proved fatal to them."

A change in depot organization which foreshadowed the territorialization of the regiments of the line took place in March, 1879, when the depot companies of the 100th and 109th Regiments, which had been attached to the 109th since its return from India, embarked in H.M.S. *Assistance* for conveyance to Ireland. The destination of these companies was Birr where they formed the 67th Brigade Depot under the command of Major Lucas. One result of this step was the disappearance of a large part of the German element of the 109th. The Germans did not relish this new organization and very many of them whose time was up took their discharge, a notable exception being the quartermaster whose intriguing signature, " A. Just Quartermaster " became well known throughout the army. The Regiment still, however, continued to include a German strain owing to the fact that in the late '70's a few Anglo-Germans joined as six year men : but though apparently pure Teutons these claimed to be Heligolanders and were therefore not regarded as being connected with the old German Legion. The Regiment was at this time known throughout the army as the Jägers, and the last Jäger was generally supposed to be a Simeon Addlestay or Adelstein who lingered on till the '80's. As a matter of fact this Simeon was neither a Jäger nor a Heligolander, but a Pole who hated the Germans like poison and who regarded it as an insult to be associated with the Fatherland. In his way this man was something of a celebrity, for though totally illiterate he spoke English, French, German, Yiddish, Polish, Russian, Arabic, Pushtu, Punjabi, Bengali and several Indian dialects. It was said of him that he could acquire the spoken language of any country in a month and his gift was of great service when he served with the 100th in India. John Meyers, another comparatively old soldier in the '80's was popularly supposed to be a genuine Jäger ; but as a matter of fact he was merely a stranded Hamburger who managed to join the 100th as an Englishman and who served a very short period, if at all, in the 109th. A well-educated man who rose to the rank of sergeant, Meyers made history in a curious way. He asked the commanding officer for the hand of his daughter in marriage. " H.M.S. *Pinafore* " had recently been produced but alas ! Ralph Rackstraws made happy matches only on the stage. An indignant Captain Corcoran had Meyers brought before a prosaic medical board who invalided the swain as an imbecile.

That there was no organized sport for the rank and file until well on in the '80's seems now almost incredible, yet it is quite a fact. With the exception of a very occasional game of cricket between regiments, in which the players were mostly officers, the rank and file had no games. How then did the men spend their time ? In most barracks there was a recreation room which contained a bagatelle board, a few daily newspapers for those who could read, the *Illustrated London News*, the *Graphic*, *Punch* and *Judy* for those who could only read pictures, and an extraordinary collection of old books called " The Library " to which the soldier was compelled to pay a monthly subscription of 2d There were also a skittle alley and a ball alley and if these attractions were not sufficient to exercise both body and mind, in barracks, well, the private soldier could go anywhere he liked outside barracks, within boundary limits, and for other attractions, of course there was always the canteen to fall back on, where beer at 1½d. per pint could be obtained so long as he had money to pay for it.

How many people know that in 1879 the pay of the soldier had not changed since pre-Crimean days? His gross pay was only 1s. per day with an additional penny after two years' service, twopence after six years, threepence after twelve years and fourpence after sixteen years, provided he managed to keep his name out of the regimental defaulter book—a very difficult thing to do. Men who were allowed to complete twenty-one years' service also received what was called the " re-engagement penny " on completion of twelve years' service. But the gross pay of the bulk of the men was only 1s. per day. Moreover there were compulsory stoppages and a soldier was a very careful and a very fortunate man if he ever received in cash an average of sevenpence per day. There were five pay days in the month—four weekly and one settling up day and if a man got four shillings on each of the first, second, and third pay days, three shillings on the fourth pay day and a couple of shillings with a few coppers over or under at settling up he was very lucky indeed. There were compulsory monthly stoppages *viz.* :—8s. 9d. messing, 1s. 3d. washing (in a thirty day month), 2d. library, 1d. haircutting, and the most careful man had to get something on payment from stores every month (no part of the free kit of necessaries issued on enlistment was ever again renewed except on payment) such as a pair of socks, a towel, a knife, a fork, a sponge, a razor, a comb, a piece of soap and occasionally even a shirt had to be purchased, or the repairing of a pair of boots had to be paid for. Looking back on our average of sevenpence a day one often wonders how we managed to buy a pennyworth of butter and a penny bloater daily to supplement our messing, and at the same time keep ourselves in tobacco and beer. Yet we did it, and some of us even paid an occasional 2s. 6d., 5s., 7s. 6d. or 10s. fine for official over-indulgence in the latter, and now and again, managed a " bust outside."

Some idea of games provided in barracks has already been given, from which it will be seen that anything in the nature of sport or entertainment outside barracks was—well—at least a change ; to look on at a game of cricket was something, to see a regimental athletic sports meeting was a delightful way of spending an afternoon, but the joy of a good soldier's life was a stroll on the sea front with a swagger cane, wearing " made-over " boots, and defying regulations by wearing " taken-in " trousers and a " taken-down " Glengarry cap with about twelve inches of tails instead of the regulation five inches, and thus being equipped for " glad-eyeing "—or whatever was then the equivalent. Such a soldier was a swell or a masher if you like but his army cognomen was " square-pusher." The square-pusher was the *élite* of the rank and file.

Another class were those who spent a great deal of their time in " Soldiers' Institutes " which were in the late '70's becoming popular ; they provided a mild form of indoor recreation with occasional lectures, addresses and concerts but of a kind rather too straight-laced to draw big crowds. Notwithstanding this and the fact that one soldier, at least, was publicly ordered off the platform for attempting to sing a mildly humorous song, one has no hesitation in saying that they did a great deal of good in the army and they eventually destroyed the low-class public-house music hall which then infested most garrison towns. Indeed they were the fore-runners of the very fine regimental institutes now to be found in every barracks.

A third class (of whom the less said the better) were those who spent their evenings at the music hall public-houses referred to above; these places were absolute dens of iniquity with a certain outward appearance of respectability; so long as "order" was kept no one in authority ever interfered with them. Here is a description of one of them. The hall, attached to a public-house, was about thirty feet by forty with a small dirty looking stage at one end, in front of which at table sat a burly "chairman"; the floor of the hall was covered with deal tables, and groups of soldiers of all arms sat at them on chairs or benches. Attendants moved among the tables and saw to it that men did not "loaf" in the hall with empty pots; one or two tenth-rate professionals had been engaged for the week, but for the most part it was the soldiers themselves who provided the programme. When a soldier's "turn" went on to the stage, he was announced by the chairman thus:—

Rapping his table with a mallet—

If an infantryman. "Order, Order! A *bloke* of the line is going to sing."

If an artilleryman. "Order, Order! Do keep order. A *man* of the artillery is now going to oblige."

If an engineer. "Will you please keep perfectly quiet while a *gentleman* of the engineers obliges the company."

How he would have announced a cavalryman or a guardsman cannot even be conjectured.

The uniform of both the 100th and 109th was of the ordinary infantry pattern, the only difference being in the full dress head-dress, facings and badges. The head-dress of the 100th was the old shako, the facings were royal blue and the badges were the Prince of Wales's plume very much the same pattern as worn by the Regiment in 1922. The 109th head-dress was the, then, new pattern helmet, the facings were white and the badge was a royal crown.

Great changes have taken place since 1879 in both quality and pattern of the uniform as well as the number of garments allowed to the soldier; the quality then was very much better and the design or pattern was neat (the comparison is with pre-khaki clothing) and what the soldier lacked in quantity he had in quality.

On enlistment, in addition to receiving a free kit of necessaries—not anything like the number of articles he now receives—he was issued with two pairs of boots, one pair of leggings, one pair of cloth and one pair of serge trousers, one kersey frock, a Glengarry cap, a great-coat and cape; and on being dismissed recruit's drill he was given a full dress tunic and a full dress helmet; thereafter on each 1st April and 1st October he received a pair of boots, and annually on the 1st April a pair of cloth trousers and in addition on every alternate 1st April he received a full dress tunic and a pair of serge trousers. The helmet, great-coat, cape and leggings, which were "public property," were only renewed when worn out but new articles were not necessarily issued in lieu, all other articles of clothing were the soldier's "personal property" when they had lasted the prescribed period, *i.e.*—when renewed.

The arms were the ·45 Martini-Henry rifle and long bayonet (known a year or two later as the "corkscrew"); sergeants carried a long sword-bayonet—a very substantial weapon which was never "fixed" on ordinary parades. All staff-sergeants carried a handsome leather and brass-mounted slung sword; drummers and bandsmen carried a heavy dagger-like straight sword with a heavy brass hilt; pioneers in addition to carrying saws, axes, and other articles of various trades, carried a special sword with a saw-like back.

The "pack" had just been abolished and we were beginning to get used to the most complicated collection of bags, belts and straps called the "Valese Equipment" that ever the army was blessed with, before or since; we did guards in it, we did musketry drill (then called "poking drill") in it, we did skirmishing in it, we did field days in it, and we did route marching in it, and we also spent most of our spare time in barracks trying to put it together correctly and to keep it clean. The straps were of heavy, buff leather with many runners, buckles and rings, (pipe clay and brass ball)—there were two black leather ammunition pouches, (heelball, beeswax, rags and polishing bone) one black expense pouch, (special black polish), there was the valise itself, which was of strong leather and had to be kept polished so that it could be used in emergency as a looking-glass, and there was a mess tin in three pieces (bath brick) with an American leather cover. To keep all these articles in a state to satisfy a captain or an adjutant required all the spare time of a young soldier and the expenditure by him or the old soldier of the cost of many " pints " ; it would take too long to describe how the valise equipment was put together but it would perhaps be interesting to the present day soldier to know what the soldier of '79 was bound to carry on the equipment or in his valise—all on his back ; *i.e.*, haversack, Italian water-bottle, greatcoat, cape, a pair of boots, a pair of socks, a pair of trousers, a holdall complete, a towel, soap, three brushes, a tin of blacking and amongst other cleaning necessaries, at least the following : — heelball, brass ball, pipeclay, chalk, bathbrick, beeswax, buff-stick, polishing bone, buff-rubber, oil bottle, oil rags, jag, sight-protector, besides various descriptions of cleaning rags. A route march of seven or eight miles twice a week under the C.O. was not exactly a pleasant walk, neither indeed was the weekly brigade route march under the brigadier any more pleasant, but a divisional field day on the Fox Hills once a week, with perhaps at the end of the day, a march past in column at the shoulder (the long shoulder) over the sands of the Long Valley was a joy (?) that never can be forgotten.

One of the features of that old-time soldiering was the absolute mania to obtain discharge which sometimes obsessed soldiers. Those were the days when every sentry box was a mass of pencilled appeals " Roll on

1885" or whatever was the year when the scribbler's time was up. Some men would go to extraordinary lengths to "work their ticket." In the Cambridge Hospital records of 1879 will probably be found the case of Private John Hoare, 109th Regiment, who claimed relationship with John the Baptist. One night the barrack-room was startled by an unusual noise; it was John Hoare standing in the middle of the room calling us all to "repent" and proclaiming that he was John the Baptist. John was perfectly sober, but was at once transferred to the safe custody of the sergeant of the quarter guard and "crimed" with "creating a disturbance in the barrack-room after tattoo." The following morning he went before the C.O. and was "admonished"; that night the performance was repeated and the same action taken, but on this occasion John was awarded some slight punishment; then began an intensive campaign of preaching "repentance" to all and sundry from the sergeant-major down to the provost-corporal. John soon had many days' C.B. to do and became the bane of the provost-corporal's life, for all his pack-drill movements (he boasted that he was the only man in Aldershot who could give words of command in such a way that his "command" could execute fifty evolutions in fifty seconds) failed to persuade John to resign his position of "John the Baptist"; compulsory sick reports were then resorted to, but time after time these came back marked "Medicine and Duty," but medicine had no effect; neither "Medicine and Duty" nor "C.B." including sometimes twenty-eight of "all sorts," *i.e.*, 7 days' cells, 7 days' pack-drill and 14 days of answering his name to the sergeant of the guard every half hour from retreat to tattoo, stopped John from preaching repentance. At last, there was nothing else for it, John was admitted to hospital, the usual statements of his "peculiarities" being collected, and sent to a medical board, eventually discharged and sent to his home as a harmless lunatic. John afterwards wrote a letter, stating that John the Baptist rôle was a difficult one and that he found work on a farm much easier and more congenial; he had then, of course, his discharge in his pocket.

Similarly in Portsmouth in 1879 a malingerer tried the " deaf dodge." He suddenly became to all intents stone deaf; he rather over-acted the part and consequently got no sympathy from any of his comrades; he had a pretty rough time of it in barracks but nevertheless stuck it until admitted to hospital for observation which meant that every possible test and trick known to surgeons and orderlies was tried on him, but all failed to catch him. Regretfully his discharge papers were made out and sent to hospital to be given to him on discharge; the victorious smile on his face on receiving the hard-earned document rather annoyed the M.O.—especially when he turned about with a grin to leave the M.O.'s office—but the doctor had him! " Oh, by the way, Brown, I'm not quite sure whether the discharge of yours is properly made out, just let me see it a minute please." The malingerer at once halted, looked at the discharge and handed it to the M.O. " I thought so," said the M.O., " this will have to be prepared afresh." " But, Sir——." " Put him in the guard room, corporal." Result, court martial and deafness permanently cured.

The Regiment had been recruiting well both in Ireland and England but the strength was still well below establishment and such establishment was low; and a drain on the Regiment was caused by the response to a call for volunteers for the Zulu War. Over a hundred men offered their services of whom about half went to the 58th Regiment and a score to the 24th. The efficiency of the corps at this period is vouched for by a letter from the commander-in-chief who wrote that " he was glad to learn that the inspecting officer is able to give a most satisfactory account of the Regiment." The weakness of the Regiment in numbers was, however, a great disappointment to the new commanding officer who complained that it was impossible adequately to train a unit of under 500 men. After more than one interview with the War Office he decided to send in his papers, and did so in spite of the invitations to remain made to him by the authorities who recognized his value. He was succeeded by Lieutenant-Colonel A. W. Lucas who arrived from the 67th Brigade Depot on the 23rd September, 1879. Three days later the Regiment moved to Aldershot.

Until the days of the Crimean War Aldershot was merely a small village situated on the southern edge of an immense heath-covered plain, sparsely marked by fir copses, and was practically undiscovered until the construction of the South Western main line of railway. In 1853 a training camp had been formed on Chobham Common and the value of this instruction, emphasized by the lessons of the Crimea, led the War Office to consider the practicability of establishing a permanent training camp where adequate room for manœuvre would exist and where large bodies of the three arms could be handled. The choice fell upon the great expanse near Aldershot, an important consideration being that Aldershot was well situated strategically, lying as it did on the flank of a possible invader's march on London from the south coast.

In those days Aldershot was of course a vastly different place from what it is now. Except for the permanent barracks in the town, the hospital, and one or two similar buildings, there was nothing but miles of huts built during the Crimea and intended to last some ten years. These huts, it may be said, were made to do duty for four times their allotted span; and similar habitations at the Curragh were actually occupied as late as 1910. The rooms were roughly eleven feet square and a subaltern was allotted one, a captain two, and a field officer four. They were by no means weather-proof and during a blizzard one winter long lines of snow were forced through the rat holes and lay upon the floor. In addition to the permanent barracks there were a north and south camp, the Basingstoke canal forming the dividing line. The

Regiment went to the south camp and formed part of the 1st Brigade. The Aldershot District was then under the command of General Sir Thomas Steele K.C.B.

Changes in the headquarters of the Regiment took place during its two-years' stay at Aldershot. In the end of 1879 Lieutenant Murphy resigned the adjutancy and was succeeded in that appointment by Lieutenant St. John St. Leger. In the following year Lieutenant-Colonel Lucas retired and was succeeded by Major Bartholomew who, however, soon went on half-pay, and command of the Regiment then devolved upon Lieutenant-Colonel Charles Forbes who succeeded to the command on December 1st, 1880.

Meanwhile the Regiment had for the first time the honour of appearing before its sovereign, for on the 5th May it paraded with the Aldershot Division before Her Majesty Queen Victoria on the Queen's Parade, and two months later it marched from Aldershot to camp on Ascot racecourse whence it marched to Windsor with the troops from Aldershot and paraded before the Queen in Windsor Park. The Regiment returned to Aldershot on the 15th July and on this occasion the following telegram was despatched by Her Majesty : " Her Majesty has been graciously pleased to make kind enquiries as to the health and condition of the troops in camp and hopes they have not suffered from the inclemency of the weather." Her Majesty's enquiry was due to the fact that on leaving Windsor Park the Aldershot troops had been caught in a terrific downpour and on returning to Ascot the camp was seen to be a regular quagmire. A regular river flowed through the officers' mess tent and every one was wet through. The march to Aldershot should have taken place the following day but it was decided to wait until the men's things had dried a bit. Accordingly the men, taking our neighbours the 42nd as an example, divested themselves of their trousers—which they hung up on the bushes to dry—and walked about with the capes of their great-coats utilized as kilts. Much amusement was caused by the apparition of these sham Highlanders but anyway the trousers dried which was the main thing.

The great advantage of our lines in Aldershot was that they were close to the officers' club, garrison cricket ground and tennis courts. We had in those days still a very good cricket team led by Captain Mackinnon who was a "class" player. All the other battalions at Aldershot went down before us rather easily except the 82nd with whom we won and lost alternately. Several of our regimental eleven played for the Aldershot Command. Except for two field days a week, an occasional review before the Duke of Cambridge or some other royalty, and some minor operations the work was not excessively hard. The field days were always on the same two days each week so that it was always easy to arrange a jaunt to town, although leave other than the C.O.'s twenty-four hours was by no means easy to obtain. The field days, be it said, were very uninteresting to the junior officers who were never, in those days, enlightened as to what was going on. We would march out to the Fox Hills or some other ground, remain for a long time halted in some hollow, and then receive orders to extend for attack or to take up a position for defence. This would last until the cease fire sounded when we would march past the G.O.C. and so home. Those were the days of absolute precision when things were done in one way and in one way only. Distance had to be kept to a foot and dressing to an inch; the words of the drill book had to be used and no others.

There was one curious review in 1880. The troops were being inspected in the Long Valley by the Duke. On the command "Officers and Colours to the front" it was found impossible for the officers to advance although they were propped up by colour-sergeants. This is no reflection on the sobriety of the Regiment; the cause was a hurricane. An attempt was then made to march past; but the appearance of the Long Valley that day with helmets bounding over the sand like footballs was so unlike a ceremonial parade that the function was wisely abandoned.

x

The summer of 1881 was very hot the temperature frequently rising to over ninety in the shade, and one field day when the Duke of Cambridge was present several men collapsed with sunstroke and died. The matter was raised in Parliament and the Duke was called to account. His reply was that he had not considered the heat excessive, but there is all the difference in the world between sitting on a horse on a hill-top where any air that is can be found, and sweltering in one of the close and oppressive valleys on the Fox Hills and toiling from one to the other on foot. Two of our sergeants went down and although they escaped with their lives they had to be discharged as permanently unfit for further service. In those days of course the men wore red, as did the officers. As the latter had no red uniform except tunics these were worn on all field days and manœuvres. Think, reader, what it must have been like fighting over the Fox Hills in a heavy and padded tunic, tightly buttoned at the neck and in a temperature of over ninety in the shade. The custom was, however, to linger on for several years longer.

It was during this summer that an immense change was wrought in the organization of the Infantry of the Line. The old regimental numbers disappeared, and linked regiments were amalgamated into one unit with a territorial title. So far as the 109th Regiment is concerned its future was laid down by the following order of July 1st, 1881, " The 109th Regiment (Bombay Infantry) will from this date be designated the 2nd Battalion The Prince of Wales's Leinster Regiment (Royal Canadians)."

This amalgamation and territorialization of regiments were the logical outcome of the system of " linked battalions " which had now been some years in existence, but the effects were much more far reaching. Henceforth, except in the case of the first twenty-five regiments of the line, the honours, distinctions and traditions of individual regiments had to be pooled ; and the pool was to be shared by two partners who were united not as the result of mutual overtures but in consequence of orders from above. It is admitted that the authorities charged with the delicate task acted with judgment and tact but it was of course impossible to please everyone. Of all the conservative features of human society there is none more wedded to the past, more jealous of privilege and none more exclusive in its interests than a British regiment. Those who were responsible for the compulsory union of pairs of individual regiments were far-seeing enough to know that the great healer Time would sooth away the initial wounds to regimental pride and self-esteem, but probably failed to realize the dislike with which the amalgamations were regarded at the time. Now that nearly half a century has elapsed since the amalgamation of the 100th and 109th Regiments, and now that the colours of the Leinster Regiment rest in the cloistered immobility granted to the emblems of a disbanded regiment, there is no harm in relating that the union brought about in 1881 was pleasing to neither corps.

It had been possible in the case of a good many regiments to find some common denominator of local or historical signification which rendered the pairing comparatively simple; but in these respects the 100th and 109th were poles asunder. There was no possible connexion between a regiment which had been raised in Canada and one which was the youngest born of the Honourable East India Company. The 100th Foot felt an intense and legitimate pride in the fact that it was the only regiment in the British Army with a colonial origin and title; it was in a sense the successor to the famous Royal Americans who had become a battalion of the 60th Rifles, and it was the only regiment of the line which enjoyed the honour of the double title "Prince of Wales's" and "Royal." Jealous of its unique position the 100th viewed with disfavour a compulsory amalgamation with a unit to which Canada was a mere geographical expression. As for the 109th its origin and sympathies were Indian. Whatever may have been the faults of the old East India Company it was at any rate

X 2

able to inspire its military servants with a strong sense of *esprit de corps*, and it must never be forgotten that the older European regiments of the Company had a record of service dating back almost to 1660. From the mere point of age—and the claims of long descent are always extremely powerful in a conservative institution like an army—there were few Queen's regiments to vie with the old Europeans of Bombay, Bengal or Madras. The 109th itself was but a young regiment ; but it regarded itself as intimately connected with the 103rd Bombay Fusiliers, a corps of immense antiquity, from which it had, indeed, sprung. The old Anglo-Indians of the 109th Bombay Infantry viewed with dismay a compulsory union with a young colonial regiment. And it must be mentioned that the word "colonial" had then a disparaging significance ; so much so that in course of time the word fell into disfavour owing to the strong representations of the inhabitants of the overseas dominions themselves.

The feeling which existed in the 109th at the time can be gauged from the following letter submitted by Lieutenant-Colonel C. P. Forbes the officer commanding. The copy from which the letter is reproduced is undated but from internal evidence it is clear that it was forwarded between the 6th April, 1881, and the 30th June of that year.

" Sir,

I have the honour to forward for favourable consideration of H.R.H. the F.M. C. in C. this the claim of the Regiment under my command to be linked with the 103rd Bombay Fusiliers, as a 2nd Battalion, in place of to the 100th Royal Canadian Regiment, and trust that the same may be submitted to the Army Committee now sitting on Formation of Territorial Regiments.

" In 1853 when the H.E.I. Company found it necessary to increase the European Regiments in the Bombay Presidency from 2 to 3 the 3rd Bombay European Regiment was raised in Poona by Lieutenant-Colonel

David Forbes on 15th November, 1853, and consisted chiefly of volunteers from the 1st Bombay European Regiment (now 103rd) and 2nd Bombay European Regiment (now 106th). Several of the officers of these regiments came over with their men and these formed the 3rd Bombay European Regiment (now 109th Regiment). This regiment served all through the Central Indian Campaign under Sir Hugh Rose (Lord Strathnairn) and any work on that campaign will testify how well and bravely they performed their duties and won " Central India " on their colours. In 1862 the 3rd Bombay European Regiment was amalgamated into the line, and became the 109th Regiment of Foot, and returned from India in 1877-78 for the first time. The old colours of the 3rd Bombay European Regiment are deposited in the Bombay Cathedral and I feel I am expressing the wishes of all ranks of the 109th Regiment in putting forward this claim to be rejoined to the old Regiment from which they were formed, and with which they have many associations.

" I trust this may meet with approval.

" I may add that I brought this matter to the notice of H.R.H. when attending his levee on the 6th April 1881, and also that the C.O. of the 103rd is most anxious that the two old Bombay Regiments 103rd and 109th may be linked together."

The appeal, however, was without effect. It must be borne in mind that the Committee making the unions of individual regiments were faced with a special difficulty in the case of the 100th Regiment. For obvious reasons there was a case for retaining the title of " Royal Canadians " in the nomenclature of the Army List—a fact which necessitated the 100th being the senior in whatever pair it should be assigned. For it was not to be expected that, if it were amalgamated with any Regiment from the 26th to the 99th, the senior partner would take over a colonial title with which it had no connexion whatever. There were then left the Regiments 101 to

109 taken over from the Honourable East India Company, and as none of these would voluntarily become part of a Canadian regiment the good old rule of taking the junior regiment was put into force. There was indeed one possible solution of the difficulty. It so happened that, when all the pairs had been told off, there must be one regiment over, and a good case could have been made out for leaving the regiment with such unique features as the Prince of Wales's Royal Canadian Regiment as the one to maintain its individuality intact. The one selected for this distinction proved, however, to be the 79th Cameron Highlanders with whom the 109th thought they might perhaps be amalgamated. There was of course not at first sight much in common between a young regiment of John Company and a much older one from the highlands of Inverness; but on the other hand the officers of the 109th were to a large extent of Scottish origin and the bearers of Scottish names. This possible solution was rejected by the authorities, and the amalgamation of two regiments one from Canada and one born in India, one with a pronounced French strain and the other a strain more pronounced of Germans (this, too, a mere ten years after the Franco-German War) took place; and the 100th and 109th became respectively the 1st and 2nd Battalions of the Prince of Wales's Leinster Regiment (Royal Canadians). As might have been expected this title proved rather cumbersome on ceremonial parades and the difficulty was solved by the adoption by the 1st Battalion of the caution "Royal Canadians" while the 2nd Battalion employed the one word "Leinsters."

Marriages, it is said, are made in heaven; but it is a matter of common knowledge that those arranged by kind-hearted and experienced friends of the families often prove the happiest. Certainly this was the case in the union of the two regiments to form the Leinster Regiment. Although in the hearts of old 100th and 109th officers there sometimes reigned a fierce partisanship for their old unit, a community of interest and the frequent transfer on promotion of officers from one battalion to another gradually soothed away the asperities of 1881. In a few years officers joined the Regiment who knew no more of the old East India Company than they had gleaned from a holiday task of Macaulay's "Warren Hastings" (and that was not much); and as recruiting for the 1st Battalion had long ceased in Canada, the Canadian tradition—though cherished by every officer of the 1st Battalion—became too dim to have any practical influence. Year by year the Regiment grew more and more preponderatingly Irish and this national homogeneity eventually welded the Regiment into one solid whole. Long before the fatal year of disbandment the 1st and 2nd Battalions thought of themselves not as Canadian or Company units but as integral portions of one and indivisible Prince of Wales's Leinster Regiment.

Meanwhile the militia had been undergoing an important constitutional change. It was part of the new army system inaugurated in 1871 that the control of the militia should be removed from the hands of the Lord-Lieutenant of the County and vested altogether in the Crown. It accordingly virtually ceased to exist as an independent body and in 1881 became a part of the regular forces with a limitation as to the time and area and other conditions of service. Thus the militia was at this time liable for service only in the United Kingdom. Most regiments had by the new organization of 1881 only one militia battalion but the case was different in Ireland where, even with the formation of new Irish regular regiments, there was a surplus of militia battalions. Three were now amalgamated with the new Leinster Regiment namely the King's County, Queen's County, and Royal Meath Militias which henceforth became the 3rd, 4th and 5th Battalions respectively of the Regiment. The emblem of the new Regiment was devised by a union of the insignia hitherto borne by the 100th and 109th Regiments, the former contributing the Prince of Wales's plume and the maple leaves, while the 109th brought the laurel wreath and the honour "Central India."

The following is a list of the officers who were serving with the 109th when the Leinster Regiment came into being :—

Commanding Officer, Lieutenant-Colonel C. P. Forbes.

Majors, J. S. Mordaunt, D. W. Mackinnon, J. H. Campbell, J. R. Atkin.

Captains, L. E. C. Inglefield, A. S. Woods, E. F. Owens, E. W. Murphy.

Lieutenants, H. Martin, A. K. Huddart, W. W. Battiscombe, T. H. Stavert, H. R. Brander, C. W. Tribe, W. H. Greenwood, A. F. G. Foulerton.

Adjutant, Lieutenant St. John J. St. Leger.

Quartermaster, A. Just.

The strength of the Regiment at this epoch was 19 Officers; 42 Sergeants; 49 Corporals; 15 Drummers; 456 Privates.

The tumult and the shouting died. The 109th Regiment woke up on the 1st July, 1881, to find itself the 2nd Battalion of the Leinster Regiment, and the usual routine of Aldershot work continued. It is pleasing to note that the very first entry in the records of the newly named Battalion is to mention the winning of the shield presented by H.R.H. the Duke of Connaught at the Aldershot Rifle Meeting, which was won for the Battalion by a team consisting of Colour-Sergeant F. Casbard, Sergeant A. Duckworth, Private C. Cockbill, and Private J. Smith. Then in the autumn there was a command company shelter-trench competition—shelter trenches being the great "stunt" caused by the Russo-Turkish War of 1877-78—in which a company of the Battalion reached the final and would possibly have won were it not that the company was numerically very weak and the trench correspondingly short. In those days when a regiment came home from abroad it went to the bottom of the foreign service roster and was given a low establishment, so low that when the drafts for India left in the trooping season the 2nd Leinster Regiment was a mere skeleton.

There was in those days an officer's guard at Aldershot for the instruction of young officers. It was situated in the centre of the South Camp opposite Truefitt's shop, and when one was on guard most of one's friends in the Battalion and all acquaintances getting their hair cut at Truefitt's would drop in alcoholically inclined. The officer of the guard was allowed to go to his own mess for meals and after the captain and the field officer of the day had paid their last visit the young officer invariably turned in. This sometimes led to an awkward predicament when a restless G.O.C. took it into his head to visit the guard in the small hours, but as a bed and bath were provided officially the custom was winked at by the authorities.

The Battalion was very popular at Aldershot our chief friends being the 32nd and the 42nd, or to give them their new titles, the 1st Battalion The Duke of Cornwall's Light Infantry and the 1st Battalion Royal Highlanders (The Black Watch). With the other Irish battalions there were a couple of scraps which, as they led to no permanent ill feeling, may be safely mentioned. The 87th who were in the next lines to us were under orders for Egypt and in order to bring them up to strength the War Office called for volunteers from other units, offering a bounty of £1. Several of our men volunteered and one night one of them, flown with insolence and beer, called for three cheers for the 87th, adding parenthetically " To hell with the Leinster Regiment." Immediately the renegade was landed with a pint pot and then the fun began. The lines of the two battalions were quite close to the canteen and soon large contingents of Irish Fusiliers and Leinsters were hard at it. We heard the shindy in our mess and with the officers of the 87th ran down to see what we could do to quiet things down. With the help of the inlying piquets of the two battalions the situation was soon controlled but the next morning the canteen and the neighbourhood looked as if there had been an earthquake. There was, however, no further trouble and the 87th left soon afterwards.

The other disturbance was with the 18th Royal Irish commanded by Lieutenant-Colonel Gregorie and took place on a field day. Our brigade was holding a position on Cæsar's Camp and the 3rd Brigade was attacking, the Royal Irish being directly opposite us ; and when the umpires decided that the attack of the 3rd Brigade had failed they ordered it to halt. The Royal Irish, however, did not comply but continued to advance with the result that within a few minutes the two battalions were blazing away at each other at close quarters. The officers of both battalions and some of the staff rushed in between the combatants but could not get the Royal Irish to retire and of course we had no orders to do so. The situation looked ugly for a moment until our brigadier ordered us to fall back. By this time the men had become very excited but the discipline of the Battalion stood the strain and it at once obeyed.

After the summer of 1881 we were busy packing up for we were under orders to proceed to Preston. We left Aldershot late at night on December 2nd—an unsatisfactory arrangement as the men had the whole day to say good-bye to their friends and were not as steady as they might have been. Fortunately, however, the night was very dark and the Battalion escaped notice to a great extent. Nearly every band in camp came to play us out and most of the generals met us somewhere to say farewell.

Preston does not bulk large in the history of the Battalion. In 1882 war broke out with Egypt—or rather with the rebel Arabi Pasha and his followers—and in the same year occurred the terrible tragedy of the Phœnix Park murders when Lord Frederick Cavendish and Mr. Burke were assassinated. These events led to a considerable movement of troops with the result that the stay of the 2nd Battalion in Preston lasted merely some seven months.

We were quartered in Fulwood Barracks which were situated some distance from the town. These were built like many barracks in the form of a square with the officers' mess and quarters on the north side, men's quarters on the west and east and the church, school and gateway on the south. With us at Preston were the depot of the Loyal North Lancashire Regiment and a squadron of the 5th Dragoon Guards. Preston was in the Northern District which was then commanded by General Cameron, a fine old soldier but a perfect terror at inspections. It is believed that he had been in the ranks and certainly he was a veritable drill sergeant in his ways. He expected all the officers to be able to drill their men just like a drill instructor and to know all the "detail" of the drill book by heart; and he was also insistent upon every officer being able to call over his company by name. The subaltern of the first company having got into hot water at this stage of the inspection, the remaining subalterns hurriedly requested their men to answer to any name, a sensible arrangement which worked extremely well.

Those were the days when messes were usually run by messmen who charged so much a meal and bled the officers as much as possible. The charges were high and as little as possible was given for the money. We had a veritable ruffian who treated the younger officers with contempt so that many a subaltern had not enough to eat. At Preston as in most barracks of those days there was a large mess room but the ante-room was very confined the idea being that officers would sit over their wine and drink a deal of it till it was time to go to bed. As no one was supposed to leave until the senior officer present gave the word mess became somewhat of a trial when some garrulous old die-hard discoursed about his grievances or his reminiscences, over his port. Fortunately, as a battalion we were very fond of whist and had besides some good billiard players so we never stayed very long at the dinner table. We played a good deal of cricket in the summer of 1882, our chief opponents being Stonyhurst College, Southport, Lytham, etc., and we won most of our matches. We introduced afternoon dances at Preston which were so popular that they were held for a time once a week, and on the whole Preston was an enjoyable if a rather quiet station. Our stay there was suddenly interrupted by the news of the Phœnix Park murders and on 31st July the Battalion left for Ireland, the move having been brought about by the error of some War Office official who misread " Leicester " for " Leinster "—at least such has always been the legend in the Battalion. We crossed from Liverpool to Kingstown in the Pacific liner *Iberia* and marched thence to Dublin passing on the road a battalion of Coldstream Guards *en route* for Egypt, the band of that unit playing the rather inappropriate popular melody *We'll never come back any more.*

CHAPTER XXV

THE 2ND BATTALION—IRELAND 1882-1887.

IT was a hot march into Dublin and as we had experienced rather a rough crossing we thought it unkind that an empty train on the wharf could not have taken us into the city. Worse still the authorities subsequently refused us the marching allowance alleging that the distance, as the crow flies, to Richmond Barracks was under ten miles; it certainly seemed more but then we were not crows. Arrived in Dublin we found that the Powers that Be were by no means pleased to see another Irish regiment, such being the very last thing they wanted at such a disturbed period, and it was then asserted that we had been sent over in mistake for a battalion of the Leicestershire Regiment. As a matter of fact we spent just a week in Richmond Barracks waiting for our fate to be decided, and as all our things remained packed up we were not very comfortable. Finally Lord Clarina who was on the staff and an old friend of the Battalion told us that we might either stay in Dublin, go to the Curragh, or go to Birr where our depot was. As we had had a very happy time at Aldershot, and in our simplicity believed that the Curragh was something of the same kind of station, we volunteered to go there. Nothing happened during our brief stay in Dublin except garrison duties of which there seemed to be a great deal and guard duties, there being officers' guards at the Castle, Bank and Magazine. At the latter place a man of " F " Company created some alarm by opening fire while he was on sentry-go at night, alleging afterwards that he had seen a ghost. The rocket by which the garrison could be alarmed was that night in charge of a colour-sergeant of the Battalion who luckily kept his head thus obviating a fruitless turning out of all the troops in Dublin.

In 1882—and for many years after—the troops at the Curragh were housed in huts of the same old type as at Aldershot but they were not in such good repair, and as the camp was situated on the top of a ridge the wind and rain used to beat into them. On one occasion in a gale the skylight in the mess-room roof was wrenched off and went sailing away into the unknown.

When we arrived the weather was fine, everything looked well and we hoped for a pleasant tour like that of Aldershot. The nearest battalion to us was the old 52nd, but as it was a regimental custom of theirs not to make any units honorary members except those which had formed part of the famous Light Division we went to the 94th on the other side of them and became great friends. This was the regiment which had the year previously been cut up in the disaster of Bronkhorst Spruit in the Transvaal, when the colours had been saved by a young ordnance subordinate, Egerton by name. Egerton for his valour was given a combatant commission and eighteen years later when he was serving in a battalion of the West India Regiment the officers of the Battalion had the pleasure of making his acquaintance at Barbados and Jamaica. As it was the summer when we arrived at the Curragh we of course plunged at once into cricket upholding the reputation of the Battalion; as for work the field days were a farce. They took place on the open ground of the Curragh and were carried out just like a parade manœuvre—with such exactitude that after each attack every man was supposed to be in his original place in his company and every company in its original position in the Battalion—this be it remembered not two years after Majuba. It required another long and a costly war in South Africa before we were able to rid ourselves of precision merely for precision's sake.

The Battalion was weak in numbers at this time and the strength while at the Curragh was still further reduced by the necessity of finding two detachments at Boyle and Carrick-on-Shannon respectively. The fine weather lasted just about six weeks and then it began to rain as it can rain at the Curragh. With short intervals of comparative fine weather it must have rained for two months, and as we were perched on a ridge in the middle of a plain " grassy, wide and bare " and miles from anywhere there was absolutely nothing to do. We used to go for cross-country runs, as a relief from boredom, coming back wet to the skin. When Lord Clarina came in October to inspect us he asked us how we liked the Curragh, to which question with one voice we replied that we hated it. He then asked us if we would like to go to Birr as that station was still vacant and we literally jumped at the offer. So the move there was soon arranged.

While at the Curragh an innovation was started in the officers' mess. We had been living under the tyranny and inefficiency of a messman but some zealous spirits wished to try the experiment of the officers running their own show. Lieutenant Stavert took on the important though thankless office of caterer, and in defiance of the wishes of some of the older officers who wanted the charge to be so much a meal, stuck out for an inclusive charge of so much a day. After a careful investigation of prices Lieutenant Stavert startled the mess by declaring that he could give three good meals and coffee for 4s. 3d. a day; a prediction which was scouted by many as the messman had been charging about 7s. for the same meals. Lieutenant Stavert, however, proved as good as his word and not only delivered the goods but shewed a handsome profit as well, consequently the reformer was allowed to run the catering in his own way. The subalterns scored immensely by the introduction of this new system and the mess of the Battalion owes much to the foresight and energy of Lieutenant Stavert. For years, however, there rankled in the bosom of the catering officer a complaint made by the mess sergeant that one young officer had eaten eight eggs for breakfast " Gather ye rosebuds while ye may."

On the 17th November, 1882, the Battalion left Newbridge by special train for Birr, or Parsonstown as it is called in the Battalion records. We had now reached our regimental home and the fact that we were met by a welcoming crowd at the station was a good augury for our stay in the place.

In the territorial system which had recently been introduced, and by which we became the 2nd Battalion of the Leinster Regiment, the " area " of the Regiment was laid down as the counties of King's County, Queen's County, Meath, Westmeath and Longford—broadly speaking Central Ireland—and the depot, or headquarters of the Regiment was to be at Birr; while of the counties in our area the militia regiments from the three first named above became battalions and integral portions of the Regiment. Our move to Birr brought us therefore not only into our home area but to the very headquarters of the Regiment and to the headquarters of our senior militia battalion, the King's County Militia, now the 3rd Battalion. The people of the neighbourhood were pleased to have a regiment of their own and soon shewed that they had adopted us in the most hearty manner. Our title the Leinster Regiment did not, however, indicate much intelligence on the part of the committee which had been responsible for the new territorial designations. Three other Irish regiments had areas which included parts of Leinster and one of them, the Royal Dublin Fusiliers, had an area, like ourselves, entirely inside the province. Inasmuch, however, as our area included five counties it was not possible to give the Regiment a purely county designation—much jealousy would have been aroused in the counties not selected for the title, and at any rate the title Leinster Regiment was preferable to the Central Ireland Regiment which might have been the alternative.

During the three years which the Battalion passed at Birr it was undergoing a profound if silent change. It had come home from India full of old soldiers—very many of them Germans—and with officers who had grown old together in Indian traditions. At that time the officers from the colonel well down into the list of subalterns had been of much the same service and the position of younger officers joining the mess—and also that of recruits in the barrack room—had been a very subordinate one indeed. Since the arrival home of the Battalion there had been a great number of retirements and by the time we went to Ireland there were only four of the old Indian officers left. The introduction of the territorial system was gradually sapping the Indian tradition, and the Irish character of the Regiment was coming to the front. Of the old soldiers who still remained the most interesting were the handful of survivors of the old German Legion—the Quartermaster Just, Colour-Sergeant Cramer, Sergeant Hartmann and about half a dozen privates. In another respect, too, a change and one to the good had come over the Battalion. The relations with our first battalion were continuously growing better. Though we had for some years been linked battalions under the Cardwell scheme each battalion had kept to its own customs and traditions and it was natural that when they were turned into one regiment under the territorial system there should be some difficulty in settling down. But as the seniors retired and officers were transferred from one battalion to the other—and the same change over occurred of course with the non-commissioned officers and men—the *esprit de corps* of the Battalion was gradually merged into that of the Regiment. Young blood, too, began to permeate the arteries of the Battalion. Before 1880 promotion had been very slow. One officer had actually been nineteen years a subaltern; but as the older officers were entitled to Indian pensions many of them went on attaining field rank. This brought about a run of promotion, and, although several officers were brought in from outside, many subalterns of the Battalion got their companies in six years.

We were nearly three years at Birr and the officers had

a very easy time as we had hardly any men; we kept the Battalion thoroughly efficient and always got a good inspection report but numerically we were too weak for strenuous training. For instance when we were inspected by Major-General Lord Clarina on the 18th September, 1883, the state of the Battalion read 21 officers, 39 sergeants, 2 warrant officers, 15 drummers, 345 rank and file, and our " establishment " of rank and file was only 450, though subsequently raised to 520. Still we kept the reputation of the Battalion up, our musketry was good and we got the third prize in the army for signalling, this success foreshadowing the triumphs which later came to the 2nd Battalion in flag-wagging all over the world. Those were the days of setting up drill each spring. The whole Battalion would start at the beginning of the drill book, working from the " correct position of the soldier " through squad and company right up to Battalion drill. It was an amusing sight to see some of the real " old soldiers " solemnly practising the goose step or marching round the barrack square saluting by numbers.

So much for work. As regards play the officers had a splendid time. The people were most hospitable and we must have known everyone within a radius of thirty miles. There were constant dances, paper chases and tennis parties; and hardly a week passed without some show in barracks to our friends. There was a first class tennis club in the town which held an annual tournament and a gun club which met at several houses where we tried our skill at clay pigeons. The dances whether in barracks or outside were carried out with great spirit; beginning punctually they went on till late, and on one occasion guests were leaving as recruits were falling in for 7 a.m. parade. Once some of us drove thirty miles to a hunt ball in Galway getting back just in time for a hurried change for C.O.'s parade. Then of course we went to all the race meetings within thirty miles and hunted regularly with the King's County and Ormonde. On at least one occasion we had thirteen officers of the

Battalion at a meet which was not bad for an infantry battalion. *Praeteritos referat si Iuppiter annos!*

Cricket of course we had in plenty. We won practically every match, though on one occasion we were humbled to the dust by the boys of a Roman Catholic school, a boy who bowled underhand grubs bringing ruin to our side. Our bowling and fielding were generally the chief elements of our success, as we generally got our opponents out for a small score which we easily topped. We once got a Roscrea team out for seven, and on another occasion dismissed a team of Galway gentlemen for fourteen, after which we went in and hit up over two hundred ourselves. Some of our games were two-day matches and as we used to put our opponents up there were some noisy but enjoyable evenings in consequence. Once we drove thirty miles to Athlone for a two-day match with the battalion stationed there; and on another occasion, in order to make the most of the event, we arranged with the G.O.C. Curragh to have no field days for a week and we went there and played three two-day matches and won them all although our team was composed almost entirely of officers. We dined with a different battalion each night and had rather a strenuous time of it as may be imagined.

The 3rd Battalion came up for training every year at Birr and made things very lively as it was an extremely hospitable corps and combined training with something like a long picnic.

It was not only the officers who had an enjoyable time at Birr. The non-commissioned officers and men were in their home station and had very many friends in the neighbourhood. The Battalion was becoming every day more distinctively Irish so far as the non-commissioned officers and men were concerned, and the construction of the barracks at Birr did much to gather in fine recruits from the territorial area. The barracks were in duplicate having been built originally for two battalions, but now the depot occupied one half and one battalion—in this case ourselves—was quartered in the other. The depot and the 2nd Battalion were therefore like two members of a family sharing a single house, although of course administratively the two were quite distinct. The arrangement was a thoroughly happy one. A recruit on joining was quartered in one wing of the double barracks and did his recruit's drill at the corresponding end of the barrack square. On completing his recruit instruction he simply collected his traps and moved to the other end of the barracks and did his young soldier's instruction at that end of the parade ground. There was a kind of happy family feeling about this arrangement which was all to the good as regards recruiting and did much to lay the foundations of an extremely territorial and " happy " regiment which the Leinster Regiment grew to be.

In the autumn of 1885 these good days came to an end, and we left for Fermoy on the 19th September. We said good-bye to Birr with the greatest regret and everyone seemed sorry to see us go. More than one old 2nd Battalion officer, reviewing all the stations he has served in both at home and abroad in a long regimental service, has been heard to declare that of all the stations where he was quartered there was none to beat Birr.

The stay of the Battalion at Fermoy was brief, but there were several changes in the Battalion during our six months' stay. Captain St. Leger, the adjutant, was appointed adjutant of the 2nd Royal Jersey Militia, and was succeeded in the Battalion by Captain Herbert Martin. A couple of months later—on 1st December, 1885, to be exact—Colonel C. P. Forbes after five years in command, and twenty-seven years' service in the 109th, was placed on half-pay, and was succeeded by Lieutenant-Colonel and Colonel C. H. P. Ducat. That officer, however, did not remain long with the Battalion, retiring in March, 1886, with the honorary rank of Major-General. The new commanding officer was Lieutenant-Colonel and Colonel G. G. Stewart.

We were quartered in the Old Barracks the Royal Welsh Fusiliers being in the other barracks known as the New

Barracks. Our stay in Fermoy was short and little occurred there worth narrating. There was a garrison pack of hounds which, however, was rather an unnecessary expense as there were other packs quite close at hand; and what with farmers' lunches, a point-to-point race meeting and other expenses most of our spare cash went to the hounds. Apart from the hunting the river provided us with the most of our recreation. We got over from the Thames two rather fine river boats but we were not long enough in Fermoy to get much value from them. The Battalion was not at its full strength in Fermoy all the time owing to the fact that in November, 1885, two companies, each made up to one hundred non-commissioned officers and men, were sent on detachment to Limerick. The remainder of the Battalion followed in May, 1886.

The people of Limerick had made things unpleasant for a battalion quartered there—as well as can be remembered a battalion of the 60th Rifles—and as a consequence the military had been withdrawn. No sooner had this happened than the shopkeepers began to realize that they had killed the goose with the golden eggs, for it was said that the presence of a battalion in the city was worth £60,000 a year. The shopkeepers then petitioned the authorities to send another battalion and it was decided to see how an Irish battalion would meet the situation. At first two of our companies were sent as a detachment and then as nothing happened the whole Battalion united there. The townspeople of Limerick as a matter of fact were never very friendly to the Battalion, but except for a few small disturbances nothing noteworthy occurred. There were two barracks at the east end of the city and the Castle in the slums of the west end. We occupied one of the barracks and had a company at the Castle. The officers from the Castle came to mess at the barracks and sometimes had things thrown at them on the way.

Shortly after our arrival a meeting for the purpose of unveiling a memorial to the " Manchester Martyrs " was proclaimed by the Government and the troops were held in readiness to assist the police in stopping the meeting. Another battalion was sent to help us and both battalions were formed up on the barrack square each man having forty rounds of ball ammunition. The arms were piled and we were allowed to fall out but were warned to be ready to fall in at a moment's notice. However, after the officers of the two battalions had hung about our mess for some thirty-six hours the police unveiled the memorial and the trouble was over. On another occasion a company was sent out to a village about seven miles away to hold the place during the trial of a priest. When we got there the village was surrounded by a large crowd armed with hurley sticks, and the resident magistrate said that, to prevent an attack on the village, no one was to be allowed to enter it. Nothing serious happened though the company had to assist the Royal Irish Constabulary to drive back the mob. The priest was found guilty and was sent back to Limerick under a cavalry escort. Some of the mob cursed us and threw stones at us, one man receiving a nasty cut. We got back about 7 p.m. after a long and tiring day on a haversack ration.

Other companies had to attend evictions and altogether the soldier's life was not a pleasant one in Limerick of those days, but after all, on looking back it seems a veritable picnic compared with the orgy of assassination which marked soldiering in Ireland a generation later.

Not long after we got to Limerick things had become rather serious in the West and several outrages and murders had taken place. The Battalion was ordered, in consequence, to send two companies on detachment to Tralee, and another detachment was sent to Clare Castle. The night before the Tralee detachment left Limerick there was a big fire in the city at which the Battalion was present with all their engines and hose—a fortunate thing for Limerick, as the fire was in a big block of buildings in the main street and the city fire-engine was a miserable affair. The building in which the fire occurred could not be saved but owing to the exertions of the troops the fire was prevented from spreading. It was raining hard and the men were wet through and filthy, much of their clothing being irretrievably destroyed. But though the civic authorities sent a formal letter of thanks to the military they declined to pay a farthing compensation for damage to the men's clothing, and worse still, a hotel-keeper whose hotel was saved from the flames and who stood the men a drink afterwards had the meanness to send in a bill for " refreshments."

We had a visit from Prince Edward of Saxe-Weimar who was commanding at Dublin and came to Limerick to inspect some forts there. He visited us and stayed to lunch, and seemed to enjoy himself so much that he needed little persuasion to return to dinner somewhat to the embarrassment of the P.M.C. who had no previous warning. It was amusing to see the Prince with Mr. Just the Quartermaster; they began by telling each other that they had forgotten all their German and ended by jabbering away in that language all the evening. Talking of Germans it may be mentioned here that when any of the old Germans took their discharge application had to be made to the German Emperor if they wished to return to the Fatherland. The request in each case was made through our Foreign Office and the invariable reply was that, owing to the good service of the applicant in the British Army, His Majesty the Emperor was pleased to accord the necessary permission.

We had some good friends round Limerick and there were a good many entertainments. Also we brought with us from Fermoy our two river boats so that we had many river picnics, but we soon learnt that it was impossible to row against a Shannon tide. The fishermen of the Battalion used to go and stay at Castleconnel—an angler's paradise, and a regular excursion was to visit the companies at the musketry camp on the top of Woodcock Hill some distance from the city. Limerick itself was quite a fair sized place with good shops and boasting of such amenities as a theatre and Turkish baths both of which we freely patronized; still none of us cared very much for it as a station and, after Birr, Limerick seemed an inhospitable spot. The fact is that the kindness and friendliness of the Birr people spoilt us for any other place.

As for the detachment at Tralee the regimental district there was commanded by an officer who was not very fond of the detachment. The officers of the depot on the other hand were our very good friends. The depot was commanded by Major Barnard and afterwards by Major D. Johnston who has always been a great friend of the Battalion. The townspeople did not like having our men sent there to keep order and were always making trouble, especially when the militia came out for training. The duties were not hard and only once were we called out to help the police. A meeting was to be held in the town at which several Irish members were to speak, and it was proclaimed. The detachment was ordered out to assist the police and when we got to the town early in the forenoon we found some 400 police, half with rifles and half with batons. We were formed up in the Park in reserve and remained several hours there, but, when the train came in, there were no Irish members so we were sent back to barracks.

The militia were a very lively lot, commanded by Lord Headley, and there was some trouble between them and our men but nothing very serious. The officers were very good to us and were always asking us to dinner or some other entertainment; the training was rather a picnic. The country was in a bad state, all hunting was stopped and there were many outrages and some murders at Castle Island about six miles from Tralee. We got some fishing and some rough shooting and the people who remained in the district were good to us.

One of the officers at the depot had a small yacht in which we sometimes went fishing and we had a good ball court in which we played squash racquets and a drill shed in which we played badminton. There was also a good library. There was a fairly good club in the town and as the town was some distance from the barracks this made an excuse for a walk, but sometimes on our return we had things thrown at us from behind walls, etc.

During our stay in Limerick the strength of the Battalion had been increasing for at an inspection in July, 1886, the total of all ranks was exactly 800, though this had fallen a year later to 688. As regards changes in command and administration of the Battalion Lieutenant-Colonel D. W. Mackinnon left to assume command of the 1st Battalion in India the date of his appointment being 29th September, 1886. In the 2nd Battalion Lieutenant-Colonel and Colonel George Gilbert Stewart, on completion of six years as a regimental lieutenant-colonel, was placed on half-pay, being succeeded in command by Lieutenant-Colonel Lucius Joseph Collum, the latter being gazetted on the 13th October, 1887. On the 20th July of that year Lieutenant W. S. Riach became adjutant *vice* Captain Herbert Martin seconded for service with the auxiliary forces.

CHAPTER XXVI

THE 2ND BATTALION.

ENGLAND 1888–1894.

THE Battalion having received orders to move from Ireland to England, headquarters and "A" to "F" Companies proceeded by special train from Limerick to Queenstown on the 18th January, 1888. Here "G" and "H" Companies which had come from Tralee were picked up and the Battalion then embarked on board H.M.S. *Assistance* for conveyance to Dover, Shorncliffe being the actual destination of the Battalion. The *Assistance* was an old worn out ship whose early demise was always being expected, and a vessel which had an extraordinary affinity for bad weather—it was a well-known meteorological fact at Kingstown in the '70's and '80's that her arrival always brought wind and rain. This voyage was one typical of those usually experienced by her, for fogs, head winds and a breakdown of the engines protracted the passage to five days and some anxiety was felt by the advance party until the old troopship was descried limping along the south coast. As most of the men came from the centre of Ireland, and had never even seen the sea previously, they were not sorry to arrive at Dover especially after the rolling which was a feature of the old *Assistance*.

It was now six years since the Battalion had been in England and during that time it had changed considerably. When we left Preston in 1882 we still called ourselves the 109th and were inclined to jeer at our cumbrous territorial designation. Now we were the "Leinsters" and proud of the fact. Our strength too was gradually rising. There was only a small sprinkling of old soldiers left and the ranks were full of the best class of young Irishmen who were destined to show in the next few years what they would do in the competitions of garrison life. The other troops in the station were the 14th Hussars, two batteries of Royal Artillery and the 1st Oxfordshire Light Infantry, the latter being soon relieved by the 1st Lincolns. We settled down quickly to a very pleasant stay of three years, and the men soon made their way with the people of Sandgate and Folkestone who at first had been somewhat inclined to be scared by the " wild Irish."

The station was commanded by Sir Baker Russell, a fine old cavalryman with a great voice. In the soldiering of those days ceremonial was still the great thing though at times there was a weak strain of field work running through it. Thus there were many field days, just round the camp or on the cliffs between Shorncliffe and Dover, sometimes with the garrison of the latter place as the enemy. The general usually had some ladies riding with him and the field days always finished with a march past for their special benefit on the garrison parade ground. After one rather long day, when we had been nearly to Dover, an officer of the Battalion who was doing galloper ventured to hint that as the men were rather tired the march past might be dispensed with, to which Sir Baker replied in a voice of astonishment " Stavert, Stavert, what *would* the ladies say ? "

Both at ceremonial and field work the Battalion held its own well, and it was at Shorncliffe, too, that we first seriously went in for competitions and started the tug-of-war and bayonet teams which later brought such prestige to the Battalion. The Company Shield was also inaugurated about this time for cricket, shooting, football, and bayonet exercise (afterwards physical drill). We had a great many changes in personnel while at Shorncliffe. By death we lost Colonel Collum, Captain Cole and Captain Lane. Sergeant-Major Hartree and many of the old non-commissioned officers left us. Majors Hart and Prior and Captains Wathen, Davidson and Evans-Lombe joined us from the 1st Battalion, the first named retiring soon after.

A constant succession of subalterns also came to us though most of them drifted off to India, many subsequently going to the "Staff Corps" as the Indian Army—or rather the officer part of it—was called in those days. Lieutenant-Colonel Collum was succeeded by Lieutenant-Colonel G. Poignand in command and the new sergeant-major was Colour-Sergeant J. Gallehawk. The strength of the Battalion at the first inspection, held on July 23rd, 1888, was 22 officers, 2 warrant officers, 40 sergeants, 15 drummers, 747 rank and file, total 826 of all ranks.

We were quartered in huts at Shorncliffe and these were in extremely bad repair, and as the camp was on the top of a wind-swept hill the cold at times was very severe. Our first winter was a very cold one with much frost and snow and we had a good deal of fun tobogganing, etc. One night there was a regular blizzard and the field officer when going his rounds fell into a great snowdrift and had to be pulled out by his boots. A sentry box was overturned by the gale the same night, with the sentry inside. The snow used to drift into the huts through doors and windows although these were tightly shut. There was often snow on one's bed in the morning and always in the passage where the matutinal tub was enjoyed.

We played a fair amount of cricket with other units in garrison but the zenith of the reputation of the Battalion at the game had been passed; many of the famous eleven had left and the departure of Colonel Mackinnon to the other battalion was a severe loss. We saw something of the Dover garrison and had some very pleasant interchange of hospitality with the 89th Royal Irish Fusiliers, they staying with us on their way to the musketry camp at Lydd and we with them when in Dover for field operations. A piece of plate was presented to the mess by the officers of the 89th to commemorate the friendly relations and was a treasured article of the mess silver up to the disbandment of the Battalion. In those days there was a prevalent idea that the men of two Irish battalions could not meet without a fight, and on one occasion when we were quartered with the 89th it is said that a staff officer was sent round to ascertain the number of casualties. The only quarrel, however, had arisen from the men of the 89th insisting that our men should use the beds while our men absolutely refused to put their hosts to any inconvenience. The difficulty was solved by both battalions sleeping on the floor, while the beds remained unoccupied by either. We went to Dover, actually to be quartered there as part of the garrison, for a few weeks in 1890, the bulk of the Battalion being in the Shaft Barracks and a detachment at Fort Burgoyne. The last time we were inspected at Shorncliffe was by H.R.H. the Duke of Cambridge, the Commander-in-Chief, on the 4th October of that year the strength of the Battalion on that date being 570 of all ranks, this small number being probably accounted for by the fact that the inspection was actually held at Dover and some details had been left behind at Shorncliffe Camp; for at another inspection just two months earlier the total strength was 752. An important event so far as sport is concerned was the posting to the Battalion of 2nd Lieutenant Frederick Guthrie Tait, who was even then probably the best golfer in the army and destined later to win the amateur championship. When the list of reliefs for 1890-1891 was published we saw that we were to proceed to Aldershot and reluctantly we prepared to say good-bye to Shorncliffe where we had spent a very pleasant three years.

As the Battalion was destined to spend four years at Aldershot, and as Aldershot was in those days the hub of the British military machine, a brief description of the conditions of soldiering there over thirty years ago may be of interest.

Both in military and other respects the place was far different from the Aldershot of to-day. To-day it is a vast town; a generation ago it was a camp; and, when the 2nd Battalion went to it, in place of the fine red brick barracks now existing there were row upon row of wooden huts originally destined for the Crimea; the so-called permanent barracks now known as Wellington Lines were, however—and had been some time—in existence and pretty uncomfortable they were. The officers' messes were characterized by unnecessarily large mess-rooms and by inconveniently poky ante-rooms. This arrangement was due to an inspiration of the Prince Consort who, with his German recollections of officers' life, visualized officers as three bottle-men, sitting an immense time at table, and requiring an ante-room merely as a place for assembly for dinner. Even in the new barracks the rigid conservatism of the Royal Engineers and the Barrack Department was evident. There were no bath-rooms of any kind. Although electric light was fairly common in those days such generous illumination was unknown in Aldershot; even gas, introduced in 1816, had not found its way to military Aldershot. Both mess and barrack-rooms were lit by the old, wasteful, dangerous and smelly system of oil lamps. Needless to say there were no telephones although these instruments had been for years in common use elsewhere. When the 2nd Battalion found itself soon afterwards in the Western Hemisphere great was the astonishment of all ranks to find, even in a remote spot like Bermuda, every house furnished with an apparatus unknown in the new military buildings of Aldershot.

From the military point of view the chief difference between soldiering at Aldershot when Plancus was consul and in these days lay in the absence of several factors now commonplace. Aerial work was, of course, practically unknown. The Royal Engineers indulged a little in the old gas-bag balloon, but for all practical purposes the air was an unexplored element. Wireless had not even been dreamt of. Mechanical Transport was in its earliest infancy, an infancy rendered ricketty and unhealthy owing to the then diet of steam, which had not yet been replaced by the more highly efficient petrol. Khaki was a kit seen only on a rare Indian Army officer—or Staff Corps officer as they were termed in those days—blown in by a chance attachment; the army at Aldershot was a red army in those days though recruits had begun to wear a blue jumper, and a similar jacket—*mutatis mutandis*—was struggling for recognition as undress for officers against the maledictions of the Powers that Were. The official undress was a heavy blue garment called a patrol jacket, garnished in front with heavy braiding, in which we looked unutterably modish and in summer felt uncomfortably hot. Quite a sensation was caused and some alarm amongst Die-hard authority by the introduction of the " Red Serge." This was in effect a tunic minus the ornate and expensive embellishments of the latter, and was invented to enable an officer to take the field without a plaster of gold lace and to enable him to pass through a field day without irretrievably ruining at least twelve guineas worth of uniform in an afternoon.

The helmet or " war-pot "—that awful heritage of the Franco-German War—had replaced the more French shako, while for undress, there was the smart but uncomfortable forage cap with its peak pressed against the forehead, forming in warm weather a fine conductor of sweat into the eyes of the wearer. For drill order there was the Glengarry, now seen only in Scottish regiments, replaced during the stay of the 2nd Battalion in Aldershot by the " stream line " or " fatigue" cap now worn only by the Royal Air Force. As for armament we thought ourselves tremendously efficient by the possession of a magazine rifle—the old long-barrelled Lee-Metford which had replaced the Martini-Henry. There were many who decried the passing of the latter with its simplicity of mechanism, its wide calibre and man stopping powers. But it had no magazine and it had a " kick." In the artillery the quick-firing gun had not yet come and indeed it was not so very long since muzzle loaders had been in use.

An officer in marching order in those days wore the spiked helmet, covered with blue cloth, with the helmet plate in front containing the badge of the Regiment. The jacket was the " red serge," identical with the scarlet tunic except that it was made of serge, not cloth, and that all gold lace and such frippery were absent. Badges of rank were the metal stars etc. as worn to-day; but in those days the signification of these emblems was different *i.e.*, a captain wore but two stars, a lieutenant one, and a second lieutenant walked the world with shoulder straps unadorned, which caused him to be mistaken at times for an army schoolmaster. A crimson sash was worn over the left shoulder and the sword was slung from a white buff belt, worn outside the red serge round the waist, and secured in front by a particularly handsome buckle on which was in silver gilt the Prince of Wales's plume inside a wreath of maple and laurel leaves, the latter it is said having been granted the 109th for distinguished service in the Mutiny. On both this buckle and the helmet plate was displayed the honour " Central India." The haversack was pipeclayed white, and on the back of the belt was a rolled cape or greatcoat of dark grey cloth, the greatcoat being a far smarter and more tasteful article of clothing than the khaki coloured greatcoat which succeeded it. The sword was worn with a steel scabbard, the Sam Browne conglomeration coming later with khaki, and in those days the hilt was of brass work and smaller than that in use to-day. Trousers of blue cloth with narrow red piping, as worn in mess kit now, low black gaiters which reached just above the ankle and stout black boots (by regulation " without toecaps," but in practice never actually so disfigured) completed the outfit. Brown dogskin gloves were worn and gloves were always *de rigeur* in every kit.

The officers' mess jacket was fitted with a high collar of the colour of the regimental facings and was furnished with thick gold-braid shoulder straps and an immense number of tiny buttons in front for show and not for use. Field officers wore spurs, and scabbards, of brass and a perfectly useless appendage to the sword slings called a sabretache—popularly supposed to be a receptacle for maps or despatches. The name was ever a stumbling block to the rank and file, and once Captain " Paddy " Reeves, temporarily commanding the Battalion during the leave season, was disconcerted on being asked by his servant " Will you be wearing your *parasol* to-day sorr ?"

If the Great War did nothing else at any rate it brought into being a living wage for the officers of the British Army. Nowadays it is not easy to imagine the time when not even a pretence existed that an officer could exist without an allowance or private means. The pay of the Army had, in spite of a considerable depreciation of the value of money, remained precisely as it had been in the reign of Queen Anne, and almost up to 1914 a second lieutenant received the fourth of a guinea, 5s. 3d. a day to be exact, or some £95 a year. There were practically speaking no allowances whatsoever, and as even the most economical of mess bills was never under £10 a month this clearly left an adverse balance in a monthly wage of little over eight pounds. There was, therefore, an unwritten but practically universal law that a subaltern must have a private income of £100 a year over and above his pay; not all, indeed, were so fortunate and many was the career of perpetual financial shakiness and many a worried heart beat behind a glittering mess jacket in those days. There was, however, always " the other battalion " in India where rumour stated that living on one's pay was actually within the bounds of possibility; and tailors, blessed be their names, were a long-suffering race. Some accounts were indeed stretched almost to infinity but it was the proud boast of Flight that he had never run in an officer, and a proud tribute to the integrity of the sweated officer of those days that it was almost unknown for a tailor to have a bad debt.

Aldershot was a large straggling place to get about in but in spite of this the bicycle as a means of transport was absolutely unknown. And yet in the late nineties the push bike was no new and untried invention ; even the present " safety " shape had been in use for some years, and pneumatic tyres had come to stay. Nevertheless, the use of the bicycle was anathema and taboo. It is difficult indeed to give any comparison which will bring home to readers of to-day how the bicycle was regarded

z

in the years the 2nd Battalion was at Aldershot. You, gentle reader, hurrying perchance through some London by-street, have perchance been incommoded by a grimy urchin, ragged in kit and shod, not with a pair, but with *one* rusty and half broken roller skate. As you cursed his rough dot-and-carry-one gait did it ever occur to you to visit Pall Mall thus clothed and equipped, and solemnly, in the severe portals of the Senior or the Rag, to remove the underlying wheels from your foot and then unwashed and in rags to penetrate to the Smoking Room ? And yet the courage required for such operation to-day would be no more than that required to be seen on a push bicycle in Aldershot as late as the year of grace 1894.

Of course even that conservative stronghold had to bow to the storm of 1896 which blew the bicycle into the four corners of the United Kingdom. It was then that Society with a large S used to disport itself with gravity before breakfast in Battersea Park astride a wheel, and of course, with this lead, Aldershot had to follow suit. But even then this new invention had like matrimony to be approached not wantonly nor unadvisedly but with soberness and discretion. In those days of Form a correct and suitable kit had to be evolved for this new pastime. Anxious deliberation eventually fixed on a Norfolk jacket, knickerbockers, riding leggings and above all things a hunting stock, immaculately white, exquisitely tied and with gold safety-pin complete. There was still the faint recollection of horse about these garments and a spin through Aldershot must be carried out with the solemnity and precision of hacking in the Row. Those of us who returned to Aldershot about 1896 for a course or what not would gaze with admiration at these solemn knuts pedalling sedately along at some eight miles an hour. It was thus that the push-bike was admitted after years of blackballing to the inner life of Aldershot.

With push-bicycles taboo, and the petrol age still to come, walking held a place as an exercise absolutely unknown in these softer days. In the early nineties there were giants, in the pedestrian line, in the Battalion.

It was quite a common thing for Lieutenants Craske, Tait and Colquhoun to walk to Guildford and back between lunch and dinner, averaging six miles an hour for the distance of 20 miles out and home. To-day this statement will appear incredible, but it is an incontestable fact. Even the present writer, fond of walking but not of violent physical exertion as that of the three heroes referred to above, can remember a solitary Sunday afternoon stroll out to Hartford Bridge Flats, then on to Basingstoke, back by train to Farnborough, and thence back to barracks on foot. A map and dividers show this walk to have been nineteen miles. Every one walked a good deal in those days and kept extremely fit in this way.

"Form" was indeed a tyrant in those days. In uniform to be "improperly dressed" was the mortal sin. It might be that the impropriety consisted of nothing but a sleeve button a sixteenth of an inch in excess or otherwise of size, or a mess vest opening a shade too low, or a sword knot varying a trifle from accepted custom. You had one of these things. You were "improperly dressed." You received a memorandum from the orderly room to "give your reasons in writing" for the enormity—the offence being too serious for mere verbal reprimand; and if you were a comparatively junior officer you were exposed to personal violence at the hands of your outraged fellow subalterns. The same iron rectitude of Form ruled your clothing in "running up to town." A lounge suit and bowler might conceivably do for mere shopping in the Strand; but should your journey take you to the West-End a frock coat and topper were *de rigeur*. Even an afternoon's constitutional across Cæsar's Camp and home by Laffan's Plain was often undertaken in the propriety conferred by a bowler hat. Such sartorial laxity as is represented to-day by the Homburg hat or the cloth cap was unknown in those days. The soft collar would have thrown many officers of that time into paralysis and what came later to be known as "ratcatcher kit" was unknown in the Aldershot of the nineties.

The truth is that in those days the army was a comparatively small body of men forming a distinct caste of its own and with its own rigid if unwritten conventions. Splendid as the new armies of the Great War proved themselves in the hour of trial of the Great War, there is no use denying the fact that by their very numbers they swamped and bore away many of the minor traditions and conventions of the old Red Army of pre-war days. In those days the Army regarded itself not so much as the fighting representatives of the nation as the armed retinue of the sovereign. The uniform was above all things the " Queen's uniform " ; and the fact that the sovereign was a woman and that there was scarcely a single surviving officer who held his commission except at her hand led to a sentiment of chivalrous loyalty which is never likely to be equalled. Above all things the army was a royal institution and the officers of those days felt in a very real way their royal connexion. Apart from the peculiar sentiment of loyalty to the old Queen the hierarchy of the army had in those days a royal strain unknown in these days. The Army Council, " an abstraction I never very much cared about "—as Charles Lamb remarked about the Inland Revenue—had then no existence. The Commander-in-Chief was the Duke of Cambridge, a cousin of Her Majesty, and even the newly gazetted subaltern might receive an official communication in which some big-wig scribe would begin by stating gravely that he was " directed by His Royal Highness the Commander-in-Chief," etc. etc. At Aldershot in 1894 the royal connexion of the Army was emphasized by the fact that the station was commanded by a son of the Queen, H.R.H. the Duke of Connaught. No subaltern who joined the Leinster Regiment at Aldershot about that time could fail to be permeated with the spirit of this royal connexion. Did he but go on a route march he felt conscious of wearing the Queen's livery of red—could anyone think of khaki as a royal livery ?—while his badge and facings brought home to him the royal title of the Regiment and its connexion with the

Queen's eldest son. On the march he was as likely as not to see another of the Queen's sons, the Duke of Connaught—a fellow sojourner in the great camp at Aldershot ; and, later on in the day, a slight check might occur, word would be rapidly passed to march to attention, there would be hurried whispers of "the old Duke," and the subaltern would find himself passing under the eyes of the old Commander-in-Chief, and as likely as not would hear a gruff commentary if that eagle eye had detected something in that young officer's turn-out not quite *comme il faut*.

Undoubtedly it was a royal army in those days. An officer had the "Queen's commission" ; a man became a soldier by taking the "Queen's shilling" ; both wore the "Queen's uniform" ; the 2nd Leinster Regiment, proud though it was of its old John Company connexion, felt even a stronger pride at being now a "Queen's regiment." When we thought of war it was in a strain somewhat different from that of recent years. The splendid millions who crossed the seas between 1914 and 1918 went—at least so the Press yelled—" to make the world safe for Democracy." We were content to think that we should fight "the Queen's enemies." To be quite frank no one in the old Red Army cared a straw for Democracy but everyone did care and care a great deal for the old Queen.

It must be confessed, however, that in those days we had a great deal to learn about marching. The 2nd Battalion prided itself and justly that it could march any other battalion in Aldershot off its feet. But looking back one remembers features which seem bizarre to-day, or which at any rate were unknown ten years or so after we left Aldershot. In those days when the troops were route marching, even lightly equipped, provision was made for quite a number of stragglers. Every company officer went on such parade with a bundle of "falling-out slips," little certificates which stated that Private So-and-So marched off with the battalion but "was unable to keep up," and these tired warriors, on being retrieved by ambulances or rear-guard, would hand over these chits as their authority for quitting the ranks. It must be remembered of course that the great bulk of the rank and file of home battalions were little more than recruits and young in age, but the same remark applies to ten years later. Those who were with the 1st Battalion at Devonport will remember the manœuvres in Wiltshire and Oxfordshire in 1909 when we did sixty-six miles in three days, the men carrying full marching order, and not one fell out. Graduated training had, however, by then come into being whereas at Aldershot no such system prevailed and the young soldiers were often taken literally from barrack square drill for long and tiring manœuvres.

It is true that the bulk of the rank and file were young and immature soldiers, but curiously enough in those days the private aged at a terrific rate, and when quite a young man would have all the appearance of antiquity. There were in the 2nd Battalion in those days patriarchal old men who looked almost seventy. Who does not remember Private Dooley the old pioneer with his grizzled beard whose sole duty was to provide the packets of ball ammunition on guard mounting and to take over similar packages when a guard had completed its tour of duty? And big Harry Quinn of " D " Company who looked as old as many a man of sixty to-day. And yet even assuming that these venerable soldiers enlisted at the maximum age and that they were " over their twenty-one," their ages could in very few cases have been over forty-five, in other words the very prime of life. This premature ageing was a very marked characteristic of the Victorian soldier, and many causes have been assigned for it. The present Lord Plumer once expressed to the writer his opinion that the excessive and monotonous guard duties of those days had much to say to it, but this could hardly have been the sole cause. It is probable that the Indian service of those days with its long spells of hot weather in the plains, and its epidemics with the inevitable nerve strain thus brought about, was a distinctly predisposing cause. Added to this it must be said that a copious indulgence in beer, especially in a tropical climate, could scarcely have been as rejuvenating as monkey glands. Whatever the cause or causes the "old soldier" of the Victorian days has no counterpart in the present times.

Beer, indeed, played a part in soldiering thirty years ago difficult to realize to-day. There was a fixed belief that without Beer the British soldier could not march or fight. The dominating feature of manœuvres was the provision, transport and issue of Beer. Towards the end of a long, hot, tiring march a whole brigade might be held up, and if you moved forward to investigate the block you would meet Beer again. Drawn athwart a hill would be one or two great contractor's vans, the sullen horses in a state of mutiny, and under the great white waggon tilt—visible of course to the enemy a dozen miles away—peeped out those fat, dull, comfortable-looking casks inside which was stored the glorious British Beer. The delay might be long, the tactical scheme might be ruined, rations, ammunition and other useful impedimenta might be kept back but no one ever thought of that. There was the British soldier and there was the Beer.

A bucket let down into the well of memory has some other drops of recollection worth gazing into. Bridge was unknown at the time the 2nd Battalion was at Aldershot in the '90's; whist, however, was played a good deal, but chiefly by the seniors. The standard of play was extremely high, and as a battalion the 2nd Leinsters had rather a reputation for whist. The game was played with a seriousness not to say a solemnity quite different from the atmosphere of ordinary bridge to-day. The junior officers played billiards and pool to a much greater extent than their successors. There were then of course no picture palaces nor hippodromes and probably officers, certainly at Aldershot, "dined in" more than at the present time, and the absence of motor-cars, motor-buses, motor and push-cycles kept one indoors rather more than to-day.

Another point that perhaps deserves recording is the comparative rarity, and consequently the enhanced value, of "ribbons" in those days. An officer with even one medal was almost conspicuous, with three he was remarkable, and once, at a review, an officer with five was described in the local Press as "multi-medalled Murray." It was generally believed in the Battalion that the then Major Willcocks of the Regiment shared with Lord Wolseley the distinction of being the most beribboned soldier living. So far as can be remembered now Major Willcocks's number was eight, just the number that a smart young liaison officer, or an "A" or "Q" brass-hat at St. Omer or Montreuil, might with luck have garnered in the last war. Two other points of interest may be recorded. There were pipes in the Battalion as far back as the '90's; but they were the "Union" pipes —not inflated by the mouth but by leverage of the arm, and were very difficult to manipulate. The Battalion had, at that time, a very large proportion of Scottish officers as the names Winton Seton; Kenneth Mackenzie Drummond; Thomas Sinclair Davidson; Ronald Gower Campbell; Julian Campbell Colquhoun; and Frederick Guthrie Tait will show.

It was on the 11th February, 1891, that the 2nd Battalion left Shorncliffe for its new station its strength on arrival being 25 officers, 2 warrant officers and 640 other ranks, and on the same day a new establishment was ordered to bring the Battalion up to 1,009 of all ranks. At that time Sir Evelyn Wood, a veteran of the Crimea, was in command of the station and the Battalion joined the 1st Brigade in the South Camp, then under Major-General Gregorie, who had commanded the 18th Royal Irish in their distinguished service on the Nile. General Gregorie had the reputation of being a severe martinet and this, with his rather forbidding expression, gained him the soubriquet of "The Bogey Man" amongst irreverent subalterns and others; but his knowledge of an Irish regiment made him a splendid brigadier to serve under. The 2nd Battalion was one of the last units to serve in the old wooden huts so long characteristic of Aldershot, but so soon as the new barracks were complete the battalion moved into Albuhera Barracks in the Stanhope Lines. About this time the Battalion suffered a severe loss in the death of its adjutant Captain W. S. Riach who died in Switzerland of tuberculosis. He was succeeded by Captain T. St. C. Davidson.

The four years at Aldershot showed the Battalion at its best. It was soon up to strength; the physique of the men was very noticeable and the fact that both the brigadier and the divisional commander were Irishmen spurred on the Battalion to show its mettle. During the first year the present ex-German Emperor visited England, and the 2nd Battalion was one of the units selected to march to London, to line the streets and to take part in a review on Wimbledon Common. The Battalion was posted in St. Paul's Churchyard and Cheapside where the crowd was immense and several times it seemed as if the pressure would swamp the men of the Battalion. An attempt was made to form a barrier by rifles held horizontally, but as bayonets were fixed the commanding officer Lieutenant-Colonel Poignand considered this method might lead to casualties and ordered the men to drop their rifle-butts on the toes of the front rank of the crowd—an order which was greeted with some booing from Cockneys ignorant of the first principles of crowd management. Later in the year the Battalion had its first experience of Aldershot manœuvres which that year took place in the neighbourhood of East Meon. The march down was carried out in very hot weather but the 2nd Battalion worthily maintained its reputation as a first-class marching regiment, not a single man falling out. Other manœuvres in which the Battalion took part were at Frensham in 1892 and on the Berkshire Downs in 1893. Both in marching and in the field the Battalion always gained credit, and on one occasion was specially fallen in to receive the thanks of General Chapman, the commander of one side, for a rapid and well-executed advance to a position.

Meanwhile Lieutenant-Colonel Poignand had been succeeded in command by Lieutenant-Colonel A. S. Woods under whom the Battalion maintained the high reputation it had won. Without any incident of outstanding importance the further stay of the Battalion in Aldershot was marked by a succession of ceremonial and manœuvres interspersed by the steady and continuous barrack square drill of those days, while in military competitions the 2nd Leinsters more than held their own, especially in physical drill, bayonet fighting and tug-of-war in which their record was unique. In the first named " G " Company in 1892 won first place in the Bronze Medal Competition at Aldershot and obtained second place at the Royal Military Tournament at Islington. In the following year " B " Company won second and third places respectively in these competitions, while in bayonet exercise the Battalion team in 1892 was second both in the District Competition at Aldershot and the Army Meeting at the Royal Military Tournament. In bayonet fighting " A " Company scored two highly meritorious firsts in 1894 at both these places.

In tug-of-war the record of the Battalion was even higher. In 1892 the Battalion team won the 120-stone competition and the officers were similarly successful, both these events, though held at Aldershot, being open to the whole army. The following year was one of especial triumph, for the Battalion team gained first place at Islington and followed this up by two more firsts at Aldershot where the officers also won the Officers' Inter-Regimental event. Further successes followed in 1894 and in these competitions the reputation which the Leinster Regiment gained in tug-of-war in the four quarters of the globe was worthily upheld. It may be noted that the officers during their stay at Aldershot not only were never beaten but in fourteen pulls were never once pulled over the line.

In the summer of 1894 the Queen visited Aldershot as did also the ex-German Emperor in whose honour a big review was held on Laffan's Plain, with a field day also during his stay. In this exercise the 2nd Battalion was in reserve but was suddenly ordered to debouch from a wood to carry a hill against which the attack of other units had failed. Those were still the days of close formations but as the 2nd Battalion, under the eyes of the ex-German Emperor, dashed up the slope in quarter column, against a murderous magazine fire from the defenders, the Imperial shoulders shrugged themselves up nearly to the Imperial ears. It was St. Privat and the Prussian Guards over again ; and even such an advocate of close order tactics as William II was evidently startled by the sacrifice of a battalion.

For Her Majesty—whose visit though it took place the same summer did not coincide with that of her grandnephew—the Battalion furnished the Irish guard of honour, this being the second time during its stay at Aldershot that the 2nd Leinster Regiment had such a privilege, the former occasion being when Queen Victoria visited Aldershot to open the new church in Stanhope Lines. In this year the Battalion did not take part in the autumn manœuvres for in the programme of reliefs for 1894-5 the Battalion was down for Malta. An inspection was held by General Gregorie who in a farewell speech declared that if he were about to take the field in command of an army there was no regiment he would rather have under him than the 2nd Battalion of the Leinster Regiment. Coming from a commander who had a well-justified reputation of meaning what he said and by no means given to conventional compliments these words meant much. On the 9th November the Battalion entrained for Southampton, H.R.H. The Duke of Connaught honouring the Battalion by coming to the station to bid it a personal farewell, and the Highland Light Infantry pipers playing the Battalion out with a pibroch—a send-off which was a very high honour indeed. Including the advanced party, which had gone on the previous day, the strength of the Battalion on proceeding overseas was 20 officers, 541 non-commissioned officers and men, 34 women and 59 children.

CHAPTER XXVII

THE 2ND BATTALION.

THE MEDITERRANEAN, 1894–1895.

THE trooping season of 1894–1895 was marked by a new departure in the transport of troops overseas. The old " lobster pots," as the troopships manned by the Royal Navy were called, were withdrawn and their place taken by passenger steamers chartered by the Admiralty. These were officered by their usual personnel of the merchant service, the Admiralty being represented merely by a commander whose duty was " to form a channel of communication between the master of the vessel and the officer commanding the troops on board." As a matter of fact the channel had nothing whatever to do except to doze in the smoking room, though every day at noon he religiously took some private sights—which the ship's officers always swore were inaccurate. It was the rooted conviction of the Admiralty that the officer commanding troops would need an interpreter to translate such mystic terms as " bow," " stern," " port," " starboard " etc. but in practice the military dealt direct with the ship's captain and in course of time the channels were abolished.

The vessel chartered to convey the 2nd Battalion was a fine P. and O. liner of some 6,000 tons, the *Victoria*—a name of ill omen, for the frightful disaster to the battleship of that name was still fresh in people's minds. There was, however, nothing in the initial stage of the voyage to alarm the most superstitious for the first afternoon out was one of bright sunshine and smooth sea. But the next day a gale was brewing and at dinner that night there were very many vacant places indeed. By turning-in time there was a tremendous sea running, but the passage of the Bay would only take twelve hours and when morning came the worst would be over. With this comfortable reflection even the poorest sailors on board sank to sleep.

When morning did come on the 12th November the ship was rolling in a terrible manner and with a lifeless air not at all in keeping with an early exit from the Bay. To every cabin steward was put the same query "Are we out of the Bay yet?" and to every questioner came the same reply "No, sir, blowing a gale, sir, since four o'clock. Steering gear just carried away, sir." We now noticed—at least those who were in a condition to notice anything—that the engines had stopped and as the stewards were sceptical as to whether breakfast could be served or not many of us remained in our bunks. Little comfort was this for as time went on the motion became so violent that only by wedging oneself in with pillows could one avoid being thrown upon the cabin floor. The rolling at times was distinctly alarming; further and further would the vessel heel until it seemed impossible she could ever right herself again, and then for a sickening moment she would lie on her beam ends as if deliberating whether it was worth while to keep up the fight. Soon from the alleyways there was the sound of swirling water and at times a piece of a wave would look in through the half open cabin door and gleefully seize a pair of boots or a suit-case, merrily toss these to and fro, and then disappear.

On deck the sight was one of absolute grandeur. The *Victoria* seemed to be amidst a range of snow-capped mountains, and from the bottom of the frequent valleys the crests could be seen towering far above the funnel tops. With her steering gear carried away the ship was out of all control and when she fell away broadside to the waves she rolled at times till her boats on the lee side lay upon the water. Some of these rolls were of 45 degrees and when, as frequently happened, a squall caught the *Victoria* in this position the pressure on her exposed side held her down in a manner to take the breath away even from the most experienced traveller. There were moments when it looked as if the end of the 2nd Leinster Regiment had come, for it seemed impossible that any vessel could survive such buffetting for long. One moment at least will live for ever in the memory of one who passed through it. The *Victoria* had just risen wearily from her beam ends, when right ahead was seen a mountain of water—a very Everest of waves—reared right in the vessel's path. Slowly this colossus among billows curled over as if contemptuously viewing the cockle shell beneath. Then with a roar like an explosion it flung itself upon the ship and one third of the *Victoria* simply disappeared ; what was happening under those fathoms of seething waters no one could tell, but gradually—like a submarine nowadays breaking surface—our bow reappeared and we knew that this time we had escaped. But no ship ever launched could stand much of that battering without having her decks burst open.

Meanwhile every effort was being made to repair the steering gear and to get the vessel once more under control. When the steam steering gear had parted the emergency hand-gear had been immediately shipped but this carried away almost at once, and the great quadrant of steel at the rudder head was banging backwards and forwards in a way which threatened to tear the stern out of the ship. The first thing to do was to muzzle this great mass of metal and a fatigue party of a hundred men working under the ships' officers set out to lasso the quadrant with stout ropes. The work was extremely difficult and hazardous but at length the quadrant was secured ; but only for a moment, for the hemp cable snapped like thread and the task had to be tackled once more. Finally an immense wire cable—a veritable king amongst ropes— was brought to the fray and at long last the rudder was secured. By this time the gale shewed signs of subsiding and with the improvement in the weather and the securing of the rudder the worst was now over.

Later an extract from the ship's log was, by permission

of the captain, copied and entered in the records of the Battalion. It runs as follows :—

"November 11th *A.M.* 4. Moderate gale with high sea and hard squalls. At times ship rolling and lurching heavily. 7.30. Shipped a heavy sea in starboard waist which carried away a collapsible boat and broke after accommodation ladder. 8.00. Fresh gale with very high sea; ship rolling heavily and shipping quantities of water. 10.50. Eased to half speed. Noon. Fresh gale with very high sea, ship rolling very heavily and taking in large quantity of water in waists. *P.M.* Sun obscured. Glass of starboard lighthouse and electric light broken by sea. 4.00. Gale still blowing hard, ship pitching and rolling heavily, and shipping heavy sprays forward. Midnight. Strong gale and high sea.

"November 12th. *A.M.* Gale still blowing with hard squalls of hurricane force. Shipping heavy water over forecastle; rails, stanchions, anchor securing shackles and projector box broken. 6.00. Shift of wind to west with mountainous sea. 7.30. Ship pitching and lurching very heavily; steam steering gear carried away. 7.38. Shipped hand-gear. 7.50. Ditto carried away also brake lever. Set tarpaulin in mizzen rigging. 10.00. Fore hatch washed away. Endeavouring to secure quadrant with towing hawsers. Using engines as requisite to keep ship out of trough of sea. Hawsers parted, striking and tearing compasses from deck. Noon. Strong moderating gale with mountainous sea. *P.M.* Scuttle frame and glass on after lower troop deck burst in. Plugged ditto. Still at work securing quadrant. 4.00. Ship labouring heavily and rolling heavy water on board. 7.30. Steering chain secured round quadrant. Proceeded easy. 8.00. Full speed. Midnight. Fresh breeze and fine with heavy westerly swell. The ship touched 45 degrees in rolling."

In all the *Victoria* had spent over sixty hours in the Bay and the captain stated that never had he experienced such a passage. Down in the troop decks while the storm was raging the condition was indescribable, and for forty-eight hours any attempt at cooking or issuing rations was impossible. The ship's commander spoke in the highest terms of the pluck and endurance of the men and of the valuable assistance they rendered to the *Victoria's* officers and crew during the perilous time. Of four horses on board three were killed by the violence of the gale. The gale once over the remainder of the voyage was without incident. Gibraltar was passed during the night, and four days later right ahead were the battlements of Valetta and all around was a faint pungent odour we were to know so well—garlic. Later in the day the Battalion was conveyed in steamers and native boats to Gozo.

Gozo bore to Malta proper somewhat the same relation as Alderney does to Jersey, that is to say it was a younger member of a group of islands, and the station of a detachment instead of a battalion headquarters. That was the normal arrangement, but conditions were altered for the 2nd Leinster Regiment. The official legend was that the new barracks in the centre of Malta—Imtarfa—not being completed it was necessary as a temporary measure to station the whole of the Battalion in Gozo. What really happened was that the staff in Malta were frightened at the prospect of " wild Irish " in Valetta and, contrary to all fairness, decided to maroon the Battalion *en bloc* at Gozo. This timidity led to a gross injustice. At Malta where there were barracks good and bad, healthy and decidedly the reverse, there was an excellent custom by which whenever a new unit came out there was a kind of general post, the last joined unit going to the least favoured barracks while everybody else " moved up one." From this excellent system the Leinsters were carefully excluded, for although it was the first battalion to arrive in the trooping season of 1894–5 it remained at Gozo even when, months later, other units arrived from the United Kingdom. During the whole of its stay in the command, except for such absolutely necessary moves to musketry camp and manœuvres, the 2nd Leinster Regiment was isolated at Gozo, rather rough treatment of a battalion which had won and deservedly won golden opinions at Aldershot.

Gozo is an island some nine miles long by four and a half in breadth with the typical terraced cultivation of the Maltese group, practically speaking without a single tree and one might almost say without a single blade of grass. An uninviting station indeed at first view, though it must be said that in summer when Malta looked like faded brown paper, Gozo, though it also looked like faded paper, bore some resemblance to paper of a bilious grey-green hue. All the inhabitants without exception were peasants, priests, fisherfolk or grog-shop keepers (there was a "Welcome Leinster" caravanserai when we arrived) and English was neither spoken nor understood by a single soul, except by an excellent and charming priest—Father Magri. Of social life there was, therefore, absolutely none whatever, and even for games or amusements *inter nos* the island was very unsuited. There was a concrete cricket pitch on the barrack square and you could—if you were reckless and thought nothing of broken bones play soccer on the same terrain amid ridges and rocky out-crop. Sailing was possible, but the coast was rocky and inhospitable and—at any rate in the cooler months—violent and sudden squalls were a deterrent. Lieutenant Colquhoun, bringing over a sailing-boat from Malta, capsized but was fortunately rescued. There was in fact practically nothing whatever to do at Gozo, except to bathe in the warm weather. That was the one unfailing resource in summer—in the cool of the evening to clamber down an appallingly steep path to a great rocky and tideless cove for an hour's grand exercise, and then, the one-in-one ascent breathlessly accomplished, to quaff as an *aperitif* before dinner a glass of really excellent Marsala—cost one penny.

Even from the point of view of accommodation Gozo was quite unsuited for more than a detachment. There was a large old fort just above, and commanding, the so-called harbour, dating from the old days of the Knights of St. John. This was Fort Chambray inside which there was accommodation for two or three companies and for married quarters, the remainder of the Battalion being under canvas outside. There was no proper officers' mess though quite a passable native house with a fair garden formed a reasonable substitute. Except for a couple of rooms therein there were no officers' quarters at all, and practically the whole of the officer personnel were in large E.P. and staff sergeants' tents. These, however, were by no means uncomfortable and as their occupation meant field allowance the arrangement was quite popular.

Compared with Malta proper Gozo was practically a penal settlement. Valetta was quite a lively garrison; apart from a large number of gunners there were in those days eight battalions in the command so that things were by no means dull. Add to this that the Mediterranean Fleet was then our most important squadron and that it spent the winter months in the Grand Harbour, and that numerous English visitors used to come out for the season, and Malta will be seen to have had the elements of quite a good station. There was a first-rate club, the opera, and lots of polo and cricket. From all these delights we felons at Gozo were practically cut off. Though only four miles from the nearest point of Malta, to reach Valetta meant a voyage of some twenty miles in rather trying conditions. Twice a day two steamers sailed each way, the smaller being merely a large launch and the swagger craft a kind of doll's steam yacht. Often it was decidedly rough and only the most seasoned sailors could contemplate the journey in unsettled weather with equanimity.

We had, however, some compensations. In the first place we were left alone. There were no generals or staff to come prowling unexpectedly round corners; a surprise visit was impossible, and a visit in roughish weather most improbable. Then there were no garrison duties whatever, a marked difference from Malta with its numerous guards. But it was in health that we scored most. Before the cause of Maltese fever had been tracked down Valetta was a notoriously unhealthy station and Gozo was in comparison a regular sanatorium. These two factors enabled the Battalion, when it was made up to strength, to have some splendid barrack square drill, it being quite a common occurrence to have nearly a thousand men on parade. In the hot weather the officers had all their meals out of doors under a large awning in the mess garden—a boon compared with the barracks in Valetta; and last but not least, from the point of view of the impecunious subaltern, the place had distinct merits—it was practically impossible to spend money outside one's mess bill and the field allowance represented a substantial increase to the exiguous pay of those years.

Looking back over an interval of nearly thirty years three occurrences seem to stand out from our twelve months' stay in the island; the passing through of the 1st Battalion on its way home from India; the boat race for the Governor's Cup; and the leave season, seven months being devoted to two spells of this great boon.

The normal system being that one battalion should be at home and one abroad it followed that when the 2nd Battalion was ordered to Malta the 1st Battalion was to return to the United Kingdom. It had now been some eighteen years in India and on the 6th January, 1895, it reached Malta on the hired transport *Dilwara* on its way home. It is not often that the two regular battalions of a regiment meet, and on the rare occasions when such an event happens there is naturally a joyful reunion. Unfortunately our exile at Gozo prohibited a real fraternizing between the two battalions though as many as could be spared from the 2nd went to Valetta to meet the 1st Battalion and to make the most of the few hours the *Dilwara* stayed in port.

As the 1st Battalion was coming on the home establishment while we in the 2nd were beginning our foreign tour a large number of non-commissioned officers and men were transferred at this time from the former—429 to be exact. These men might easily have been transhipped to Gozo without delay, but for some reason they were kept one night in Valetta, most inadequate arrangements having been made by the staff for their accommodation. The fact that they were not to proceed home with their comrades was apparently sprung upon these four hundred as a surprise, and accordingly there was a tendency among them to drown their sorrow by making a night of it. Four hundred Irishmen straight off shipboard, and who had not known Bacchus for over three weeks, and with a legitimate grievance had all the elements of a little " divarshion " and the Maltese police had rather an exciting night. The men of the 400, accustomed to the humble native of India, could not understand the pertinacity of the little saddle-coloured constables of Valetta who would try to spoil the fun, and many of them were uproariously upended by the Irishmen. Of course next day there was rather a to-do ; the staff were horrified at this outbreak of " wild Irishism " and there was a small crop of miscreants, who had been secured by the Malta police, to be dealt with by the civil power. The little Maltese constables were, however, good sportsmen and gave their evidence without a trace of vindictiveness and the Maltese magistrate made every allowances for Irishmen out for a night's " rag," so that a few fines settled everything. No damage had been done and the whole thing was simply an Irish spree though the staff for the moment were inclined to look upon it with an affectation of horror.

Instructions were soon afterwards received that two companies should proceed to Malta to undergo three weeks' instruction in gun drill, and accordingly " A " and " H " Companies left for the main island and marched inland to the lines of Bengemma and Deuira respectively. A trifling omission on the part of the staff resulted in the companies finding neither tents nor blankets on arrival and in the words of a contemporary record they " had to be content for that night with the canopy of Heaven for a covering." On 25th March five companies proceeded to Musta camp, five miles from Valetta to take part in the annual manœuvres where they encamped with their old friends the Lincolns, the East Surreys and 60th being also in camp. After the Aldershot Command manœuvres the training at Malta had its amusing side. There was no open country whatsoever, and, as the so-called cultivation was sacrosanct, the opposing forces merely marched along roads. When contact was established the opposing sides would each hoist a red flag which meant " I am deployed." Deployment or formation into column of route were therefore but matters of seconds. As no firing was allowed upon roads and as the troops could move nowhere else the value of the training was not very evident.

The stay of the Battalion in Malta proper was, however, marked by a memorable incident connected with these manœuvres. An advanced party of one company had been sent a few days ahead to draw camp equipment etc. and to pitch camp for the main body of the Battalion. After a strenuous morning in Valetta drawing stores the little column marched up the Strada Reale, the gear being conveyed on local Maltese carts. The native drivers were most indifferent packers, and constantly the load, especially on an up-hill, threatened to slide off the tail of the carts. All went well, however, till the middle of the Strada Reale. As luck would have it, just as the convoy was passing the club, down the steps strolled the general officer commanding surrounded by the most glittering of glittering staffs. The officer commanding the company—Lieutenant Colquhoun—was in front and missed this galaxy, but his subaltern in rear saw clearly that this was a case for a salute. Calling the men to attention he drew his sword and thundered out "Eyes right." At that very moment the load of the cart immediately opposite the general slid tailwards, and by the inflexible law of leverage elevated the mule into mid air. Taken by surprise the sorry jade squealed loudly, madly pawing the air meanwhile, and then, as bundles of blankets finally dropped upon the pavement, it crashed loudly to earth once more. For the next few minutes that subaltern had a confused impression of a snorting general, horrified staff officers, screaming Maltese drivers and a neurasthenic mule. It was a dramatic salute if a trifle overdone.

The boat race for the Governor's Cup was the chief

sporting event at Malta and the 2nd Battalion of course decided to enter for it. They were lucky in having in Lieutenant Taylor, who had done much rowing at Bedford, a capable stroke and there were many others who had wielded an oar on the Thames or the Aldershot canal. The race was for crews of six in clinker built racing boats with fixed seats, and the course was always the length of the Quarantine Harbour in Valetta, a distance of roughly a mile and a half.

From the very first Fortune refused to smile upon the Battalion. The first thing was to get a racing boat. Captain Drummond most generously provided this from his own pocket ; but although the order was placed early in February it was not until April that the craft was ready, just a short time before the race. Meanwhile training was carried out in an ancient craft, but the lack of shelter at Gozo militated against regular practice, and unfortunately our stroke was an extraordinarily bad sailor and by no means at his best when there was the slightest suspicion of a sea. We did not get any chance of real training until early in April when we were at Pembroke Camp, Malta, for musketry, but as we were still three miles from the harbour we were at a disadvantage as compared with the battalions in Valetta itself. The race was rowed on 18th April, 1895, on a wild and windy day which caused a really heavy swell at the mouth of the harbour and made the luck of the draw a very real factor. As will be seen the Battalion was unfortunate in this respect the position of the crews beginning at the more sheltered side of the harbour being as follows :—

        North Staffordshires.
        Gloucesters.
        Malta Militia.
        Leinsters.
        Royal Artillery.

There was some considerable delay in starting owing to the roughness of the sea, and during this time two waves broke over the stern, drenching cox and adding considerably to the weight of the boat. Eventually, however, we got off with a capital start and nearing the half-way post we were level with the Gloucesters the remaining crews being from one to two lengths astern. Here, however, disaster overtook us; the swell and the water in the boat causing our craft to roll a great deal with the result that stroke caught two crabs in succession and within a few seconds we were almost last. The crew quickly pulled themselves together, but a stern chase is always a long one and the most the Battalion could do was to cut down three of the other boats, finishing second to the Gloucesters after a gruelling race. The winners were a fine crew, but had had the advantage of the sheltered position and all those who rowed in the Leinster boat still think, nearly thirty years after, that with luck we might have won.

The names and "latest weights" of the crew were as follows:—

	Name.	Height.	Weight.
Bow	Lt. G. I. P. P. O'Shee	6 ft.	11 st. 7 lb.
2	Lt. J. C. Colquhoun ...	5 ft. 10½ in.	11 st. 6 lb.
3	2nd Lt. F. E. Whitton	5 ft. 11½ in.	12 st. 3 lb.
4	Capt. K. M. Drummond	6 ft. 2 in.	14 st. 1 lb.
5	Capt. T. St. C. Davidson	5 ft. 11 in.	11 st. 7 lb.
Stk.	Lt. G. A. Taylor ...	5 ft. 8 in.	11 st. 7 lb.
Cox.	Capt. & Adjt. W. T. M. Reeve	5 ft. 7½ in.	10 st. 3 lb.

Average height of crew	...	...	5 ft. 11⅛ in.
Average weight of crew	...	...	12 st. ½ lb.

The crew was therefore on the light side and there were too many under the average weight to make it a really co-ordinated six.

There is little else to tell of the stay of the Battalion in Gozo. Early in 1895 inside information began to trickle in from the beer contractors of the canteen—in those days the military authorities communicated all secret things to military tailors and brewers first—that during the winter trooping season the Battalion would proceed to Bermuda. This was a disappointment to the more adventurous spirits, for Bermuda was but a station in the " Colonial " tour where the chances of active service were *nil*, and most officers had hoped that the Battalion would follow the more usual round to Egypt or India. This, however, was not to be, and soon the dark secret became official information. The best thing about Gozo was the leave season—three and a half months of the hot weather at home, and the remaining three and a half months at Gozo being a welcome contrast to the stifling heat and smells of Valetta. It was at Gozo that the 2nd Leinsters wore khaki (drill) for the first time although curiously enough the officers were not allowed to wear it but did all parades and duties in the hot weather in white. Gozo, too, saw the last of the Glengarry, these caps being worn by the draft from the 1st Battalion but were then replaced by the field service cap as worn by the remainder of the Battalion.

On the 15th November, 1895, the Battalion marched down from the fort to the tiny Marina below and embarked for Malta. Taking a last look at the island a private was overheard to remark " The back of me hand to you, Gozo " and this trite remark echoed the feelings of most. At Malta the Battalion immediately embarked on the hired transport *Pavonia* of the Cunard Line. The Battalion was now under a new commanding officer for on board was Lieutenant-Colonel J. G. Glancy who had come out from the 1st Battalion to take over command *vice* Lieutenant-Colonel Woods whose time had expired. Captain Reeve had also succeeded Captain Davidson as adjutant.

CHAPTER XXVIII

THE 2ND BATTALION.

BERMUDA, 1895–1897.

THE voyage to Bermuda was without incident and, as from Gibraltar onwards it was across an expanse out of the usual highway of traffic, there was nothing to relieve the inevitable monotony of shipboard. The *Pavonia* was quite a comfortable vessel of some 5000 tons and must have been one of the last of Atlantic liners to carry sails in addition to steam power, these being set most of the way and providing the tug of war team with ample exercise in hauling on various mysterious ropes. The weather was fine throughout, though a beam sea was experienced all the way across the Atlantic and in this the *Pavonia* literally wallowed. There never was a vessel to beat her at rolling and from Gib. the whole way to Bermuda the fiddles were never off the tables for a single meal, a unique record in a voyage during which not a drop of water came on deck.

Early in the morning of the last day of November Bermuda rose upon the horizon and as the *Pavonia* drew near it was seen that our new station was quite different from the island which we had left a fortnight earlier. The whole place was a mass of green, and thick clumps of cedars were in refreshing contrast to the ghastly brown-paper hue of Malta and Gozo, while here and there houses of snowy whiteness peeped out from the dark background. Altogether a cheerful looking station and as, to reach the anchorage, it was necessary to coast along the whole length of the island a panorama of the place was displayed to us before we actually landed.

There is a popular belief that Bermuda, or the Bermudas, consists of 365 islands, and therefore, one is apt to conceive a vision of a great archipelago. Nothing, however, could be further from the truth. Imagine a great sea fish-hook some thirty miles from shank to barb, and imagine, further, projecting halfway down the shank an arm reaching halfway to the point. With this Bermuda is visualized. Where the projection joins the shank is Hamilton the chief town, and above it is the breezy camp of Prospect the military headquarters. At the barb were the naval dockyard, the headquarters of our North American Squadron—and the island of Boaz, connected with the main curve of the hook by causeways, where was stationed a detachment of one company of infantry. The butt of the hook was formed by the old capital of St. George's where were all the Garrison Artillery and another detachment of two companies of infantry. Inside the bight formed by the projection mentioned above and the curve of the hook were many wooded islands. Actually the area of the whole group was somewhere about 21 square miles and as the greatest length was nearly thirty it follows that the island in places was less than a mile wide, but so skilfully had nature laid it out with little hills and valleys that it was as deceptive as a landscape garden and the narrowness across was never unduly evident. And though the whole command was tiny yet the Battalion was very split up, for the distance by road to the two outlying detachments was over twelve miles in each case.

Here the 2nd Battalion relieved the 1st Royal Berkshire Regiment and was destined to pass two years, happy years on the whole though at first things seemed to go a bit awry. Before we had actually landed one subaltern had shewn such symptoms of melancholia that he had to be sent home immediately and never rejoined the Regiment again, while soon afterwards a young officer—Second Lieutenant P. F. A. Leahy—went down with tuberculosis and was invalided, to die a few months later in France. The climate, too, in the summer months was peculiarly enervating and depressing; it used to be said that five years' sojourn in Bermuda could be thus summarized:—First year, sailing; Second year, cutting walking sticks; Third year, collecting shells; Fourth year, madness; Fifth year, death. The Battalion had, too, a new commanding officer—one who had never served a day in it and who had practically never served a day out of India. Added to this the exile in Gozo had rather blunted the social side of the officers' mess and made its members possibly a trifle *farouches*, and as it happened Bermuda was pre-eminently a station where tact was called for, and in large quantities.

There were simply two classes of inhabitants—the black and the white. The former were the regular African negroes but orderly, civil, industrious and prosperous and as different from the West India pongoes as chalk is from cheese. The remainder were the white people amongst whom there were practically no social gradations whatever, and this absence of the accepted order of things was at first a bit perplexing for a newly arrived unit. When you went into a tiny draper's shop, to buy a pair of white gloves to wear at a dance at Government House, you did not expect to find the shopman, who supplied you with these necessary articles, present at the same function that night—and this mark you no *omnium gatherum* but a gathering of Bermuda Society with a big S. Practically speaking, with the exception of Government officials, the leading white inhabitants were all shopkeepers, but they were the direct descendants of the earliest colonists of two centuries previous and more than one name which was imprinted over a small outfitter's or grocer's shop was to be found in the list of governors of this small but ancient colony. This rather abnormal condition of things was due to the economic situation of the island. The tiny area of the place precluded a land owning class; there was for the same reason no mineral or manufacturing wealth; and these representatives of old English families if they did not actually live " by taking in each other's washing " did live by selling necessaries of life to the naval and military forces. Charming, hospitable and cultured people they turned out to be, and when you had been in the island a few months there seemed nothing odd about the system. But to a unit almost fresh from England and with officers whose only experience of foreign service was the rigid social system of India the conditions of Bermuda society were undoubtedly a little baffling.

For a man whose ideals of happiness were bound up with horse and hound, or rod and gun, Bermuda was a poor station indeed. There was of course no hunting, nor was there any space large enough and level enough for a polo ground. A horse was rather like a black swan in Bermuda, although there was a little, Heath Robinson " race meeting " where a syndicate of local " sports " would sweep the board with some old broken down selling-plater imported from the United States. There was no game to shoot and a rod was unnecessary for there was not a river, nor a stream, nor even a well in the island, drinking water being obtained by saving the rain water, which trickled off the roofs, in immense tanks. But in other respects there was a deal of amusement and recreation to be had. The cricket was excellent, as indeed it always is where Anglo-Saxons have settled in tropical or semi-tropical places, and taught the black man to play. Lawn tennis, too, was of a distinctly high standard and the garrison had a thriving club in the Happy Valley, a small depression near barracks where the moist heat in summer provided a fine test of physical endurance and induced a most alarming inclination for iced lime squash. No mention of lawn tennis in Bermuda would be complete without reference to two ladies prominently connected with it, Miss Mary and Miss Bessie Gray daughters of the Attorney-General of the island. Fine players themselves, by their skill and enthusiasm they held high the torch of tennis in the colony. They had a " day " once a week at their house to which all new arrivals whose form appeared satisfactory were invited, and if your skill and keenness passed the ordeal you were henceforth among the select. Your first " day " was the acid test, and woe unto you if you succumbed to the enervating climate and played a trifle languidly—you were thereafter an outcast fit but for a pat-ball four. Regiment after regiment of the British Army was in time thus vetted and on the veldt of South Africa, in the jungles of Hindostan, amid the mud of Flanders, or the horrors of Gallipoli officers of different units meeting—and finding in Bermuda a common topic—would infallibly blurt out " Did you play in the Miss Grays' lot ? "

The real sport, however, of Bermuda was sailing, and few places could be more suitable for picnic yachting, and amongst the officers three or four had in their young days acquired the yachting art. The craft were peculiar to the place and the *Dauntless* which was acquired by the officers of the Battalion was a typical example. The *Dauntless* was built throughout of cedar, a wood of everlasting wear, and was in size something less than an old three tonner ; she had a large cockpit and a trunk hatch which gave headroom of some five feet. On account of the reefs all ballast was inboard. The rig was that peculiar to the place—Bermudian, that is to say the mast which was of great height raked sharply aft the " mainsail " being of leg of mutton shape, hoisted by a single halliard, and with a boom projecting far over the counter. The headsail was a great foresail set on a long bowsprit which with a fiddle bow gave the old *Dauntless* a smart appearance. In many ways she was a beautiful boat to handle. The rig was of quite extraordinary service in luffing up to pass through a short channel between two coral reefs—and these were frequent, and the single halliard and absence of gaff to the mainsail made reducing sail in a squall a simple operation. The necessary absence of outside ballast had, however, to be remembered and when the *Dauntless* had her covering board under it was time to think about the fore sheet.

The coral reefs made a paid hand with local knowledge —or as he was always called there a " pilot "—absolutely essential, and the pilot of the *Dauntless* was a fine old coloured man Telfer Simmons, with the skill of a Cowes skipper and the dignity of a member of the Royal Yacht Squadron. The skill of these local pilots was amazing ; by day they would take a yacht through a maze of reefs, simply sitting forward and chanting out every now and then " Luff a little, sah," " Keep her off now, sah " and the helmsman, perspiring freely, would, over the lee quarter, discern grisly masses of coral whizz by two or three feet below the surface. Even at night these pilots, working half by bearings and the other half apparently by instinct and memory, would take the most audacious short cuts. An accident with them was almost unknown so highly developed was their skill.

Looking back over a generation ago was there ever anything better than a Thursday in the old *Dauntless* ?—for our new commanding officer had introduced the grand old Indian custom of a ." Europe morning " on that day. There was the leisurely holiday breakfast in flannels, the ancient marinery study of wind and sky by the old salts of the Battalion and then the minute instructions regarding a hamper to Sergeant Shummacher, the mess sergeant and prince of picnic providers. One slid easily by push-bike down to the little yacht club and from the balcony would watch the faithful Simmons getting things ready just below, and then we are off. An English hot summer's day, a breeze with just a bit of weight in it at times, and we fly past the Princess Hotel, waving our hands to our lady friends on the verandah above. Past Agar's Island where we shout derisive greetings to the subaltern on guard, loafing about his tiny domain in shirt sleeves and looking like a youthful Robinson Crusoe. An extra punch in the breeze, a long gentle luff and we are through Two Rock Passage and out in Grassy Bay, and here there are dainty little mischievous white horses which prance on board now and then and drive old Simmons aft, growling a trifle morosely at the helmsman's seamanship. It is only eleven o'clock so appetites, even sharpened as they are by the tang of sea air, must put away visions of the hamper down below. Still there is great virtue in bottles of Kola—from the Battalion soda water machine—with three fingers of froth and a block of ice chinking against the glass—does that god-like nectar exist to-day one wonders ? And so with a long lazy run here and a succession of tacks there, close hauled with the covering board a wash, and there is Darrell Island right ahead. That emerald glade amid the cedars seems just the place—and who said lunch ? In a trice we shoot up alongside a rough stone pier and an hour later four white men are lying replete, supine and somnolent in the sun and an old coloured man is asking sarcastically whether we intend to spend the night there.

And then with a lighter wind we glide across to Boaz and " draw " the detachment there for tea, and after a pipe and a yarn embark once more for home. The wind has fallen lighter still and a lotus-land drowsiness is over all the crew. Even the helmsman nods and the other idlers are shamelessly strewn and stertorous on the deck, even the necessity of having to pole through Two Rock Passage scarcely galvanizing these loafers to activity. Soberly we drift up the harbour and at last the moorings are aboard. It is stiff work push-biking up to Prospect and not much time to dress. In four brains the same wicked thought has been brewing and four tongues simultaneously gasp out " I vote we dine in the Mess Office." And so we do, with red copper faces and in our yachting flannels, sequestrating from frightened waiters the daintest tit-bits *en route* to those respectable folk beyond who really did look upon mess or even " Thursday supper " as a parade. Yes, those were good days in the old Bermuda *Dauntless*, but a perfect day required that furtive mess office meal to round it off.

There were several yacht races, while we were at Bermuda, for which the *Dauntless* entered, but without much luck ; in fact unkind people used to assert that she got her name from her indomitable resolution in competing even after defeat. At any rate the crew had some fun. Racing canvas was carried ; the shrouds were removed to allow scope for the spinnaker boom—and in consequence the mast would bend like a whip ; and shifting of ballast was allowed. All this made for smart handling in a breeze.

There were other yachts too, the *Nautilus* of Lieutenants Bullen-Smith and O'Shee, with a fine turn of speed, one too in which Captain Reeves and Lieutenant Mather were wont to make deep sea fishing voyages to the outer reefs and the *Juno* of Captain Canning. With the last was associated a tragedy. Captain Canning was going home on leave and the day before—it was a Sunday just after church parade—asked an officer if he would care to buy his boat. The latter was not a buyer, but just at that moment Second Lieutenant Buchanan was passing and impulsively—as was his wont—said " I'll buy her." The deal was completed and Buchanan who knew nothing about sailing, and who but five minutes previously had no idea of being a yacht owner, found himself the possessor of the *Juno*. That evening was dark and squally, but the new owner offered to take Lieutenant Stuart, who was the officer on duty for the week at Agar's Island, back to his command. Inexperience and a black squall did the rest. Lieutenant Stuart managed to swim ashore, land, fortunately, being but a few hundred yards off but, though he swam about first looking for his companion, no trace of Buchanan could be seen. It was some days before his body which had been entangled in the mainsheet was recovered. An officer of striking personality, handsome, and six foot three in height Second Lieutenant Buchanan was a splendid specimen of the young British officer. He lies buried in the little cemetery on the summit of windswept Prospect, and a simple cross erected by his brother officers tells the story of " Duncan Reginald Ross Buchanan. Drowned by the capsizing of the yacht *Juno*, 28th February, 1897. Aged 20 years."

From the social point of view there was much to recommend Bermuda. It was in those days a regular winter resort for Americans and Canadians and this livened things up a good deal. Each of the two large hotels had a dance once a week and it is a fact that in the elevated railways in New York were to be seen advertisements describing the advantages of Bermuda as a pleasure-resort and ending up with two strong recommendations " Malaria unknown. Officers attend hotel dances in uniform." Both statements were true, but whether the scarlet or blue and gold mess jackets brought any additional visitors must always be a matter of conjecture. At any rate the two services were by no means unpopular with the visitors. Another pleasant feature of Bermuda was the opportunity we had of making friends with naval officers. In those days there was a North Atlantic and West Indies Squadron consisting to a large extent of small sloops and gun boats for fishery duties off Newfoundland. The *Crescent* and later the *Talbot*, was the flagship. There was a floating dock at Ireland Island which was rather a rarity when it had been first installed.

The non-commissioned officers and men liked Bermuda although as they did not share the joys of the leave season they had no break during their stay. There were few garrison duties, the barracks, partly stone and part huts, were by no means uncomfortable and soldiering, especially in the detachments could hardly be described as strenuous. There was lots of cricket, excellent bathing and many were enabled to make friends with the Senior Service during our stay. The engineers had a kind of permanent lien on the infantry for building a pier, an arrangement not unpopular with the men as it was a paid fatigue and cut into the days available for drill. Lieutenant-Colonel Glancy was, however, not the man to hand his battalion to a C.R.E. or anybody else without having something to say in the matter. Colonel Glancy had a passion for barrack square drill ; he had been seven years adjutant of the 1st Battalion in India and had there gained a great and deserved reputation. Always well mounted, immaculately turned out, with a fine seat on a horse and that rarest of possessions a perfect word of command, he had many natural advantages for the work. Added to this he had a knowledge of all Red Books—the

Infantry Drill included—encyclopædic in character. He took over the Battalion with the prestige of the best drilled battalion at Aldershot and for five years he polished it up to impeccable perfection. Twice a week at least there were commanding officer's parades, always ceremonial and invariably ending with a march past, and as he took only one day's leave during the tenure of his command a simple calculation will show that the Battalion from 1895 to 1900 must have practised this operation hundreds of times. If ever there has been a battalion to beat the 2nd Leinster Regiment at handling arms and marching past the present writer has missed seeing it. These parades at Bermuda were held on the cricket field and attended by American visitors in their hundreds. Kodaks clicked like magazine fire while the Battalion marched past and invariably at the end of the " Bayonet Exercise in Quick Time " there were rounds of enthusiastic applause. Some of us were inclined to affect an air of disdain for these parades and to talk contemptuously of a " circus " ; but they were a fine thing for an Irish battalion, and brought out that spirit of " showing off," in its best sense, which is such a marked characteristic of the Irish soldier.

From the purely military point of view there was no event of outstanding importance during the stay of the Battalion at Bermuda, although for a short time tension existed with the United States over the question of pressure by England and Germany on Venezuela for payment of debts. At any rate dusty mobilization and defence schemes were dug out of long sealed pigeon holes and there was a mild flutter amongst the American visitors over the prospect of internment. Everything, however, was settled peaceably, and not even a single ball at the " Princess " or " Hamilton " was suspended. At Bermuda we celebrated the Queen's Diamond Jubilee, and at Bermuda alas ! our invincible tug-of-war team was humbled by the garrison gunners from St. George's—lusty men who played with mighty coast defence cannons every day. It was during our stay that the old colours of the 3rd Bombay Europeans, which had been carried through battle after battle in the Central India campaign were received from the military authorities in India and deposited in the officers' mess. It is worth mentioning, as shewing the versatility of the British soldier, that the three Lloyd's signal stations in the island were run by men from the signallers of the infantry battalion in Bermuda for the time being. The only other military item worth recording is that the establishment of the Battalion which had been reduced to 892 of all ranks was from the 1st April, 1896, increased to 1012.

The next station on the colonial tour was Halifax, Nova Scotia, and, orders having been received, the Battalion embarked on board H.M.T. *Avoca*, on relief by the 2nd Battalion Worcestershire Regiment, on the 19th October, 1897. The actual strength was 22 officers, 2 warrant officers, and 868 non-commissioned officers and men.

CHAPTER XXIX

THE 2ND BATTALION.

HALIFAX, 1897–1898.

OUR next station would be a great and welcome change from Gozo and Bermuda. We had been in two small islands and were now going to a continent; and from the enervating climate of Bermuda we were looking forward to the bracing effect of a Canadian winter. Also there was something in the prospect of being once more in a city with a theatre, a club, street cars, evening papers and all the adjuncts of civilization. The stay of the Battalion in Bermuda had on the whole been pleasant, but the moist heat of the summer months was wont to produce a most depressing and lowering effect and every one felt in need of a change. How damp the air in Bermuda can be will be understood when it is remembered that a pair of boots taken off at bedtime would be found in the morning covered with green mildew. Smoking was in the Bermuda summer almost a forgotten luxury; one did smoke of course but inhaling the fumes of cigarette or pipe tobacco covered with vegetable fungus can scarcely be called smoking. Further, Bermuda though a small station had been distinctly expensive. There was no colonial allowance and as the inhabitants lived chiefly on the Navy and Army prices were high.

The experience of the Battalion as regards heavy weather during the voyage to Malta in 1894 was almost equalled by the trip to Halifax as the following extract from the log of the *Avoca* will shew. " October 22nd 0.30 a.m. Hard gale and high sea, brought ship to N.E. ½E., slowed engines and hove to. Wind and sea increasing with terrific rain squall. 4 a.m. Whole gale, mountainous seas running, terrific rain squalls, vessel labouring heavily and shipping quantities of water." We remained hove to for about twelve hours but the *Avoca* was a fine sea boat and she came through the ordeal without serious mishap. On coming on deck a curious testimony to the violence of the gale met one's eyes. A large steam launch which rested in chocks on the promenade deck, to which it was lashed by stout ropes, had been lifted bodily from its bed and deposited against the smoking room door, a gaping hole in its side telling of the violence to which it had been exposed. After the storm, however, came the calm and on the 24th October we steamed up the harbour at Halifax.

Wellington Barracks overlooked the landing place and were brick buildings of the old " prison " type of barracks, that is to say the officers' and men's quarters confronted each other across a large barrack square the whole being surrounded by a wall in the old-fashioned manner. As regards the officers' mess the sapper officer responsible for it had been given the instructions " Build the most unsuitable type of mess you can possibly conceive." At any rate on no other supposition can the peculiarities of that building be understood. In any mess it is desirable that officers should be able to proceed from their quarters to the mess proper under cover. At Wellington Barracks this was not the case ; many of the occupants had first to emerge into the open, walk some twenty yards in front of the building, and then enter the mess by the front door. What this meant in a blizzard, or with four feet of snow on the ground, or the temperature 18 degrees below zero—remember we wore patent leather boots for mess—can be imagined. The intelligent sapper had also so arranged all water pipes that they were in a chronic state of bursting, with immense inconvenience to everyone concerned and repaired at great and frequent expense to the State. And of course he steeled himself to an adamantine firmness against the installation of electric light—and this in a country where electric light was as common as " water laid on " over here. We did indeed gain permission to install electric light at our own expense in the mess, being solemnly informed that it was an " encroachment " and that all " encroachments " lapsed to the War Office. But even this robbery was more tolerable than the reek of paraffin all and every day.

But it was in the mess wine cellar that this sapper wrought his masterpiece. That vast cavern had the maximum of exposure to the icy elements and the minimum—nay the complete absence—of any warming arrangements. One can just say that whisky and brandy remained fluid during the winter, but wines gave up the struggle and died. The wine caterer, on descending to draw champagnes and clarets, would find these generous cordials frozen solid, and the afternoon before a guest night the kitchen would be crowded with bottles ranged near the fire, while the wine caterer wondered what would be his fate if the generous grape juice hung icily on the bottle lip and refused to flow into the goblet of the honoured guest. How any one except either a raving lunatic or a prohibition maniac could have passed the plan of that wine cellar passes human comprehension. But there are depths of imbecility impossible adequately to fathom.

Halifax was a two-year station but as the 1st Royal Berkshires whom we had relieved would drop out of the colonial tour after their stay in the West Indies we, as we were unofficially informed, would remain three years in our new station. Those were the days when Government supplied practically no mess furniture and, as at Gozo and Bermuda we had no need for much more than wicker chairs and other tropical outfit, now was the time to furnish more solidly and comfortably. Accordingly the anæmic mess fund was bled to the tune of a couple of hundred pounds before we secured a really comfortable home—and just as we were settling down to a three year enjoyment of our new possessions the whole roster was altered. We got £19 for what had cost us more than ten times that amount and of course not a penny of compensation from "The Public." This is, however, to anticipate somewhat and the actual stay of the Battalion in Halifax can now be described.

There was a special kit for winter in Halifax the officers wearing a special greatcoat with astrakhan collar and cuffs, an astrakhan cap with flaps which could be tied over the ears, and huge gauntlets of the same material. The boots for walking through snow were immense brown leather ones reaching to the knee and in appearance exactly resembling those worn by employees of the London County Council who work in sewers; and in order to secure a grip when moving over a frozen surface small instruments called creepers, which resembled miniature harrows, were strapped under the instep. Non-commissioned officers and men wore their ordinary greatcoats but were served out with thick woollen mufflers, fur gauntlets and caps of a serviceable pattern and boots as worn by the officers. The officers' kit was expensive and represented a severe drain upon five and threepence a day—the pay of a second-lieutenant—but in practice each regiment passed on the greatcoats, etc., to their relief at a very reduced price. For route marching the officers' kit proved too warm even in the severest weather, especially the astrakhan cap, and it was not uncommon to see officers on the march holding the caps in their hands while the perspiration on their heads, induced by the caps, was freezing on their hair, giving quite an old world effect. But for sentry-go for the men no kit could be too warm and in the regiment we relieved a sentry, even with a one hour relief, had been frozen to death.

We had heard great things of sport in Canada and the hearts of the big game men and flyfishers had burned within them in anticipation, but we were soon to find that there was nothing doing within a reasonable distance of Halifax. Moose were to be had in strictly limited quantities, due to Governmental regulations, and the venture necessitated much organization, considerable travelling, the engagement of an Indian hunter, and no little expense. Captain Craske was not the man to rest easy for a moment so long as there were a rifle and a wild beast left in the world and he made a winter hunting trip ; but for the great majority of the officers sport in Halifax in the winter was simply skating.

Here, however, we were again to a certain extent disappointed. We knew of Nova Scotia as a land of immense lakes and many looked forward to mile after mile of fine rightaway skating. What really happened was that no sooner had the lakes frozen than the snow descended and lay three feet thick, and lake skating was at once ruled out. Skating at Halifax was really confined to two rinks in the town in which you could on some days have the rapturous waltzing with the fair sex, and on other days enjoy the great Canadian winter game of ice hockey. The game has already been mentioned in the narrative of the 1st Battalion's stay at Halifax and all that need be said here is that the 2nd Battalion, officers and men, took up the game with the greatest enthusiasm, a sunk tennis court outside the officers' mess being flooded to form a regimental rink. Our first game upon it was somewhat remarkable. The garrison gunners from the citadel rather patronizingly agreed to give us newcomers a game and play duly started, the gunners with a couple of winters' experience distinctly fancying themselves. But before the play had been long in progress one of the Battalion's side whizzed through the opponents like forked lightning and the " puck " hurtled through the goal with the rapidity of a whizz bang. It was Lieutenant Heneker, an officer who had joined the Battalion, while it was at Gozo, from the military college at Kingston. A good man at all games Heneker had spoken once or twice about the ice hockey we could get at Halifax but had said nothing to prepare us for his form. As for this particular game it was soon seen that, by our expert, we could score a goal whenever we chose ; it was just as if Melbourne Inman or Smith had joined in a subalterns' game of snooker or if Lieutenant Kershaw and Commander Davies had taken the field against a preparatory school which rather fancied itself at rugger. Sheer modesty and nothing else prevented Lieutenant Heneker scoring a hundred goals that day. Later we learnt from ice hockey giants of the place that Heneker was one of the star players of Canada and recognized as the best shot at goal in the whole Dominion ; at any rate the gunners in that match were up against something they had not bargained for. When the big league matches between the local teams took place Heneker was generally asked to referee, a high but well deserved compliment to his reputation.

The 2nd Battalion had left Aldershot with a big reputation and the behaviour of the men both at Gozo and Bermuda had been exemplary ; but we had not been long at Halifax before we discovered that there were alarming symptoms of wind over the arrival of an Irish regiment in the place. One day all the officers of the Battalion were summoned to the headquarter office. Speculation ran high as to the meaning of this order, the bulk of the opinions hardening round either a decision from home that the Regiment was to be turned into Canadian Guards or that war had broken out between England and the United States. At headquarters all was solemnity and silence till General Montgomerie-Moore—a fine old cavalry soldier who had the unique experience of rising to full general without securing a single " ribbon "—began to speak. To our utter amazement he referred in ponderous terms to the " state of utter indiscipline of the Battalion " and mentioned how shocked he was by his investigation of the company defaulter sheets—these had apparently been impounded by his staff who gazed solemnly upon us with the expression of serious, low-church looking hens. It must be admitted that some of the sheets would seem alarming documents to-day, more than one containing records of 50 " drunks," but one swallow does not make a spring and certainly one or two old soakers in an Irish regiment need not damn that unit for good.

The dear old general read us a lecture which we listened to with becoming gravity although we knew full well that the old man's alarm was ridiculous. The interview closed with a fine speech by our commanding officer Lieutenant-Colonel Glancy who indignantly combated General Montgomerie-Moore's statements and emphasized the reports which the Battalion had gained while under his command at Bermuda. The words were spoken with earnestness and dignity and made a great impression even on those officers of the Battalion who did not always see eye to eye with their colonel. Never a popular commanding officer John Grogan Glancy had nevertheless this sterling quality: he would never allow an officer or man of the Battalion to be done down by superior authority.

All's well that ends well and as will be seen later the G.O.C. put on record his high appreciation of the conduct of the Battalion while in Halifax, and, what was even more satisfactory, before we had been many weeks under his command, he apologized to Colonel Glancy privately in the most handsome manner for the strictures he had mistakenly made against the Battalion. And so we regained our reputation. But nowadays it is difficult to describe the terror which an Irish regiment used to inspire long ago in stations where dear old gentlemen were found pleasant and lucrative shelving billets. Some of our Haligonian friends told us later that the shopkeepers had seriously thought of barricading their shops for some days after our arrival.

If we looked forward to some bracing weather after Gozo and Bermuda assuredly we were not disappointed for the winter of 1897-98 was abnormally severe in Halifax. It was the boast of that city that it was Canada's natural winter port inasmuch as the harbour was always ice free; but alas, this proved to be fiction for that winter the harbour froze in the most unmistakable way. The temperature at that time dropped on several days to 18 degrees below zero and brought home to some of us what real cold means. So long as the air was still and there was sunshine no very great inconvenience was experienced, but with a tearing north wind the sensation was the reverse of agreeable and one felt on emerging into the open as if one's ears were plunged into molten lead. With the thermometer at that low level curious things would happen. You started to walk across the barrack square; in five seconds your moustache would feel like a wire frame; in ten seconds it was a block of iron; and before you got back to the ante-room fire great tusks of ice from your frozen breath were pendant on your chest. Perhaps you had lit a pipe while outside; if your hand incautiously touched the silver band you would know it. Instantly the flesh would turn dead white and after you had jammed the frozen member into its gauntlet, and shoved gauntlet and all under the other armpit, you would know the physical pain of restored circulation. This little episode over you might remove your pipe a moment from your mouth; on reinserting it you could not make it draw, for your saliva in the stem had frozen solid. Of course if you ever went out skating, and in putting on your skating boots (which had skates permanently screwed in to them) were fool enough to touch the steel for a second, you were hopeless; at any rate you were not likely to do it again. These little things will perhaps convey a better idea of real cold than a whole page of meteorological statistics.

On the whole Halifax was an enjoyable station. It had the great merit of being cheap. The price of food was extraordinarily low, best meat being 5d. a pound, game at something the same figure, and as for oysters we used to consume barrels of them for a mere song. Further, the garrison was allowed to import wines and spirits duty free and the best whisky cost the mess only one and tenpence a bottle. Subalterns whose banking accounts were in need of a rest cure could therefore do themselves proud without gargantuan mess bills, especially as tobacco and cigarettes could also be obtained on these terms. In some respects, however, Halifax was rather a disappointment. There was a curious Puritan element in the place, and though there was a theatre it had to be camouflaged under the more elevating title of "Academy of Music," and the performances were in keeping with this austere title. Apparently while the Battalion was in Halifax the place was suffering from a commercial depression; at any rate money seemed to be tight and the inhabitants, hospitably inclined though they were, did very little entertaining for a place of the size of Halifax. We were told that, pleasant though the winter was with the skating, the real charm of Halifax was the summer months, but these we were destined never to experience. Two other features of the place are worth recording :— it was extraordinarily healthy; and its proximity to the United States where wages were very high was a temptation to desertion on the part of the garrison. Two small detached posts about twenty miles out kept a sharp look out on a main road and the railway which led from Halifax, and there were of course elaborate precautions at the steamer landings. We did not, however, suffer any loss of *personnel* in this way.

While we were stationed at Halifax friction existed between the United States and Spain over Cuba and one day a thrill of excitement was caused by the news of the blowing up of the U.S.S. *Maine* in Havana Harbour. War between the two Powers was not long delayed and the British Cabinet decided in the circumstances to maintain for the time two battalions in the West Indies. It was about this period that the movement, referred to earlier, for the repatriation of the 1st Battalion was in full swing, and accordingly orders were sent by cable that the 2nd Battalion would embark early in May for the West Indies and that it would be relieved at Halifax by the 1st Battalion. Thus it happened that on the 5th May, 1898, the two battalions were drawn up together on the parade ground at Wellington Barracks on which occasion General Montgomerie-Moore addressed the men of the 2nd Battalion as follows :—

"Men of the 2nd Battalion Leinster Regiment you are ordered suddenly and unexpectedly to Jamaica, and I, seeing you for the last time, can only say I am sorry to lose you from my command. Your conduct during your stay in Halifax has been exemplary and creditable to the British Army and your corps. I attribute this to the judicious measures taken by your commanding officer in many ways and in instituting in barracks counter-attractions to the public house outside and the liquor bar inside. The branch of the Army Temperance Association may be particularly mentioned and I trust that the good work begun and so successfully carried on may be continued and I believe it will. I also wish to compliment you on your courtesy especially noticeable in the town, and your smart appearance on all occasions. I wish you good luck and prosperity wherever you may be."

It was with this stirring *amende honorable* ringing in our ears that we marched out of the barrack gate and embarked on the transport *Dilwara*.

CHAPTER XXX

THE 2ND BATTALION.

JAMAICA, 1898.

THE two battalions were destined to soldier together at the same station—for a day at least—for although the 2nd Battalion embarked during the evening of the 5th May the ship did not sail until the evening of the following day. This was in consequence of the receipt of a cablegram from the Adjutant-General due to the fact that there was some trouble in West Africa whither it might be necessary to send troops; and of course the easiest troops to send are always those all packed up and on board a ship. Bermuda was reached on the morning of the 9th and the *Dilwara* was again detained by another cable from home. During the day some of the leading residents of the island came on board to renew their acquaintance with the Battalion and in the most flattering manner stated how they missed the 2nd Leinster Regiment. Towards evening another cablegram arrived directing the ship to proceed and accordingly the *Dilwara* sailed on the morning of the 10th May, arriving at Kingston, Jamaica, early on the morning of the 14th after an uneventful voyage. The actual strength of the Battalion on disembarkation was 23 officers, 2 warrant officers, 849 non-commissioned officers and men, 10 women and 14 children.

To those who disembarked that steaming May morning at Kingston the recollection of the famous march up country—the Leinsters' Anabasis—will be with them to the grave. With the exception of three companies which were to be quartered at Up Park Camp—where the headquarters of the West India Regiment were, in the "Plains" just outside the city—the Battalion was to march to the hill station of Newcastle. This could be descried clinging to the steep slopes of the Blue Mountains, almost up in the clouds and some fifteen miles away. The invariable rule in the West Indies is that white troops—except in circumstances of urgency or as part of their training and when the men are in good condition—march at night; but some reason—most probably the old bogey of an Irish regiment—made the staff decide otherwise. They accordingly in their wisdom directed that a battalion on its very first day in the tropics, "soft" from ten days on board ship, and tired out with handing in blankets and stores from about 4 a.m., should make a fifteen mile march in the hot season, five miles at least being up mountain paths.

Colonel Glancy was a commander who believed in having band and drums playing throughout a march but this craze robbed the Battalion of any chance of performing the journey. It is difficult to give a real impression of the effect of a band on West Indian niggers. All that can be said is that every nigger within earshot leaves his job, rushes to the sound of music, and then becomes afflicted with a rabid form of saltatory mania. If there is one thing a battalion on a hot march needs it is air, but with a thousand odd shrieking niggers barging into the ranks breathing becomes less easy. Also the air must be fresh, and, apart from the suffocating dust raised by a thousand pair of naked dancing feet, there is no use glossing over the fact that niggers heated by violent exercise smell most damnably. To a battalion already rather fatigued the first mile or two of these conditions through the sweltering streets of Kingston were worse than three times the distance in open country.

Up Park Camp was reached with some of the men already shewing signs of distress and a senior medical officer strongly deprecated the continuance of the march, urging that the men should rest in the shade of the trees at the camp till sundown, when the march could be resumed. Colonel Glancy, however, felt that as no arrangements had been made for rations or cooking the lesser of two evils was to let the indifferent staff arrangements take their course, and to plug on to the mountains. This was accordingly done, and the Battalion made its way under a pitiless sun to Gordontown where the climb up the mountain begins, many having fallen by the roadside utterly exhausted. A long rest was made and some refreshment was obtained—there was for long a legend that one officer consumed fifteen bottles of ginger beer—and then after the strenuous march in the sun the real physical test began, five miles in the dusk up a steep mountain path, much of the going being in single file with exhausting checks every now and then. This was the final undoing of the Battalion and when in the darkness it straggled on to the tiny barrack square of the hill station it was found that but a handful had survived. For three days the authorities were picking up men, many too exhausted to walk and the bill for wheeled transport was a fine one. It is worthy of record that not a single officer, nor the sergeant-major, fell out though some of the former had vomited from the terrific heat several times *en route*. The officers were of course more lightly equipped than the men but a meed of praise is due to the two second lieutenants carrying the cased colours—with the old pattern poles be it remembered, which made their burden a strenuous one.

The hill station at Newcastle had many amenities and was delightfully cool, but it needed the enthusiasm of an Alpine climber to appreciate it. If the Blue Mountains be considered for the moment as a seated giant, the ridge on which Newcastle stood or rather clung was the giant's shinbone, the cantonment clinging vertically to it from ankle to knee. At the top were the officers' mess and quarters, and zigzagging thence downwards by cunningly engineered paths one passed the men's barracks, a tiny barrack square which at any rate had a glorious view, until one reached the uttermost limits of outlying married quarters and company barracks, to find on looking back that one was a long way and the deuce of a climb from the mess and lunch. The place was rather cut off for, although a marvellously engineered road crossed the mountains from Kingston to the north coast of the island, its twistings to and fro, following the contours of the spurs, made it too long in distance. The only real way to get to Kingston was by the five mile mountain paths to Gordontown ; on the return journey it was the custom to hire a pony for the ascent to Newcastle, and those who have done that journey after dusk in deepening blackness with unseen *khuds* trending away sheer from one's very stirrup will not forget it. There was just one thing to do—drop the reins on the pony's neck and leave it to him. He never made a mistake, his plan being to walk at the extreme edge of the path and apparently to feel occasionally with a hoof to see if the *khud* was there all right.

On the 30th June, 1898, Major-General H. Jardine commanding the station made his annual inspection of the Battalion and expressed himself as very pleased with what he saw. Addressing the assembled officers he said that " he could find no fault, and on the contrary he had nothing but praise for the Battalion, the high state of efficiency of which was evident." The conduct of the men while in Jamaica was exemplary and the station appealed to them in many ways. It was a change from the usual rather drab barrack life and had a flavour of picnicking about it which the men appreciated ; barrack square drills necessarily gave way in some degree to route marches through the hills, and there was instruction in the use of mountain artillery which was a diversion from unending physical drill and bayonet exercise. The climate too was delightful, a relief both from the intense cold of Halifax in winter and the enervating drippiness of Bermuda in summer.

As for the officers opinions of the place were divided. If you liked wearing low collars—not to be dreamt of in a big station— old flannel trousers and Norfolk jacket, and really liked a four hour foot-slog through jungle paths " o'er crag and torrent " then Newcastle had much to be said for it ; but to the more poodle-faking inclined Newcastle could be exceedingly dull. Barring a married doctor or an occasional marooned sapper there was not a soul there but ourselves, and except that it was thick with verdure instead of bare like brown paper, and in the sky instead of being by the sea, it rather reminded one of Gozo. There was a concrete tennis court and a squash court, but, except for a small band of enthusiasts who resented any trespass on their preserves, these were not much used. People from the Plains did of course come up in the hottest months but the accommodation available was not very great and the place was never really more than a station for the Battalion. The normal disposition of a white regiment in the West Indies in those days was that the headquarters and four companies were at Barbados, with detachments of one company at St. Lucia and three at Newcastle in Jamaica, but the Spanish American War, which led to two battalions being in the West Indies, upset this, and the whole of the 2nd Leinster Regiment was for the time in Jamaica where it had relieved a detachment of the 1st Royal Berkshire Regiment. One consequence of this was that the accommodation in the hills had to be increased to allow for a whole battalion and this was done by erecting hutments on another ridge called Greenwich about a mile away. Here the remainder of the Battalion was quartered and an interchange of hospitality to supper on Sunday nights was a regular social feature.

If Newcastle could be dull, at times it was exquisitely and entrancingly beautiful. The view from the mess—perched on the edge of a jutting knoll—looking down the steep valley which died away below Gordontown, and with Kingston and the harbour as a background, was superb; and when as often happened a fine sunset took place the scene is beyond description. Not Turner himself, in his boldest moments, could have done justice to those blood reds, and golds and brilliant turquoise colours. No less remarkable was the scene at night when the fireflies came out, and after a torrential rainstorm—and it could rain in the Blue Mountains—when the dusk gave way quickly to a velvet blackness the Blue Mountains looked like fairyland. Imagine an ebony darkness stabbed in millions of places by little moving golden lights and you will have a faint conception of the view from the mess at Newcastle night after night. Still, when all is said and done, there is a great deal of truth in the old saying " You can't live on a view," and it must be confessed that there was a certain monotony about the place. Some little excitement was caused by the despatch of a small mobile column under Major St. Leger, our second in command, to the north of the island owing to a disturbance among the natives; but nothing happened and the force was soon back at Newcastle. The physical fitness stalwarts of the Battalion worked off their energy by great treks through and over the mountains, Captains Craske and Colquhoun doing some amazing feats of 50 mile scrambles in phenomenal time at the expense of their footgear. On one occasion these heroes arrived back triumphant but almost barefoot. Others less active did less extensive journeys on ponies, and the orderly officer on the Battalion pony had always as much horse exercise as he wanted in going his rounds on the day he was on duty. To many it came as a welcome break when on the 17th September a cable was received from the Adjutant-General of which the following is an extract—" 2nd Battalion Prince of Wales's Leinster Regiment distribute headquarters and following numbers of companies, four Barbados, three Jamaica, one St. Lucia."

This time the staff acted on commonsense lines and the march to the coast took place at night, headquarters, " A," " B," " C," " D," and " F " Companies leaving Newcastle about 11 p.m. on the night of the 24th October, 1898. The following morning they embarked on board H.M. hired transport *Avoca*, with the newly formed 3rd Battalion West India Regiment bound for Saint Helena. After an uneventful voyage St. Lucia was reached on the morning of the 29th, and " C " Company disembarked to be there quartered. The *Avoca* was now detained by a cable from home a crisis having risen between England and France over the Fashoda question. It appeared that the British, pushing south after the victories at Omdurman and Khartoum, had come in contact with an exploring party under a French officer, Major Marchand on the upper waters of the Nile, and a delicate situation had arisen which very quickly reached an acute stage. There was much big noise in the French Press and for a time it looked as if war might be the result. Anyway we were kept stewing alongside the wharf at Castries, and we heard later that an expedition against the neighbouring French island of Martinique was contemplated. The situation was not unfavourable to us for there were ourselves and the 1st Royal Berkshires practically on the spot, while the 2nd Worcestershires from Bermuda and our 1st Battalion from Halifax could have been brought quickly to make up the Expeditionary Force. Alas! things calmed down and on the evening of the 31st we set sail, arriving at Barbados the following morning.

CHAPTER XXXI

THE 2ND BATTALION.

BARBADOS, 1898-1901.

LOOKING from the deck of the *Avoca* as it lay at anchor in Carlisle Bay, just south of the capital Bridgetown, it was clear that in many respects Barbados was quite unlike Jamaica. The island was much flatter, there were no signs of jungle or forests and the place had a singularly untropical appearance.

At any rate there was to be no long and strenuous march up-country. Disembarking by lighters at a small wooden jetty, just at the distant firing point of a poorish looking rifle range on the sand dunes, we moved inland but a few hundred yards and saw our new home before us a short distance off. We were now at the edge of the Savannah, the great characteristic of Barbados—a circular expanse of really good and green grass some thirty-five acres in extent. Right under our eyes were four or five excellent grass tennis courts flanked by what looked to be a really good cricket pitch, while to the right front was a large smooth well kept polo ground. Round three sides of the Savannah were the barracks for ourselves and a detachment of two companies of the 2nd West India Regiment, headquarter offices, and an imposing guard room with a really handsome clock tower. The whole appearance was one of solidity and reminiscent of the old days when the West Indies were the " brightest jewel in England's crown " and when a large fraction of the army used to be distributed through the islands. We did not bother much about this, but were mightily glad to find that we would be living on the flat and that we could get cricket, tennis and polo just under our windows.

As a station we were soon agreed that Barbados would be all right for a short time, eighteen months to two years with a good slice of leave thrown in—at the most. The great drawback to Barbados was that it was too small. There was a legend that it was merely the size of the Isle of Wight, and another thing against it was that the island had fallen on evil days. We had read a lot about the princely hospitality of planters with fabulous wealth, but what we found was a number of kindly but broken down people with tiny sugar estates and rotten old windmills. In the good old days of protection these small properties would maintain a house in Park Lane and all the sons at Eton, but free trade and the cultivation of sugar elsewhere had made poor old Barbados a back number. It looked decayed, and money had drifted from the hands of the old island aristocracy—who thought no small beer of themselves and reminded one rather of Southerners in the States—into those of the mercantile community who lived chiefly by making money out of the Navy and Army and then advancing it on mortgage to the impoverished planters. It was an extraordinarily densely populated place and there were probably more niggers to the square mile than on any other portion of the earth, and the Barbados nigger was a very different creature from the polite and well-to-do coloured gentleman in Bermuda. As for the climate it was not bad. The temperature very seldom went above 86 or 88 in the shade but on the other hand there was no cool season, the only difference between June and December being that in the former month you could play games till 6.45 p.m. while at Christmas time you had to knock off about a quarter to six, with nothing to do till dinner time except drink cocktails—or the indigenous "bitters." The temperature, too, at night was practically the same as by day and this made the place exhausting after a year or so. It was just like a perpetual English heat wave, but on the other hand there was glorious compensation in the trade wind which blew all and every day throughout the year.

From the regimental point of view the most serious objection was the way the Battalion was split up. It is difficult to get people to realize over what an immense area the West Indies are spread. Some have probably a secret idea that most of the islands are connected by a bridge and there are certainly millions of otherwise blameless people who actually think that *Bermuda* is a West Indian island (an error about as gross as to put Madeira in the Hebrides). To come back, however, to the 2nd Battalion, headquarters and four companies were now at Barbados with only a regular fortnightly mail ; one company was at St. Lucia, 90 miles off; while the remaining three companies were at Jamaica. Jamaica is roughly a thousand miles from Barbados and was actually a different command altogether, so that it will be easily realized how difficult it was to keep up that homogeneity so necessary in a battalion.

At first we really liked Barbados. All parades had to be over by breakfast, company work and orderly room put in the morning well enough ; after lunch the invariable custom was to get into pyjamas and sleep till tea time when it was cool enough for games, which as mentioned could be had just outside the mess. We felt that we could enjoy this for a short time, and before we had been many weeks in the island the next season's reliefs were published and we saw that we were then to move on to our next station in the colonial tour, South Africa. This was certainly being kept on the move with a vengeance. We had left Aldershot in the autumn of 1894 and by Christmas 1899 we would have voyaged from England to Malta, from Malta to Bermuda, from Bermuda to Halifax, from Halifax to Jamaica, from Jamaica to Barbados and from Barbados to the Cape. Add to this that practically every officer had been home on leave at least twice during that period and it will be seen that we had done a bit of travelling. We had now just twelve months only to put in at Barbados and we felt that the place would keep us going for that time. Consequently all went merry as a marriage bell. Everyone who could hit a ball at all kept himself fit and hard with tennis and cricket, or with rackets (for there was an excellent court on the edge of the Savannah) and some went in for polo though the expected shortness of our stay in the island deterred some from taking up the game. Of the polo it can be said that it was most extraordinarily cheap, a good Jamaica pony, sure footed as a goat, and " pleasant to ride and drive " being obtainable for £20 and often less ; while at cricket the islanders white and black were very good performers indeed.

Barbados had in many ways an English appearance, due chiefly to the numerous parish churches which might have been transferred bodily from any English countryside, while the waving fields of green sugar cane looked extraordinarily like English wheat when viewed from any commanding piece of ground. The eastern or windward side was somewhat in contrast with the tamer aspect of the greater part of the island and from its comparatively rugged appearance was known as Scotland. A primitive narrow gauge railway ran across the island from Bridgetown, and then turning sharp to the north ran along the coast for some eight or ten miles. Only two trains ran each way daily, but the lack of trains was got over by trollying. All you had to do was to ring up the engineer for permission to use one and then impound two nigger boys and there you were, with the whole railway system at your disposal. It was extraordinary what the local youths could do in this respect. On one occasion when the Battalion was at manœuvres at Belle Plaine, the railhead, two officers thought they would like to dine at the club at Bridgetown for a change, and after dinner came back the whole 20 odd miles by trolly. Imagine being quartered at Aldershot and coming down from Waterloo late at night on a platelayers' trolley propelled by two urchins casually picked up near Hungerford Bridge.

On this Scotland coast lived a curious race, the remnants of the unfortunate Englishmen exiled to the island—or

Barbadosed—as contemporary chronicles put it—to work as slaves on the sugar estates. This happened in Cromwell's time and the unfortunate descendants of these exiles still preserved the racial characteristics of Britons, that is to say they had apparently refrained from intermarrying with the African negroes, and from their colour were locally known as "Redlegs." A poor washed-out looking crowd they were whose status approximated much more closely to that of the nigger than of the local white population, and indeed they were, except in colour, exactly on a par with the black man. At least one was a private in the detachment of the 2nd West India Regiment quartered in the island, and it came with something of a shock to see in the midst of a row of ebony negro faces the lineaments and colouring of a white man.

Hurricanes are the scourge of Barbados and we just missed one which played havoc in the island a few weeks before we arrived. Still, the accounts in the English papers gave a ludicrously exaggerated account of the damage done. So many thousands of natives rendered homeless, etc., etc. As a matter of fact the houses of the niggers were simply large packing cases of matchboarding which could be, and sometimes were, moved by hand, or many hands. None of them would have stood up against an ordinary English gale, and when they went down like a pack of cards it was no hardship for the tenants to spend a few nights *à la belle etoile* in a temperature of about 80° until they were re-erected. We, ourselves, never experienced a hurricane although we had warning more than once. We had, however, on one occasion a rain storm with one inch of rain in five minutes. It is mere waste of time to try to convey an idea of what rain like that is to anyone who has not experienced it. Stand under a fair sized waterfall and keep on saying "This is rain"; that is the only way to realize it.

The days slipped by quickly and Barbados seemed a real good little station. Like Jamaica, Barbados meant extra pay in the shape of a colonial allowance and there was servant allowance for a negro servant for every officer. Both these allowances made for one's comfort and, although there was nothing to shoot nor hunt, cricket, tennis and polo could be had for surprisingly little outlay. The Battalion too had earned high praise from the general officer commanding, General Fowler-Butler—a splendid specimen of the old English officer—who inspected us on the 10th February, 1899, and expressed himself as follows : " Colonel Glancy, officers, non-commissioned officers and men of the 2nd Leinster Regiment it will afford me great pleasure to make a most favourable report in connexion with my inspection of this fine battalion. Its discipline is excellent, and since its arrival in Barbados there have been practically no offences. Its drill and general appearance are also excellent, and the smart appearance of the men under arms and at all times is a matter for remark. The institutes, interior economy, etc., are very good indeed."

On the 16th March, 1899, the period of tenure of the adjutancy by Captain W. T. M. Reeve expired and he was succeeded by Lieutenant F. E. Whitton who had been acting adjutant since the arrival of the Battalion at Barbados.

The Battalion continued to earn golden opinions in the island and on the occasion of the Queen's Birthday Parade in 1899 H.E. Sir James Hay was pleased to convey his appreciation of the smart and soldierlike appearance of the Battalion at all times, and, in special connexion with the parade, to say that the steadiness of the men in the ranks, their precision of movement and their handling of arms he had never seen excelled. And a couple of months later General Fowler-Butler who was about to relinquish command of the station, made an equally flattering address. " You are " he said addressing the Battalion " a mature seasoned body of men, well disciplined, probably the best drilled in the army, and in musketry, fire discipline etc., very efficient. Of your behaviour in quarters I have nothing but good to say. Since you have been here your offences against discipline have been practically *nil*, and your appearance under arms and at all times is creditable alike to officers, non-commissioned officers and men."

It was a double farewell. General Fowler-Butler's long and honourable service was drawing to a close and the Battalion was under orders for South Africa. "Shortly you will proceed to South Africa and I feel sure that in the event of active service at the Cape you will be at once called upon" were his words. Alas! the hardest of hard luck was about to descend upon a Battalion which had just called forth such generous approbation from the commander of the garrison.

The causes of the Boer War and a short survey of the events which led up to it have been dealt with elsewhere, and all that it is necessary to say here is that naturally events in South Africa all through the summer of 1899 were eagerly followed by all ranks in the 2nd Battalion. It seemed at last as if luck—the luck of active service—were about to fall our way. To a generation accustomed merely to the Great War, which sucked every one into the vortex, it is difficult to convey an adequate idea of what active service meant to a battalion in those far-off days. Until the Boer War the wars in which British troops were engaged had for several decades been small campaigns in which comparatively few regiments took part, and consequently there was a distinction and a *cachet* conferred by having taken part in one. There was the chance of securing one or more honours for the colours and the certainty of a "ribbon" in days when ribbons were something more than five a penny. A "lucky" regiment was one which managed to be at the right place and the right time for a "show" and in this respect the Leinster Regiment, through no fault of its own, had been very badly served by Fortune. The 2nd Battalion, as a five year old, had been through a very fine campaign, but since then, except for a punitive operation in Arabia, it had no experience of active service and the selection of it for the "colonial tour" had practically put it on the shelf so far as war in those days was concerned. Had the Battalion proceeded east instead of going west after its tour in Malta a different story might have been told, for several of the battalions in garrison with us there had come in for a good deal of the fighting in Egypt which ended up at Omdurman.

Now, however, things seemed shaping in the right direction as we breathlessly followed events in South Africa. Field kits, bullock trunks and the smaller paraphernalia of war began to be ordered by the more practical and far seeing. There were smiling whispers of a " ribbon," people began to talk about a strange honour called a " brevet," and the impoverished spoke shamelessly of a curious windfall called *batta*, which might reach the sum of twenty pounds—but the sceptical laughed such wild idea to scorn. Then right in the middle of the growing excitement came the detailed programme of reliefs and the adjutant swelled with importance when he found himself for the moment the possessor of the information that the Battalion was actually due to arrive at Cape Town on 26th December. This was in August and for the next few weeks the Battalion scarcely knew whether it was standing on its head or its heels. Every evening the post corporal would bring up a transcript of the cables from England and these, read out at mess, were the subject of excited comment. Day by day the prospect of war seemed more certain ; every one frantically tore books on South Africa from the shelves of the garrison library, and the Colonial Secretary Mr. Ralph Williams, who knew the whole country from Cape Town to the Zambesi and had been a friend of Cecil Rhodes, came to be regarded as a veritable oracle. Some said of course that the Boer would climb down at the last moment, and every one knew of course that we would be in Pretoria in six weeks. The real agony was that the war might be over by Christmas. And so the suspense was unbearable and there was almost a shout of delight one day in October, 1899, when it was definitely stated that the Transvaal and the Orange Free State had declared war.

Then came the awful anti-climax. The chill blighting

intelligence. The frightful, the incomprehensible, the unbelievable news. A cable arrived from the War Office with these dread words " All colonial reliefs are held in abeyance."

Hope deferred maketh the heart sick, and there were many sick hearts at Barbados in those closing weeks of October, 1899. For a moment there was a flicker of expectation when in the following month an amended itinerary of reliefs arrived. The 2nd Battalion was evidently to remain for the present in the West Indies but there was a glorious hint of good fortune in the intelligence that the 1st Battalion was to return to the United Kingdom via the West Indies, dropping a draft of 400 non-commissioned officers and men at Barbados. Excitement ran high once more and when the news flew round that a naval and military board was ordered to assemble to survey the Royal Mail steamer *Atrato* as to her suitability for carrying troops even the most pessimistic brightened up considerably. The board was duly assembled, but with the most curious secrecy, and no hint as to its verdict ever leaked out though there was a very widely repeated statement that a military member condemned the ship for having no helmet racks. The *Atrato* be it noted was almost a brand new ship of some 5000 tons and a score of workmen could have rigged her up for trooping in a week ; the voyage would be for the most part in tropical latitudes and the Battalion would have slept on deck to a man rather than miss active service. But it was not to be.

Day succeeded day. The weeks passed by and swelled to months but still no news came as to the departure of the Battalion. As the early reverses suffered by the British became known we felt sure that at any moment a cable might arrive ordering us to the front ; but none ever came. Fresh troops poured into South Africa ; India was sending battalions of white troops ; other colonial stations were being denuded of their garrisons ; even militia regiments were being hurried to the Cape, but still we remained. Then we learnt that the

Worcesters at Bermuda, two stages behind us on the colonial tour were off, and later came the news that our 1st Battalion at Halifax was on its way home to England to be made up and equipped for service in South Africa. We were heartily glad that at any rate one of the battalions of the Regiment should be represented in the war but it was only human to think it hard luck that the 2nd Battalion, which was so to speak on the verge of departure for South Africa, should be the one to remain behind.

Why was the 2nd Battalion left " holding the baby " ? Well, there were several reasons which perhaps we did not appreciate at the time. Colonial garrisons, which were denuded of their regular garrisons, had, as a rule militia battalions sent to them for garrison duty. But the militia of those days was liable for home service only. It could not be sent abroad against its will and though militia battalions did volunteer they volunteered solely for active service or for a " good " station like Malta or Gibraltar. The West Indies had an unenviable reputation for yellow fever and there were no takers amongst the militia for those islands. Again, the Battalion was split up in three islands and time would be required to collect the various parts. Time was just what England could not spare. As usual she was unready ; there was no expeditionary force in those days ; everything was being hurriedly improvised ; and the initial reverses (which we thought were " disasters " in those days) got on the nerves of the politicians who preferred to send out any raw troops from home rather than pick up a seasoned battalion from a distant station. Then, too, the various governors in the West Indian Islands probably demurred at the prospect of having their commands either denuded of troops altogether or at best having them garrisoned with raw militia battalions from home. What hit us hardest was that we had no general at Barbados to take up the cudgels on our behalf and to persuade the War Office not to leave us out in the cold. General Fowler-Butler had gone home, the command of the troops was temporarily in the hands of Colonel Glancy, and nothing was done.

And so we were destined to put in two more years of hoping against hope at Barbados though in the end we did not actually miss the war. Doubtless the Powers that Were knew what they were doing when they left us marooned in Barbados, but that they passed by a really efficient battalion there is no doubt whatever. The verdicts of the general officer commanding and the governor (also an old soldier) on the efficiency of the Battalion have been given above and speak for themselves. For mere figures the following may be quoted. The strength of other ranks was 794, of whom about 740 were medically fit for active service. The average service of the privates was 5½ years, and their average age 25 years. Figures of merit in musketry and signalling convey nothing nowadays but the Battalion was a "good" shooting regiment and a super excellent one in signalling (an important point in South Africa). The average height of the men was 5 feet 7 inches, all well salted against tropical ailments and, with the accession of 400 selected men from the 1st Battalion, we could have quitted Barbados a fine battalion over 1100 strong.

It was indeed a bitter disappointment to the Battalion thus to be cheated out of its chance of active service, and our feelings may be imagined when we read in the papers of the recruiting of absolutely untrained young men as Imperial Yeomen at five shillings a day when the regular private received but a shilling. We felt as if we could never hold our heads up again and the non-commissioned officers and men took the whole thing very much to heart. But their behaviour was splendid. However disappointed they were they always maintained that the chance might still come and that they must be ready for it. And so we began what seemed like a second tour in Barbados, going through the old round again and with the prospect of an indefinite stay in a place which we had thought we were leaving in a few weeks. For a time we followed the operations of the war keenly enough, but when Ladysmith was relieved, the Boer general Cronje forced to surrender at Paardeberg, and Pretoria the Boer capital was occupied by the British, we thought the war was over. The politicians of the day with a General Election in the offing circulated this statement and Lord Roberts was ostentatiously recalled to shew that all the fighting was finished. Incredible though it may seem the politicians actually issued the "ribbon" for the campaign a year before peace negotiations began.

Those two years 1900 and 1901 seemed unending in Barbados. The island was small, we soon exhausted all its capabilities and our disappointment over South Africa soured us against our present station. In August, 1900, the tenure of command of Colonel Glancy expired ; he had received an extension of a year in command in 1899 and had been promoted brevet colonel. He was now succeeded by Lieutenant-Colonel St. John St. Leger who as second in command had been left at Jamaica in command of the detachment of the Battalion there quartered.

What the Battalion wanted at this time was an infusion of new blood, and luckily it got this so far as the officers were concerned. The authorities at home thought it just as well to bring regiments up to the proper establishment and consequently for about eighteen months there was a steady drizzle of second lieutenants on the Battalion. As these young gentlemen came neither by way of Sandhurst, nor by any other recognized avenue of entrance, but blew in so to speak from 'Varsity and Militia and Colonies, and later from the very battlefields in South Africa, they were christened "Frauds," from the short title conferred upon soldiers guilty of the crime of Fraudulent Enlistment. With this rapid succession of entrants the Battalion soon became as rejuvenated as if it had inoculated itself with monkey glands, though the adjutant was sore puzzled how to deal with lordly young men from Oxford and Cambridge, veterans of half a dozen trainings of raffish militia regiments and finally young warriors fresh from veldt and kopje.

There were just twelve of them in all, T. W. Butler-Kearney, C. M. B. Hamilton, J. L. Richards, N. G. Burnand, H. W. Weldon, C. Harman, B. Ussher, E. H. Wildblood, R. G. Currey, A. N. Bredin, E. B. L'Estrange. Some had left the Regiment or had transferred to the Indian Army before the Great War came upon us, but those that remained gained distinction for themselves and honour for their Regiment.

There is little to say of the doings of the Battalion during those two years. There was of course polo, cricket and tennis in abundance. No golf was played by the islanders but we made a six-hole links on the Savannah and thus introduced the game. We saw a fair amount of the Navy as there was generally a small cruiser or other anchored in the bay and at Christmas the whole North American Squadron would come down. The American Atlantic Fleet also paid a visit now and then and constantly a foreign man-of-war, European or South American, would drop in for a few days which led to an excessive amount of ceremonial calling the first day and an excessive amount of cocktails or foreign pick me-ups the next. In cricket there was a curious match, the officers against one of our third class cruisers in which Captain Cochrane took every one (15) of the visitors' wickets which fell in the match, surely a cricket record. By the middle of 1901 everyone had of course given up all thoughts of getting to the war—which though " virtually over " seemed to have a good deal of kick left in it, and advantage may be taken of this long dreary spell to see how the detachments of the Battalion had been faring at Jamaica and St. Lucia..

Three companies (" E," " G," " H ") were in Jamaica and the detachment was commanded by Major C. S. B. Evans-Lombe, who succeeded Major St. Leger, with Captains Sangster, O'Shee and Twist as company commanders. The only other white troops on the island were a company of garrison gunners at Port Royal on the coast near Kingston. This was a most unhealthy spot which formerly had been a hotbed of yellow fever. The

2D

original Port Royal had boasted a church and a small town but owing to the abnormal wickedness of its inhabitants Providence, so the story tells, had, as a punishment, submerged most of the buildings under the sea. To this day in clear water one can discern the church steeple still intact standing some fathoms under the water.

Newcastle was a delightful spot some 5,000 feet above sea level, and for those who like a hilly country it had great deal to recommend it. The orderly officer, however, used heartily to curse the place as the last barrack-room was some 500 feet below the mess and seeing " lights out " was no joke especially when the orderly officer was in the middle of a game of snooker. The climate was ideal and our men kept very fit though they were there over three years. There were no native bazaars near but a certain amount of rum still found its way into barracks.

In Newcastle there were few facilities for soldiering. Mountain warfare was out of the question as the hills were densely covered with undergrowth and trees. There was a 300-yards range, but the annual course was fired at Up Park Camp, Kingston. Route marching, signalling, knotting and lashing, and bridging were the chief forms of military occupation. For games the men had a small parade ground which was used for football, a gymnasium, and a handball court which was in much demand, and dog fights. Plenty of exercise, however, was afforded the men by a thoughtful Government in the shape of a perpetual wood-cutting fatigue. All fuel was wood and the infantry soldier had to supply it. At first sight one might imagine that a hundred men with saws, axes, etc. would cut enough wood in a week to last the garrison for six months. But why go to the expense of providing saws and axes when you could get soldier labour for nothing ?

No ! the Barrack Department issued *machetes* and nothing else for woodcutting. Now a *machete* is a home-made cutlass without a handle ; in other words a thick piece of hoop iron which the natives use for cutting sugar-cane and other soft substances. Our men had to cut trees up to six inches diameter with these implements. That's why it took so many men so long to create a wood supply. One wonders if this still goes on? Perhaps it does. Only the other day (1920) in an out station in Malabar the contributor of these notes religiously handed over amongst other magazine stores an ancient gun-metal hammer. On enquiring what on earth it was for, the writer was solemnly informed that it was for opening barrels of gunpowder and was made of gun-metal to prevent ignition by sparks! It was formally handed over and signed for; and probably will be for another two hundred years. Needless to say the woodcutting fatigue was extremely unpopular with the soldiers as the jar on the hands was most painful every time a stroke was made with an unprotected handle, but our men were strong, uneducated and well disciplined so the thing went on. But Newcastle though lacking in excitement had its compensations. The companies there were wonderfully fit and an extraordinary big set of old soldiers. From an officer's point of view life at Newcastle was not unpleasant. We all kept ponies and could ride to the foot of the hills and thence drive into Kingston a distance in all of about fifteen miles. Arrived at Up Park Camp one always found a warm welcome in the West India mess whilst for those who could afford it polo was good and there was plenty of first class tennis and cricket. Good pigeon shooting could be obtained on the marshes outside Kingston provided one could endure the mosquitoes which were the biggest and most vicious ever known.

In Kingston itself, besides a very cheery garrison gunner mess at Port Royal, was an excellent civilian club where one could get a room for the night, but we were always glad to get back to the cool of the hills after a short sojourn with the hardy soldiermen who lived perpetually in that enervating climate.

Historically, Up Park Camp was interesting. *Tom Cringle's Log* is full of anecdotes of the military life there of two hundred years ago ; in the days when the chief drink was brandy and water and when officers died daily of yellow fever. There is still the old mango tree outside the West India mess mentioned in *Tom Cringle's Log*, whilst the " crow's nest " outside the same mess was a time-honoured institution. There it was that one used to sit after an afternoon's hard exercise and imbibe the insidious cocktail before dinner.

As an exchange of hospitality the gunners and West India Regiment officers were always welcome in our small mess in Newcastle, and the making of many a pleasant evening was frequently the outcome of a week-end in the hills. As most of the married ladies lived at Newcastle there was always a certain amount of society there, but occasionally one ventured as far as Kingston to attend social functions. On these occasions one met people outside the garrison and obtained a better insight into the social life of the island. No one will ever forget the delightful week-ends which the Governor and Mrs. Raper were kind enough to ask us to spend at their charming residence. Glimpses of English home life which one was beginning to forget. We would have done anything for the Governor, his wife or their daughter.

Officers' servants of course were natives and very good servants too. One dear old waiter we had in the mess was a regular " Uncle Tom." His name was Berger and on one occasion when he was told to telephone to Government House he rather startled those who overheard him thus begin : " Am you dar ? Am you dar ? Dam you dar ! Who de hell you are ?" and so on. The addressee was the Governor himself, who later on used to recount the conversation with great gusto.

The story of the detachment at Jamaica would be incomplete without a reference to the great Altitude Ramp. A new map of the island was being prepared, and the sapper officer while lunching at Newcastle one day, remarked casually " I see you are exactly four thousand and ten feet above sea level here." For a moment there was silence and then shrieks of hysterical laughter floated up to the very peaks of the Blue Mountains.

The figures " 4010 " which the map-maker had seen displayed in huge figures on a rock had nothing on earth to do with datum lines or elevations but were the insignia, the unofficial crest, the emblem and trade-mark of the Leinster Regiment. It was common to the two battalions. Wherever the Leinster Regiment served that number will be found. Europe is full of it. Asia knows it well. Africa displays it. America has it too. From the banks of the Bramaputra to the Jordan, from the Vaal to the Rhine that mystic symbol will be seen. Jungle and veldt ; kopje and beach ; desert and pass, all record it. When the Martians conquer the Earth their archæologists can verify the wanderings of the Regiment not by this history but by a patient search for " 4010's " in each quarter of the globe. Wherever one or more Leinster soldiers stayed, were quartered or passed through, he or they wrote those four digits on everything within reach. It is an historical fact that when H.M.S. *Crescent* the flag-ship at Bermuda, left for home it was with " 4010 " chalked on her stern ; and when her relief H.M.S. *Talbot* arrived it was to find the great mooring buoy in Grassy Bay similarly adorned. If ever a triumphal arch is erected in memory of the Leinster Regiment the figures " 4010 " will be found upon it within an hour of its unveiling.

The origin of the symbol is wrapped in mystery. No explanation is really satisfactory. That, most usually accepted, is that a private of the 2nd Battalion whose number was 4010 (or forty-ten) was once the fiftieth man on parade and when the numbers 46, 47, 48, 49 were rapidly called out in " numbering off " he, in a moment of confusion, shouted out " Forty-ten " instead of " Fifty," and that the ludicrous error became a catch word. This solution is, however, open to several objections, the chief being that the regimental number 4010 would " date " the origin of the craze in the late nineties. But the patient historian has been assured that long before that the emblem was used by the 1st Battalion in India where it was supposed to be a corruption of a trail-blazing mark of the old Canadian *voyageurs*. The real origin of the symbol will never be known. All we can say with truth is that its signification always has been " The Leinster Regiment has been here."

As for St. Lucia it was not one of the good stations which the Leinster Regiment met in its tour of colonial service. It is a small, exceedingly hilly, almost mountainous island with no carriage roads, except the two-mile winding road from Castries (called after the first French governor) to Morne Fortune, the headquarters of the military ; the island, however, can be traversed in most directions, except to the south, by a multitude of bridle paths leading in most directions to the various sugar and cocoa estates and the few misnamed towns. The southern area where there are practically no paths was a very thorny matter after the British captured St. Lucia, being full of French slaves and partisans who gave endless trouble to the British troops. The inhabitants speak a bastard French fairly easily understood, but difficult for an Englishman to acquire. The importance of the island consisted in the fact that it was a coaling station for the Navy. The troops at Barbados were intended to reinforce the garrison in an emergency, pending the construction of great new barracks which were being erected in the late nineties.

The garrison was a large one for such a small place, and the harbour, though small, was one of the best in that part of the world. The garrison in those days consisted of one Royal Garrison Artillery company in which the present Air Marshal Brancker was a subaltern, one native garrison artillery company which was very smart and had a really good band which helped a lot to enliven things in a very dead place, one white company of infantry found by the Battalion at Barbados (in this case " C " Company of ours) and two West India Regiment companies. There was also a company of Royal Engineers engaged building new barracks at a fabulous cost which were never occupied, and about one hundred armed police under the command of Captain Ponsonby, one of Lord Desborough's sons.

The Administrator was Sir Harry Thomson who with his charming wife did their utmost to make things less lonely for the military and naval officers who were stationed in or called at the island. The officer commanding the troops was Colonel Egerton of the West India Regiment who had gained his commission for wrapping the colours of the 94th Regiment round his body, when that regiment was treacherously attacked outside Pretoria in 1881, and so escaping with them. He was succeeded later by Major Seton of the Leinster Regiment. Principal recollections of the place are polo, really good cricket, the great paucity of white ladies—they could be numbered on two hands, and the antediluvian defence scheme which must have been taken over from the French when the place was captured and had never been much more than modified. On one occasion an officer was told that he was not playing the game at some manœuvres because, instead of coming up some of the various bridle paths, he elected to capture one of the batteries by climbing one of the concreted rain water drains running out of the fort.

Those of us who served at St. Lucia have a very nasty recollection of the outbreak of yellow fever there, which started with the deaths of three members of the warrant officers' mess at Morne Fortune and was rather typically put down to too much beer, but when an officer and teetotaller died the right cause was diagnosed and Dr. Low, from the Liverpool School of Tropical Medicine who happened to be in Barbados was sent to us. The deaths were many and sudden for ten days or a fortnight, and it was not until the, as we thought then, rather drastic step of segregating all the troops on Vigie Peninsula, and putting a cordon of troops to prevent ingress and egress, was adopted that the epidemic came to an end. There were many and various theories for the outbreak, one being that the earth which was turned up by the engineers while road making and clearing had excavated some hundred-year-old yellow fever remains; another that it was imported in fruit from Central America; but it was remarkable that none of the civil inhabitants got it, although as most of them were blacks who are supposed to be immune, this can be understood. A black doctor who was sent to the island elected to escape in a sailing-boat, but as the island was strictly quarantined it is difficult to understand how he hoped to score.

Two rather disconcerting events were that we knew that officers by name were ear-marked at Barbados to take our places when we pegged out, and the daily taking of the blood test to see if we had got fever. We generally tried this ourselves at the West Indian livery hour of 10 a.m., and as most nights were spent at smoking concerts and suppers until one and two in the mornings in order to keep up the spirits of the troops, we were usually feeling particularly yellow feverish the next day.

A particularly brave, unsparing man in those days was the head Roman Catholic priest from Castries whose name is unfortunately forgotten. He kept a change of clothes in Captain Mather's room and was in the hospital at all hours of the day and night, and in some cases had to help the doctors to get the corpses ready for burial.

Such a thing as an epidemic is of course a glorious opportunity for finance wallahs. Captain Mather had been advised by the doctors to burn some twenty blankets, which he did and was eventually charged with the cost of same when the company left the island. After three years' correspondence, amounting to some twenty-seven letters he compromised by paying a few shillings to close the affair. This, be it remembered, when the Government was pouring out millions on barracks which were never occupied and doubtless lie derelict to this day.

While we were in St. Lucia there was a gunner subaltern called Graham who had started life as a medical student at Edinburgh, on leaving which he had promised to send the Edinburgh medicos some poison of various snakes as he travelled around the world; so on arrival in St. Lucia he advertised for a *fer de lance*, one of the most deadly snakes in existence. In course of time one was brought alive, with its head fastened in a loop which passed through the side of a box in which its length was coiled. The question now was how to kill it without bursting the poison bag. There was a brilliant proposal to drown it, and the box was immersed under water for twenty minutes. When brought out and opened and the rope removed from the snake's neck the latter promptly wagged its tail. One officer climbed up a solid iron post on to the roof, a rather stout artillery captain dropped over the verandah, and Graham fled. Fortunately the snake's wriggle was only a muscular contortion, but the incident got reported outside and there was a small panic for some time, particularly in the line the snake was reported to have taken. A *fer de lance* bite, it may be mentioned, means instant death. They were introduced by the French to check the desertion of slaves who would take to the jungle; but so formidable did the snakes become that mongooses were then imported to keep them down. In our day they were fortunately very rare.

Another exciting episode was when Major-General Hilton, resplendent in uniform, was inspecting a machine-gun battery and unknowingly was standing on an ant hill. A few seconds later he had to have his nether garments removed by an A.D.C. while he tried to clear himself of the small pests. Talking of machine guns the Leinster company had eight, practically all on different mountings, and as not a soul on the island knew much about them it was a long time before anyone could be persuaded to fire more than two rounds at a time.

To return now to headquarters at Barbados. One day in October, 1901, a cablegram was handed to the adjutant at lunch. It was in code from the commanding officer who was on leave and read merely "Nubifer November." The adjutant put it in his pocket thinking that it referred to the date the colonel was returning from leave, and that it could wait till he went back to the orderly room for the Unicode book. An officer, however, happened to have a copy and volunteered to fetch it from his quarters. The adjutant consulted it and then with a shout read out " The Battalion will embark for South Africa in November." Instantaneously the news flew to the furthest corner of the barracks and it seemed as if the clock had been put back two years and that we were looking forward to active service with the eagerness of 1899.

There followed a strenuous period of route marching and musketry, everyone wanting to walk impossible distances or to spend the whole day on the range so as to be in the pink of condition to meet brother Boer. The Battalion was re-armed with Lee-Enfield rifles and the old Lee-Metfords with their corroded barrels and erratic shooting powers were returned to store. Though Fortune had at last smiled upon us it was a bleak and friendless smile, and it still seemed that we might be disappointed. Although the official intimation from the War Office arrived on the 14th October stating that we were to be prepared to embark on relief by the 3rd Lancashire Fusiliers, probably in November, delays took place and we were at last informed that we would not leave till Christmas—grievous news inasmuch as the war had been " virtually over " for two years and it might really peter out any day. Then yellow fever broke out in St. Lucia which meant quarantine for the detachment there, and we groaned lest we might all be tarred with the same brush. However, all's well that ends well and on the 26th December, 1901, the headquarters and four companies at Barbados embarked on H.M. hired transport *Sicilia* where there was a great *rapprochement* with our comrades from Jamaica who had been picked up by the ship some days earlier. The unfortunate " C " Company was left at St. Lucia and the strength of the Battalion on sailing from Barbados was 19 officers and 578 other ranks.

CHAPTER XXXII

THE 2ND BATTALION.

SOUTH AFRICA, 1901-1905.

THE *Sicilia* was a comfortable ship, an intermediate P. and O. normally, without luxurious frills but with what was far better—solid comfort, instead. As there were only some garrison gunners on board in addition to ourselves every one had lots of room and even captains had large airy cabins to themselves. The ship's officers were a good lot and before we had been many days out they informed us that Neptune had signified his intention of coming on board when we crossed the line. It appeared that his majesty, recognizing the service and age of the field officers and captains, had been pleased to grant them immunity, and every one above the rank of subaltern thought this a very satisfactory arrangement indeed.

Some error had, however, occurred for on coming in to lunch on the fateful day the captains of the Battalion were much alarmed to find on their plates peremptory summonses to appear at two o'clock with the significant intimation " Herein fail not at your peril." One or two affected to treat the missive as a joke but it was noticed that all slipped off to their cabins after a hasty meal and reappeared very lightly clad—all that is except the senior captain who was misguided enough to think that Father Neptune could be bluffed. This was a mistake.

The ceremony of initiation was to take place in the break of the ship between the saloon deck and the poop which gave fine opportunity of witnessing the ceremony to those looking on. At 2 p.m. the ship was stopped, Father Neptune clambered over the bow and with his satellites made his way aft to the scene of initiation.

Some rather alarming looking preparations were made with what seemed quite unnecessary ostentation and the prospective victims did their best to look unconcerned. Some of the captains began to wish they had been as brave as the senior company commander, Captain Rooke, who, in all the defiance of uniform—and a wrist watch—had secured a fine coign of vantage and was looking on with considerable satisfaction. All initial ceremonies having finished the real rite was about to begin. For a moment there was dead silence and the hearts of the captains— who were to be initiated first—could be heard all over the ship. Then from the throat of a horrid-looking satellite came in trumpet tones :—

"*Captain Rrrrrrrooke*" (with about forty-five R's in it).

About one second of law was allowed the victim, but as there was no sign of acceptance on his part a storming party consisting of two six-foot subalterns under the command of Captain Colquhoun (all of whom had basely enlisted in Neptune's service) dashed up the companion way. There was a struggle but only for a moment. Some genius on the poop realized that the moment for a snapshot had come and so long as copies of it remain there can be seen the fate of one who was rash enough to defy the bidding of the monarch of the ocean. The remaining captains went like sheep when they were called. They were brave men, but even the bravest would rather not provoke Captain Colquhoun, Lieutenant Ussher, and Lieutenant Burnand.

Seeing the old year out was the next excitement. Colonel St. Leger professed to hold the secret of making punch peculiarly adapted for such a festival. It consisted so far as could be seen in boiling several bottles of neat whisky in a copper, adding from time to time some of practically every alcoholic ingredient to be found on board and " serving hot." As an obliterator of any sad memories of the year which had expired it had its points— not poppy nor mandragora could have brought such welcome oblivion. But as an invigorator for the year to come it failed completely. On the 1st of January, 1902, the officers of the Battalion were divided into two jaundiced schools of thought—those who believed that the war would be over before we arrived, and those who thought that it would still be on but that they would be killed in the first engagement.

The *Sicilia* put in to St. Helena where we saw our first Boers, prisoners of war who had been sent to the island. Eagerly we enquired from such officers as came on board for news of the war but were met with guarded replies. We guessed at once that negotiations for peace were in the air and that our ill-luck had dogged us still. But when the ship had started the colonel assembled the officers and informed them that he had been informed, under a pledge of secrecy not to divulge the intelligence till we were at sea, that a disaster had just occurred—a force of yeomanry having been surprised and scuppered in a night attack. We did not know whether to look elated or dejected at the news but every one was remarkably cheerful at dinner that night. On the 16th January we arrived at Cape Town and after a strenuous day's unloading ship entrained for " the front."

When the Battalion arrived in South Africa the war which originally was to have been " over in six weeks " had been in existence for just two years and three months. All precedents of European warfare had been discredited and the chief task of the British military authorities had for long been to devise some method for terminating a war which seemed to have in it the germs of immortality. By all the rules of the game the enemy had been defeated long ago. His field armies had been consistently worsted when once their early snatch victories had been lived down ; the capitals of both the Orange Free State and the Transvaal had been in our possession for nigh on two years ; the whole immense territory from the Cape to Rhodesia was traversed by British columns ; scarcely a single piece of artillery remained in Boer hands. Nevertheless the war was in no respect whatever really over, and the ultimate victory of the British—though as certain as anything in war could be—still seemed a long way off. The struggle was now and for some time had been one of guerilla war. At the beginning of 1902 the three chief Boer leaders were still at large. Delarey was lurking in the difficult kloof of the Western Transvaal; in the high veldt of the Eastern Transvaal Botha was still on the watch; and the greatest of the three, Christian De Wet, was biding his time in the north-east of the Orange River Colony. In round numbers the British had about a quarter of a million men against 30,000 of the Boers.

The two great assets possessed by the Boers at this time were their extraordinary mobility and the way in which a Boer force when in difficulties would completely dissolve to reappear later, perhaps a hundred miles from where it had vanished. How to counteract these features had long been the problem and the solution was one borrowed from the realm of sport. In game shooting there are for all practical purposes two methods by which the birds can be laid low; when they are plentiful and slow on the wing they can be walked up and shot " over dogs," but when scarcer, wild and strong in flight a surer method is to have them driven over stationary guns.

It was the latter method which was now in operation in South Africa and for this system the very daring and activity of the Boer commandos had worked to their undoing. In order to protect the railway and the so-called roads, which wandered across the immense area of veldt, from the constant raids of enemy columns it had been found necessary to protect these lines of communication by small corrugated iron blockhouses rendered proof against musketry fire. These blockhouses were, as a rule, sited about three quarters of a mile apart and were garrisoned generally by a non-commissioned officer and eight or nine men, the headquarters of larger formations such as a battalion usually being in a larger work protecting some particularly vulnerable point as a bridge or ford. It was a simple task to join up these blockhouses by barbed wire fencing and when this was done there were hundreds of miles of "butts" against which even the wildest game might be driven. Some of these blockhouse lines were indeed constructed, not to protect lines of communication, but frankly as butts and there was one in Cape Colony some three hundred miles in length from the railway to the Atlantic Ocean. When as sometimes happened, either from chance or design, two great blockhouse lines intersected it is easy to see that good results might be obtained by shepherding the game for some weeks and gradually forcing the birds up into the apex of barbed wire thus formed. It was warfare of this kind which the 2nd Battalion was now about to experience.

After a long journey of four days and four nights the 2nd Battalion detrained at Elandsfontein—the Clapham Junction of South Africa—and went into camp among the gold mines of Germiston, an outlying suburb of Johannesburg. The move up country had not been without excitement for while passing through the Orange River Colony we had been warned by the military authorities at one station, at which we arrived about dusk, that it was very probable the train would be attacked by a Boer column during the night. All preparations were accordingly made for a rapid detrainment to repel attack, but in the end nothing happened, rather to our relief as the initial step in these encounters was usually the derailment of the train. We spent just over a fortnight at Germiston during which time the Battalion was reclothed with khaki serge in lieu of the drill in which we had arrived, poor covering for the cold nights of the high veldt. There was little to be done for beyond finding a few guards the Battalion was not utilized. This rather damped our spirits, eager as we were to see some real active service, an eagerness which had apparently evaporated amongst those who had been in the country a long time. Everyone seemed to us rather stale, and the unexpected duration of the war seemed to have produced a general listlessness. Our bloodthirstiness seemed rather to amuse the old hands and there was amongst them the air rather of " Spare me your callow enthusiasm my friend."

At last on the 6th February we were under way to take part in active operations moving on that day by rail down into the Free State, as the Orange River Colony still continued to be called. If reference is made to the map it will be seen that the branch line to Heilbron forms with the main line from Cape Town, via Bloemfontein, to Pretoria an angle acute ; and it was into this that a great sweep was to drive as many Boers as possible still at large in the north-eastern portion of the State. The task of the Battalion was by means of small posts to fill up the spaces between the blockhouses on the Heilbron railroad, so that when the Boers were driven against it they might be met by a line of fire all along the railway. The drive proper had started on February 3rd. De Wet, who on 10th January had had a hurried interview with Steyn near Reitz, was lying at Elandskop where he had concentrated his burghers and was planning an escape with them to the south across the Kroonstad-Bethlehem blockhouse line. Two days later a British force of some 9,000 men under Elliot, Rawlinson, Byng and Rimington formed up on a line stretching from Frankfort to Tafel Kop ; this force had very few field guns but no less than 2,200 horse and field artillerymen were acting as mounted rifles. The drive lasted three days the columns reaching the main line of railway and penetrating the " angle " on 8th February. It was so far effective that but few Boers broke back through the driving line but when the " bag " was examined it was found that among the 300 or so prisoners De Wet was missing. That leader had succeeded in forcing his way through the southern blockhouse line between Kroonstad and Bethlehem with a herd of live stock and retired to his old haunt in the Doornberg.

The rôle of the 2nd Battalion during these days, or nights rather, was exciting for small parties of Boers " felt " the railway to Heilbron, and in one or two cases a few of the enemy probably got through. We quickly learnt two things; one, if in the darkness—and no one who has not experienced it can realize the velvety blackness of night upon the veldt—fire was opened on some moving object, possibly cattle or wild horses, grave reproofs as to waste of ammunition came next day from functionaries who had spent the night quietly in bed perhaps twenty miles off; and, secondly, if fire was not opened and a few Boers sneaked through, why then the Battalion was evidently asleep. It was thus rather a thankless job and there was a good deal of " Catch him you there by the hedge " on the part of the driving columns. Readers of " Alice in Wonderland " will understand the allusion.

As soon as the drive had petered out De Wet and his followers again crossed the southern blockhouse line and quietly returned to Elandskop where he dispersed them for the time being. We, of course, did not know this and took our place at once in further driving operations, acting as reinforcements to the blockhouse line between Heilbron and Frankfort on the 14th and 15th of February and between Frankfort and Tafel Kop from the 16th to the 19th. Nothing of real interest occurred in these operations and we then returned to Frankfort—or what had been Frankfort for the town was simply one great ruin—to take our place in a great super-drive

For all practical purposes the area of the drive may be regarded as the whole of the north-eastern portion of the Free State, that is to say that portion bounded by the River Vaal, the Drakensberg Mountains, the Harrismith-Bethlehem-Kroonstad blockhouse line and the main line of railway from Kroonstad to Vereeniging. It was to be a combined operation in which 30,000 British troops were to be directly or indirectly employed and was to range over an area of some ten thousand square miles. Inside that area De Wet was known to be, and the real object of the drive was to capture that elusive leader. The actual operation was to be twofold, that is to say it was to consist of two movements by two sets of columns. One force under Elliot was to start eastwards from Kroonstad and the Doornberg, resting its right first on Lindley

2E

and then on Harrismith, while a group of columns commanded by Rawlinson, Byng and Rimington was to work down between the Vaal and Wilge Rivers, and the net was to be drawn on board about Harrismith when it was hoped the De Wet fish would be soon discovered. The initial pressure of Elliot's advance would force Boers across to the east of the Wilge River and to prevent these worthies breaking back was the task of the 2nd Leinster Regiment. The Battalion was to move up the river with a mounted column and drop a stopping force at every drift or ford until its supply of men ran out. This would straggle the Battalion out over some twenty-five miles of the Wilge valley, and the one question which concerned us was how were we to get back to Frankfort once the driving columns had passed on towards the Drakensberg.

This may seem to require some explanation nowadays, but those who took part in the South African War will remember how it had come to be an axiom in that campaign that an infantry column moving without mounted troops was simply " asking for it." There was not such a thing as a dismounted Boer in the country and the wonderful mobility possessed by the enemy put mere infantry at a disadvantage not to be underrated. The Boer tactics in these circumstances were to gallop round the unfortunate infantry in wide rings and to dismount every now and then under cover and open fire upon the foot soldiers. The great object of the Boers was to bring the infantry to anchor on an exposed spot and then methodically to " sting it to death," an operation for which the Boer marksmanship was ideal. In this kind of fighting the Boers had no superiors in the world. Trained to ride from infancy, fine shots, and mounted on hardy ponies sure footed as goats and trained to stand while the rider dismounted and opened fire, a party of Boers could give a really nasty gruelling to an infantry force four times its strength. We at that time were rather green in South African fighting but we were not so green as to underestimate the mobility and marksmanship of Brother Boer. The Wilge valley too seemed just the place for Boer tactics, the track which led up it being commanded everywhere by heights from which all movement in the valley could be watched and where an ambush could be laid every quarter of a mile.

The Battalion marched out of Frankfort on the morning of the 21st February acting with a mounted force, Kitchener's Fighting Scouts, who were some 160 strong. This was an ideal combination for veldt warfare, the mounted troops scouting far ahead and to the flanks while the infantry could afford a fine rallying point should opposition be encountered. We crossed the river by a drift two or three miles from Frankfort, the water being nearly waist high. The approaches were steep and muddy and considerable time was required to get the transport across. As we moved up the valley we began to drop detachments at drifts a task which possessed great difficulty. The river wound about in extraordinary loops, sometimes being close to the track and at other times out of sight, a mile or so away. It was almost impossible to locate drifts, for the map issued by the Intelligence was about as accurate as Marco Polo's charts and the two ex-enemy guides with us knew apparently less about the country than we did ourselves, and were probably spies to boot. However, we were not worried by the enemy and late in the afternoon we bivouacked on a knoll overlooking the river. Here descended upon us a terrific thunderstorm of the most virulent South African brand with a deluge of rain which scraped the proofing off raincoats as a man would scrape paint off with a knife.

Next day we continued our move up the valley, the Battalion shedding itself in detachments on the way. Still no sign of the enemy, but we rounded up about fifty head of cattle and thousands of sheep, most of the latter being slaughtered to deny them to the Boers. That night we bivouacked at Bamboo Spruit some twenty-five or thirty miles from Frankfort and from the other bank came the sound of machine guns and pom-poms shewing that the driving line was engaged. Next morning the drive passed on taking with it our friends, Kitchener's Fighting Scouts. Headquarters and about half a company of the Battalion now moved over the river to some high ground overlooking a drift feeling a little alone in the world.

We remained there two or three days amusing ourselves rounding up wild horses and signalling to Tafel Kop about fourteen miles away, the atmosphere being so clear that even on a dull day when the helio could not be used it was possible to read the large flag through a telescope. A rather amusing incident of red tape enlivened our stay even on this lonely kopje. Before the detachment which had been quartered at Jamaica had left that island there had been some trouble over the accounts of the Garrison Canteen at Newcastle where the non-commissioned officer in charge had gone wrong. Now apparently a cable had come from the War Office demanding a copy of accounts from the officer who had been canteen president, and the order had flashed up country by telegraph and visual signalling until it trickled in to us by a flag message from the top of Tafel Kop fourteen miles away. The command was peremptory—the information was to be sent " by return." There was something delightful in receiving such an order when perched on an isolated kopje in the middle of boundless veldt; and the irony of the thing was that the officer concerned had been invalided from Jamaica and was at home, as the War Office might have well known if that fine old institution had but lived otherwise than in watertight compartments.

The supplies which we had brought up the valley with us in the Battalion transport were now running short and unless we received orders to return to Frankfort very shortly we would have eaten everything we had. There were still flocks of sheep roaming about and some were captured and killed; but it was not safe to move too far from our camp and short rations stared us in the face. Accordingly Major Drummond, the second-in-command, with Sergeant-Major Smyth and two yeomen who were attached to us were sent back to Frankfort to draw more supplies and to arrange for some method of getting the stuff up the valley. It was a pretty exciting day's journey for the quartette for they were early on chased by a band of Boers and in riding for safety to one of our own posts on the drifts they were received by a very heavy fire, the officer in command of the post urging on his men to rapid efforts with the words "It's De Wet trying to break out!" Luckily there were no casualties and the party arrived eventually at Frankfort. The authorities who had apparently forgotten all about us now sent a signal message via Tafel Kop ordering the Battalion to collect itself and return to Frankfort as quickly as possible.

The Battalion headquarters started next day very early. In order to shorten the time till the nearest post could be reached it was decided to do without all the usual precautions of advanced and flank guards, to put all the personnel on the empty waggons, and to move as rapidly as possible, not following the bends of the river but taking a short cut across country. This was the really tricky part of the return journey. There was the whole of the Battalion transport with merely headquarters and about half a company, and the first few miles led through the most beastly country from the ambush point of view. However, our luck held and we got into touch with the first post on the drifts without incident, and as the Battalion would grow stronger as we moved down the valley to Frankfort we hoped soon to be out of the wood. We, therefore, outspanned for breakfast, rather foolishly doing so just short of a donga which would have to be crossed and was commanded by a steep conical hill; but as it was the most convenient spot at which the post from the nearest drift could rejoin we let it go at that.

Soon, however, our look-outs signalled "enemy in sight" and from some high ground on our left Boers could be seen galloping round to our rear, while at the same time the conical hill commanding the donga in front was seen to be held by the enemy. There was only one thing to be done and that was to clear the Boers off the conical hill at once, to hold the passage over the donga while the transport was being inspanned, and to do this before our tail was twisted by the Boers from behind. Once across the donga we would be in more open country and might be able to push on rapidly. This we knew as we had been wise enough to take note of the various features while journeying up the valley a few days before, "in case."

All was now bustle though—as they say in the papers after a shipwreck—" there was no panic." The mules were quickly collected and inspanned and meanwhile the adjutant had galloped forward to the donga where a picquet of the Battalion had been posted and ordered the non-commissioned officer in command, Sergeant Gaffney, to take the conical hill at once, telling him at the same time that the remainder of the company would be sent in support at once. Bullets were now dropping pretty thickly on and round the donga but the picquet responded at once to Sergeant Gaffney's "Come on boys" and extending rapidly went for the hill followed soon after by a party under Captain Sangster. The Boers were evidently unprepared for this movement and after some further firing rapidly quitted the hill; and, when Captain Sangster was seen signalling from the top, the remainder of the force, increased now by the post which had joined up from the drift, hurried across; the transport—luckily the waggons were nearly empty now—being sent across at a gallop. In front was now a long gentle glacis-like slope of about a mile not commanded by any important feature within decisive range, and up this the Battalion —or what there was of it at the moment—moved as rapidly as it could, a small reargroup under Lieutenant Fox being left to watch the passage over the donga and the conical hill—now evacuated by our people—to his right front.

The Boers immediately re-occupied this hill, and were evidently reinforced by the party which we had seen galloping to our rear. It was impossible to tell—so cunningly did the Boers utilize cover even within 500 yards range—how many were now on the conical hill but from the firing it was clear that the enemy easily outnumbered our rearguard. Things now began to get rather lively. There was no cover on the glacis slope and the main body had disappeared over the crest leaving the rearguard in a rather unhealthy position and distinctly " in the air." The Boers took in the situation in a flash and redoubled their fire. For a moment the position of the rearguard looked as if it might become serious. Lieutenant Burnand got a bullet through the forearm, luckily not touching the bone; the transport officer, Lieutenant Richards, who was shepherding some recalcitrant mules had a bullet through his haversack; the adjutant, while looking through his glasses, had his jacket cut by a bullet, and seven or eight men were knocked over. It was just about this time that a mule carrying part of the machine gun thought that the time had come to go over to the enemy and started to gallop over " No Man's Land " being, however, very pluckily retrieved by Sergeant Kavanagh. Fortunately the Boers had too much respect for our fire to leave their cover and advance up the glacis, and Lieutenant Fox coolly and skilfully extricated the rearguard, most of the wounded being able to carry on till all were out of range and had closed up on the Battalion. It was now late in the afternoon so we headed for the spot where we had bivouacked when coming up the valley, and where we had thrown up a shallow circular trench. It was quickly brought home to us that a dead horse which we had left unburied had got rather offensive in the interval and life became unbearable until the quadruped had been put under ground. Boer picquets rather ostentatiously occupied some of the neighbouring heights but the night passed without any incident.

Next morning we sent a signal message to Frankfort via Tafel Kop asking for a few mounted men to be sent up the valley to scout for us, since if the Boers were to hold the drift over which we would have to cross the river, we might easily be delayed a day and we were now eating our last ration. A reply came back ordering us to remain where we were till morning and that a mounted force would leave Frankfort at dawn. This force consisting of an officer and 25 yeomen did not arrive, however, until the evening of the following day having failed to find us. They did not like the look of the valley and had returned to Frankfort, whence they were despatched again with peremptory orders not to return until they had found us. At dusk we saw them moving slowly in widely extended order a mile or two away and managed to attract their attention and they closed in upon our bivouac.

We had our last piece of bully and our last biscuit that night and determined to push off just before dawn and to move in a great square in single rank with the transport in the centre, half of the mounted men scouting in front and half being with the rear face. We still had almost half of the Battalion to pick up, but with mounted men to scout for ambushes we had a much easier task than two days before. The plan worked well, for although immediately it became light Boers began to harry the rearguard and continued the annoyance till the afternoon they kept at a respectful distance and we had merely one or two men wounded. The yeomen were simply invaluable, for, thanks to their scouting to front and flanks, the Battalion was able to keep moving briskly, while the dozen or so with the rear face would hold a position as a temporary rearguard when required, and then mount and gallop back to rejoin the Battalion. By the time we got near the drift some miles from Frankfort the whole Battalion had been collected and the mounted men were sent ahead to scout. The drift was found unoccupied and the yeomen then forded the river and held the further bank, the Battalion then crossing protected by a strong rearguard which was, however, not attacked. Late in the afternoon we reached Frankfort safely, pretty hungry after a long day without food Rations were immediately issued to the men and the officers were entertained to a champagne dinner by the officers of the Royal West Kents which regiment formed the garrison of a fort constructed just overlooking the ruined town.

This little scrap—which in casualties seems hardly worth mentioning to people whose memories are stored with recollections of the Great War—has been described somewhat at length as it is in a way unique, being probably the last occasion in the war that infantry was called upon to move without mounted troops. A series of "regrettable incidents" had long ago shewn that, against a highly mobile enemy, infantry stood a very good chance of being scuppered, and we felt we had got out of the Wilge valley very cheaply indeed. When the war was over and De Wet published his book *The Three Years' War* we discovered that while we were returning down the valley he and a number of his followers, who had burst out of the net, were moving parallel to us and within easy striking distance. Our presence and scattered condition were apparently known to him, but when peace came Boers told us that the sight of infantry without mounted troops in the valley so mystified the enemy that they thought there must be something behind it. Anyway De Wet decided to refrain from tickling us up which was pretty lucky for us as anyone with experience of South African warfare will admit.

After a few days' rest at Frankfort we moved out towards Tafel Kop to strengthen the blockhouse line for a reverse drive between the 5th and 7th March, and next day marched to Heilbron and did a same service on the branch railway line between Heilbron and Wolvehoek from the 9th to the 13th. One night was rather exciting as some Boers attacked the line and some managed to get through. There was rather a fuss about this next day the authorities alleging a want of vigilance on the part of the particular post concerned but the reflection was grossly unwarranted. Those whose experience of war is confined to France will probably visualize "wire" as a regular maze which had to be battered down by days of shell-fire, but it must be remembered that wire in South Africa meant merely a plain fence such as one may see round a field in England. The Boers would carefully reconnoitre a small sector between two reinforcing posts, well away from a blockhouse, during the early hours of darkness and later would shepherd a mob of cattle up to the line and at the last moment send the beasts full tilt against it. Away would go everything and in the confusion the small party of Boers would slip through, in spite of the hurried fire brought to bear upon them. This is just what happened in this case, one Boer being killed while probably some twenty or thirty got through. The irritating thing was that these reinforced blockhouse lines were always expected to stop anything, although when as frequently happened fairly large parties would break back through the driving lines at night nothing was said. However, the drives had been a great success, the one in which we were concerned on the Wilge River having netted near Harrismith a great number of prisoners and a large quantity of stores.

These drives having concluded we were ordered to entrain for Pretoria where we arrived on the 14th March, relieving the Cameron Highlanders in the Staats Artillerie Barracks, the Camerons leaving to take part in operations in the Transvaal. In the western portion of that State rather a regrettable incident had occurred, a Boer force under Delarey having fallen upon a British force under Lord Methuen and severely defeated it. Methuen's mounted troops were not of high quality and many of them took to flight; the regular infantry stood fast to the guns but were soon overwhelmed and as a result four guns and 600 prisoners fell into the hands of the Boers, among the prisoners being Lord Methuen, severely wounded. Some time earlier in the same country a British convoy escorted by 700 men and two guns had been ambushed and captured, the booty including half a million rounds of ammunition. These were the kind of things still happening in a war which had been " virtually over " for nearly eighteen months and for which a ribbon had long been issued. Fourteen thousand British troops were now required to sweep the Western Transvaal.

THE 2ND BATTALION

Pretoria seemed exceedingly dull after the movement and excitement of the veldt, and the Battalion was now very much split up. Headquarters were at the Artillery Barracks but a great portion of the Battalion went into garrison in the forts and blockhouses round Pretoria and along the railway running north to Pietersburg. On 15th April " C " Company arrived from St. Lucia, and now for the first time for over three and a half years the whole Battalion was together; though only on paper for as mentioned above it was really dispersed round Pretoria.

Peace was now in the air and the indomitable remnant of the Boers, convinced at last of the futility of a prolonged resistance, agreed to come under safe conduct to Pretoria there to discuss the question of surrender. There we saw De Wet for the first time in person, striding moodily along the verandah of the house where the delegates were quartered. Six weeks passed away in negotiations and then a conference was held at Vereeniging as a result of which articles of peace were signed at Pretoria on the 31st May and the South African War was a thing of the past.

Those members of the Regiment who served in both the South African War and in the Great European War have often been asked, by those whose experiences are confined to the latter struggle, how the two wars compared. This has always been a very difficult question to answer as not only were the conditions of the two wars entirely dissimilar, but each war had phases which differed widely between themselves. Looking at the first few weeks of both wars there is perhaps not such a noticeable difference, for the fighting at Mons, Le Cateau and the Marne differed in degree rather than in kind from the fighting on the Tugela and the Modder River. There was much more artillery action in the first named battles; but as regards rifle fire and the casualties inflicted and endured thereby a man fighting at Mons went through very much the same ordeal as his predecessor at Colenso. In the latter phases the two wars diverged sharply—one drifted into a deadlock and warfare by attrition, with a rigidly defined front, immobility, vast numbers and colossal supplies of ammunition; the other war was mobility above all else, and there was no " front." Nothing could be more unlike the far-flung operations of the British columns in the guerilla period of South Africa than the long, wearisome and bloody stalemate in France.

The comparison can, therefore, at best be but a negative one, that is to say the relative conditions of the two wars will be better grasped, not by collecting a few rare points of similarity, but by emphasizing the factors in which they differed *in toto*. Perhaps the most interesting point to mention is that in the guerilla stage in South Africa the very word " front " was unknown. In a sense the whole immense area of South Africa was all front. A soldier in the trenches in France might suffer infinite danger while in them, but remove him ten or fifteen miles back and he was as safe as if he were in London, for the air raids over the rest areas were probably no worse than the attacks on England. In South Africa this relative immunity was unknown. The Boers may have been but 30,000 in all, but they were everywhere in twos, or threes, or tens, or scores, or hundreds, or thousands. The region of safety was definitely limited to the immediate perimeter of a town actually garrisoned by the British or to a narrow strip either side of a blockhouse line. It would have been a perfectly truthful warning if a newcomer to South Africa in those days was thus addressed : " Here on this map is a patch of the continent fifty thousand square miles in extent. Every bit of it is in our possession, nominally. The war has been over, on paper, for nearly eighteen months. Nevertheless I must tell you this, if you wander half a mile away from a blockhouse line anywhere in that area you run distinct risk ; if you wander to twice that distance you will be in serious danger ; a two mile stroll is simply suicide." This, then, was the condition which above all things distinguishes South Africa from France, and it exercised a distinct influence on everybody. It made one impatient at the restraint, irritable over the apparent impotence imposed on us by the enemy, and exasperated at the Boer for what we were inclined to think was not "playing the game." It would be, perhaps, an exaggeration to say that this kind of thing got on our nerves but it certainly prevented one from getting real rest. Where a Boer or Boers might be encountered anywhere over an area half as big as Europe the great thing, after dark, was to shoot first and find out afterwards. It became, indeed, an unwritten law that outposts once posted could not be visited at night. The least sound of footsteps and the sentry fired, making "visiting rounds" too unhealthy a system to last. Not only was the Boer everywhere but he was extraordinarily "slim" or cunning, and for stealthy night work and stalking required some beating. In a word he was a hunter from childhood and working in a country and under conditions with which he was thoroughly at home.

In casualties the difference between France and South Africa in the guerilla period was enormous. It is true that columns were now and then surprised and "scuppered" with a very heavy percentage of casualties, indeed, but in actual fighting a loss of one quarter the effectives on the British side would have been considered serious. On the other hand disease took a toll far beyond that experienced in France and the losses by enteric probably outnumbered deaths from wounds in action. The water on the veldt was rare and usually contaminated by dead animals. Just before we left Barbados one of the officers of the Battalion received a letter from Major Foulerton of the 1st Battalion then in South Africa full of tips for us newcomers. One phrase lingers in the present writer's memory. "It's a grand country if only you keep off water." Long before the letter reached the West Indies poor Foulerton was in his grave. The water had added his name to the tens of thousands of "died of disease."

As regards rations conditions were on the whole far better in France. The war in Europe being, after the first few months, a stationary one the troops got "their victuals regular"; and even in 1914 there were bacon and cheese and jam (plum and apple), and even an occasional tin of marmalade which had escaped the non-combatant harpies on the lines of communication. But in South Africa it was a different story. The blockhouse garrisons did not do too badly, but for the columns on trek it was very largely an affair of mere biscuit and bully, and there was, even for the garrisons of towns and posts, nothing like the abundance of eatables which made service in France bearable. The South African Field Force canteens did, it is true, an enormous amount of service in supplying the troops with goodies to supplement the frightful monotony of the rations, but alas! how often was one fifty miles away from the nearest branch of that invaluable institution. In South Africa, too, it was often the case that a column ate up its available supplies before it could refill and there were probably as many flapping belts in South Africa in a week as there were in France in a whole year.

Talking of rations brings back to mind a feature of South African warfare which did not seem to exist in France—the vogue of sparklets. Soda water being impossible to obtain—and impossible to carry about even if it had existed in oceans, those who liked to dilute their rare whisky with something fizzy invariably had recourse to a Sparklet apparatus. The fashion grew until it spread from Table Bay nearly to the Zambesi and every bivouac could be traced by dozens of leaden bulbs in which the charge of gas had been contained. In shape these were not unlike bullets, and it was said that at first the Boers, searching abandoned camping grounds, were indignant at the employment of what seemed to be a new explosive bullet and that they actually made formal representations against this breach of the laws of war.

Another question often asked is—How did the Boer compare with the Hun? i.e. as an enemy. Here the answer is easy, the Boer was always a gentleman and fought clean, whereas the Hun was—well, a Hun. There never was the slightest trace of that contemptuous loathing with which we came to regard the Germans ; on the contrary there was very often a feeling of real admiration for the gallant way in which the Boers fought a losing game for so long ; although it is quite true that this very toughness of the enemy caused a feeling of exasperation amongst the British who wanted to finish off the war and get home again. Nor was there any of that antipathy which in France we felt for the Germans as a race ; on the contrary, deep down in the hearts of many on our side there was sometimes an uneasy feeling that after all it might not be a particularly just war. It was impossible altogether to forget that after all the Boers were fighting for their country, and that apparently we wanted to take their country from them. And it needed a very convenient strain of casuistry to disguise the fact that had it not been for the gold in the Transvaal we would never have been fighting there at all. Originally there had been a lot made of the way British subjects in the Transvaal had been treated in the Kruger regime. Some time before the war our hearts had burned within us over these wrongs and we had thrilled at that glorious venture made to avenge these sufferings — the Jameson raid. But alas ! a walk through Johannesburg—or Jo'burg as it was the fashion to call it then—was sufficient to dispel these generous enthusiasms of youth. Were those greasy cosmopolitans of Hebraic type the downtrodden British of our imagination ? Just Heaven, are women and children being imprisoned in concentration camps, and farms given to the flames day by day in the Free State and the Transvaal, in order that that mottle-faced alien may dabble in diamonds or gold ? Those of us who thought of these things felt that the answer might have to be in the affirmative, so we told ourselves that our job was just to do as we were bid and not ask, even of ourselves, rather troublesome questions.

A herd of Boer prisoners compared very favourably with a similar collection of Germans, and even in their tattered clothes—the Boers of course wore no uniform—the former were an immense improvement on the square-headed, truculent looking blonde beasts we got so familiar with in " cages " in France. Even in adversity the Boer preserved a dignity and bearing peculiarly his own. Once while we were at Heilbron at the finish of a drive a hundred or so prisoners were caged, and the inevitable crowd of bored-looking Tommies stood round the barbed wire looking over the captives within. The Boers were of all sorts and all ages; here was a white-bearded patriarch who as a middle-aged man may have fought at Majuba, there was a barefooted lad of some fifteen summers. Some wore rough homespun country suitings, others, and they were the majority, had clumsy corduroy breeches, some had coats, a few were in shirt sleeves, most wore the typical slouch hats of South Africa, but there was some incongruous headgear—a disreputable bowler, and in one case a boater straw which had seen better days and from which half the brim had disappeared. Many wore home-made makeshifts of ox hide as footwear which was a combination of grotesqueness and ingenuity. A more ragged, tatterdemalion lot of scarecrows it would be difficult to imagine and to a military eye there was something absolutely offensive in their disreputable and slovenly appearance. And yet those ragged, hungry and dirty travesties of soldiers bore themselves with a proud and simple dignity that was almost pathetic. As they conversed one with another in the cage an onlooker unconsciously got the impression that he was looking on a woodcut of an ancient family Old Testament. There one saw the bearing of members of a race long dominant amongst hordes of uncivilized natives, of men who had ridden from childhood and had lived all their days in the open air. Gaunt, haggard, ragged, and dirty though they were there was yet a something about those caged Boers which not even a century of boasted Prussian *Kultur* could impress upon the soldiers of the Fatherland.

To return, however, to the 2nd Battalion. Peace was

officially declared on the 1st June and as the coronation of King Edward VII had been arranged to take place upon the 26th of that month the Government immediately recognized that it would be an extremely fitting adjunct to the ceremony if the victorious army in South Africa could be represented. The time was very short, but it was just possible that a contingent could be selected from every unit in South Africa and sent home "non-stop" in time to take part in the great event. The cables were busy and all over the veldt in South Africa orders were sent for units to send post haste to the railway a contingent of one officer and ten men. From the 2nd Leinster Regiment the following accordingly left Pretoria for Cape Town on the 3rd June :—Captain and Adjutant F. E. Whitton; Sergeant F. Bailey; Lance-Corporal Luckett; Privates Mines, Ford, Lamport, Deacon, Cummins, McKenzie (3676), McKenzie (3677) and McCaul. By the 7th June the last contingent had arrived, and the *Bavarian* sailed from Cape Town on that date, the ship's engineers having pledged themselves to get us home in time or to burst all the boilers in the attempt. Fortunately the weather was ideal but heavy fog in the Bay of Biscay and onwards made it seem as if our chances of arriving in time were poor. The captain, however, took some risk and we pushed on up the Channel right through the pall and when the fog cleared away on the 24th June, lo! there right ahead were the Needles and Hurst Castle, a tribute to some super-excellent navigation.

There was a man semaphoring vigorously at Hurst Castle as we passed and soon the news flashed through the ship—the King was ill and the coronation was postponed.

We were all immensely relieved to hear when we tied up alongside in Southampton a few hours later that His Majesty was convalescent and we were informed unofficially that we would proceed to London next day there to go under canvas in the parks until the coronation should take place. Next day the whole contingent paraded in the docks, some 2,200 strong, for inspection by the Commander-in-Chief, Field-Marshal Lord Roberts, who was accompanied by Mr. Brodrick the Secretary of State for War. Lord Roberts at the conclusion of the inspection made a short speech and then proceeded to inform us of the arrangements for our immediate disposal. These came as a surprise. The Colonial troops were to proceed to London and to remain there for the coronation; the Regulars and Militia " would not be wanted and were to proceed at once to their depots."

Every Regular officer, non-commissioned officer and man on that parade felt as if he had been struck with a lash. No one of course moved, but the silence was impressive. Lord Roberts seemed a trifle ill at ease and even Mr. Brodrick — a singularly complacent-looking individual—appeared abashed. The parade was then dismissed and the units returned to the ship where there was some pretty straight talk by the Regulars on board. To have been selected as representatives of the old Regular army and then contemptuously sent to the right about while Colonial and Irregular units were to be welcomed in London as " the men who won the war " seemed incredible. But it was only too true. In order to save a few hundred pounds, and there being no General Election pending, the Government had decided that the Regulars and Militia " were too much bother." But imagine an old Regular officer like Lord Roberts allowing himself to be a party to such a transaction. That seemed the bitterest and the most incredible part of the whole concern. However, there it was; the Regulars went to their depots and when the coronation took place they played no part in it and thus lost the Coronation medal. No one attached much importance to a Piccadilly decoration, least of all in those days when medals did mean something, but the Coronation medal had a special significance to the South African contingent, testifying as it did that the wearer was one of a small band selected from the whole of his unit at the end of a victorious war. So ended the hopes of the contingent of the 2nd Battalion.

Captain Whitton returned to South Africa as soon as he could get a passage.

Pretoria after the war was quite a good station as South Africa went. There was a theatre in the town and quite a good restaurant. The garrison was big enough without being too big, and curiously enough the infantry formed just a Union Brigade there being an English, a Scottish, a Welsh and an Irish battalion, the Welsh Regiment being our especial friends. Polo began to be played and there was a sufficiency of tennis and cricket, the latter game receiving a great impetus by the visit of the Australian Eleven from its tour in England. Sport, however, in the sense of game shooting proved a great disappointment and those who had been looking forward to thinning out rhinoceroses or even springbok had to put their rifles and guns away, for a long close season was ordered to enable the fauna to get over the rough times of the war. Some of the animals had suffered severely, for of course in the drives animals were forced into the bottle necks along with Boers and afforded a useful change of diet to Briton and Boer alike.

As for training everything was in a state of transition the chief object now being to profit by " the lessons of the war." The war, however, was too recent to enable it to be viewed in the proper perspective and there was a tendency to consider that the wars of the future would be more or less on South African lines, a hopelessly erroneous conclusion. Everything now was to be given up to secure " initiative " on the part of the private soldier, and in the efforts to secure this desideratum there was a perfectly deplorable craze for doing away with steady drill, the very foundation of the Regular soldier's efficiency. A still more absurd idea was the conviction, which in the cases of some generals mounted to an obsession, that frontal attacks were henceforth absolutely impossible and there grew up an extraordinary system of tactics by which infantry were expected to carry a position by crawling on their stomachs obliquely to the enemy's line. The great thing about war apparently was that there should be no casualties or as few as possible. The old saw about omelettes and eggs was forgotten. The younger school in the army openly derided the perverted wisdom of their seniors but would never have carried the day had not the Russo-Japanese War come as a ray of illuminating light in this dark tactical era. The war in Manchuria afforded an object lesson to all the armies in Europe, and the British army ruefully remembered how British columns had been held up in South Africa after trifling loss on the pretext of " the destructive effect of modern fire." Both Russians and Japanese once more illustrated the cruel necessity for heavy sacrifice of life when a nation stakes its existence on the battlefield. Had it not been that the great conflict in the Far East came just in time to sweep away the South African heresies the Old Contemptibles in 1914 might have made a sorry show.

At the end of the year Captain Whitton resigned the adjutancy to proceed to the Staff College. He had passed the entrance examination during the long period of abeyance in Barbados, in 1901, and when at last news came for the Battalion to be prepared to embark for South Africa he had applied to have his entrance deferred for a year. This had been refused by the War Office and Captain Whitton thereupon resigned his claim. The War Office, however, now informed Captain Whitton that a vacancy had been reserved for him and he accordingly proceeded home to take it, being succeeded as adjutant by Captain J. C. Colquhoun.

While at Pretoria we took part in the very impressive peace celebration, some companies attending the service and others lining the streets. After this came the transition from war to peace conditions under difficult circumstances. We sent home a large draft of time-expired men, and received in exchange a number of men from the 1st Battalion which was returning home. These men had been detailed at the last moment and arrived in a very bad frame of mind. They completely swamped the young soldiers remaining with the 2nd Battalion, and for some time the maintenance of discipline was a hard task. This state of things culminated in an outbreak by a few men in a barrack-room in which one man was shot. One of the ringleaders was sentenced to death, but afterwards reprieved and others received severe sentences. Soon after this we left the Artillery Barracks and on the 8th April, 1903, headquarters marched out to a camp at Quagga, and three companies went on detachment to Pietersburg. Quagga Camp was in most insanitary surroundings, being bounded by a sewage farm, a leper hospital and a dump of condemned tinned meat. New cantonments were being built, but there were many delays in the work. The Pietersburg detachment was camped outside the town, and its time was devoted to the usual training. There also some cantonments had been put up, but just as they were ready for occupation the order came that they were to be sold for what they would fetch. This happened in many places all over the country. It seems that after the war a long occupation was contemplated, but that the country settled down so quickly that it was found unnecessary and very expensive to keep many troops there. General Clements had taken over command of the Pretoria district from General Barton.

On the 14th June the Pietersburg detachment rejoined headquarters at Quagga. Mounted infantry was looked on as very important during these years and we had a detachment training at Potchefstroom. We then moved to a camp near the new cantonments until they were ready, when we moved in. The other battalions in the place were Northamptonshires in the Artillery Barracks and Welsh Regiment encamped on the other side of the city. During all this time we had a monotonous life of garrison duty and training. Manœuvres were carried out at Klip River, and the Battalion held its own both at work and play. Our cricket team started again at Pretoria. Lieutenant Ussher was its mainstay, a very good all-round cricketer. At tug-of-war we had a team that beat all comers, trained by our quartermaster Smyth. In the spring of 1904 we lost Colonel St. Leger who went home on leave pending retirement. On the 7th May we left for Middelburg, Transvaal, with a detachment under Major Evans-Lombe at Barberton. We were in good cantonments at Middelburg with a battalion of the Middlesex Regiment alongside us, and later a detachment of Mounted Infantry. Brigadier-General Kenyon Slaney commanded the troops. We had a pleasant time there, devoted to routine work, with no outstanding events. Lieutenant-Colonel W. Doran, from the 18th Royal Irish, took over command in succession to Lieutenant-Colonel St. Leger. There is very little to write about these years in South Africa, which were occupied mainly in the transition from war to peace conditions and in training in the light of experience gained from the war.

A word must be said about mounted infantry particularly as this arm is now defunct. For some years after the South African War mounted infantry was retained and in South Africa every infantry battalion furnished one company as mounted infantry. Three of these companies, each from a different regiment, constituted a mounted infantry battalion which was commanded and staffed by selected officers, the commanding officer being generally a major.

" H " Company was the mounted infantry company of the 2nd Battalion and was posted to the 2nd Battalion Mounted Infantry commanded by Major Luard D.S.O. of the Durham Light Infantry. At this time Captain G. F. Boyd (now Major-General, and who had been posted to us from the East Yorkshire Regiment) commanded our mounted infantry company, which was organized in four sections, each of thirty men and horses under Lieutenants N. G. Burnand, M. Heenan, F. B. Lefroy and H. Goold-Adams as section commanders. Our men were chiefly drawn from the disbanded 3rd Battalion Mounted Infantry which had fought through the war with the King's County Militia, the men themselves having re-enlisted for regular service at the termination of hostilities. They were a hardy lot, good horsemen and very proud of their sections which were graded into chestnut, grey, bay, and mixed. The other two companies of the 2nd Battalion Mounted Infantry were found by the 3rd Middlesex Regiment and the Loyal North Lancs, with both of whom we were on the most friendly terms.

In 1904 the 2nd Battalion Mounted Infantry was transferred from Ladybrand to Harrismith, Orange River Colony. This was a small station consisting of one infantry battalion (The Buffs), one battalion Royal Garrison Regiment (shortly afterwards disbanded), a battery Royal Field Artillery and the 2nd Battalion Mounted Infantry.

The work in mounted infantry was naturally most interesting for those who liked horses, and the country round Harrismith was ideal for mounted work; in fact you could ride a hundred miles in any direction without meeting a fence of any description. Our ponies were mostly country bred or Argentine, and none of them over fifteen hands high. Each officer was provided with two chargers besides which he was able to play his groom's and servant's ponies at polo. In this way one got about six chukkers three days a week. There was little amusement for the men outside barracks, but of course tug-of-war was our forte. Although no man on mounted infantry was supposed to weigh over ten stone we yet managed with our "H" Company team to beat the regimental team of the Buffs in an all-over pull. Not bad for a company team, but of course some of our men did weigh over ten stone. Private Breen, for instance, our anchor man, weighed between thirteen and fourteen stone. How he ever was sent on mounted infantry was a mystery. We couldn't mount him, and he was on perpetual duty as stable orderly.

One of the most pleasing memories of the mounted infantry was a tactical ride which Captain Boyd organized. One company rode off into the veldt for a fortnight, and lived on the country. Every march we made had some tactical object which gave interest, and much amusement was always obtained in dealing with Boer farmers for supplies. A bottle of whisky went a long way with the farmers at that time, so we generally managed to get what we wanted. During this ride we visited the little town of Vrede (Orange River Colony) where we found many graves of the 1st Leinsters. As these were in a bad state of repair we purchased paint and in an amateur way every man lent a hand in renovating the crosses.

In 1905 the 2nd Leinsters moved to Mauritius so " H " Company had to rejoin, and became infantry again much to the disinclination of all ranks.

CHAPTER XXXIII

THE 2ND BATTALION.

MAURITIUS, 1905-1907.

EARLY in 1905 the 2nd Battalion moved from Middelburg, South Africa, to Mauritius. The mounted infantry company, "H" Company, under Captain G. F. Boyd, D.S.O., D.C.M., with Lieutenants Burnand, Heenan, Goold-Adams and Lefroy joined the rest of the Battalion at Durban. The Battalion was now all together, and this was one of the few advantages of our new station. Mauritius was originally a French colony and was acquired by us after the Napoleonic wars. There were still many of the old French laws in existence, one of which was that no employer was allowed to give a servant other than a good character ; if he did he was liable to civil action for libel. By this means it was very hard to select servants, grooms etc. The island is known as the Pearl of the Indian Ocean, and is looked on by the Indian Army as one of their health resorts. It certainly is a beautiful spot with some fine mountains and the usual tropical vegetation, and breeds about the largest and most venomous mosquito ever seen. They have even been known to move officers' furniture about at night so powerful are they when working in teams. The health-giving proclivities of Mauritius are slightly exaggerated as there is a peculiarly virulent type of fever on the island which during our stay was gradually working up into the higher altitudes, and, in fact, shortly after we left, had reached the European barracks and necessitated the withdrawal of half of the Loyal North Lancashire Regiment to South Africa to recuperate.

The white inhabitants are almost entirely French with French customs, dress and manner of living, also French is the universal language, whilst the native speaks a sort of patois. The British national anthem, known to the populace as "ze Godsave," is only played in public as a compliment to us. The chief industry is cane growing and sugar manufacture, while in slack seasons a game known as "hidden treasure" is started. It is the old trick. Someone hears of a pirate's hoard somewhere, promotes a company and issues shares, etc. Needless to say the treasure has not yet been discovered, but apparently pigeons can always be found to put their money into the gamble and have their feathers plucked. They were just starting a fresh one as we left. It keeps money in circulation, and is no more expensive than buying building plots round Johannesburg, of which no doubt some of the Regiment still have happy memories.

On arrival at Port Louis we were met by the adjutant of the outgoing regiment who duly handed over to his "opposite number" (Captain Colquhoun) the usual percentage of ready-dug graves in case of accidents. The European barracks were situated some 2,000 feet up, and were approached by a narrow-gauge railway, which was of French construction and a most self-important little concern. The carriages were built with seats on the roof like a tram, which will give one an idea of the speed attained by the railway. This was before the universal introduction of motor cars, and most of the business men went daily to town by the *Grande Vitesse,* as the train was called. One of our soldiers has been known to "shake off" the top of a carriage without hurting himself, run on, and catch the train at its next stop, the man being later brought before the commanding officer for assaulting a railway employé who tried to stop him running after the train. At one time there was a certain amount of discontent amongst the season ticket holders as to the speed attained by the *Vitesse,* so after much deliberation the company imported an English engine driver to see whether he could not "ginger up" the service. He did. He only drove the train once from the country into Port Louis and let her go all out down the hill the whole way. The scene on arrival at the terminus, they say, was most impressive. All the frock-coated business men embracing one another, offering up thanksgivings to their Maker, cursing the driver, and congratulating each other on their safe arrival, to the intense disgust of the Yorkshire driver whose return passage to England was promptly secured. That was the last effort at speeding up the *Grande Vitesse de Meurice*.

The Battalion was now complete and had a good opportunity for smartening up which was taken full advantage of by Colonel W. R. B. Doran, D.S.O., who was considered the best commanding officer the Battalion ever had. We also had a most splendid battalion sergeant-major (Brooks) an ex-guardsman who after his first few months became a general favourite with all ranks. He was a man of iron discipline and integrity. As an Englishman he always had some difficulty in pronouncing some of the men's names; his efforts frequently gave a comic touch to the rather electric atmosphere of the orderly room. Such names as O'Hara and O'Shaughnessy altogether beat Sergeant-Major Brooks; he could not pronounce them other than " HO'Ara " and " HO'Shockennesy." To the deep regret of all ranks poor Sergeant-Major Brooks died in Jullundur after three years' good work with the Battalion, his death being due to the fact that he would not go sick when suffering from pneumonia.

Under Colonel Doran every officer, non-commissioned officer and man was made to work hard and play hard. It was no Battalion of specialists. The veriest "dud" in each company had to do something and Thursday mornings were devoted entirely to company or sectional games and sport. There was no staying in bed in the morning, and no resting in the afternoons for officers, with Colonel Doran, and under his supervision we turned out quite a respectable cricket team, whilst our future boxing successes had their origin in Mauritius. This intensive activity kept the Battalion fit and we had little sickness in a climate which was conducive to all the ailments encountered in the East.

Polo and racing was encouraged among the officers though the class of pony was miserable, as owing to frequent epidemics of horse sickness we had to rely entirely on shiploads of third-rate ponies from Australia, which were only imported for work on the cane fields but which we used to buy unbroken in the open market and hope to train either as racing or polo ponies or both. There were two race courses on the island, one managed by the military and the other and larger course managed by the civilians. The meetings at the latter were most amusing; the great race of the year was for horses over a mile course and had to be run the best of three races on successive days. Imagine such a thing! These unfortunate brougham horses were probably driven to the course in the family barouche, had to run a race each day for three days in succession, and then pull the family home after the day's sport. The winner, the *beau cheval*, was always garlanded with a wreath of flowers round his neck. That's about all he got out of it.

On the military course our races were run more or less under English racing rules. Every officer owned and ran some sort of pony. Secret trials were carried out on the Limekilns (our training ground) and one never quite knew what surprises an owner had up his sleeve.

During our stay in Mauritius new Colours were presented to the 2nd Battalion and a very fine parade was carried out which deeply impressed the civilian populace who were invited to attend. All who served with the Battalion at this period will probably agree that we were fortunate in having a very fine set of officers, and guest nights were generally of a most hilarious nature, horse-play being encouraged by the commanding officer as a safety valve for an excess of spirits. After one experience of a guest night our guests never again came in their best uniform, nor did they leave their traps or cycles in the vicinity of the mess for obvious reasons. On one occasion a subaltern drove off in the Governor's car late in the evening, and as bad luck would have it the engine broke down in the middle of the polo ground some half-mile from the mess. The miscreant had to hurry back and find the chauffeur before the car could be brought round for His Excellency, who by this time was becoming impatient, whilst the commanding officer was suggesting all sorts of excuses but at the same time fearing the worst. He really *was* angry with that subaltern when eventually the latter returned.

There was a certain amount of shooting on the island, and big game was to be found in the shape of a large deer known as the *gros cerf*. These animals were almost as big as our red deer with quite a fine head, and to shoot them one had either to become a member of a *club de chasse* or wait to be invited. The stags were driven up to the guns who were in extended order waiting in butts or sangars, and a shoot of this description was an exciting experience as the French sportsmen thought nothing of shooting straight down the line ; and as they were armed with H.V. sporting rifles most of one's time was employed in taking cover. Beaters were shot each year, but no one seemed concerned about it. Probably there was an old Napoleonic law exonerating the *chasseur* from the charge of manslaughter or less when shooting the *gros cerf*. On one shoot as it was getting near lunch time and no stag had been shot our host sent down word to all the guns to " shoot onyzings " as he evidently did not want to return with an empty bag. In consequence a fusillade commenced, and several doe were slaughtered and incidentally a beater got a " blighty." As Commander Scroggs the Port Trust officer afterwards remarked when he found his trap laden with about 3 cwt. of fauna as a present, " I wouldn't mind the shooting so much if it wasn't for this bloody meat they always give me." Goodness knows what he did with it all.

One does not wish to appear ungrateful to our French friends by making fun of some of their little peculiarities, and without doubt they had their laughs at our attempts at speaking French and at some of our customs too. We received much hospitality on the island, and many a pleasant Sunday morning some of us have spent with a charming French family playing Bridge at their house, followed up by a heavy *déjeuner* and then tennis.

Another and less dangerous form of sport was the gentle art of catching cray-fish. These were a large and very succulent kind of prawn with claws like a lobster and were to be found in the streams. The method of catching them was this. You got a noose of fibre on the end of a bamboo, threw bait into the water and then waited for the cray-fish to swim through the noose towards the bait. The rest was simple. A rather Heath Robinson form of amusement, but one with its thrills. Two years on the island was as much as the ordinary man could stand; besides, there was no competition for a Battalion, and in 1907 we were delighted to hear that we were to move to India, our station being Calcutta.

CHAPTER XXXIV

THE 2ND BATTALION.

INDIA, 1907-1911.

TO reach Calcutta we sailed round Ceylon on an Indian Marine boat, only putting in at Madras *en route*. We had with us on board an Indian infantry regiment who carried their meat " on the hoof," as the butchers say, in the shape of some hundreds of goats which were herded in the fore end of the vessel. The older the goat and the more strong in flavour the meat is, the greater the delicacy. Well! if that's what they liked that regiment must have done themselves remarkably well. As the voyage progressed the goats diminished in numbers, till on arrival at Calcutta the last billy had disappeared and the atmosphere of the ship had become bearable.

Going to Calcutta from Mauritius was like going to London from Birr. We were stationed in Fort William and our men very rarely left the fort to go down town. Whether it was on account of the trouble of getting into red serge and belts or whether they were frightened that they would not find their way back one never could find out. At any rate their conduct was exemplary, and there never was a case of a man misconducting himself outside the fort. The duties of orderly officer, the reader will be interested to know, were much sought after at Fort William, the reason being that some old gentleman years previously had left a legacy of £1 a day to the orderly officer for having been rescued by that functionary from thieves. There was no trouble in getting a substitute to take one's duty.

We arrived at the beginning of the cold weather and left at the beginning of the hot, a period of about six months, and a very delightful time we had. Six months was about as much as most of our purses could stand, but it was worth it! There was a race meeting almost every Saturday after which, win or lose, you invariably dined at the Bengal Club either to spend your winnings or to drown your sorrow. On most Sundays there was an all-day cricket match at one or other of the private clubs, whilst the late Rajah of Cooch Behar frequently invited us to play on his private ground where we would probably find ourselves opposed to his team on which were two Sussex professionals.

Few of us could run to polo or paper chasing, but there was any amount of other sport and games including dancing, and a delightful institution known as the Saturday Club presumably because the dances were held on Fridays. There was excellent snipe shooting to be had outside Calcutta, and Major Craske and Lieutenant Harman made it their invariable practice to supply the mess with game. Harman always maintained that it was the cheapest shooting in the world as on one occasion he peppered four coolies for eight annas; and they were quite satisfied. The civilians were most hospitable and friendly, several of the older ones having known the 1st Battalion when it was in Calcutta in the eighties. The Viceroy at this time spent the cold weather in Calcutta as also did the Commander-in-Chief, Lord Kitchener; so with these two celebrities and the Governor of Bengal in residence there was plenty of entertaining.

We had one little excitement in the shape of a strike by the European railway employés on the East Indian Railway. All the white engine drivers and other grades ceased work at a most important junction called Asansol, some 300 miles north of Calcutta. Troops were called out to keep the peace and stop any excesses at Asansol and also to prevent drivers still unaffected from being persuaded to join the strike as their engines arrived at the junction. For this purpose Lieutenant Burnand and another subaltern with half a company received secret orders to proceed by train at night to Asansol, where they were to arrive unexpectedly and by their sudden appearance so to astonish the strikers that they would immediately return to work. The party proceeded to entrain at Calcutta in the evening with the following orders. Before arrival at Asansol the men were to fix bayonets and keep low so as not to shew themselves; immediately the train stopped the troops were to spring out onto the platform and further developments would depend on the action of the strikers. All this, provided the strikers were there to meet the party, and hadn't been warned of its arrival. If they were not there things would fall rather flat.

The journey was uneventful, and the next evening as the train steamed into Asansol everything was ready, bayonets fixed, etc. etc. The train stopped. Now for it. The troops were prepared to spring out of the carriages, but the unforeseen happened. The doors on the platform side of the train were all locked. This rather put things awry, and the troops began to laugh. Whilst, to make matters worse, one heard sounds of welcome as of the reunion of old comrades. What was to be done? The enemy had started to fraternize, and Lieutenant Burnand was still locked in his carriage. Whilst he was trying to attract the attention of a guard to let him out, one of the strike leaders, evidently an ex-non-commissioned officer, approached and most respectfully asked whether the men would have tea now, as it was all ready for them. The officer had to decline the hospitality as politely as possible, and said that they were there on duty. The employés evidently appreciated the awkward position, and apologized by informing Lieutenant Burnand that nearly all the strikers were old soldiers and that he hoped the detachment would be able to give the strikers a game of football next day.

The party stayed at Asansol for some days, living on the fat of the land at the railway restaurant which was managed by a German firm, who produced, under pressure, their best Burgundy, foie gras, caviare, etc. These luxuries were only produced on special occasions when Rajahs and railway managers, etc. were travelling, and the German manager did not like wasting his good stores on mere subalterns. We returned to Calcutta without having sustained any casualties, and found that the Mohmand Campaign (Willcocks's week-end campaign) had broken out. The Battalion was ordered up to Jullundur (Punjab) and the Gordons relieved us in Calcutta. Everyone was hoping that we were for service especially as General Sir James Willcocks had been in the Leinsters and Lord Kitchener had rather a liking for us. Unluckily we were under strength and could not be taken ; though some of our non-commissioned officers went in different capacities.

We remained over two years in Jullundur, having one company on detachment in Amritzar, whilst our hot-weather station was Dalhousie.

Jullundur was a good little station with very little society outside the garrison which consisted of one battery Royal Field Artillery, one Indian cavalry regiment, two Indian infantry regiments and ourselves. Life there was pleasant and uneventful; officers could afford to keep ponies and play fairly good polo ; and most officers preferred to remain in the plains during the hot weather rather than go to the hills with the Battalion headquarters. Dalhousie itself was an ideal spot, the climate was perfect and inclined to be rather cold at the beginning and end of the hot weather. No one stayed there in the winter as there were several feet of snow for some months' duration. In Dalhousie one had the advantage of meeting other European regiments, two of which besides ourselves sent headquarter wings to that station.

The work was hard generally speaking, as after manœuvres in the plains including "Kitchener Tests," musketry, etc. etc. one had to practise mountain warfare on arrival in Dalhousie and performed operations with the Gurkhas who were stationed nearby. Amritzar was our plague spot ; each company which went there was absolutely incapacitated by fever. Every precaution was taken against mosquitoes, but with a disgusting native town of half a million inhabitants within a stone's throw of barracks it was impossible to keep men fit. Major J. Craske, D.S.O., who commanded the detachment there for most of the time was not one to take things lying down; but even he could not improve matters much. To this day men who were in the Amritzar detachment still complain of recurrent fever.

Major C. S. B. Evans-Lombe assumed command of the 2nd Battalion in about 1910 and continued to encourage a high standard of efficiency in work and play throughout the Battalion. He was most enthusiastic about the boxing team, which was just beginning to make itself felt in the big meetings at Simla, Lucknow, etc. On 18th February, 1911, the Battalion was inspected at Jullundur by Lieutenant-General Sir James Willcocks, commanding the Northern Army. He expressed his great pleasure in meeting his old regiment again and reminded his hearers that it was at that very station thirty-two years earlier he had joined the 1st Battalion. Sir James Willocks's speech made a great impression on all ranks and he was given a tremendous send-off when he left the station that afternoon. Soon afterwards we were informed that the Battalion was to take part in the Delhi Durbar at which the King was to be present during the following cold weather. Much money was spent in fitting out the Battalion suitably, but news arrived that we were to proceed home early in the trooping season, and that the 1st Battalion was coming out to India. So the Durbar was " off." Everyone was disappointed, though we were glad to be going home as the Battalion had been abroad just seventeen years. We had still one or two members who had left England with the Battalion on its foreign tour. Two of these were Captain Grainger the quartermaster, and Battalion Quartermaster-Sergeant Boyer, both as fit as fiddles but getting a bit big in the girth. The 1st Battalion from Plymouth were to arrive in India as we left, so we sent them a draft of some 6 officers and 300 non-commissioned officers and men and in return received on our arrival in Cork a good draft of their young soldiers.

CHAPTER XXXV

THE 2ND BATTALION.

CORK, 1911–1914.

THE Battalion landed at Queenstown on the evening of the 14th November, 1911, and entrained for Cork, marching from the station to Victoria Barracks.

Thus finished a tour of foreign service which had lasted almost exactly seventeen years, and had embraced the four continents of the globe, the stations where the Battalion had been quartered being Malta, Bermuda, Halifax, Jamaica, Barbados (with detachments at Jamaica and St. Lucia), the South African War (Transvaal and Orange Free State), Pretoria, Middelburg, Mauritius, Calcutta and Jullundur. Such a tour had always been a rare one and, with the closing down of Halifax, and later South Africa, as stations for Imperial troops, will possibly never be repeated in the future. To commemorate it some old officers of the Battalion presented the officers' mess with a centre piece in the form of an Irish round tower flanked by allegorical groups representing Europe, Asia, Africa, and America.

After the sunshine and glitter of the gorgeous East, Cork seemed a drab, dismal and depressing station. One diary remarks that the writer of it can never forget " the dark, damp, dismal mornings with the bugle of a light infantry battalion playing *reveillé* round the barrack square. No wonder the people in Ireland drink." The barracks matched the climate and had not even the virtue of accommodation, two companies with musketry recruits having soon to be sent to Birr owing to overcrowding at Cork.

MESS PLATE OF THE 2ND BATTALION

On the disbandment of the Regiment in 1922 this Plate was deposited with the Mayor of Colchester with the intention of presenting it to the National Museum, Dublin, when conditions should permit.

From a soldiering point of view the three years' stay of the Battalion was unmarked by any outstanding incident other than the great change brought about by the four company organization which was introduced on 1st October, 1913. By this innovation the whole infantry system of the army was profoundly affected, and the company was put on a par, theoretically, with the cavalry squadron and the battery of artillery. From a tactical point of view there is not a shadow of doubt that the change was all to the good, although against this was the fact that the initiative which was fostered in a young company commander in the eight-company days was not so likely to flourish in his new position of second captain in a company of double the size. There was an enormous advantage, too, in the separation of fighting from administrative duties, the second captain of a company being charged with the latter; and the old-time colour-sergeant, who was always submerged in company accounts, etc., now handing over those duties to the company quartermaster-sergeant, a new grade. A great blunder was made by the higher authorities, who, probably from some fear of a trifling additional expense, refused to make company commanders *ipso facto* field officers, although they were now mounted officers by the new scheme. The absurdity and injustice of the ruling are apparent when it is remembered that whereas the war establishment of the squadron and field battery were respectively 158 and 198 of all ranks, that of the infantry company was now 227. Yet the commanders of the two former were majors, while in the infantry the company commander might be, but was not necessarily, of field rank. When the 2nd Battalion took the field in 1914 three of its company commanders were merely captains although each of these had twenty years' service.

The officers hunted with the United, although sport and also the Point-to-Points were greatly spoilt by the prevalence of foot and mouth disease. But it was in boxing that the Battalion really distinguished itself while at Cork. Its career was one of splendid triumphs, and the enthusiasm and hard work of Colonel Doran and Captain Burnand in South Africa, Mauritius and India now bore splendid fruit. In April, 1912, the Battalion won the Irish Inter-Regimental Challenge Cup at Dublin with its team of nine; and Private Delaney won the heavy-weight and Private Halpin the light-weight championships of Ireland. These two privates later in the year pulled off the light heavy-weight and light-weight championships of the army respectively at Aldershot and at the King's Own Yorkshire Light Infantry tournament open to the Cork garrison. Private W. Delaney won the novices middle-weights, and the feather-weights fell to Private T. Byrne. In 1913 and 1914 the Battalion again won the Inter-Regimental competition at Dublin, and the cup became the property of the winners; and in these years championships were won by the Battalion in heavy, welter, light and feather-weights.

Delaney and Halpin in Cork were the " sure thing"; there were picture post cards of them for sale in the town. Delaney fought a twenty-round draw with Packy Mahoney (who was an aspirant for the English heavyweight championship) in Cork, giving Mahoney a stone in weight, and fighting the whole time with a bone in his jaw broken from a previous contest in Aldershot. Delaney would always draw a house, for everyone knew he would fight to the last ounce; he was never knocked out. Plymouth used to wire to Cork offering him £30 win, lose or draw, and he generally won.

There are three figures round whom boxing in the Battalion centres, Colonel Walter Doran, Captain Burnand and Private " Jack " Delaney. It was the first named who really started it and it was Delaney who brought the glory to the Battalion; yet there was no one who by example, inspiration, pluck, iron nerve, and imperturbable coolness—all pearls of boxing strung on the silken string of a sense of humour—did more for boxing in the Regiment than Norman George Burnand.

Boxing, however, by no means exhausted all the sporting activity of the Battalion while it was at Cork. In bayonet fighting Sergeant Burke won the open pool at the Dublin tournament, and at the Curragh in 1913 the open and old soldiers' events were won by the Battalion. There is an entry in the Battalion records of a brigade gymkhana that year in which " the Battalion won all the competitions," i.e. cross country race, bayonet fighting and fire direction and control. In hockey the Battalion won the South Munster Hockey League championship and the Irish Army Cup ; and reached the semi-final for the Army Cup, which it lost only after extra time.

On the 6th June, 1914, the Battalion marched 27 miles to Kilworth Camp to undergo battalion training, and a few weeks later Sergeant-Major H. O. Squire succeeded Captain J. Grainger as quartermaster. Then occurs the curt entry " 4/8/1914. Orders received for the Battalion to mobilize for war." That earth-shaking cataclysm will form the subject of another volume. Meanwhile it is necessary to trace the story of the Militia, later the Special and Extra Reserve Battalions of the Regiment.

CHAPTER XXXVI

THE 3RD, 4TH AND 5TH BATTALIONS.

IT is quite outside the scope of these volumes to do more than give the very briefest outline of the old Militia; and beyond saying that this Constitutional Military Force, raised, by general compulsion or otherwise, for home defence dates from very ancient times it is merely necessary to add that when Charles II was King the National Militia was re-established and the chief command was vested in the sovereign. It was in this reign in 1683 that Sir Lawrence Parsons, the first Baronet, was appointed to command " all the Militia fforces that are or shall be raised " in the King's County and this writ may be taken as containing the first reference to what was later to be the 3rd Battalion of the Leinster Regiment. As a matter of fact, there is no record to show that any militia was actually raised at this period in the King's County. The whole question was allowed to drop, and it was not until the reign of George II that it was revived. In Ireland, during this reign, a number of independent troops of mounted militia (probably akin to the more modern yeomanry) were brought into existence, and Sir Lawrence Parsons, grandson of the first baronet, was in command of the troop in King's County. Later, when George III was on the throne the volunteer movement spread through Ireland, which had been drained of troops by the American War, and there are references to ephemeral corps such as the Parsontown Loyal Independents, the Tullamore True Blues, the Mountain Rangers, and so on. The military value of these flamboyantly named corps was probably not very high, and it was

1793-1855]   THE 3RD BATTALION   457

probably due to this fact that in 1793 the Irish militia infantry was revived when the greater part of what were later to be known as Special Reserve Battalions came into being.

The order of preference of the various militia battalions was decided by lot, and the number drawn for King's County was 19, and thus in old Irish Militia lists is found the 19th King's County Regiment, known later as the 98th King's County Royal Rifles. The new regiment had Sir Lawrence Parsons for its first colonel. This Sir Lawrence became the second Earl of Rosse, and for over 200 years the family of Lord Rosse was intimately associated with the control and command of the King's County Militia. Many other county families were also intimately connected with the Regiment, amongst them being the Westenras, the L'Estranges of Moystown House, the Rollestons of ffranckfort Castle, Bernards of Castle Bernard, Warburtons of Garryhinch, Bennetts, Roches, Hacketts, Frenches, and others.

Within five years of its formation the King's County Militia was called upon to take the field, the occasion being the bloody and misguided rebellion of '98. The Regiment served under Colonel L'Estrange at Vinegar Hill, Enniscorthy, and a detachment distinguished itself in the defence of Newtownbarry, where L'Estrange had under his command 230 of the King's County Militia, a troop of dragoons, and about 100 yeomanry. During the Peninsular War the Regiment was embodied ; and having volunteered, its services were accepted in 1815. Some of the Regiment had actually embarked on board ship when peace was declared.

For the next 40 years the life of the King's County Militia seems to have had no outstanding incident to distinguish it. It was the period of the long peace after Waterloo when the nations of Europe were concerned chiefly in repairing the immense damage caused by the Napoleonic Wars. Then the vision of a universal golden age was shattered by the outbreak of the Crimean War. In common with other militia battalions the King's

County Militia was embodied in 1855 and so continued till 1856. The Regiment again volunteered for the front, but peace was concluded before its services could be utilized. Nearly half a century was to elapse before a third opportunity was vouchsafed the Regiment, and this time with more fortunate results. Two events during the period are of importance and should be here related. In 1859 the militias of the United Kingdom became formed into one whole, and in 1881 when the Territorial Regiments of the Line were formed the 98th King's County Rifles became the 3rd Battalion of the Prince of Wales's Leinster Regiment, with headquarters at Birr.

In October, 1899, the South African War broke out, and early in the following year the 3rd Battalion Leinster Regiment was moved to Woolwich for garrison duty. The need for more troops at the front was pressing, and it was imperative to set free such Regular and Colonial units, as were tied to lines of communication, by second-line troops from home. Accordingly, on 8th February, 1900, Colonel Holroyd Smith, commanding, received a telegram asking if the Battalion would volunteer for active service. It was immediately paraded, and, in response to the question put, the whole Battalion with but two dissentients volunteered with acclamation. On the 7th March the 3rd Leinsters formed in six companies, embarked on the *Kildonan Castle*, arriving at Cape Town on the 26th, whence the ship proceeded four days later to East London. The Battalion disembarked, proceeding to Queenstown, about a hundred miles to the northward and an important depot on the eastern railway system.

Here the 3rd Battalion remained five months. Although there was at this time no real " front " in South Africa, and enemy bands might be met everywhere, still Queenstown was a long way from any fighting area and no enemy were seen during the Battalion's stay. On 8th August a move was made to Stormberg, still in Cape Colony, the left half battalion under Major Barry being detached to Aliwal North, some sixty miles away. An attack was expected at Stormberg on 3rd October, and all arrangements were promptly made, including the "recall of some officers who were at a charity ball at Molteno, eight miles away"; but greatly to the disappointment of the Battalion nothing happened. The left half battalion, however, on 27th December, had an engagement with some Boers at long range. At Stormberg the right half battalion for some time found the crew of a small armoured train, *The Leinster Lily*, whose career was for a time checked by collision with a mail train, fortunately without any loss of life.

From Stormberg the Battalion moved north to Kimberley, which by this time had been relieved. Here life was at the same time more martial and more pleasant. On the martial side there were treks with convoys and small mobile columns, and a mounted infantry company was formed. On the side of pleasure there were an excellent club, polo, race meetings and band performances. It was during the stay of the Battalion that Colonel Holroyd Smith was invalided home, and from Kimberley the Battalion had its first experience of blockhouse duty. A change took place to the Modder River in December, 1901. Hard by the railway station was a little cemetery holding the bodies of those who fell at the Battle of the Modder River in 1899. Amongst them lay an officer of the Leinster Regiment who at that time was fast achieving fame, Colonel H. P. Northcott, chief staff officer to Lord Methuen. He had been amongst the first to fall, and had thus ended a brilliant career.

The war in South Africa, as has been said in another chapter, had a strain and anxiety peculiar to itself; nevertheless, with the recent experiences of a much greater war fresh in the mind of the reader, it is curious to find in a history of the 3rd Battalion in South Africa " by the end of 1901 . . . the Battalion was beginning to feel the effects of its strenuous and harassing work." The quotation of this sentence is not to be construed as in the smallest way reflecting on the 3rd Battalion, whose work on the lines of communication was consistently well done; but it is an interesting index of the way in which war was regarded at the beginning of the twentieth century, and the words show clearly how little anyone realized the sacrifices which would have to be made—and were gallantly made—less than fifteen years later. Those who served with either the 1st, 2nd or 3rd Battalions of the Regiment in South Africa, and later served in France, will, when comparing the two campaigns, regard the former as almost a rest cure when put *vis-à-vis* with the Western Front. In fact, it is hardly too much to say that South Africa was as bad a training for continental war to the British Army as North African warfare was to the French Army in the years before Sedan. Fortunately for the Old Contemptibles the Russo-Japanese War had obliterated the false lessons of South Africa some years before the British Army was called upon to act in a really great war. The adverb is necessary, for the struggle in the Free State and Transvaal did for a time arrogate to itself the title " The Great Boer War."

This is, however, leaving the 3rd Battalion ready to embark at Capetown, where they went on board the *Canada*, reaching Queenstown on 25th May, 1902, entraining next day for Birr. Five days later peace was declared. Between that date and 1914 there appears to have been no outstanding incident connected with the Battalion.

The 4th Battalion was originally the Queen's County Militia, and like the other Irish militia regiments it was raised in 1793, the date of appointment of the colonel, John, Earl of Portarlington, being the 23rd April of that year. In the ballot for regimental precedence held a few months later the Queen's County Militia drew the number 25, a figure it held till 1833, when it appears with the numeral 104. The establishment of the Regiment was six companies, and this continued in vogue for well over a century. The uniform was scarlet with blue facings. During the Irish rebellion the Regiment was certainly employed in the west of Ireland, and it seems that at least a portion of it took part in the Battle of New Ross. In a list of officers dated 1st July, 1799, appears the name of

Map Illustrating 1st and 2nd and 3rd

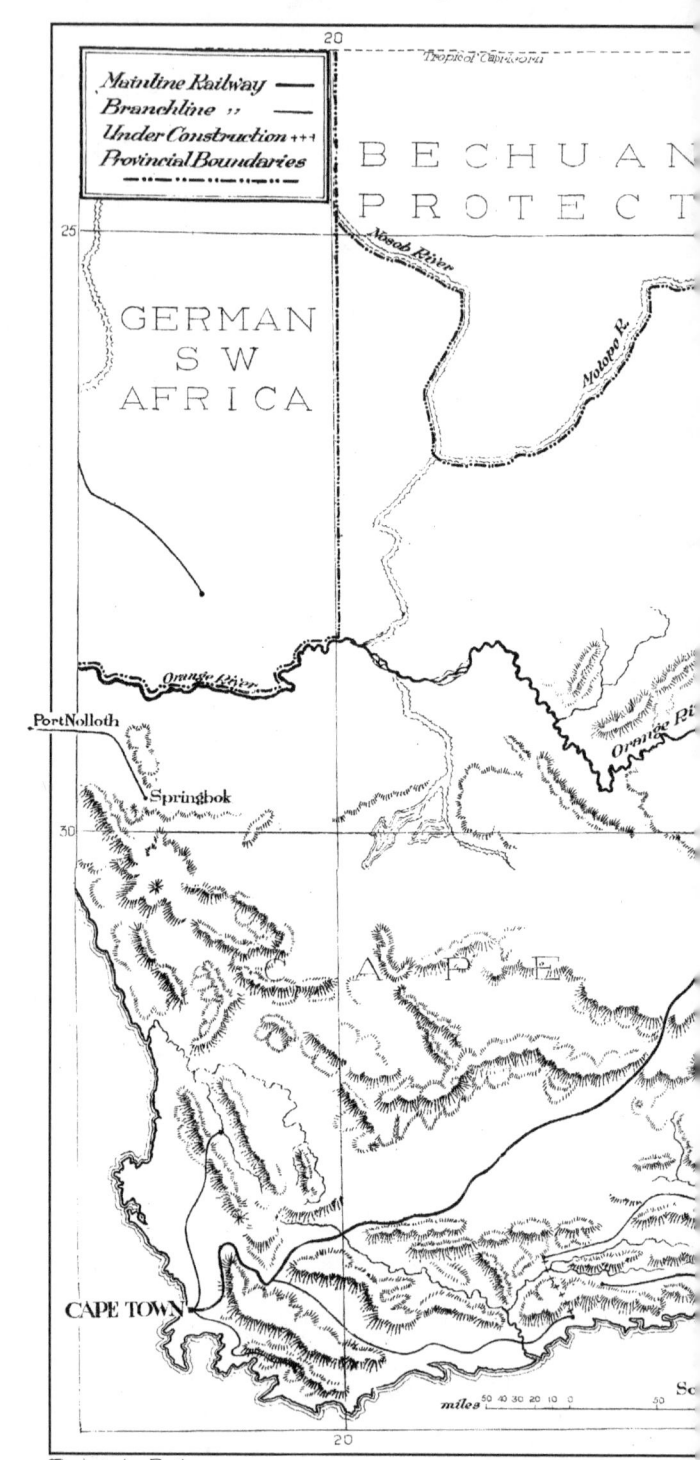

The Leinster Regt.

Battalions in South African War of 1899-1902.

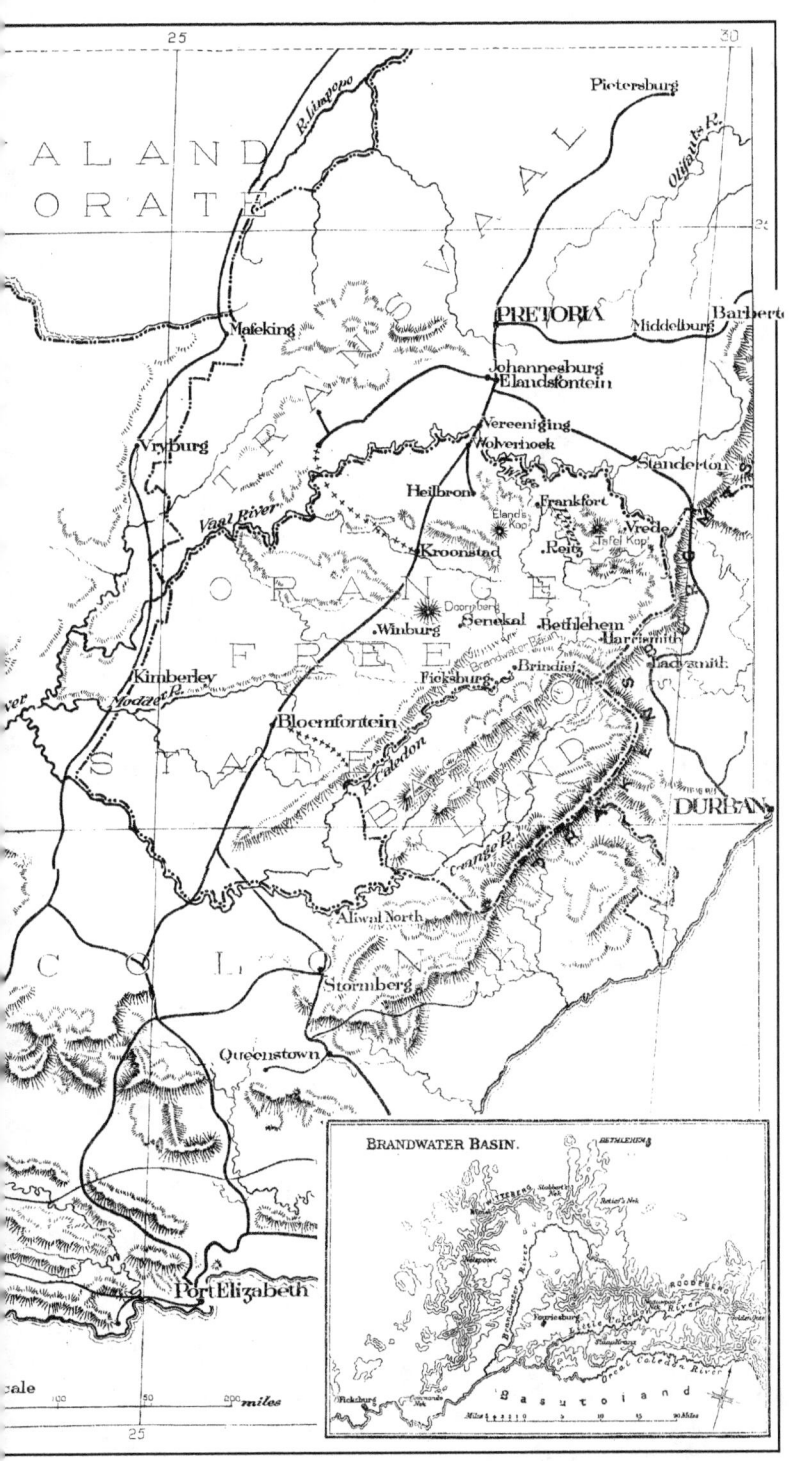

Lieutenant-Colonel Stewart Weldon, whose portrait in the uniform of the Regiment is at Kilmorony.

During the Napoleonic wars the Queen's County Militia was several times embodied and was quartered at various dates at Maryborough, Mullingar, Naas, etc., frequently with outlying detachments. During this period it seems that a property qualification was required of all officers above the rank of lieutenant, and the yearly value appears to have been £200 for a captain and £300 for a major. By a curious regulation it would seem that any officer who was absent, no matter from what cause, automatically came to be in arrest and his pay was mulcted. A feature of those days appears to have been the reluctance of authority to pay allowances due and the downright dishonesty of paymasters in embezzling such emoluments as came their way. There are extant several memorials on the subject either from officers or other ranks, and in one, *circa* 1815, twenty-six officers signed a document appealing for the payment of sums due to them amounting in all to nearly £1,100.

A few items selected from the records of the Regiment of those years are not without interest. An order sent from Naas on 8th October, 1815, for orderly room stationery, to be sent to Naas by the next coach, was for " Ten Quire of Best Fools' Cap paper, two quire of a coarse sort for covers, 2 Inspection Returns, four quire of letterpaper, 50 weekly states, one box wafers and 2 sheets of wax." There is an entry of how the commanding officer " placed the Paymaster under arrest and reported his defalcation." The same month, a letter, almost incoherent with despair, is sent to higher authority concerning " the distressing situation of the married officers who are in want of any place to cook in, there being but two kitchens, the Mess one and one for the Field officers." It was hoped " that by your representing it to my Lord Lieutenant that something might be done for the comfort of those officers who have families." The pay of an ensign of this time was £8 a month, a sum paltry enough, but slightly in excess of the starvation wage given a second lieutenant eighty years later. The pay could not have gone far towards the officer's wine bill—and wine seems to have flowed pretty freely. Spirits, of course, were not a gentleman's beverage, but everyone appears to have done himself well in wine which came down to Naas in canal barges. One of the wines was "Teneriff" (possibly an innovation on "Canary"); it cost 57s. per dozen, and apparently, for a dozen, thirteen bottles were given.

There seem to have been fines for most things. If you were absent from the mess you were fined. A captain who was away from 25th August, 1815, to 10th January, 1816, was mulcted for "one day per week, making twenty weeks," or £10 10s. 0d. You were fined if you were promoted and a newly-fledged captain had to disgorge £22 15s. 0d. It was also resolved "That the officers on entering the Regiment shall pay a fine to the Band Fund, on entering the Regiment," the rates varying from £5 13s. 9d. for an ensign and a quartermaster to £22 15s. 0d. for a surgeon, paymaster, captain or major, up to £113 5s. 0d. for a full colonel. It may be mentioned that the Queen's County Militia attached great importance to the band and when in 1917 the question of bands for Special Reserve Battalions was raised the 4th Leinster Regiment was able to prove that it had possessed a band for over a hundred years, extorting from the authorities the verdict "the 4th Leinster Regiment is entitled to a band."

The period of enlistment in those early days was for five years. In 1819 unserviceable greatcoats to the number of 274 were disposed of at prices ranging from 10d. to 1s. 6d. to "those recommended by the minister and churchwardens of contiguous parishes as proper objects" to receive them. Two years later there was a slight scandal when non-commissioned officers and drummers of the permanent staff " opened houses for the sale of ale and spirituous liquors, which is contrary to law." It is interesting to note that in 1822 the War Office was still corresponding about men who had volunteered for the line as far back as 1798, and there is an indignant official refusal to grant a pension to "the said Hogan" who served from 1793 to 1814 "which is only twenty-one years and besides he was eleven months out of the Regiment during that period." Dear old F Branch of the dear old War House. In 1832 a roll of subalterns shows the average age to have been about 45; the list is topped by a patriarch of 52 but this is offset by a mere child of 36; possibly, however, these elderly gentlemen were a kind of reserve of officers. In 1833 the number of the Regiment became 104 and about this time it was first called the Queen's County Rifles, to which the affix "Royal" was added later.

There seems to have been very little training in the long post-Waterloo peace and the next we hear of the Regiment is during the Crimea. It was then embodied and found to be "completely inefficient, but one sergeant being fit for any duty." It soon, however, came to be a useful unit again and from it many men volunteered for the line. After the fall of Sebastopol the militia regiments were disbanded and the Queen's County did no training till 1861; while in the period 1866-1870 the annual training was suspended owing to Fenian trouble. In 1873 there broke out a feud with the North Corks caused by a Queen's County rifleman asking loudly in the canteen "Who killed Father Murphy? The North Cork Militia by jabers." Father Murphy was a priest prominent in the Irish rebellion of 1798 but the meaning of the reference to the North Corks is uncertain. It may be mentioned that in 1900 it was considered inadvisable to quarter the two battalions together on Salisbury Plain owing to the feeling caused by those ten words. They had been uttered twenty-seven years before, and the incident they referred to was over a century old. But the military mind is as tenacious as glue.

In 1878 the Queen's County Rifles trained on the Great Heath, Maryborough, which became their habitat practically up to 1914. In 1884 the Battalion (for in 1881 it had become the 4th Battalion Leinster Regiment) was presented with colours. During the South African War the Battalion was embodied and proceeded first to Salisbury Plain and thence to Dover. On 1st February, 1901, it took part in lining the streets on the occasion of the funeral of Queen Victoria. Irish pipes, the gift of Lord Castletown were introduced in 1903 (they had been adopted by the 2nd Battalion at least ten years earlier); and in that year the Battalion took part in the military ceremonies which marked the visit of King Edward VII to Ireland. There is about this time a reference to Colonel Glancy, who commanded the Regimental District. " He usually referred to the Great Heath as ' the Savannah,' or ' the Maidan.' " Old 2nd Battalion officers of the late '90's will be tickled by this Wackfordism. After 1908 the Battalion ceased to be militia and became the 4th Special Reserve Battalion of the Leinster Regiment continuing to earn very high praise from the officers who inspected it. In 1911 a detachment was present at the ceremony of the coronation of King George V and Queen Mary; in the same year the system of attaching line officers to the Battalion, which had been brought in with the Special Reserve organization, was discontinued.

As for the 5th Battalion, it was also raised in 1793. It drew the number 17 in the ballot; and there is no reason to be found in the archives consulted why it subsequently became junior in precedence to the 3rd and 4th Battalions which had drawn the numbers 19 and 25, but possibly a later renumbering is the explanation. It was raised as the Royal Meath Militia, the denomination " Royal " being due to the fact that Meath had at one time been the residence of an Irish king. The first commanding officer was Viscount Headfort; afterwards Earl of Bective, and subsequently Marquis of Headfort. The Regiment marched from its county in August, 1793, and occupied Cashel. Later it moved to Cork, its establishment being eight companies of 70 rank and file.

In 1796 when a French fleet appeared off Bantry the Royal Meath Militia was one of the first regiments to

COLONEL CHARLES PEPPER, M.B.E.
Commanding the Royal Meaths from 1896–1901

oppose the landing. On the retirement of the enemy the Regiment was quartered at Youghal and Waterford, the companies being now augmented to 100 rank and file. In the rebellion of 1798 the Royal Meaths also played a part. They were sent to the relief of Wexford and suffered the first considerable loss sustained by the King's troops, one company being surprised and cut up by the rebels. It was also engaged at the Battle of Vinegar Hill and the following year it moved to Connaught and occupied Castlebar. The Royal Meaths marched back to their own county in 1802 and were disbanded at Kells on the 16th March.

In the following year the Regiment was again called out, moving in 1805 into Ulster, in 1809 to Tullamore and to Cork in 1810. In the following year it volunteered its services for England and embarked on 26th January, 1812, disembarking at Harwich, whence it proceeded to Ipswich, subsequently moving to Chelmsford and Bristol. It was disembodied at Kells, County Meath, on 1st August, 1814.

During these years the social life of the officers was governed by "The Rules and Regulations of the Mess by Thomas Pepper, Lieutenant-Colonel" (who was connected with the Regiment for the phenomenal period of fifty years). Every member had to pay half a guinea a week for his mess, " for which he is to be found in good small beer." The " strictest decorum " was to be preserved in the mess and any defaulter in this respect was liable to a penalty of three bottles of wine. Even the President or the " Vice for the President " had to mind their p's and q's for if they failed to sign the wine book daily they likewise were liable for three bottles. There were, of course, fines—monetary ones—for every step in promotion. One pint of wine was to be brought into the room for every member at dinner. " As soon as the quantum is finished the Vice, who opens the wine, is to inform the President, who is to inform the mess." All bets in the mess room had to be in wine, and the wine had " to be drunk at the mess." Mess bills were settled weekly, and no dogs were allowed into the mess, an exception, however, being made for " Chany."

For nearly thirty years after Waterloo there is little extant about the Regiment but it seems to have been quartered in England in 1841 and 1842. It was embodied during the Crimean War and new colours were presented at Trim on 10th May, 1856. Thereafter, the record of the Regiment is one of consistently good service and it appears to have been pre-eminently a " county " regiment. The leading landowners of Meath were always identified with it and the colonels of the Royal Meaths, from its foundation, were Viscount Headfort, Earl of Bective, Marquis of Headfort, Marquis of Conyngham, Marquis of Headfort, Hon. Hercules Rowley and Colonel Charles Pepper, who had commanded the Regiment from 1896 to 1901. A detachment of the Royal Meaths proceeded to London in 1897 on the occasion of the Diamond Jubilee and in the following year the Battalion—for it was now the 5th Battalion of the Leinster Regiment— crossed to England to take part in the manoeuvres in the south. Here it did extremely good work which was described in flattering terms in the English Press ; the strength of the Battalion on these manoeuvres was 534 of all ranks. During the South African War the Royal Meaths were embodied and proceeded to Aldershot. On the retirement of Colonel Charles Pepper in 1901 the command passed to Lieutenant-Colonel Nugent Everard who was in turn succeeded by Richard Taylor Woods, Edward F. Farrell, and John McDonnell. The headquarters of the Battalion had, some years before the Great War, been shifted from Navan to Drogheda.

Such is the tale of the Battalions of the Leinster Regiment up to the *annus mirabilis* of 1914. How these five Battalions, augmented by two more raised on the outbreak of the Great War, played their part now remains to be told

INDEX

A.

ABDHALI Arabs, 259
Abdul Nejid, Sultan, 197
Abercrombie, Sir R., 175
Abercromby, A., 12, 13
Aberdeen, 11, 42, 173, 174
Aberdeen, Earl of, 125, 174
Aberdeenshire, 175
Abyssinia, 266, 269, 271
Abyssinian War, 267
Addlestay, or Adelstein, S., 295
Addington, C. J., 90, 94, 96
Addiscombe, 183
Aden, 255, 256, 257 sqq., 266, 269
 ,, Crater, 257, 258, 259, 265
 ,, Isthmus, 257, 259
 ,, Steamer Point, 257
Affleck, W., 284
Afghan Wars, 99. 100, 101, 189
Afghanistan, 99, 104
Agamemnon, s.s., 254
Agar's Island, Bermuda, 366, 368
Agra, 112, 113, 114, 116, 117, 168, 271
Alabama, the, 71
Alameda, the, Gibraltar, 72
Albemarle, Earl of, 4
Albert, Prince Consort, 64, 247, 334
Albert Victor, sailing Transport, 265, 266
Alberta, 85
Albuhera Barracks, Aldershot, 345
Alderney, 352
Aldershot, 57, 62, 64, 89, 96, 97, 114, 133, 153, 154, 155, 247, 294, 301, 303 sqq., 317, 318, 333 sqq., 353, 370, 377, 391, 392, 454, 466
Alderson, E., 153, 154
Alexandria, 258
Algeciras, 73
Alighur, 283

Aliph Cheem, 156
Aliwal North, 458
Allahabad, 97, 168, 197
Allan, —, 54, 55
Allardyce, —, of Dunottar, 175
Alma, Battle of the, 77
Almora, 159, 162
Amaxosa Kaffirs, 249
Ambala, *see* Umballa
America (*see also* United States of), 58
American War of Independence, 456
Amery, L. S., 156
Amritzar, 450, 451
Anantpoor, Fort, 9
Arabi Pasha, 314
Arabia, 395
Archibald, —, 224
Arcot, 181, 188, 189
Argyllshire, 2
Armstrong, J., 79
Armstrong, W., 220, 225, 226, 233, 258, 264
Army Enlistment Act, 1870, 278-9
Army Purchase, Warrant Abolishing, 281
Arundel, 152
Asansol, 448-9
Ascot, 304
Ashford —, 77, 79
Ashton, —, 89
Assaye, 188
Assistance, H.M.S., 294, 330
Atahualpa, 176
Atherley, M. K., 254
Athlone, 323
Atholl, Duke of, 171
Atkin, J. R., 312
Atlantic Ocean, 85, 361
Atrato, R.M.S., 397
Auckland, H.M.I.N.S., 266
Australia, 111
Austria, 86, 213, 258, 277
Austrian Succession, War of, 180

468 INDEX

Avoca, H.M.T., 371, 372-3, 387, 388, 389
Aylesbury, 170, 171
Ayr, 88

B.

BAIGRIE, —, 228-9, 240
Bailey, F., 433
Baker, Sir S. W., and Lady, 263
Balaclava, 49
Baldwin, T. H., 51
Ball, —, 29
Ballyglass, 122
Bamboo Spruit, 419
Banaghong Gate, Jhansi, 227
Banda, 197
Bankipore, 284, 286
Banpore, 212
,, Rajah of, 210, 212
Bantry, 464
Barbados, 3, 132, 318, 386, 387, 388, 389 sqq., 391, 406, 409, 410, 436, 452
Barberton, 438
Bareilly, 159, 163, 164, 168, 196
,, Khan of, 196
Barnard, —, 328
Barodia, 204, 205
Barrackpore, 189
Barrett, R. A., 100, 103, 105
Barrett, W., 51
Barry, —, 458
Bartholomew, —, 304
Bartleman, —, 108
Barton, —, 437
Basingstoke, 339
,, Canal, 303
Bastia, 11
Basutoland, 137, 147, 148
Batavia, 35
Battersea Park, 338
Battiscombe, W. W., 312
Bavarian, H.M.T., 433
Bayliff, R. L., 50
Bazaine, 89
Bective, Earl of, 464, 466
Bednore, 9
Beena River, 204, 205
Beer, 343
Behar, 196
Belknap, —, 73
Bell, —, 117
Belleisle, 171
Belle Plaine, Barbados, 392
Belloc, H., 156
Bengal, 177, 242, 308
,, Lower, 187

Bengal Army, 178, 179, 182, 184, 189, 190, 194
,, ,, Cavalry, 182
,, ,, Infantry, 192
,, Club, Calcutta, 448
Bengemma, Lines of, Malta, 356
Bennett family, 457
Bently, —, 66
Bently, Dr., 142
Benwell, F. W., 50
Berger, —, 404
Berkshire Downs, 345
Berlin, S. Africa, 250
Bermuda, 123, 128, 334, 360, 361 sqq., 372, 374, 377, 378, 385, 388, 391, 398, 405, 452
Bernard family of Castle Bernard, 457
Bertie, Canada, 36, 37
Bertram, A., 12
Bethlehem, S. Africa, 141, 145, 148, 149
Betwa River, 213, 218, 221
Beville, —, 262
Bhopal, 201, 202, 204
,, Begum of, 201
Biddulphsberg, 134
Bingley, A. H., 110
Birr, 105, 123, 124, 294, 317, 319, 320, 321, 328, 447
Biscay, Bay of, 349 sqq., 433, 458, 460
Bisset, —,
Blackdown, 153
Blackheath, 96
Black Rock, 35
Blackwater River, Co. Cork, 150
Blair Castle, 171
Blake, G. P., 50
Bloemfontein, 133, 134, 148, 416
Blue Mts., Jamaica, 383, 384, 386, 405
Boaz Island, Bermuda, 362, 367
Boer Prisoners of War, 413
Boer War, see South African War
Boers, the, 134 sqq., 430 sqq.
Bombay, 7, 97, 118, 119, 159, 178, 179, 187, 241, 245, 266, 269, 308
,, Army, 182, 184, 189, 190, 197
,, ,, Cavalry, 182
,, Arsenal, 264
,, Cathedral, 204, 309
,, Island of, 176
,, Presidency, 117, 177, 181
Bonet, J., 93
Bonus, —, 233
Bordeaux, 264
Borny, 89

INDEX 469

Botha, L., 414
Boulton, C. A., 51, 78, 79
Bourke, G. T., 42, 45
Bourke, M., 45
Boyce, C., 73
Boyd, G. F., D.S.O., D.C.M., 438, 439, 441
Boyer, —, 451
Boyes, —, 135
Boyle, 94, 319
Brabant, Duke of, 258
Brady, —, 230
Brancker, —, 406
Brander, H. R., 312
Brandwater Basin, 137, 138, 146-7
,, River, 137, 147
Branksome Park, Bournemouth, 161
Bredin, A. N., 401
Breen, —, 439
Bridgetown, Barbados, 389, 392
Brindisi, S. Africa, 138, 147, 148, 149
Brink, Dr., 252
Bristol, 171, 465
British Columbia, 85
Brodrick, Rt. Hon. St. John, 434
Broke, sloop, 22, 23
Bronkhurst Spruit, 318
Brooks, —, 443
Broughton, J., 5
Brown, Maj.-Gen., 37
Brown, Major, 256
Brown, —, 302
Brown, Dr., 212
Brown, R., 5
Brown Down, 247
Browne, Capt., 136
Browne, Lieut., 142
Browne, A. A. P., 286
Browne, G. T. D., 110
Browne, H. G., V.C., 50
Bruce, T., 8
Buchanan, D. R. R., 368
Buck, —, 37
Buena Vista Barracks, Gibraltar, 65
Buffalo, 34, 35, 36
Bullen-Smith, G. M., 368
Bullock, —, 29
Bullock, —, 30
Bundelcund, 197
Burke, Mr., 314
Burke, Sergt., 455
Burlington, 27
,, Heights, 24, 25, 36, 37
Burma, 116, 189, 196
Burnand, N. G., 401, 412, 423, 438, 441, 448, 449, 454

Burnley, 89
Burntisland, 175
Butler, D., 93
Butler-Kearney, T. W., 146, 401
Byng, —, 416, 418
Byrne (1858), 230
Byrne (1912), 454

C.

CACHAR, 111
Cæsar's Camp, Aldershot, 314, 339
Calcutta, 108, 110, 111, 112, 160, 176, 195, 251, 284, 285, 446, 447, 452
,, Monsoon Skye Race, 110
Caledon River, 137, 147, 148
Calicut, 7
Calpee, 197, 231, 232, 234, 235 *sqq.*, 241, 242
Calpee-Jhansi Road, 237
Camberley, 153
Cambier, —, 84
Cambridge, Duke of, 83, 114, 198, 246, 247, 255, 276, 294, 305, 306, 308, 309, 333, 340, 341
Cambridge Barracks, Portsmouth, 92, 93, 294
,, Hospital, 301
,, University, 400
Cameron (1902), 149
Cameron, General, 315
Campbell, Capt., 206
Campbell, Maj.-Gen., 134, 143, 144, 146, 147, 148
Campbell, C., 2, 3, 5, 9
Campbell, J., 5
Campbell, J., 89, 90
Campbell, J. (42nd), 10
Campbell, J. C., 344
Campbell, J. H., 111, 112, 312
Campbell, N., 2
Campbell, Sir C., 195, 197, 198, 210, 217, 231, 232, 236, 240, 241
Campbell, W., 81, 84
Canada, 12, 19, 24, 26, 42, 43, 44, 45, 46, 51, 52, 62, 64, 65, 68, 75, 81, 82 *sqq.*, 93, 115, 124, 125, 126, 129, 130, 247, 307, 310, 311, 378
,, Dominion of, 84-5
,, Lower, 85
,, Upper, 18, 45, 66, 85
Canadas, the, 16
Canning, A., 368
Canning, Lord, 186, 191, 243
Cape Breton, 13

INDEX

Cape Colony, 250, 252, 458
„ Comorin, 178
„ of Good Hope, 6, 131, 132, 249, 391, 413
„ Town, 133, 148, 250, 396, 398, 413, 433, 458, 416, 460
„ Verde Islands, 6
Cardwell, Lord, 278
Cardwell Scheme, 321
Carlisle Bay, Barbados, 389
Carnarvon, Earl of, 111
Carrick-on-Shannon, 319
Carrick-on-Suir, 96
Carriere, C. H., 51
Carter, Dr. N., 259
Carter, H., 111
Casault, L. A., 50
Casbard, F., 312
Cas de Navire, 3
Cashel, 464
Castlebar, 465
Castleconnel, 327
Castlegate, Aberdeen, 173
Castle Island, 328
Castletown, Lord, 464
Castries, St. Lucia, 388, 406, 408
Catherine of Braganza, 176, 179
Cavagnari, Sir L., 101
Cavendish, Lord F., 314
Cawnpore, 194, 195, 217, 276, 283, 284
Central America, 408
„ Asia, 117
„ India Field Force, 197 sqq., 371
Ceuta, 72
Ceylon, 447
Champlain town, 23
Chanderi, 212
„ Fort, 213
Channel, the, 433
Chapman, —, 345
Charles II, 176, 179, 456
Charles St., London, 279
Charlotteville, Canada, 24
Charlton, —, 30
Chatham, 41, 271
"Chatsworth," race-horse, 111
Chaubatia, 159, 160, 161, 162, 163
Chaudierè Falls, 41
Chauncey, —, 19
Cheapside, 345
Chelmsford, 465
Chesapeake, the, 22
Chichester, 154
Chillianwallah, 287
China, 196

Chippawa, 35, 37, 39
„ Creek, 37
„ River, 38
Chittagong Hills, 108
Chobham, 96
„ Common, 303
Chunar, 284
Church Plateau, Aldershot, 96
Civil War, U.S.A., 76
Clare Castle, 326
Clarina, Lord, 317, 319, 322
Clark, E., 73, 93
Clarke, —, 39
Clarke, C. J., 50
Clarke, J., 50
Clarke, W. P., 51
Clary, J., 50
Clements, —, 139, 437
Clerk, F., 84
Clifton, Karachi, 253
Clive, Lord, 177, 180, 181
Clonmel, 96
Clyde, River, 88
Cochrane, J. K., 401
Cockbill, C., 312
Colchester, 247
Cole, —, 331
Colenso, 427
College Street Barracks, Montreal, 82
Collum, L. J., 110, 329, 331, 332
Colonial Office, 75, 86
Colquhoun, J. C., 339, 344, 353, 357, 359, 387, 412, 436, 442
Colt, A., 9
Coningham, H. J., 117, 118
Conker, —, see Whirlpool
Connaught, 465
Connaught, Duke of, 90, 150, 151, 312, 340, 341, 347
Conroy, —, 230
Constantinople, 96, 197, 285, 287, 289
Continent, the (*see also* Europe), 89
Conyngham, Marquis of, 466
Cooch Behar, Rajah of, 448
Cooke, H., 50, 82, 84, 86, 89, 90, 96, 97, 100
Coondapore, 9
Coote, Sir E., 7, 181
Cork, 151, 254, 451, 452 sqq., 464, 465
„ Exhibition, 151
Cork Woods, the, 71
Cornelius River, 141
Coromandel Coast, 7, 180
Coromandel, s.s., 265, 266

INDEX

Corsica, 11
Cossigny, —, de, 10
Coulson, G. B., 50, 69
Cowes, 79
Cox, Mair and Cox, 5
Cracklow, H., 183
Craig, —, 279
Cramer, —, 321
Craske, J., 339, 376, 387, 448, 451
Creasy, Sir E., 181
Crescent, H.M.S., 369, 405
Crimean War, 43, 44, 45, 46, 65, 66, 68, 70, 77, 193, 197, 211, 245 *sqq.*, 251, 303, 333, 457, 463
Crocodile, H.M.T., 97, 207
Cromwell, Oliver, 393
Cronje, 400
Cuba, 4, 126, 380
Cummins, —, 433
Curragh, the, 95, 303, 317, 318-19, 323, 455
Currey, R. G., 149, 401

D.

DALE, T., 9
Dalhousie, 450
Dalhousie, Marquis of, 186, 188, 191
Dalrymple, Sir H., 279
Darrell Island, 367
Dartmoor, 156
Dauntless, s.y., 365 *sqq.*
Davidson, H. E., 51
Davidson, R. V., 110
Davidson, T. St. Clair, 110, 147, 149, 155, 331, 344, 345, 359, 360
Davies, —, 206
Davies, —, 377
Davies, E. D., 79
Davis, —, 32, 33
Dawson, —, 29, 30, 33, 35
Deacon, —, 433
Deane, —, 163
De Bellefeuille, L. C. A. L., 50
Deesa, 116, 117
Delaney, J., 454
De Lange's Drift, 144
Delarey, —, 414, 426
Delaney, W., 454
Delhi, 159-60, 194, 196, 272, 273, 274, 275
„ Durbar, 451
Denison, A. C., 110
Denison, S., 105
Denmark, 277, 291
Deolali, 97

Dera Ismail Khan, 271
Derbishire, P., 51
De Rottenburg, Baron G., 26, 48-9, 50, 57, 60 *sqq.*, 68, 73, 76
Desborough, Lord, 407
Detroit, 18, 19
Deuira, Lines of, Malta, 356
Devonport, 155, 156, 157, 158, 342
De Wet, C., 137, 141, 142, 144, 414, 416 *sqq.*, 425, 427
Dhamoni Pass, 210
Dhurub, 261
Diamond Jubilee, the, 124, 466
Dick, J. G., 224
Dickinson, —, 143
Dickinson, N. H. C., 110
Dill, J. G., 149, 155
Dilwara, H.M.T., 120, 127, 133, 355, 382, 383
Dinapore, 276, 284 *sqq.*
Disraeli, Rt. Hon. B., 285, 286
Dix, S. H., 149
Dogra River, 168
Dominion Day, 83, 122
Dongola, s.s., 158
Donne, —, 233
Donovan, —, 76, 77
Dooley, —, 342
Dooly, J., 50
Doornburg, 416, 417
Doran, —, 224, 230
Doran, W. R. B., 438, 443, 454
Dover, 152, 330 *sqq.*, 464
Downs, the, 154
Drakensberg Mts., 142, 417, 418
Drogheda, 466
Drummond (1858), 224
Drummond (1861), 74
Drummond, J., 83
Drummond, K. M., 344, 358, 359, 420
Drummond, Sir G., 26, 27, 28, 33, 34, 35, 165
Drury, —, 156
Dublin, 11, 94, 96, 126, 316, 317, 318, 327, 454, 455
„ Bank, 317
„ Castle, 123, 317
„ Magazine, 317-18
„ St. Patrick's Cathedral, 149, 166
Ducat, C. H. P., 324
Duchesne, H. T., 51
Duckworth, A., 312
Dufferin and Ava, Countess of, 109, 110
„ Earl of, 109
Duffield, J., 292-3, 294

INDEX

Dugan, F. R., 123, 148, 158
Duncannon Fort, 96
Dundalk, 234
Dundee, 6, 175
Dungarvan, 96
Dunhallow, 150
Dunn, A. G., 77
Dunn, A. R., v.c., 47, 49, 50, 66, 69, 76, 77, 78
Dupleix, 177, 181
Durban, 441

E.

EAGLE, vessel, 22
East, the, 285, 289
East Indian Railway, 448
East London, 250, 458
East Meon, 345
Edinburgh, 408
Edward VII (Prince of Wales), 59 *sqq.*, 65, 90, 109, 125, 137, 138, 151, 165, 284, 285, 341, 433, 464
Egerton, —, 318, 407
Egypt, 313, 314, 316, 396
Elandsfontein, 45
Elandskop, 416, 417
Eland's River Drift, 145
El Khor, Forts, 262
Ellenborough, Lord, 189
Elliot, —, 23, 24, 25, 27, 30
Elliot, —, 416, 417, 418
Empress of India, 286
Enfield, 3
England (*see also* Great Britain, and United Kingdom), 14, 15, 26, 40, 44, 48, 51, 75, 82, 86, 87, 88, 89, 92, 96, 130, 132, 133, 180, 196, 245, 285, 286, 302, 330, 370, 398, 451, 465
Essex, 171
Euphrates, H.M.T., 94, 97
Europe, 40, 80
Evans-Lombe, C. S. B., 110, 331, 401, 438, 451
Everard, N., 466

F.

FALKINER, F. J., 12
Farley, —, 164
Farnborough, 339
Farrell, E. F., 466
Fashoda, 388
Fawcett, W., 12, 13, 23, 29, 30, 35, 36
Feeney, —, 230
Fenians, the, 463

Fermoy, 150, 151, 324-5, 327
Ficksburg, 135
Finlay, —, 143, 149, 159
Fisher, Lord, 129
Fitzroy, —, 3
Flanders, 365
" Flats, the," Canada, 41
Fletcher, J., 50
Flight, 337
Floriana, Malta, 81
Floriana Parade Ground, Gibraltar, 76
Foch, Marshal, 238
Fogo, 63
Folkestone, 152, 331
Forbes, C. P., 262, 304, 308-9, 312
Forbes, Sir W., of Craigievar, 173
Ford, —, 433
Forrest, —, 241
Fort Burgoyne, Dover, 333
„ Campbell, S. Africa, 147
„ Chambray, Gozo, 353
„ Davidson, S. Africa, 147
„ Delhi, 274
„ Erie, 35, 36, 37, 40
„ Fareham, 294
„ George, Canada, 13, 24, 25, 26, 27, 37, 40
„ Manoel, Malta, 80
„ Maroney, S. Africa, 147
„ Mississaga, 37, 40
„ Moro, Cuba, 4
„ Niagara, 27, 28, 30-1, 33-4, 36, 37, 40, 165, 169
„ Ricasoli, Malta, 77
„ Royal, Martinique, 3, 4
„ Widley, 90
„ William, Calcutta, 109, 111, 112, 447
Fortescue, Sir J., 241
Fortune, —, 39
Foulerton, A. F. G., 143, 149, 312, 429
Fouriesberg, 138, 139, 145
Four Mile Creek, 27
" 4010," 404-5
Fowler-Butler, R., 394, 395, 398
Fox, Lieut. (1858), 224
Fox, Lieut. (1902), 422, 423
Fox, G. M., 79, 93
Fox, M. F., 154, 155
Fox Hills, Aldershot, 300, 305, 306
France, 10, 14, 15, 89, 171, 180, 187, 268, 273, 279, 286, 290, 310, 362, 388, 425, 428, 429, 430, 432, 460
Franco-German War, 89, 94, 272, 273-4, 277 *sqq.*, 281, 289

INDEX 473

Frankfort, S. Africa, 250, 416, 417, 418, 419, 420, 421, 423, 424, 425
Fraser, E., of Woodhill, 174
Fraser, J., 5
" Frauds," the, 400
Frederick the Great, 90, 180
French East India Company, 177
French family, 457
French, Sir J. (Earl of Ypres), 153, 154
Frend, —, 24
Frensham, 345
Frere, s.s., 270
Frimley, 153, 154
Fry, C. B., 156
Fudhli Arabs, 259 *sqq.*
Fulwood Barracks, Preston, 314
Futteghur, 274
Fyzabad, 107, 108, 113, 168, 169

G.

GAFFNEY, —, 422
Gale & Polden, Messrs., 156
Gall, —, 232
Gallehawk, J., 332
Gallipoli, 96, 365
Gallowgate Barracks, Glasgow, 88
Galowlee, 236, 237
Galway, 322, 323
Ganda-mak, Treaty of, 100-1
Garibaldi, G., 80
Garland, V. J., 110, 117
Garrakota, 206
Garvock, Sir J., 89
George II., 456
George III., 12, 173, 456
George V., 159, 451, 464
German Crown Prince, the, 213
German Emperor, the, 286
German Legion, the, 68, 245 *sqq.*, 291 *sqq.*, 295, 321
Germans, the, 272, 321, 327, 430 *sqq.*
Germany, 3, 89, 187, 250, 273, 370
Germiston, 415
Ghauts, the, 9
Ghizri, 253
Gibbon, 39
Gibraltar, 11, 64, 65 *sqq.*, 75, 76, 79, 83, 86, 115, 121, 352, 361, 398
 ,, Bay, 73
 ,, Straits of, 121
Gillman, —, 224
Glancy, J. G., 96, 102, 110, 360, 369, 378, 383, 384, 394, 399, 400, 464

Glasgow, 88
Glasgow, —, 159
Golden Gate, the, S. Africa, 145
Goodfellow, —, 224
Goodwin, H., 83
Goodwood River, 41
Goold-Adams, H., 438, 441
Gordontown, Jamaica, 385, 386
Gorman, H., 45 *sqq.*
Gosport, 12, 289, 290, 294
Gozo, 120, 352 *sqq.*, 361, 363, 372, 374, 376, 378
Graham, —, 408-9
Grainger, J., 451, 455
Grand Trunk Road, India, 276, 283
Grant, Colonel (Grenadiers), 4
Grant, G., 51
Grant, Maj.-Gen., 152
Grant, Sir H., 90
Grant, U., 17
Grassy Bay, Bermuda, 366, 410
Gravelotte, Battle of, 89
Gravesend, 6
Gray, Miss B., 364, 365
 ,, Miss N., 364, 365
" Great Boer War, The," 460
Great Britain, 4, 10, 172
Great Heath Maryborough, 463, 464
Great Lakes, the, 17, 18, 180
Great War (1914-18), 34, 39, 337, 340, 395, 401, 425, 427 *sqq.*, 436, 455, 460, 466
Green, Messrs., 254
Greenwich Ridge, Jamaica, 386
Greenwood, Cox, and Hammersley, 12
Greenwood, W. H., 312
Gregorie, —, 313, 344, 347
Greville, —, 159
Grierson, J., 153, 154
Growler, vessel, 22
Guadeloupe, 2, 3
Guildford, 339
Gujerat, 188
Gwalior, 197, 241, 242
Gwynn, S., 156

H.

HACKETT family, 457
Halifax, N.S., 45, 85, 115, 123, 126, 127, 128, 129, 133, 246, 247, 371, 372 *sqq.*, 385, 388, 391, 398, 452
 ,, Harbour, 129, 132
Hall, —, 35
Halloran, P., 93

Halpin, —, 454
Hamilton, —, 21, 29, 30, 31, 35
Hamilton, Bermuda, 362
Hamilton, C., 12
Hamilton, C. M. B., 401
" Hamilton," Bermuda, 370
Hammonia, 134, 135, 136, 138
Hand, —, 224
Happy Valley, Bermuda, 364
Harley, —, 139, 140
Harman, C., 401, 448
Harris, Lord, 118
Harrismith, 140, 141, 142, 144, 145, 146, 149, 418, 426, 439
,, District, 148
Harrismith-Bethlehem-Kroonstad blockhouse Line, 417
Harrison, W. H., 24
Harrow, 170
,, School, 66
Hart, J., 110, 331
Hartford Bridge Flats, 339
Hartmann, —, 321
Hartree, —, 331
Harwich, 465
Haslar, 247
Havannah, 4
,, Harbour, 380
Havelock, —, 195
Haviland, —, 3, 4,
Hay, A., of Rannes, 173, 174, 175
Hay, Sir J., 394
Hazaribagh, 284
Head, Sir E., 43
Headfoot, Viscount (later Marquis of), 464, 466
Headley, Lord, 328
Hearne, J. A., 12
Heenan, N., 438, 441
Heilbron, 416, 417, 425, 432
Heilbron-Wolvehoek Railway, 425
Heligoland, 247
Hemphill, —, 74
Hempstead, —, 95
Henderson, —, 74
Heneker, F. C., 376, 377
Hertfordshire, 170
Highlands, the, 170
Hilsea, 6
Hilton, J. F., 409
Himalaya Mts., 160, 161-2, 168, 197
Himalaya, H.M.S., 88
Hindustan, 181, 187, 197, 365
Hoare, J., 301
Hogan, —, 463
Hohenlohe, Prince, 65

Holkar, Maharajah, 196
Holland, 12, 31
Holroyd Smith, —, 458, 459
Hon. East India Company, 175, 176 sqq., 186, 188, 243, 278, 281, 307, 308, 310, 311, 341
,, Armies, 182, 184, *see also* Bengal, Bombay, Madras
Hong-Kong, 121
Horse Island, 20
Hoyes, —, 95
Hoyes, A., 275
Huddart, A. K., 110, 312
Hudson Bay Company, 85
Hull, W., 18, 19
Humberstone, F. MacK., 5, 7, 8, 9
Humbert, —, 11
Hume, —, 285
Hume, J. E., 183
" Hun," the, 430-1
Hunter, —, 139, 140
Hurst Castle, 433
Hutchinson, —, 79
Hutchinson, J., 51
Hyde Park, 157
Hyderabad, 251, 255, 256, 257
Hyder Ali, 7, 8, 165
Hyder Ghar, Fort 9
Hythe, 152, 247
,, School of Musketry, 290

I.

IBERIA, s.s., 316
Imperial Yeomen, 399
Imtarfa Barracks, Malta, 352
India, 52, 64, 96, 97 sqq., 158 sqq., 186 sqq., 264, 265, 278, 280, 284, 286, 289, 293, 294, 312, 329, 332, 342, 355, 364, 369, 371, 397, 446, 447 sqq., 452, 454
,, Native States, 187
Indian Army, 401, 441
,, Frontier, 75
,, Mutiny, 43, 44, 45, 75, 124, 188 sqq., 251, 291
,, Staff Corps, 105, 332
Indians, North American, 17, 27, 38, 58
Indore, 235, 241
Indus River, 270
Inglefield, L. E. C., 312
Ingram, R. B., 50
Inkerman, Battle of, 77
Inverness, 6, 310
Iphigenia, H.M.S., 41

INDEX

Ipswich, 465
Ireland, 11, 12, 94 sqq., 120 sqq., 150, 151, 290, 294, 302, 310, 321, 330, 456 sqq.
Ireland Island, Bermuda, 369
Irvine, —, 149
Isle-aux-Noix, 19, 21
Isle of Wight, 12, 65, 390
Italian Contingent, 246, 247
Italy, 80, 187

J.

JACKSON, T. S., 17
Jacob, G. Le G., 183, 189
Jamaica, 17, 126, 318, 380, 382 sqq., 389, 391, 393, 400, 401 sqq., 410, 420, 452
James, —, 22
Jameson Raid, 431
Japanese, the, 213
Jardine, H., 385
Jena, Battle of, 278
Jersey, 2, 3, 5, 175, 352
Jhansi, 197, 200, 206, 208, 210, 214-15, 217, 218, 231, 232, 240, 241
" Banaghong Gate, 227
" Fort, 214 sqq.
" Orcha Gate, 222
" Rocket Tower, 222, 225, 226, 227
" Road, 234
" Rani of, 196, 213, 214, 216, 227, 228, 229, 235, 242
Joanna, Island of, 6
Johannesburg, 415, 431, 442
Johnson, —, 39
Johnston, D., 328
Johnstone, —, 6
Jonathan, Chief (Basuto), 148
Jones, B. P., 148
Jones, Capt., 164
Jubbulpore, 97, 98, 197, 235, 286
Jubilee of Queen Victoria, 109
" Diamond, 124, 466
Jullundur, 97, 98, 99, 100, 443, 450, 451, 452
Jumna River, 197, 235, 236, 237, 238, 240, 241
Jumna, H.M.T., 97
Juno, s.y., 368
Just, A., 294, 312, 321, 327

K.

KABUL, 101
Kaffaria, 249, 250
Kalbitzer, —, 292-3
Kandahar, 101
Karachi, 251 sqq., 270
Kashmir, 100, 178
Kathgodam, 160
Kavanagh, —, 423
Kaye, —, 272
Kaye, A. G., 110
Kells, 464
Kelly-Kenny, —, 133
Kenyon-Slaney, —, 148, 438
Kershaw, —, 377
Kersteman, J. B., 78, 97
Khandwa, 97
Khartoum, 388
Kidd, —, 275
Kildonan Castle, s.s., 458
Kilkenny, 95, 96
Kilmorony, 461
Kilworth Camp, 150, 151, 455
Kimberley, 459
King's County, 456
King's County Royal Rifles, 457 sqq.
Kingston, —, 39
Kingston, F. A., 110
Kingston, Jamaica, 382, 383, 385, 386, 401, 402, 403, 404
Kingston Military College, Canada, 376
Kingston, S., 13
Kingston, Ontario, 17, 19, 21, 23, 24, 26, 40, 46, 47, 74
Kingstown, Ireland, 94, 96, 316, 330
Kinloch, —, 248
Kirby or Kerby, —, 27, 29, 32
Kirkee, 267
Kitchener of Khartoum, Earl, 448, 450
Klip Nek, 134, 135, 136, 137, 138, 149
" River, 141, 437
Knights of St. John, 353
Knowland, —, 29
Königrätz, 213
Koonch, 232, 234, 235
Kribs, —, 50, 56
Kroonstad, 417
Kroonstad-Bethlehem blockhouse Line, 416
Kroonstad - Vereeniging Railway, 417
Kruger, President, 181, 431
Kumaon Hills, 161
Kumasi, 122
Kuropatkin, —, 118
Kurram, 101

INDEX

L.

LABOURDONNAIS, —, 177
Ladybrand, 439
Ladysmith, 135, 140, 144, 400
Laffan's Plain, 339, 347
Lahore, 271
Lake, P. G. B., 50
Lake Champlain, 17, 18, 21, 22
,, Erie, 18, 19, 24, 26,
,, Huron, 16, 17, 18
,, Ontario, 17, 19, 22, 24
,, Superior, 17
Lalitpur, 212
Lally, Charles, 7, 8
Lamb, —, 340
Lamb, G., 110
Lamb, J., 50, 77
Lamont, H., 9
Lamport, —, 433
Lancashire, 86, 89
Landport Station, 9
Lane, —, 331
Lane, F. C. B., 110
Langenburg Range, 146
Laughlin, C. E. H., 118
Leadenhall Street, 187, 188, 191
Leahy, P. F. A., 362
Le Cateau, 427
Lee, —, 46
Lee, C., 17
Lee, J., 50
Lee-Enfield rifles, 410
Lee-Metford Magazine rifle, 335
Lefroy, F. B., 438, 441
Legge, R. F., 146, 156
Leicester, H. C., 144, 149
Leinster Lily, The, 459
Leinsters' Magazine, The, 156
Leipzig, Battle of, 278
Leith, —, of Freefield, 173
Le Marchant, Sir J. G., 76
L'Estrange, —, 457
L'Estrange, E. B., 401
L'Estrange family, of Moystown House, 457
Levett, —, 66
Liao-yang, Battle of the, 213
Liddard, T., 51
Liddell, —, 203, 205, 206, 211, 223, 224, 225, 230, 231
Limekilns, Mauritius, 444
Limerick, 325 *sqq.*, 330 *sqq.*
Lindley, 417
Linked Battalion System, 282-3
Lismore, 151
Little Caledon River, 137
Liverpool, 51, 52, 62, 88, 132, 316

Liverpool School of Tropical Medicine, 407
Lloyds' Signals, Bermuda, 371
Lohari, Fort, 232, 233
Lomax, —, 152, 153
London, 62, 86, 90, 157, 303, 345, 433, 447, 466
London, Ontario, 45, 46, 47
Long Common, Aldershot, 63
Longhurst Ravine, 28, 29
Long Valley, Aldershot, 300, 305
Louis XIV, 177
Low Countries, the, 279
Low, Dr. 407
Lowe, Surgeon, 225
Lower Canada, 85
,, St. Elmo Barracks, Malta, 80
Luard, —, D.S.O., 438
Lucas, A. W., 274, 275, 276, 288, 294, 303, 304
Luckett, —, 433
Luckhardt, —, 252
Lucknow, 194, 195, 196, 291, 451
,, Bishop of, 165
Lundy's Lane, 40
Lydd, 332
Lyon, —, 39
Lytham, 315

M.

McARTHUR, SIR E., 74
Macartney, G., 50, 88
McCaul, —, 437
Macaulay, Lord, 176, 180, 188
Macbean, F., 159, 163, 164
McClure, —, 24, 25, 28
McCormack, —, 108
McDonald, —, 74
Macdonald, A., 2
McDonnell, J., 466
McEvoy, —, 230
McGregor, Commissioner, 148
McGuiness, —, 230
MacHarg, J., 2, 5
Macintosh, —, 236, 240
McKenzie, — (3676), 433
McKenzie, — (3677), 433
Mackinnon, D. W., 108, 109, 110, 112, 275, 305, 312, 329, 332
McLean (1813), 29
McLean (1911), 159
Macleod, —, 7, 10, 175
McNabb, Sir A., 29
McNab's Island, 129
MacPherson, M., 13
Madras, 116, 176, 177, 180, 181, 183, 187, 197, 447

INDEX 477

Madras Army, 178, 179, 180 *sqq.*, 189, 190, 191, 308
Magri, Father, 353
Mahoney, —, 55
Mahoney, P., 454
Maine, U.S.S., 380
Majkhali Camp, 162
Majuba, 318, 423
Malabar, 403
Malabar Coast, 9
Malabar, H.M.T., 97, 288
Malta, 74, 75, 76 *sqq.*, 83, 86, 115, 120, 287, 347, 352 *sqq.*, 372, 391, 396, 398, 452
Manby, —, 171
Manchester, 88, 275
"Manchester Martyrs" Memorial, Limerick, 325-6
Manchuria, 213, 436
Mangalore, 9, 10
Manitoba, 85
Mann, —, 120, 133
"Maple Leaf," The, 114-15, 126, 127
Marchant, —, 388
Maria Theresa, Empress, 180
Marina, the, Gozo, 360
Marlborough Lines, Aldershot, 133
Marne, Battle of the, 238, 427
Mars-la-Tour, 89
Martin (1813), 23, 29, 32, 35
Martin, General, 91
Martin (1895), 123, 133
Martin (1900), 149
Martin, H., 127, 131, 132, 133, 136, 142, 143, 144, 148, 150, 312, 324, 329
Martinique, 3, 4, 5, 388
Mary, Queen-Consort, 464
Maryborough, 461
Massey, —, 149
Mather, J. D., 160, 368, 408
Matthews, —, 9
Maude, —, 254, 264, 270
Maunsell, —, 54
Mauritius, 177, 196, 440, 441 *sqq.*, 452, 454
Maximilian, Emperor of Mexico, 286
Maxwell, —, 236, 237, 238, 240
Meadows, W., 6
Mean Meer, 273
Meath, 464
Mecca, 80
Meerut, 194
Mehemet Ali, 197
Meiklejohn, —, 224
Melville, Viscount, 50, 60, 74

Meredith, J. V., 163, 168
Merewether, —, 259, 269
Merewether, J. W. B., 110, 112
Messagerie Impériale, 264
Methuen, Lord, 426, 459
Metternich, 14
Mexico, 286
Meyers, J., 295
Mhow, 197, 199, 200, 242, 244, 245
Middleburg, 438, 441, 452
Middlesex, 170
Milford, 152
Militia, the, 311, 456 *sqq.*
Miller, —, 55
Mines, —, 433
Mitchell-Innes, C., 110
Modder River, 427, 457
Mogul Empire, 180-1
Mohamand Campaign, 450
Molteno, 459
Moltke, H. von, 213, 291
Monckton, —, 3
Mons, Retreat from, 157, 427
Montezuma, 176
Montgomerie-Moore, —, 377, 378, 380
Montgomery, —, 3
Montreal, 13, 26, 40, 46, 47, 48, 82, 84, 85-7
Montreal Gazette, 84
Montreuil, 344
Montrose, Market Cross, 174
„ Rood Fair, 174
Mooltan, 269, 270-2
Moore, G., 3
Moors, the, 179
Moorson, C. McD., 51
Morar, 242
Moravian, s.s., 87, 88
Mordaunt, J. S., 262, 312
Morgan, J., 93
Moriarty, —, 230
Morne Fortune, 406, 407
Morne Grenier, 3, 4
Morne Tortensen, 3, 4
Morocco, 72, 73
Morris, F., 51
Morton, G., 113, 114
Mount Abu, 116, 117
Mounted Infantry, 438 *sqq.*
Mullingar, 461
Munro, Sir H., 174
Murphy, —, 230
Murphy, E. L., 149
Murphy, E. W., 290, 293, 304
Murphy, Father, 463
Murray (1813), 27, 28, 29, 33
Murray (1911-12), 160

Murray, D., 51
Murray, J., 12
Musta Camp, Malta, 356
Mysore, 8, 11

N.

NAAS, 461, 462
Nairne, J., 170, 171
Nairne, 3rd Baron, 170
Nana Sahib, the, 217, 235
Nanda Devi, 162
Napier, Sir C., 189
Napier, Sir R., 269
Napoleon I., 14, 15, 246, 278
Napoleon III., 89, 273
Napoleonic Wars, 441, 457, 461
Narut Pass, 210, 211
Native States, India, 187
Nautilus, s.y., 368
Navan, 95
Near East, 96
Need, —, 219
Needles, the, 433
Neptune, Father, 411-12
Newark, Canada, 24, 25, 27
New Barracks, Fermoy, 324
Newbridge, 320
New Brunswick, 17, 85
Newcastle, 2
Newcastle, Jamaica, 383, 384, 385, 386 *sqq.*, 402-3, 420
New England States, 16
Newfoundland, 13
New Orleans, 18
Newport, —, 224, 230, 233
New Ross, Battle of, 460
New South Wales, 234
Newtownbarry, 457
New World, 36
New York, 369
Niagara (*see also* Fort Niagara), 165, 247
„ Falls, 32
„ River, 19, 24, 27, 28, 34, 35, 36
Nicholls, H. L., 50
Nightingale, T., 3
Nile, the, 263, 344, 388
Nolan, —, 230
Nolan, J., 92
Norfolk, Duchess of, 152
„ Duke of, 152
North Africa, 460
North America, 26, 36
Northcott, H. P., 122, 459
North, Lord, 177
North Raglan Barracks, Devonport, 155
North West Arm, Halifax, 129

North-West Provinces, 187
Norway, 157
Nova Scotia, 85, 376
Nowlan, —, 32, 34
Nursling Common, Southampton, 175

O.

" ODETTE," race-horse, 110
O'Hara, —, 443
Ohio, 18
Old Barracks, Fermoy, 324
Old Contemptibles, the, 436, 460
Old Machar Cathedral, 174
Old and New Barracks, Queenstown, 150
Old World, 14
Omar Pasha, 197
Omdurman, Battle of, 388, 396
Ontario, Province of, 16, 18, 85
Oomree, 234
Orange Free State, 131, 135, 137, 396, 413, 416, 417, 452
Orange River Colony, 134, 137, 414, 415, 416, 439, 440
Orcha Gate, Jhansi, 222
Orontes, H.M.S., 74, 96
Orpen-Palmer, R. A. H., 155
Orpen-Palmer, G. de M. H., 164, 165
Osborne, 80
O'Shaughnessy, —, 443
O'Shee, —, 142, 149, 151
O'Shee, G. I. P. P., 359, 368, 401
Osman Pasha, 289
Ottawa, 42, 64, 82, 83, 84, 86, 110, 124, 126
„ River, 41
Ottawa Citizen, 83
Oudh, 107, 113, 187, 191, 196
Owens, —, 108
Owens, E. F., 312
Oxford University, 400
Oxfordshire, 342

P.

PAARDEBERG, 400
Pacific Ocean, 16, 17, 85
Paddington, 157
Paget, A., 153
Paisley, 88
Palaeologus, Dr., 254
Palampur, 116, 117
Palmerston, Viscount, 246
Panianee, 7, 8, 9
Panmure, Lord, 246, 248
Parandhur, 266
Parham, 152, 153
Paris, Siege of, 273

INDEX

Parle, —, 230
Parkes, H., 90
Parkhurst, Isle of Wight, 65, 79
Park Lane, 157
Parsons, Sir L., 456
Parsons, Sir L., the younger (Earl of Rosse), 456, 457
Parsonstown, see Birr
Pau, 264
Pavonia, transport, 360, 361
Pearl of the Indian Ocean, see Mauritius
Pearson, —, 37, 38, 39
Pegu, 191
Pemberton, A. J. M., 168
Pembroke Camp, Malta, 86, 358
Penguin, H.M.S., 262
Peninsular War, 16, 36, 457
Pennsylvania, transport, 81
Pepper, C., 466
Pepper, T., 465
Perim Island, 257
Persia, 188, 193
„ Shah of, 92
Peshawar, 101
Phœnix Park murders, 314, 316
Pietersburg, S. Africa, 427, 437
Pilcher, —, 163, 164
Pilkington, —, 35
Pindari War, 207
Pitt, W., 178, 187
Plains, the, Jamaica, 383, 386
Plassey, Battle of, 177, 181, 188, 192
Plattsburg, 23
Plenderleath, N.S., 13
Plevna, Siege of, 289
Plumer, Lord, 342
Plymouth, 155, 157, 451, 454
Plympton, 5
Poignand, G., 110, 112, 114, 118, 332, 345, 346
Pois tribe, 109
Pondicherry, 177
Ponsonby, Hon. —, 407
Poona, 118, 119, 184, 185, 251, 266, 267, 269-70, 308
Portarlington, John, Earl of, 460
Port Elizabeth, 133
„ Louis, Mauritius, 442, 443
„ Royal, Jamaica, 401, 402, 403
„ Said, 120, 158
„ Stanley, Canada, 74
Porto Praya, 6
Portsdown Hill Forts, 90
Portsmouth, 2, 3, 6, 11, 64, 65, 90, 92, 93, 96, 97, 171, 287, 288, 290, 294, 302
Potchefstroom, 437

Potsdam, S. Africa, 250
Potts, J., 93
Pountenay, —, 170
Preston, 314 *sqq.*, 330
Pretoria, 396, 400, 407, 416, 426, 427, 433, 435, 436, 437, 452
Prevost, G., 21, 26, 27
Price, R. C., 50
Prichard, —, 241
Princess Hotel, Bermuda, 366, 370
Prinsloo, M., 138, 140, 166
Prior, H. H., 79, 82, 110, 111, 116, 118, 331
Prior, T., 67
Proctor, —, 26
Prospect, Bermuda, 362, 367, 368
Prussia, 251, 277, 278, 291
Puerto Rico, 126
Punjab, the, 182, 187
„ Chief Court of, 276

Q.

QUAGGA Camp, 437
Quarantine Harbour, Valetta, 358
Quebec, 13, 16, 22, 27, 41, 46, 48, 51, 52, 62, 74, 82, 87
„ Province of, 17, 85
Quebec, steamer, 82
Queen's County Militia, 460 *sqq.*
Queen's County Royal Rifles, 463
Queenstown, 121, 126, 150, 330, 452, 460
Queenstown, S. Africa, 458
Quinn, B., 90
Quinn, H., 342

R.

RAINES, Mrs., 263
Raines, Gen., 258, 261, 263-4
Rajaman Droog, 9
Rajputana Field Force, 197
Rance, —, 74
Rangemuttia, 108
Ranikhet, 159, 161, 162
Ranikhet Club, 163
Raper, Governor, and Mrs., 404
Rathghur, 201, 204, 205, 206
Ratieff's Nek, 146, 147
Rawlinson, Sir H. (now Lord), 153, 156, 416, 418
Raynes, —, 149
Raynsford, R. M., 146, 156, 159, 163, 168
Raynsford, Mrs., 163
Rea, —, 39
Reay, —, 145, 146

INDEX

"Redlegs," Barbados, 393
Reeve, W. T. M., 359, 360, 394
Reeves, P. E. S., 336, 368
Reitz, 416
Renown, H.M.S., 129
Rhine, Army of the (1870), 89
Rhodes, C. J., 396
Rhodesia, 413
Rhoner, J., 93
Riach, W. S., 329, 345
Riall, B. C., 26, 35, 37, 38, 39, 149
Richards, J. L., 401, 433
Richardson, F., 156
Richelieu River, 20, 21
Richmond Barracks, Dublin, 94, 317
Richmond, Canada, 41-2, 45
Richmond, Duke of, 41
Richmond Landing, 41
Ridout, J. G., 51
Remington, —, 416, 418
Roach, —, 230
Roberts, Earl, V.C., 109, 122, 135, 137, 434
Roberts, J., 263
Roberts, M. B., 110
Robertson, I. H. C., 50
Robinson, Sir J. B., 29
Robison, —, 223, 224, 225, 230
Roche family, 457
Rocket Tower, Jhansi, 222, 225, 226, 227
Rogers, —, 224
Rohilcund, 196
Rolleston family, of ffranckfort Castle, 457
Rollo, —, 4, 46, 47
Roodeberg Mts., 137
Rood Fair, Montrose, 174
Rooikranz, 136, 138
Rooke, G. H. J., 412
Rooke, H., 5, 9
Roorki, 272, 273, 274, 275, 276
Roscrea, 323
Rose, Sir H., 197 *sqq.*, 258, 263, 309
Rosherville, Poona, 118
Ross, A., 2
Rosse, Earl of, 457
Rowley, —, 6
Rowley, Hon. H., 466
Royal Hibernian United Service Club, 123
Royal Meath Militia 464 *sqq.*
Royal Military Tournament, 346
Royal Oak, H.M.S., 78, 79
Royston, 170
Rundle, Sir L., 134, 136, 137, 138, 143, 144, 145, 148, 151
Rushmoor Bottom, Aldershot, 89, 90

Russell House, Ottawa, 84
Russell, Sir Baker, 331
Russia, 14, 96, 285
Russo-Japanese War, 436, 460
Russo-Turkish War (1877), 96, 287, 289, 312
Rykert, A. E., 51

S.

SACKETT'S Harbour, 19, 20, 21, 23, 26
St. David's, Canada, 28, 36
St. George's, Bermuda, 362, 370
St. Helena, 387, 413
St. Lawrence, Gulf of, 16, 17, 19, 20, 23, 82
St. Leger, St. J., 304, 312, 324, 387, 400, 401, 412, 438
St. Lucia, West Indies, 386, 387, 391, 401, 406 *sqq.*, 410, 427, 452
St. Omer, 344
St. Patrick's Cathedral, Dublin, 149, 166
St. Patrick's Day, 111, 122
St. Paul's Churchyard, 345
St. Privat, 347
St. Salvatore, Malta, 77
St. Vincent, Cape Verde Islands, 133
Saki, 156
Saldanka Bay, 6
Salford Barracks, Manchester, 88
Salisbury Plain, 152, 463, 464
Salsette, s.s., 270
"Sam," the dog, 62-4, 86
Samarang, H.M.S., 73
Sandgate, 54, 58, 59, 331
Sandhurst, 400
Sandwith, —, 228, 230
Sangster, T. A. G., 401, 422
Sarnia, Ontario, 45
Saskatchewan, 85
Saturday Club, Calcutta, 448
Saugor, 198, 200, 201, 206, 208, 209, 210, 212
„ Road, 201, 202
Savannah, the, Barbados, 389, 401
Saxe-Weimar, Prince Edward of, 327
Scandal Point, Karachi, 253
Scharnhorst, —, 278
Schmid, —, 252, 262, 273, 291
Schmidt, O., 252, 275, 292-3
Scinde, Punjab, and Delhi Railway, 97
Scindia, Maharajah, 196, 242
Scobell, —, 144, 149

INDEX

Scotland, 2, 6
Scotland, Barbados, 392-3
Scott, —, 149, 160
Scott, W., 38
Scroggs, —, 445
Scutari, 248
Seaforth, Lord, 8
Sebastopol, Siege of, 77, 246, 403
Second Empire in France, 286
Sedan, 286, 460
Sehore, 198, 199, 200, 201
Semmes, —, 71-2
Senekal, 134, 135, 136
Senior, H. O. R., 110
Serapis, H.M.T., 97
Servois, D. K., 29, 32
Seton, W., 110, 112, 137, 344, 407
Seven Weeks' War, 86
Shaft Barracks, Dover, 333
Shakespear, J., 110
Shannon, River, 327
Shannon, sloop, 22, 23
Sheikh Othman, 259, 261
Shepherd, T. V., 105
Sherman, P. H., 17
Sherrard, —, 39
Sherwood, A. W. C., 122-3
Ship Street Barracks, Dublin, 123
Shorncliffe, 52, 53, 58, 59, 62, 64, 72, 109, 152, 153, 247, 330 *sqq*.
Short, E. G. M., 110
Shugra, 262
" Bunder, 262
Shummacher, —, 366
Sialkot, 100, 102, 103, 107
Sicilia, H.M.T., 410, 411, 413
Sicilian, s.s., 149
Simla, 101, 103, 286, 451
" R.C. Bishop of, 165
Simmons, T., 366
Simpson, —, 247
Simpson, —, 290
Skeen, —, of Skeen, 174
Slapkranz, 139, 140, 145
Sleigh, —, 39
Sligo, 94
Small, —, 159
Smalley, —, 54
Smith, —, 46
Smith, J., 50
Smith, J., 312
Smith, M. W., 267
Smith, S., R.N., 22
Smyrna, 248
Smyth, R. W., 420, 437
Smythe, T. W. W., 50, 82, 84, 90, 102

Sohagpore, 97
Solan, 103
Sonapore, 285
Sonar River, 206
South Africa, 75, 187, 196, 251, 365, 391, 395, 398, 399, 400, 410, 411 *sqq*., 436, 452, 454
South African Republic, 130
South African War, 130 *sqq*., 166, 187, 196, 250, 269, 274, 318, 395, 396 *sqq*., 410, 413 *sqq*., 427 *sqq*., 435, 436, 452, 458, 460, 464, 466
Southampton, 133, 149, 175, 247, 250, 347
Southport, 315
Spain, 4, 70, 72, 73, 75, 380
Spanish-American War, 124, 126-7, 380
Spearman, —, 29, 31
Spicheren, 89
Squire, H. O., 455
Standerton, 141, 142, 143, 144
Stanhope Gate, 157
Stanhope Lines, Aldershot, 345, 347
Stavert, T. H., 136, 139, 142, 145, 150, 312, 319
Steele, Sir T., 304
Steinkamp Kop, 148
Stevenson, E. A. E., 110
Stewart, G. G., 324, 329
Stewart, J. F., 108
Steyn, President, 137, 416
Stirling, 4
Stonyhurst College, 315
Stormberg, 458, 459
Strada Reale, Valetta, 357
Strathnairn, Lord, *see* Rose, Sir H.
Street's Creek, 37, 38, 39
Stuart, H. C., 368
Suez Canal, 158, 286, 287
Suffren, —, 6
Sultan, the (1840), 197
Sultan, s.s., 270
Sumter, U.S.N., 71
Suraj-ud-dowlah, Nawab, 181
Surrender Hill, 145
Swiss Contingent, 246, 247
Switzerland, 345
Syria, 197, 211

T.

TABLE Bay, 430
Tafel Kop, 416, 417, 420, 421, 423, 425
Tait, F. G., 333, 339, 344

2 I

INDEX

Talbot, H.M.S., 369, 405
Tangier, 179
Tanjore, 7
Tantia Topi, 217, 218, 220-1, 232, 235, 242
Tarland, 174
Tarlingham, 247
Taylor (1813), 21, 22
Taylor (1858), 46, 49
Taylor, G., 13
Taylor, G. A., 358, 359
Tector, —, 168
Tecumseh, 17, 19, 26
Tellicherry, 7
Territorial Regiments, 290
Thames, River, Canada, 24, 26
Thames Valley, 156
Theodore, King of Abyssinia, 266, 267
Thlotsi, 147, 148
Thomson, Sir H., and Lady, 407
Thornton, Surgeon-Major R., 276
Three Rivers, Canada, 13
Three Years' War, The, by De Wet, 425
Tighe, M. J., 110
Times, The, 246, 294
Tipperary, 119, 121-2
Tippoo Sahib 7, 9, 10, 165
Tom Cringle's Log, 403-4
Toronto, 19, 66, 74
Trafalgar, Battle of, 13, 14
Tralee, 326, 328, 330
Transvaal, 130, 131, 141, 396, 413, 414, 426, 431, 438, 452
Travers, —, 276
Trench, H. W., 118, 123, 127
Tribe, C. W., 312
Trim, 94, 466
Truefitt's, Aldershot, 313
Trueman, —, 240
Tugela River, 427
Tullamore, 465
Turkey, 96, 285
Turner, J. W. M., 386
Tweedale, Marquis of, 39
Twelve Mile Creek, 27
Twist, A. W. E., 401
Two Rock Passage, Bermuda, 366, 367

U.

ULSTER, 465
Umballa, 97, 103, 105, 107, 273
United Kingdom, 80, 88 *sqq.*, 123, 149, 187, 286, 311, 355, 397

United States of America, 14, 15, 16 *sqq.*, 246, 251, 370, 380
„ Civil War of, 76
Up Park Camp, Jamaica, 382, 383, 402, 403-4
Upper Canada, 18, 45, 66, 85
Urgent, H.M.S., 65
Ussallah, 262
Ussher, B., 401, 412, 437

V.

VAAL River, 417, 418
Valetta, 352, 354 *sqq.*
Valentine, —, 39
Vancouver, 85
Vancouver, s.s., 132
Van Reenan's Pass, 144
Van Straubenzee, B., 86
Vellore, 189
Venezuela, 370
Vereeniging, 427
Victoria Barracks, Cork, 451
Victoria, H.M.I.N.S., 262
Victoria, P. & O., s.s., 348 *sqq.*
Victoria, Queen, 64, 95, 96, 109, 124, 243, 244, 247, 248-9, 281, 286, 304, 340, 341, 346, 347, 464
Vigie Peninsula, St. Lucia, 407
Vinegar Hill, Enniscorthy, 457, 465
Vrede, 141 *sqq.*, 149, 440

W.

WACHT am Rhein, Die, 292, 293
Wales, Prince of, *see* Edward VII
Wallis, B., 51
Wandewash, Battle of, 181
Wanouri Barracks, Poona, 266
Warburton family of Garryhinch, 457
War Office, 75, 86, 94, 126, 130, 132, 397, 410, 436, 462
Warrenpoint, 12
Wasp, H.M. brig, 22
Waterford, 96, 151, 152, 465
Waterloo, Battle of, 40, 245, 280, 457, 463, 466
Wathen, E. O., 110, 331
Waudby, —, 149
Webb, W. H., 275, 290
Wegwelin, T. M. L., 50, 53
Welch, J., 93
Weldon, H. W., 163, 167, 401
Weldon, S., 461
Wellington Barracks, Halifax, N.S., 129, 373, 380
Wellington Lines, Aldershot, 334

INDEX

West Africa, 382
Westenra family, 457
West Indies, 127, 128, 175, 374, 380, 386, 389, 391, 397, 398
Westmacott, —, 159, 160
Westmeath Hounds, 95
Wexford, 465
Whirlpool, —, v.c., 233, 234
White, S. R. L., 147, 163, 165, 166, 168
Whitehill, C. S., 254
Whitton, F. E., 359, 394, 433, 436
Widdicombe, G. T., 110
Wildblood, E. H., 401
Wilge Drift, 141, 144
„ River, 141, 144, 418, 419, 421, 426
„ „ Bridge, 140
„ „ Valley, 418, 419, 420, 424, 425
Wilhelm I, German Emperor, 286
Wilhelm II, German Emperor, 345, 346, 347
Wilkin, A., 110, 114, 127
Willcocks, J. L., 102
Willcocks, Lady, 167
Willcocks, Sir J., 99, 101, 102, 110, 112, 160, 164, 165, 167, 168, 344, 450, 451
Williams, —, 39
Williams, R., 396
Willing, A., 91
Willow Grange, S. Africa, 138
Willsworthy Camp, 156
Wiltshire, 157, 342

Wimbledon Common, 345
Winburg, 134
Winchester Assizes, 93
Windmill Hill Barracks, Gibraltar, 65, 70, 72
Windsor, 304
„ Park, 96, 304
Wintle, —, 169
Wintle, E. de V., 110
Wisbech, 170
Witteberg Mts. 137
Woerth, Battle of, 89
Wohlfahrt, —, 252, 270
" Wolseley Gang," 101
Wolseley, Viscount, 344
Wood, Sir G., 344
Woodcock Hill, 327
Woods, A. S., 312, 346, 360
Woods, R. T., 466
Woolcombe, —, 260
Woolridge, —, 247
Woolwich, 458
Worthing, 152, 153
Wylde, —, 169
Wyllie, Sir W., 254

Y.

YEO, J., 19
Youngstown, 29, 30, 31
York (Toronto), 19, 36, 37
Youghal, 465
Ypres, First Battle of, 268

Z.

ZABBAS Gate, Malta, 77
Zambesi River, 396, 430
Zulu War, 302

www.ingramcontent.com/pod-product-compliance
Lightning Source LLC
Chambersburg PA
CBHW061922220426
43662CB00012B/1779